*f*P

ALSO BY ELIOT A. COHEN

Supreme Command:
Soldiers, Statesmen, and Leadership in Wartime

Strategy in the Contemporary World:
An Introduction to Strategic Studies
(coedited with John Baylis, James Wirtz, and Colin S. Gray)

War over Kosovo: Politics and Strategy in a Global Age
(coedited with Andrew J. Bacevich)

Knives, Tanks, and Missiles: Israel's Security Revolution
(with Michael J. Eisenstadt and Andrew J. Bacevich)

Revolution in Warfare? Air Power in the Persian Gulf
(with Thomas A. Keaney)

Military Misfortunes:
The Anatomy of Failure in War
(with John Gooch)

Citizens and Soldiers: The Dilemmas of Military Service

Commandos and Politicians:
Elite Military Units in Modern Democracies

Conquered into Liberty

*Two Centuries of Battles Along
the Great Warpath That Made
the American Way of War*

ELIOT A. COHEN

FREE PRESS

NEW YORK   LONDON   TORONTO   SYDNEY   NEW DELHI

FREE PRESS
A Division of Simon & Schuster, Inc.
1230 Avenue of the Americas
New York, NY 10020

First Free Press hardcover edition November 2011

FREE PRESS and colophon are trademarks of Simon & Schuster, Inc.

For information about special discounts for bulk purchases, please contact
Simon & Schuster Special Sales at 1-866-506-1949
or business@simonandschuster.com.

The Simon & Schuster Speakers Bureau can bring authors to your live event.
For more information or to book an event contact the Simon & Schuster Speakers Bureau at
1-866-248-3049 or visit our website at www.simonspeakers.com.

Designed by Maura Fadden Rosenthal/Mspace

Manufactured in the United States of America

2   4   6   8   10   9   7   5   3   1

Library of Congress Cataloging-in-Publication Data
Cohen, Eliot A.
Conquered into liberty : two centuries of battles along the great warpath that made the
American way of war / Eliot A. Cohen.
p. cm
Includes bibliographical references and index.
1. New York (State)—History—French and Indian War, 1755–1763. 2. New York (State)—
History—Revolution, 1775–1783. 3. New York (State)—History, Military. I. Title. II Title:
From Albany to Montreal, two centuries of battles that made the American way of war.
E199.c67 2011
355.009747—dc23
2011023717

ISBN 978-0-7432-4990-4
ISBN 978-1-4516-2733-6 (ebook)

To my children

Contents

Dramatis Personae

Captain James Abercrombie, British officer who served during the assault on Fort Carillon in 1758, killed at Bunker Hill in 1775

Major General James Abercromby, British commander at Carillon in 1758

John Quincy Adams, American diplomat and politician, chief negotiator of the Peace of Ghent in 1814

Ethan Allen, American agitator, philosopher, hero, and possibly traitor, founder of Vermont

Ira Allen, brother of Ethan, also a founder of Vermont; if anything, wilier

Lord Jeffery Amherst, British commander in North America during the final years of the Seven Years' (French and Indian) War and conqueror of Canada

John Armstrong, American aide to Major General Horatio Gates during the war of American independence, perceptive but incapable secretary of war during the War of 1812

Major General Benedict Arnold, brilliant American officer; key leader in the invasion of and retreat from Canada and the battles of Valcour Island, and Saratoga; traitor

Colonel Jeduthan Baldwin, Massachusetts farmer, self-taught engineer, service at Fort William Henry during the Seven Years' War, and engineer of the northern army during the campaigns of 1776 and 1777

Brigadier General Jacob Bayley, American general on the northern frontier in 1778–80

Colonel Timothy Bedel, incompetent American commander at the Cedars in 1776; inveterate enemy of Benedict Arnold

Judah P. Benjamin, Confederate secretary of state, head of the Confederate secret service, responsible together with Secretary of War James Seddon for plots originating from Canada in 1864

François Bigot, venal but capable civilian administrator of Canada during the end of the French period

Louis Antoine de Bougainville, aide to Montcalm at Carillon in 1758; scientist, explorer, and commander of a French naval squadron in North America during the war of American independence

Colonel John Bradstreet, British (North American–born) logistician and commander during the Seven Years' War

Colonel John Brown, American lawyer and soldier during the northern campaigns, 1775–77

Noah and Adam Brown, builders of the American fleet on Lake Champlain, 1814

Lieutenant General John Fox Burgoyne, illegitimate son of Major General John Burgoyne, chief engineer of the British army and defense planner during the American Civil War

Major General John Burgoyne, commander of British forces in the campaign along the Great Warpath, 1777

Louis-Hector de Callières, French soldier and governor of Canada, architect of the Great Peace of Montreal in 1701

Major General John Campbell, Earl of Loudoun, British commander in North America, 1757

Major Christopher Carleton, commander of British light forces operating in the Lake Champlain region at the end of the war of American independence

Major General Sir Guy Carleton, governor and successful defender of Canada in 1775–76, returned as commander in chief in North America at the end of the war of American independence

Charles Carroll, Marylander, colleague of Benjamin Franklin on his trip to Canada, 1776

John Carroll, American Catholic priest, cousin of Charles, also companion of Benjamin Franklin

Thomas Chittenden, governor of Vermont during the war of American independence; collaborator in the secret negotiations with Lieutenant General Frédéric Haldimand

Clement Claiborne Clay, Confederate commissioner in Canada, responsible for covert operations into the United States

Lieutenant Matthew Clerk, junior engineer under British General James Abercromby

George Clinton, governor of New York during the war of American independence

Cadwallader Colden, scholar and statesman, lieutenant governor of New York for much of the late colonial period

Richard Coote, Earl of Bellomont, colonial governor of New York

Charles-Joseph Coursol, Canadian magistrate responsible for freeing Confederate raiders in 1864

Jacques-René de Denonville, governor of Canada in the 1680s

Baron Jean-Armand Dieskau, French commander at the battle of Lake George, 1755

Captain George Downie, British naval commander, Battle of Plattsburgh, 1814

Colonel James Easton, Massachusetts militia commander, enemy of Benedict Arnold

Colonel William Eyre, British engineer and commander during the Seven Years' War, architect of Fort William Henry

Jonas Fay, son of the owner of the Catamount Tavern, member of the Green Mountain Boys, Vermont official

Joseph Fay, Jonas's younger brother, negotiator with Justis Sherwood for the return of Vermont prisoners

Hugh Finlay, British bureaucrat and observer of revolutionary New England

Benjamin Franklin, American diplomat, who aspired to incorporate Canada into the new United States

Major General Simon Fraser, British commander at the Battle of Hubbardton, 1777

Louis Buade de Frontenac, twice governor of Canada and architect of the strategy of frontier terror, to include the attack on Schenectady in 1690

Lieutenant General Thomas Gage, British military innovator, schemer, and unsuccessful commander in chief in North America; veteran of the Seven Years' War

Major General Horatio Gates, commander of American forces at the battle of Saratoga in 1777

Lord George Germain, architect of British strategy during the war of American independence

Joseph-Louis Gill, adopted Indian of ambiguous loyalties

Lieutenant General Frédéric Haldimand, Swiss soldier, veteran of the Great Warpath in both the Seven Years' War and the war of American independence, governor of Canada during the negotiations for an independent Vermont

Chief Hendrick (Theyanoguin), Mohawk ally of Sir William Johnson

George Augustus, Lord Howe, founder of the British light infantry; killed at Carillon, 1758

Major General George Izard, American commander on the northern frontier during the War of 1812

Colonel William Jervois, British engineer and spy, author of important estimates on Canada's ability to defend itself against the United States during the Civil War

Guy Johnson, cousin of Sir William Johnson, Indian agent on behalf of the British

Sir John Johnson, only legitimate son of Sir William Johnson

Sir William Johnson, Anglo-Irish adventurer and feudal overlord of the Mohawk valley, dominant figure in Anglo-Indian relations from the 1750s through the early 1770s

Peter Kalm, Swedish scientist, visitor to the Great Warpath in the middle of the eighteenth century

Major General Henry Knox, George Washington's artillerist, commander of the "noble train of artillery" hauled to the siege of Boston in the winter of 1775–76

Colonel Thaddeus Kosciuszko, Polish patriot and engineer, volunteer in American service during the war of independence

La Corne St. Luc, French Canadian partisan leader, businessman, diplomat, and plotter; active leading Indians against the British, and later the Americans in three wars

Marquis de Lafayette, French volunteer with American forces in the war of independence, who failed to achieve his dearest objective, the liberation of Canada from British rule

Levrault de Langis, French Canadian partisan leader during the Seven Years' War

Jacob Leisler, seventeenth-century businessman, politician, and rebel in New York

François-Gaston de Lévis, deputy to Montcalm, one of the ablest commanders in North America during the Seven Years' War

John A. MacDonald, father of Canadian confederation

Commander Thomas Macdonough, commander of American naval forces at the battle of Plattsburgh Bay, 1814

William Lyon Mackenzie, Canadian revolutionary agitator during the 1830s

Colonel Allan Maclean, Scottish emigrant turned loyal soldier of the British Crown; defender of Quebec, 1775

Major General Alexander Macomb, commander of U.S. land forces at Plattsburgh in 1814, subsequently general in chief of the U.S. Army

Joseph Marin de la Malgue, French partisan leader in the Carillon area, 1750s

Jane McCrea, American victim of Burgoyne's Indians; her death became a major American propaganda triumph

Colonel George Monro, British defender of Fort William Henry, 1757

Marquis Louis Joseph de Montcalm, French commander in North America during the second half of the Seven Years' War

Brigadier General Richard Montgomery, British officer turned American patriot, led operations along the Great Warpath, killed during the assault on Quebec in 1775

Brigadier General Richard Prescott, British officer in Canada, 1775

Lieutenant General Sir George Prevost, governor of Canada during the War of 1812

Major General Friederich Adolphus von Riedesel, commander of Burgoyne's German forces

Colonel Beverly Robinson, loyalist colonel, liaison with Ethan Allen for the purposes of negotiating Vermont's return to the British Crown

Brigadier General Matthias Alexis de Roche Fermoy, French officer in American service at Ticonderoga, 1777

Major Robert Rogers, American founder of the ranger unit named after him during the Seven Years' War

Peter Schuyler, mayor of Albany at the time of the Schenectady massacre

James A. Seddon, Confederate secretary of war; authority for the St. Albans raid

Captain Justus Sherwood, American founder of the Green Mountain Boys, loyalist officer, and spy

Philip Skene, British officer during the Seven Years' War, founder of Skenesborough (Whitehall, New York)

Major General Arthur St. Clair, American officer in command at Fort Ticonderoga, 1777

Colonel Barry St. Leger, British officer commanding forces on the Mohawk in 1777 and the northern frontier to the end of the war of American independence

Brigadier General John Stark, officer under Robert Rogers, commander during the war of American independence, victor of Bennington, 1777

Daniel Tompkins, energetic governor of New York during the War of 1812

Major General Joseph G. Totten, American designer of the land defenses of Plattsburgh in 1814, later of Fort Montgomery, and then chief engineer of the U.S. Army during the Civil War

Colonel John Trumbull, son of Jonathan Trumbull, aide to George Washington, American officer at Fort Ticonderoga in 1776, artist

Jonathan Trumbull, governor of Connecticut during the war of American independence

Pierre de Rigaud de Vaudreuil de Cavaignal, last French governor of Canada, whose father had held the same position

François-Pierre de Rigaud de Vaudreuil, partisan leader, brother of Pierre de Rigaud de Vaudreuil

Charles Gravier, Comte de Vergennes, French foreign minister during the war of American independence

Samuel Vetch, Scottish adventurer and military leader, planner of two abortive invasions of Canada at the beginning of the eighteenth century

Thomas Walker, Montreal businessman, American sympathizer, and later exile during the war of American independence

Seth Warner, leader of the Green Mountain Boys, Vermont politician and military commander

Brigadier General David Waterbury, Benedict Arnold's deputy at the battle of Valcour Island

Brigadier General Anthony Wayne, American commander at Fort Ticonderoga during the winter of 1776–77

Major General Daniel Webb, British commander at Fort Edward during the siege of Fort William Henry, 1757

Major Benjamin Whitcomb, American ranger and scout during the war of American independence

Major General John Wool, American commander of regulars at Plattsburgh, 1814, inspector general of the U.S. Army; Eastern District commander during the Civil War

Brigadier General David Wooster, American veteran of three wars in North America, disastrous successor to Benedict Arnold at the siege of Quebec

Captain Sir James Yeo, British naval commander on the American lakes during the War of 1812

Captain Bennett Young, Confederate leader of the St. Albans raid

Author's Note

My parents' generation fought and won the great war against Nazi Germany and Imperial Japan, so World War II was very much a living memory as I grew up. As a graduate student I studied America's Cold War—then at a peak of intensity—with the vast Soviet empire, believing (as did most sober observers) that it would last decades into the future. In the new century, as a senior government official I advised the secretary of state and interagency colleagues about our wars with Iraqi insurgents, the Taliban, Iran's Revolutionary Guard Corps, and Al Qaeda, and spent a good deal of time visiting battlefields in the Middle East and Afghanistan as well as shaping strategy in Washington. But when I left government service in 2009 I eagerly resumed work on this book, which deals with America's most durable, and in many ways most effective and important enemy of all.

Canada.

For well over a century, from the colonial period through American independence, the military struggle with what is now Canada was America's central strategic fact. For at least a half century beyond that war between the United States and British-ruled Canada was a very real possibility. This contest powerfully influenced American military institutions, strategic thought, and military culture. This book deals with the central front in that conflict: what natives called the Great Warpath, the great water route between New York City and Montreal, along the Hudson and most particularly along Lakes George and Champlain. This book is a historical exploration through a careful examination of selected battles real and, in some cases, potential. Not decisive battles, necessarily, for few can accurately be termed such, but rather revealing battles—contests that illuminated both the larger conflict and some enduring features of an American way of war that it engendered.

A word about how I, a professional scholar of strategy and contemporary security policy, came to study the Great Warpath.

In the early 1960s, just before the United States plunged into a decade of urban riot, fruitless war, and more than a little historical nihilism, I visited Fort Ticonderoga, and was entranced. The stones and palisades, the eighteenth-century guns, the mountains, and the lake were, and remain, magical. I had grown up in Boston, where colonial history had surrounded me, and a bookish precocity had led me to take refuge from the turmoil of the times in Francis Parkman's depiction of Rogers' rangers, gliding in canoes "under the silent moon or in the languid glare of a breathless August day" or in the winter moving on snow shoes "in the tomb-like silence of the winter forest."[1] My parents, who had grown up in New England during the Depression, recommended to me an author of their youth, Kenneth Roberts. I succumbed to his portraits of fictional and real figures from the past: Cap Huff and Steve Nason were as alive to me as Daniel Morgan and Benedict Arnold, and all far more interesting than the baffled politicians and soldiers of my own day.

My field of study as an undergraduate and graduate student drifted toward contemporary military and strategic affairs, however, and as an academic my studies drew me to the present. I taught at Harvard, the Naval War College, and starting in 1990 at Johns Hopkins University's School of Advanced International Studies, a graduate school that included in its programs an executive education program conducted for the Department of Defense. Thus, in 1995 I came back to Fort Ticonderoga, where I planned to take a group of generals for a staff ride—a kind of historical case study in leadership used for executive education. The director of the fort, Nicholas Westbrook, who had also been enchanted with the place as a boy and had now secured the job of his dreams, took me into a vault. To my great delight, he put in my hands the original manuscript of one of Kenneth Roberts's best-known novels, *Rabble in Arms*, set largely in the vicinity of the fort. I was hooked all over again, and determined to find a way, as a scholar and writer, to revisit those woods and ancient battlefields. And the more I did so, the more interesting and significant I thought them. I freely confess, therefore, a return to boyhood fascinations in this book. And by a curious coincidence, at a time when, once again, the outside world seems caught up in obscure and violent struggles, I am drawn to the same topics.

Readers may or may not wish to know the source of an author's interest in his topic; they deserve, however, to know what he or she has to offer them. In my case, it is the perspective that has come from some thirty years of thinking, teaching, writing, and occasionally offering counsel about contemporary military issues. My students and interlocutors have included college freshmen and admirals, journalists and colonels of infantry, foreign diplomats and assistant secretaries of defense. My subjects have ranged from the uses of air power in modern war to the transformation of combat organizations by high technology, from civil-military relations to counterinsurgency doctrine. The more I have reflected upon warfare along the Great Warpath, the more it occurred to me that a student of contemporary conflict has much to learn from, and even something to say about, this particular swath of history set in a well-defined geographical area.

No historian escapes his or her time, nor should they attempt to do so, at least so far as the posing of questions is concerned. What follows explores, among other topics, the troubles that conventional armies have in coping with irregular opponents, the relationship between professional soldier and democratic politician, and the power of symbols to distort strategic judgment. The title of the book—*Conquered into Liberty*—comes from the opening sentence of a subversive pamphlet American revolutionaries spread about in advance of the invasion of Canada in 1775. It captures a paradoxical notion in which not only they, but many of their descendants to this day, have believed.

And as for the charm of the subject, if this book prompts those who read it to explore for themselves some of the places it describes I will be glad. They will discover, as I did, that with an attentive ear, a modicum of imagination, and a wholesome curiosity about the past, one can still hear the echoes of musket and cannon shot, the shouts of command, the flap of canvas and creaking of oars, and even—with some effort—the near-silent padding of moccasin-shod feet.

Note to readers: I have, in most cases, modernized seventeenth- and eighteenth-century spelling. I have, however, used primarily contemporary maps, to help retain the atmosphere of the times in which these battles were fought—and knowing that modern cartographers rely heavily on them in any case.

Conquered into Liberty

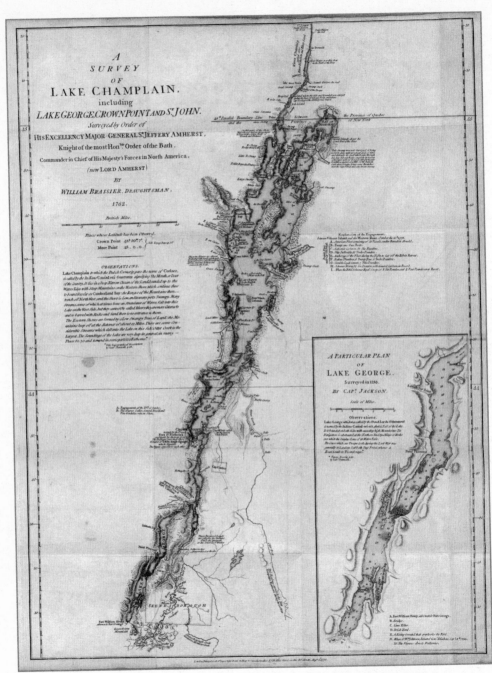

The Great Warpath. *Courtesy, Library of Congress, Geography and Map Division*

The Great Warpath

Stern hills, lonely lakes, and venerable woods

Nearly two centuries ago, a writer scrambled through the ruins of a tumbledown fort. It was a picturesque spot, framed by the pine trees of the great woods of northern New York, the crags of Mount Defiance, and the placid waters of Lake Champlain. Scattered about lay remains of burned timbers and soldiers' graffiti on the fragments of plastered walls; and all around "stern hills, lonely lakes, and venerable woods."[1] The writer had a guide, a bright young lieutenant of engineers, who expertly pointed out scarp and counterscarp, angles of fire and avenues of approach. The writer, impressed but unmoved, thought that the young officer's interpretation had "a good deal to do with mathematics but nothing at all to do with poetry." The author came back alone, and conjured up in his imagination the soldiers who had passed through Fort Ticonderoga—Canadian voyageurs, Indian war parties, gallant French aristocrats, the dour Scottish soldiers of His Majesty's forces, Ethan Allen bawling at the sleep-befuddled commander to surrender "in the name of the great Jehovah and the Continental Congress." But the reality of the present returned, and as he gazed at the pine forests that had swelled over the ruins, he mused that "the last garrison marched out, to return no more, or only at some dreamer's summons, gliding from the twilight past to vanish among realities."

The writer, Nathaniel Hawthorne, was not quite correct in imagining this the end of the romance of Fort Ticonderoga, however, for that scientific young soldier may have been none other than Robert E. Lee, and author and soldier alike were to find their own enduring places in the American story.[2] And they were by no means the last public men to fall under the spell of the fort on its lonely peninsula.

In the nearly two centuries that have passed since Hawthorne's visit, the Lake Champlain region has retained its fascination for visitors hoping to catch the echoes of drum, trumpet, and war cry. To be sure, in many places the reverberations are so faint as to be nearly inaudible. Ghastly constructions of asphalt, concrete, and plastic logs at which hawkers sell rubber tomahawks and toy muskets muffle the sounds even as they blight the view. Careening speedboats and cheap motels named after long forgotten soldiers make it hard to remember the menacing gloom of primeval woods. The conveniences of summer tourism—soft ice cream shops, package stores, and quaint bed and breakfasts—cause one to forget how grim a place this was in an age when food moved by boat, wagon, or on the backs of living things.

But with only a little exertion the traveler who desires to catch those echoes will hear them even today along the two-hundred-mile stretch from Albany to Montreal, which native Americans once called the Great Warpath. The ruined fortifications of Crown Point, much vaster than the neatly reconstructed fort at Ticonderoga, loom by the lake, watching over the ruins of an even older French fort; the lonely little battlefield of Hubbardton, Vermont, looks very much as it did in the eighteenth century, and in Canada the reconstructed strong point of Chambly or the mass grave of the United States' soldiers who succumbed to smallpox at Isle aux Noix bring one back to the days when this was the most bitterly contested piece of land in the world.

The Great Warpath, which runs from Albany to Montreal, is approximately two hundred miles as the crow flies, and not all that much longer by water and wilderness path. It is the central portion of a great arc of water that runs from New York City to Quebec, and beyond, to the mouth of the St. Lawrence Seaway. At the southern end, on the American side, New York lies about 130 miles from Albany on a route navigable by the Hudson River. In the seventeenth and eighteenth centuries the Hudson itself was accessible (other than when ice-bound) to substantial ships, including warships, well beyond West Point, and it formed a natural artery of commerce for most of the year.

On the Canadian side, navigational problems were more difficult. The St. Lawrence iced over earlier, and in the vicinity of Quebec strong tides made for tricky navigation, as English warships were to discover on at least one occasion. On the looming hulk of Cap Diamant—so named after the diamonds that French explorers mistakenly thought they had discovered there—stood the citadel of Quebec, and beneath it the lower town with its docks and wharves. Properly fortified, Quebec was a formidable obstacle for any fleet, which would have to deal with batteries as well as treacherous currents in assaulting the city. The journey between Quebec and Montreal, on the other hand, was relatively easy, some 160 miles by the broad St. Lawrence River. The Richelieu River, with its source at Rouse's Point on Lake Champlain and its mouth at Sorel, some 113 miles southwest of Quebec and 75 miles northeast of Montreal, connected the St. Lawrence with the Great Warpath.

The rivers, lakes, and lands between Albany and Montreal constitute the Great Warpath, but neither city was, in colonial times, a terminus. Rather, each was a point of departure to, on the one hand, the great West, and on the other, the seaboard cities that in turn were linked to the Atlantic system of trade and politics. The Warpath was just that—a military corridor more than a route for commerce; unlike the Danube, or the Rhine, or later, the Mississippi, it was not suited for much in the way of business traffic. But it was a convenient path for raiders and usable—although not easily so—for substantial armies.

Rivers and lakes were the true highways, and oceans the great commons of the New World until the advent of the railroad, the internal combustion engine, and the airplane. Particularly in seventeenth- and eighteenth-century North America, water dictated movement, for commercial and military purposes alike. Along the riverways traveled the Indian and European traders with bundles of furs, cloth, and tools, the heart of the economy of Indian country in the seventeenth century. Without water, armies simply could not move the mass of supplies they needed,

or could do so only with the greatest difficulty. In the wilderness, in particular, roads were often muddy, stump-strewn pathways through the wilderness; carts carried far less than a boat, and required the services of
oxen or horses, which in turn needed regular supplies of fodder not nor-
mally available in the woods. And—an important point for eighteenth-
century armies—carts meant teamsters, civilian contractors who could
prove highly unreliable under fire, and unscrupulous in their business
dealings at other times.

The preferred mode of transport for American Indians and light
troops of France and Great Britain was the bark (birch or elm) canoe—a
vessel manufactured from the materials readily found in the North American woodlands. Some of these, used for trade, could carry up to a dozen
people and a cargo of over a ton. European and colonial armies, however,
depended on the bateau, a double-ended flat-bottomed boat, up to fifty
feet long and little more than six feet wide that was the workhorse of
eighteenth-century warfare as much as the two-and-a-half-ton truck
would later be for the soldiers of World War II. But because the Great
Warpath was not simply a continuous water route, armies hoping to
move in the wilderness required wagons and ox carts to get around parts
of the rivers that were not navigable, or across tongues of land, particularly that separating the southern ends of Lake George and Lake Champlain from the Hudson River.

Access to the oceans made North America part of the Atlantic world.
Where today's Americans think of the ocean as dividing them from the
Old World, the truth is that it connected them. To be sure, journeys to
and from Europe could take months in either direction. But from the very
beginning the oceans tied the economy of North America to that of the
greater European world. Fishing fleets off the Grand Banks provided
protein-rich cod for the growing urban centers of Europe; the forests supplied masts and other ship-building materials for navies and merchant
fleets; furs fed the fashions of Paris and London, while the colonies in
turn drew not only manufactured goods but even staples from Europe.
Conversely, European goods including cloth and basic tools (knives, fishhooks, and the like) quickly became essential to Indian life deep in the
continent. The oceans made the New World part of the European state
and strategic system. Until the end of the eighteenth century, without
access to the Atlantic, no one in North America could live anything but

the most primitive existence. The woodland Indians, no less than the colonists, came to depend upon the goods of European civilization—knives, needles, pots, beads, clothes, and, of course, firearms. These Indians, like the European colonists with whom they traded, were thus linked in an intricate web of commerce and communication. And the easiest, indeed, often the only way for all of them to communicate lay along the waterways of the New World.

Four cities and one collection of villages shaped the Great Warpath: New York, Albany, Onondaga, Montreal, and Quebec. Although Giovanni da Verrazano had blundered into New York's harbor as early as 1524, it took a full century for the Dutch to found New Amsterdam at the tip of Manhattan Island. Even in its early days, New York had a mixed population, including Swedes, blacks, Indians, and even a small Jewish community. In 1664 the town fell to the English, but it retained a substantial Dutch population, and a Dutch feel, for at least another half century and beyond. Its society remained polyglot, and turbulent enough to include an uprising in 1689 by merchant Jacob Leisler against King James's governor; Leisler, after a tumultuous reign, was eventually overthrown and hanged, but the legacy of upheaval remained, and the politics of New York remained rough and occasionally violent for decades thereafter. In 1690, however, it was a city of 8,000 in a province that numbered perhaps 20,000 in all. It was, in any event, primarily a commercial capital, looking out on the Atlantic world.[3]

Quite different in outlook was the town of Albany. The Dutch established a trading post called Fort Orange in 1624, later abandoned for nearby Albany. The latter town had a population of some 500 by 1700, in a compact area surrounded by a wooden stockade.[4] It grew and thrived on the trade with Native American hunters, who brought pelts from the West down the Mohawk River. After the fall of New Netherlands in 1664 the town continued to grow, still under the domination of the leading Dutch families who had originally settled there, and whose large estates surrounded the area. It had 2,000 inhabitants by 1750, and expanded still further during the war for empire, now not so much as a trading town but as a military hub and a gateway to settlement in western New York and north to Indian country and Canada. Albany was, like most commercial towns, more interested in money than politics, and more than once during the seventeenth and eighteenth centuries, officials in New York would suspect its inhabitants of preferring a profitable trade with the enemy to a dutiful support of a war.

Not on the Warpath, but near it and powerfully influential were the villages of Onondaga, not quite the capital of the Iroquois confederacy, but something like it. The founding of the Iroquois confederacy remains, of necessity, shrouded in the obscurity that must accompany a people who did not leave a contemporary written record of their activities. At some time, however, between 1400 and 1600 five tribes—the Senecas, Cayugas, Onondagas, Oneidas, and Mohawks—came together to form a confederacy in the area of what is now upstate New York. From the Senecas in the west to the Mohawks in the east, they dominated northern New York, and, importantly, any of the fur trade that would flow from the west, south of the Great Lakes.[5]

The Iroquois were never large in number, and rarely more than twenty-five hundred warriors in total, but they dominated the trade routes, were exceptional fighters, and had a sophisticated political culture. The confederacy's tribes were not always united, but they developed traditions of negotiation and debate that made them a formidable power on the North American continent. Like many other Indians, the Iroquois were on the whole a fairly settled people, not nomads. Their "castles," as the colonists described them, were palisaded towns, inhabited during the hunting and warring seasons by women who exercised remarkable influence on the selection of chiefs and on the culture of warfare. The capital of the confederacy, such as it was, lay with the centrally located Onondaga, who maintained the council fire and presided over the deliberations of the Five Nations (who became six with the absorption of the southern Tuscaroras in the early eighteenth century).

Where Dutch merchants had founded New York and what became Albany, and Indian sachems had made Onondaga, Montreal owed its founding to the French Catholic Church. Founded in 1642 by missionaries from the Société de Notre Dame pour la Conversion des Sauvages, the town became a rival to Albany as a gateway to the West, to the Indians of the *Pays d'en Haut* or "High Country," the upper Midwest of today. But Montreal differed from Albany in important ways, in the domination of the Church (which retained seignorial rights to the island in midcentury), and in the degree of control exercised by a centralized government. Montreal served as a kind of alternative capital for the colony of New France, as a base for the extension of French power into the hinterland of North America, and as a military base. Secured in part by its site on an island in the middle of the St. Lawrence, its outskirts lay within easy reach of Iroquois raiders, who alternated between war and uneasy negotiations with the French.

At the end of the water arc was Quebec, the citadel of Canada, its capital, and the strong point whose capture was the focus of British efforts for over a century. Founded in 1608 by Samuel de Champlain, it occupies a peninsula jutting out into the St. Lawrence, and dominating it from the mass of Cap Diamant, upon which rested fortifications that would be developed over a period of two and a half centuries. Under both French and British rule, geography required yet a further maritime outpost—the fortress cities of Louisbourg under the former and Halifax under the latter, in what is now Nova Scotia. But Quebec dominated Canada well into the nineteenth century. It was the largest city under both French and English rule, a political capital, and the gateway to the entire province. To lose it permanently meant Canada's isolation from the Atlantic; small wonder that British and later American strategists focused on seizing it from their enemies.

At the heart of America's Warpath lie two substantial lakes, George (called by the French Lac St-Sacrement) and Champlain, both running on a rough north-south axis. The southern ends of each are some twenty or thirty miles, depending on the route, from Fort Edward, the last navigable spot on the Hudson. Fort Edward, in turn, is just under fifty miles north of Albany. Flowing into the Hudson less than ten miles north of Albany is the Mohawk River, vitally important as a corridor of commerce and because its valley provided some of the better farmland in upstate New York. The town of Schenectady, though today part of the greater Albany area, was once a major settlement in its own right along the Mohawk.

Lake George is the smaller of the two lakes, only a mile or two wide for most of its thirty-three-mile length. Bordering it are rugged hills and rocky shores, thickly forested with pine. Lake George meets the much larger Lake Champlain (120 miles from north to south) at a tongue of land, several miles long, where the Chute River feeds from the former into the latter. The Chute's three-mile length includes five waterfalls and a drop of 220 feet, which forced eighteenth-century travelers to portage, or carry their canoes and boats, to the site of the fort the French would call Carillon, and the Americans and British Ticonderoga. South of this point, Lake Champlain—barely a mile wide—narrows to a river, Wood Creek, before ending at modern Whitehall, earlier Skenesborough, New York.

Lake Champlain itself is a much more substantial body of water than George, its sister to the southwest. Indeed, Champlain's admirers wistfully claim it as the sixth, albeit the smallest of the Great Lakes. Although bordered by the Adirondacks on the west and the Green Mountains on the east, it abuts rather more arable land, particularly on its eastern shore, the farther north one goes. About twelve miles north of Ticonderoga, after the choke point of the peninsula that was the site of the French Fort St. Frédéric and the British Crown Point, Champlain broadens out to a width of some forty miles at its northern end. It is liberally sprinkled with small islands, and its shores on both sides abound in little coves suitable for the hiding of small craft seeking shelter from the prevailing northerly winds. The lake is about twenty-two miles from its southernmost tip (Skenesborough, now Whitehall) to Ticonderoga. A stretch of narrows in the southern lake lies between Ticonderoga and Crown Point, the last waters. From there it is something over thirty miles to what is now Burlington, Vermont, and the broadest part of the lake.

At the very north of Lake Champlain begins Canada, with the French fort of Chambly and the town of St. Johns. These towns, along the rapid-strewn Richelieu River, are little more than twenty miles overland from Montreal, a hard day's march, perhaps. By boat, however, the distance is almost five times as great, because one must travel north along the Richelieu to the town of Sorel on the St. Lawrence, and then backtrack an equal distance, and against the current, to Montreal.

Most of the land bordering the Warpath, though well watered, was not very well suited to farming. It had, however, abundant timber and pine products, all valuable for the construction of seventeenth- and eighteenth-century sailing vessels. The harsh winters—the snow and freezing season lasts from November through the end of April—made it far less appealing to farmers than the middle colonies, or even southern New England. For eighteenth-century men and women unprepared for it, a North Country winter was a brutal thing. In January 1760 Colonel William Haviland reported to Major General Jeffery Amherst that his garrison at Crown Point was suffering cruelly. "I have the misfortune to tell you that almost every man was frost bit." The surgeon, he reported, "was obliged to take off above one hundred toes this day and must more tomorrow."[6] The heavy snowfall of winter (which froze the lakes with a crust that could bear the weight of cannon) limited the mobility of conventional forces, but not of raiding parties, even large ones composed of hundreds of men. Snowshoes, skates, and sledges, all familiar to woodsmen of the eighteenth century, made movement over and along the lakes easier, in some respects, than slogging along the muddy, swampy roads of the North Country spring. But it was easier to move men than supplies, and no force beyond a raiding party numbering in the dozens could hope to supply itself with game from an area that had been well hunted even by the eighteenth century. As we shall see, in the North Country, as to a certain measure farther south, warfare was a four-season business, and hence quite different from the usual pattern of European campaigning, which usually came to a halt over the winter.

* * *

It was a very sad song

The European contest for North America began eighty years before the first battle we shall describe in detail, the French raid on Schenectady in 1690. Before that, no single Indian tribe had dominated the Albany-Montreal area: Iroquois, Abenaki, and Mahican peoples clashed along it. For Native Americans, this was a route, and also a hunting ground for wide-ranging parties of Indians. But it was a battleground, too, of sorts, as tribes clashed with one another in the combats of societies that valued individual warrior prowess as demonstrated in combat, and in which Indian groups competed for power, the resources of the forest, and slaves.

The competition, however, took a different and more murderous turn with the arrival of the white men. Here were people armed with powerful weapons—the gun, of course, but also edged weapons—who were willing to trade some of these, as well as more mundane but no less valuable goods such as caldrons and fishhooks, for the fur, in particular beaver fur, in which the land abounded. The weapons made Indian warfare more deadly; the prospects of trade made the stakes higher; and perhaps most important of all, the diseases of the white man disrupted Indian society by causing mass deaths. Historians vary in their estimates of just how much havoc was wrought by diseases like smallpox and measles, to which the Indians were acutely vulnerable, but surely hundreds of thousands perished. As tribes lost much and in some cases most of their population, the politics of Indian country became more turbulent, as tribes melted in to one another, were absorbed, or attempted to absorb others. Furthermore, the militarily powerful white man was a disruptive presence, a potential ally who could make all the difference in intertribal warfare.

The first and most famous clash of white men and red along the Great Warpath took place on July 30, 1609.[7] The great explorer and colonizer of Canada, Samuel de Champlain, had forged an alliance with Montagnais, Algonquin, and Huron Indians. With two French companions, he accompanied a band of these warriors looking for their Iroquois foe, the warriors of the Five Nations. The band of three hundred warriors shrank to sixty as they left the Richelieu River (known, ominously perhaps, as the River of the Iroquois) and proceeded south on the lake to which Champlain would give his name. The group encountered several hundred Mohawks camped on the site of what is now Fort Ticonderoga.

The battle that ensued began with a ritual exchange of challenges, war chants, and insults—a pattern that predated the arrival of the Europeans in North America.[8] But when the Mohawks stood to repel the advance of the Montaignais and Hurons they were stunned by something entirely unexpected. Champlain and his French comrades fired their arquebuses (matchlock firearms) directly at the Mohawk chiefs, killing two and wounding one. The Mohawks fled, and the grateful Hurons provided Champlain with the head of one of the slain, even as the Frenchman squirmed at the prolonged ritual torture to the death of the Iroquois prisoners, who were required to sing during their evisceration by their captors. Unsurprisingly, "it was a very sad song," Champlain recalled.[9]

The consequence of this clash, like so much of the history of the Warpath, has been distorted in popular myth, which holds that Champlain's volley cost New France nearly a century of bitter struggle with the Iroquois. This was not the case, because the Iroquois did not make war simply over grudges, and indeed, they would later conclude truces and even alliances with the French. The Iroquois thought and acted strategically, understanding their interests well. They had the human appetite for revenge, but this did not make them unique; rather, they hoped to make the French dependent on them for access to the interior, and they desired to destroy their traditional enemies, the Hurons.

Nor had Champlain stumbled naively into a fight with incalculable long-term consequences. The French had chosen an alliance with the powerful Hurons, and were quite willing to accept war with the Iroquois as a consequence. But it would be just as true to say that the Indians had chosen the French as allies.[10] In any case, the French understood that they could never gain access to the furs of the West, or to the (mythical) passages to the Asian sea without Indian aid. No early seventeenth-century European power could bull its way beyond the coast of North America without native allies. The upshot in this case was a series of brutal wars between the Franco-Huron alliance, on the one hand, and the Iroquois, on the other, which lasted through much of the middle of the seventeenth century.

The Indians were no match for the French in open warfare: European firearms, armor, edged weapons, and above all discipline saw to that. But the Indian way of war, ambuscade and raid, made it impossible to spread out and farm land even in the immediate vicinity of Montreal with any hope of security. And without peace, the French could never hope to engage in the lucrative fur trade that alone could support the Quebec colony once it had become clear that New France was neither rife with diamonds, nor the route for an easy passage to Asia.

The colony of New France struggled for existence, until the turning point came in the form of twelve hundred regular soldiers dispatched from France, chiefly men of the Carignan-Salières regiment, who arrived in 1665. They attacked Mohawk villages, and despite some occasionally disastrous blundering in the woods by these conventional soldiers of France, they overawed an exhausted Iroquois population, which had, at the same time, been fighting a no less bitter war against their Susquehannock enemies as far south as what are today the mid-Atlantic states. At the same time, however, New France's Huron allies had virtually disintegrated under the impact of disease. With both Indian allies and enemies exhausted, the French had the opportunity to make a deal that would buy the colony time to take root. By 1667 the Iroquois were ready to negotiate a peace that gave New France a window of sixteen years in which to develop and establish itself. Nor did the French confine themselves to simple negotiations: Catholic missions to the Iroquois followed in the wake of French soldiers, and by the end of the 1660s the Jesuits had missions established with all of the Five Nations. Champlain's fight had not doomed France to perpetual hostility with the Iroquois.

The myth of the consequences of Champlain's fight—the notion that it created an enduring hostility between France and the Five Nations—deserves a closer look. It reflects a view of the Indians as passive victims of European technology and military prowess. They were, no doubt, victims of European disease, but the Indians were remarkably adaptable in taking on European arms, which Dutch merchants in Albany were quite happy to supply. Confronted with firearms, the Indians abandoned the use of light armor and mass ritual displays on the battlefield, adopting instead what disconcerted white men later called "a skulking way of war."

More important, even at this early stage, the fighting along the Great Warpath showed a mixture of motives and behavior. There was, no doubt, blood feud and score settling, and ritual forms of behavior, including torture, that made little sense to European sensibilities. But there was also strategic behavior and choice, by Amerindian and European alike. Both groups faced multiple enemies, native and European. Both groups had leaders who made purposive choices, and both stumbled when confronted by the power of European technology on the one hand, and the realities of wilderness warfare on the other. The process of learning continued for a century.

The Indians could not eject the Europeans from the continent even had they so wished. Divided among themselves, with populations reduced in some cases by an order of magnitude through disease, and, no less important, unable to fully master the military technologies of the Europeans (there seem to have been few if any Indian gunsmiths, for example), they were overwhelmed by the less wood-crafty, but more rigidly disciplined, better-armed, increasingly more numerous Europeans. In 1609 Champlain needed Indian allies if he was to hope to achieve anything, indeed to survive; by the end of that century, the Indians needed European allies for the same purpose.

For the most part, the mid and late seventeenth century was a time during which the European powers solidified their initially precarious hold in North America. Early colonial ventures were harrowing exercises in mere survival, as colonies suffered the ravages of scurvy and starvation during long winters, ailments made worse by the initial motivation of European settlement—the desire to make fortunes rather than to establish new societies. The numbers that settled and maintained themselves were scanty—as late as 1650 even the two largest English colonies, Massachusetts and Virginia, had populations of only 14,000 and 18,000 respectively. By 1690, however, those numbers had climbed to well over 50,000 each. The English colonists now outnumbered the native populations by a considerable margin and, more important, had created a viable economic base for continued growth and expansion.

From the beginning the wars of old Europe had echoed in the colonies. The English, for example, seized New Amsterdam from its Dutch founders, and briefly wrested Acadia and Quebec itself from the French in 1628. These were, however, mere skirmishes along the fringes of what the Europeans viewed as unexplored wilderness. The real contest for North America only began once the Europeans had carved out for themselves relatively secure bases in the New World, had established towns that would not starve in the winter, and did not have to fear Indian raiding parties as a threat to their existence. It took until the end of the seventeenth century for the main cities of Montreal, New York, Quebec, Boston, and the like to become sturdy towns, and not mere clusters of beleaguered cabins. The counterpart to Canada's desperate struggles with the Iroquois was King Philip's War, named after the Wampanoag chief, son of Massasoit, who had welcomed the Pilgrims in the 1620s. In a desperate struggle from 1675 to 1676, the Indians of New England fought a war that probably cost them three thousand killed, while a dozen English towns were destroyed, and perhaps half of the rest suffered some kind of damage.[11] For a time it seemed to threaten the very existence of New England, and the damage was not fully repaired for several decades. In the end, however, it marked the destruction of native power in New England, although the Abenaki tribes of northern New England maintained a stubborn—and French-supported—resistance through much of the eighteenth century. Still, by the last quarter of the seventeenth century neither French nor English colonies in the New World faced threats to their survival from the Indians.

Having established themselves along the coasts and at key points inland, maintaining populations that had begun a course of natural growth and (in the case of the English colonies) substantial immigration, the colonies of England and France now became mutual antagonists on their own terms. The wars of Europe, driven by the ambitions of Louis XIV and the determination of other states, including Protestant England and Holland, to thwart them, had their echoes and reflections across the Atlantic. The war that began in November 1688 and lasted through October 1697—called by the French the War of the League of Augsburg, and by others the Nine Years' War (in the English colonies in North America, King William's War)—was the first in a series of struggles between France and a variety of opponents, always including and usually led by England, that lasted for a century and a quarter. These were world wars that brought battles in North America, the Caribbean, South Asia, Africa, and the Middle East. They reflected the tremendous military potential of France, whose able public servants included soldiers like the master of siege warfare and fortification Vauban, ambitious colonizers like Colbert, and skilled military organizers like Louvois. Beginning as a duel between William III of the Netherlands and Louis XIV, it became, following the Glorious Revolution in Great Britain that replaced the pro-French James II with the Dutch prince, a contest between coalitions led by England and France. It was a contest at once of religious faith, Protestant against Catholic, and of national interest, in which the Catholic emperor of Austria—beset by the Turks at one end of his kingdom—threw his weight in against France.

In this, as in succeeding wars, battles in Europe reverberated in the New World. In particular, the naval contests between the French and English fleets (with a varying cast of supporting naval allies) on the European side of the Atlantic had a direct bearing on the ability of New France to sustain itself against naval assault. From the point of land warfare, of course, the contests in North America were risible skirmishes between small bands of irregulars stiffened with a sprinkling of regular troops. The stakes in the Sugar Islands of the Caribbean were much larger: In the 1680s, for example, the value of British imports from the West Indies (almost all of it sugar) was roughly £330,000; from North America it was perhaps £200,000.[12] Small wonder that British and French alike were willing to expend considerable resources in taking and holding the islands that yielded such a profitable crop, which could be turned into rum and traded, in turn, for slaves.

By the end of the seventeenth century, then, European strategists may not have cared deeply about North America, but colonists cared deeply about European battles. Having driven back or subjugated the Indians as independent forces, the colonists of New France and of the English colonies of North America embarked on some seventy-five years of constant warfare, fighting that persisted even during periods of nominal peace in Europe. In these struggles the Indians were essential auxiliaries to sides engaged in a struggle whose logic pointed to a contest for mastery of an entire continent. And before King William's War was more than a year old, a French nobleman in the New World ensured that along the Great Warpath it would be waged by terror.

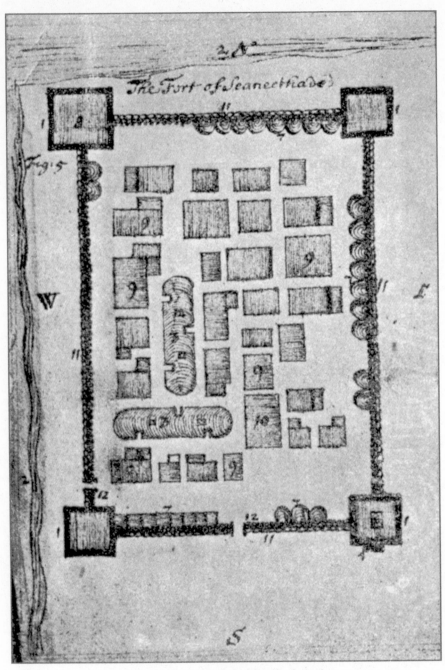

Schenectady, as rebuilt shortly after the raid.
Courtesy, University of Nebraska–Lincoln Libraries

The Schenectady Raid, 1690

---

*They dreamed that while the deep snow of winter
continued, they were safe enough*

At five o'clock in the morning on February 9, 1690, a bleeding man on a wounded horse staggered into the fortified, winter-bound Dutch town of Albany. Despite the bullet in his thigh, Symon Schermerhoorn had ridden nearly twenty miles in six hours from Schenectady to Albany through knee-deep snow. The mayor, Peter Schuyler, hastily convened a meeting of the aldermen to hear the exhausted Schermerhoorn's grim news. Just before midnight on the eighth, a party of French and Indians had stormed Schenectady, killing most of the inhabitants, carrying off others, and setting its houses on fire. In the following days some fifty survivors of the Schenectady massacre, many suffering from frostbite, trudged their way to Albany. They and their horrified hosts eventually pieced together what had happened.

There had been more Europeans than Indians in the war party—116 Frenchmen and Canadians and 92 Indians from an assortment of tribes—and together they slightly outnumbered the civilian population of the town they attacked. They had spent three weeks journeying south along the Great Warpath from Montreal, camping some six miles from the town and gathering last-minute intelligence from four Indian women they found there. The raiders had initially considered attacking Albany, but the Indians, believing the latter too well defended, pressed for Schenectady as an alternative target, and the French acquiesced.

The raiders had silently circled the town, hoping to attack simultaneously through the two gates in the palisade. In the snow and dark, however, they found only one open, and they quietly assembled opposite it. It was enough. The attackers slipped in through the north gate, dividing into parties of five or six to storm each house. With a sudden chorus of war whoops they broke into the homes, capturing or killing the inhabitants and setting the dwellings on fire. A larger body attacked the settlement's sole blockhouse, which contained some two dozen drowsy militiamen from Connecticut, sent to reinforce the New Yorkers.

The war party did not kill everyone they found in Schenectady. Shrewdly, they spared the few Mohawks in the town, partly because Mohawk converts in the raiding party had no desire to launch civil war in their own tribe, partly as a matter of policy. This forbearance, the French thought, might help wean the Iroquois from their English sponsors. And there was some genuine humanity as well. After a standoff at his fortified house, the French spared the mayor of Schenectady, who had earlier saved French prisoners from their Indian captors.

Nonetheless, when the English and Dutch relief force came to the smoking ruins two days after the raid to bury the dead, they found horrifying sights. "The cruelties committed at said place no pen can write nor tongue express," the Albany officials wrote to their colleagues in Connecticut. "Women big with child ripped up and the children alive thrown in to the flames and their heads dashed in pieces against the doors and windows."[1] The rescuers from Albany included Connecticut militia. In the ruins of the blockhouse at the corner of the palisade they found all but three of their comrades' remains, mutilated and charred by fire. The raiders had killed sixty civilians, including the town's minister, and had begun making their way back to Canada, carrying with them twenty-seven civilians.[2]

The Albany council, which deplored Schenectady's lack of watchfulness, spread the alarm. "Gentlemen, it would not be amiss if you should send post to all our towns to be upon their guard that they may not be surprised," Mayor Schuyler wrote to colleagues in New England. The officials passed the word, but not all acted on it. Cotton Mather, Boston divine and the first historian of colonial New England, somberly described the mood in the New England towns. "They dreamed that while the deep snow of winter continued, they were safe enough; but this proved as vain as a dream of a dry summer."[3] A month later Salmon Falls, New Hampshire, suffered the same fate as Schenectady.

This is the beginning of your war

The Schenectady raid was the culmination of a broader development in French strategy in North America. For years the French had waged war against the Iroquois, the extraordinarily formidable Five Nations (Seneca, Cayuga, Onondaga, Oneida, and Mohawk) whose disciplined ferocity had terrified enemies as far off as what is now Pennsylvania and Ohio. In the 1650s, for example, the Seneca, the westernmost of the Iroquois nations, had attacked a village of the Miami Indians who lived in what is now the Midwest, carrying off many of their enemies' children. Knowing that they would be followed by Miami war parties as they withdrew to their own lands, at each of their daily campsites the Seneca left the head of a Miami child impaled on a stick, looking in the direction of the pursuing Miami fathers who had arrived too late.[4] The calculated cruelty of the Iroquois turned on the French as well. Not because of Champlain's battle half a century before, but because of Iroquois desire to control the fur trade, to establish hegemony, and to gain glory, the Five (later the Six) Nations harassed and slashed at the French colony in Canada, which attempted, by turns, to appease, divide, and when unavoidable, confront them.[5]

In the second half of the 1680s Governor Jacques-René de Brisay de Denonville, a capable soldier, had reformed, strengthened, and militarized the colony in what is now the province of Quebec.[6] He began, among other practices, the commissioning of young Canadians as officers in the king's forces. After a careful survey of the situation he concluded that the previous policy of accommodating the Iroquois would fail and decided to wage war more aggressively against them. He also saw the long-term threat posed by the English and Dutch of New York, who traded with and armed the Iroquois. In 1687 he protested the French policy of friendship with England that tied his hands in the New World. "The King orders me to observe great moderation towards the English. But, My Lord, can any one wage war more openly against us than M. Dongan [governor of New York] has done, when he admits that he aids and abets our enemies with whatever ammunition is necessary to operate against us?"[7]

In 1687 Denonville launched a conventional offensive against the Iroquois, striking the Senecas in the west and the Mohawks in the east, attempting to crush the Five Nations and secure relief for New France's Indian allies to the west. Having massed a force of over eight hundred regulars, nine hundred militia, and four hundred Indians, he left first for Fort Frontenac (today's Kingston, Ontario) and then the land of the Senecas, the westernmost of the Iroquois tribes. His campaign ended as many had done before and would later, with the destruction of Seneca villages, storehouses, and crops, but without a decisive blow against the braves themselves.

Despite these inconclusive results, Denonville considered New France's best strategic hope to lie in the offensive, if it could receive adequate resources. In 1689 he communicated to the French crown a new campaign plan drafted by his deputy, Louis-Hector de Callières, governor of Montreal, that called for an attack along the Great Warpath with some fourteen hundred soldiers and six hundred militia, plus Indian auxiliaries.[8] He assumed the worst about English intentions: The English, he declared, intended to raise the Indians against Canada, ruin her trade, and then "burn and sack our settlements."[9] The strategic object was bold: Subjugate and disarm the Iroquois and shatter their ability to block or coerce New France's western Indian allies by depriving them of their Dutch and English sources of arms and trade.

The operational concept for implementing this strategy was even bolder: The French army of two thousand regulars and militia would take Albany—then a town with less than a fifth that many men to defend her. From there the army would advance along the Hudson and seize New York City, in conjunction with a naval force dispatched from France.[10] He planned to occupy and disarm the city of New York itself, treating the inhabitants mildly (or most of them—a revised version of the plan provided that Huguenots would be shipped back to France), but shattering English and Dutch ability to support the Iroquois.

It was a plan probably beyond the capabilities of the French in Canada at the time, and one that expected too much by way of naval and military coordination. And indeed, the outbreak of war between Britain and France kept Paris preoccupied with continental affairs. Absent the resources required for this bold scheme, Denonville attempted to negotiate a settlement with the Iroquois—a path opposed by France's Huron allies, who promptly ambushed a group of Iroquois ambassadors with a view to disrupting the talks. For their part, the Iroquois, backed by the English, were quite capable of fighting while talking. Still resenting the French raids of 1687, they launched a devastating stroke of their own. In August 1689 a huge Iroquois war party struck the French town of Lachine on the outskirts of Montreal. Fifteen hundred warriors killed or took prisoner over a hundred Frenchmen, and burned fifty-six of seventy-seven homes—a severe psychological blow to a French Canada composed of scarcely ten thousand souls already racked by disease and war. Denonville returned to France exhausted and depressed. His replacement would have to figure out a way of coping with both the Iroquois and the English.

On October 12, 1689, Louis de Buade de Frontenac stepped off a French warship at Quebec, returning to a colony that he had governed, erratically and often arbitrarily, for a decade from 1672 to 1682.[11] Although treated in the Canadian national myth as the great founder of New France, he was, in fact, a complicated and problematic figure. An aspiring nobleman and soldier who habitually lived beyond his means, and whose vanity and imperiousness made him more than the usual number of enemies common to viceroys in Quebec, he had used his influence at court to obtain his initial appointment as governor of New France in order to escape his debtors. He returned, however, to save a colony imperiled by Iroquois attacks (Fort Frontenac, named after him in 1673, had been abandoned), English colonial expeditions (including a rumored naval attack on Quebec itself from New England), and the larger turmoil consequent upon the first of the global wars between Britain and France.

In this dire circumstance Frontenac, though nominally under instructions shaped by the Denonville-Callières plan, decided to drop the idea of a conventional offensive. He reasoned that he would never have enough men to permanently occupy an English town, even assuming he could seize one. Of course, he clamored for more reinforcements, a plea characteristic of French governors in years to come, but he doubted that a large enough French force would ever sail across the Atlantic to definitively defeat the English in North America. From this correct premise he concluded that he should switch to a strategy of frontier raiding by Indian bands reinforced with militia and French regulars, launched from forward fortifications against English villages and towns.

This was a fateful choice. Frontenac sent bands of French, Canadians, and Indians against the English frontier not to hold ground, destroy fortified outposts, or defeat enemy forces but to burn settlements, take captives, and kill civilians. By raiding English settlements he hoped to achieve several objectives, first among them tying down substantial local forces (there were few if any regulars in the colonies) in extended defense of the frontier. Such a dispersion of effort, and the costs it would undoubtedly entail, would prevent the English from launching a direct assault on the French colony itself. Frontenac also correctly calculated that these raids would have a subtler, more political effect. The Indian allies of France would find themselves locked in perpetual conflict with the English. The inevitable losses and retaliations both sides would suffer would preclude a comprehensive Indian reconciliation with the English colonies. This was a strategic logic particularly apt for imperial frontier warfare—the stimulation of feuds and hatreds by low-level violence that would preclude one's enemies from coming to terms with one another. At the same time, moreover, Frontenac believed that eventually the Iroquois could either be brought into the French fold (overawed, perhaps, by French prowess) or, at some later date, beaten into submission. In the meanwhile, terror would serve as his policy's chief strategic instrument; hence, Schenectady.

Frontenac launched three raiding expeditions that winter of 1690: against Albany or Schenectady (his instructions with regard to targets were flexible) and against Salmon Falls, New Hampshire, and Casco, Maine. He picked Canadian-born French officers to lead these raids, among them such hardy adventurers as Pierre Le Moyne d'Iberville.[12] D'Iberville, the founder of Louisiana, was of an intrepid and ruthless type soon to become familiar to English settlers in New York and New England. In a standoff with a small group of English traders in Hudson

Bay two years before—during a time of peace between England and France—d'Iberville had prevented the English from hunting for fresh meat (dooming, thereby, some twenty-five of their number to a lingering death from scurvy), kidnapped their surgeon, and brought them as prisoners to Quebec.

Raiding warfare was psychological warfare: a combination of terror and clemency intended to demoralize and split. It did some of the former, but none of the latter. Immediately after the Schenectady raid, for example, at the behest of Peter Schuyler, mayor of Albany, the Mohawks sent a war party of over a hundred braves on the track of the retreating raiders. The French and Indians had lost only one man each in their attack on Schenectady; the pursuing Mohawks killed or took nineteen more, many of them within sight of Montreal.[13]

Several weeks after the Schenectady raid a delegation of Mohawk chiefs came to Albany not only to condole with its leaders and people, as was the Indian custom, but to put some steel in the white men's spines. The Mohawks declared that they, too, had suffered from French perfidy. The French "had broken open our house at both ends, formerly in the Senecas' country, and now here." But the Indians promised to avenge the dead of Schenectady with their own. "We will beset them so closely, that not a man in Canada shall dare to step out of doors to cut a stick of wood." The Indians urged the English and Dutch to reoccupy and rebuild their ruined village. Be patient in disaster, they counseled, and—repeating the word several times and with emphasis as they gave a wampum belt in token of their friendship—show courage. "Brethren, be not discouraged, we are strong enough. This is the beginning of your war, and our whole house have their eyes fixed upon you at this time, to observe your behavior." The Indian leaders reproached the Dutch traders who, in the interest of commerce, had formerly restrained them from waging war against the French. Let no such restraints apply henceforth; "let us now prosecute the war vigorously."

Narrowly understood, the Schenectady raid had been a substantial French success: Surprise was complete, the settlement shattered, the homes burned (in part, the French claimed, to prevent their Indian allies from looting the liquor stored within). The follow-on attacks were, by the measure of sheer mayhem, equally successful. On March 18, raiders hit Salmon Falls, New Hampshire: Thirty-four inhabitants were killed and fifty-four carried off. And at the end of May it was the turn of Casco (Falmouth), Maine, where twenty were slain and a hundred who had fled to a local fort surrendered and were then butchered.[14]

But Frontenac's raids did not, as he had hoped, paralyze the enemy. In the autumn of 1690 Sir William Phips, treasure hunter, military adventurer, and colonial leader, audaciously led a fleet carrying two thousand Massachusetts militia up the St. Lawrence to Quebec. Frontenac and his people had a narrow escape. He had strengthened the city's defenses, and although the New Englanders landed, they withdrew a week later harassed by the Canadian militia and daunted by the approaching winter. But the New Englanders did manage to seize a foothold in Nova Scotia, at Port Royal. For their part, the Iroquois were not yet demoralized by French success and continued their war on French settlements. New England and New York cooperated in defending the long frontier, and in raising forces for the struggle with Canada.

Far from dividing the northern colonies, Frontenac's raids had caused them to unite; and rather than diverting them from cooperation with the Iroquois in order to defend themselves, it intensified English efforts to play on Iroquois (and particularly Mohawk) hostility toward the French.[15] The opportunistic strike at Schenectady, a fairly innocuous settlement, rather than Albany, the hub of English and Dutch influence over the Iroquois, represented a further failure of strategic judgment. The immediate choice may have reflected the realities of commanders coping with volatile Indian allies, but the raiding strategy more broadly represented a problematic embrace of terror that doomed New France to implacable hostility from its neighbors.[16] Inevitably, raiding warfare was brutal, as Indian and Canadian raiding parties slew, captured, and tortured frontier families. No matter what measures the French took to restrain their Indian allies or to redeem captives (and they often did), the result could not be anything other than slaughter and horror. This was, moreover, not mere proxy war—the kind of indirect conflict that states wage against one another with irregular allies, whose excesses they disingenuously disavow. This was, rather, war waged against civilians by Europeans and Indians operating together. As a French prisoner subsequently confessed, it was Frenchmen who had killed the entirely innocuous Dutch minister of Schenectady.[17]

In setting aside the possibility of a defense interspersed with limited

conventional offensives (in this case to destroy Albany) in favor of a strategy of raiding, Frontenac chose a course of action that produced one feature of the American way of war—its quest for annihilating victories
against any enemy. A pragmatic determination to finish off an opponent
utterly—not so much by extermination of populations as by the dismantling of a state—began to embed itself in the American way of war. The
governor of New York groped his way to this conclusion when he wrote
to his superiors in England in 1693: "That whereas Canada is the chiefest
seat of the enemy; if they were removed, which might be done by a joint
supply from all these governments, with order and assistance from
England, would at once free these Plantations from further pressure, and
would conduce to the advantage and encouragement of all these Provinces in general, as well as the honor of their Majesties in particular."[18]
Like Cato the Elder ending every oration to the Roman Senate with the
declaration that "Carthage must be destroyed," colonial leaders, in speech,
writing, or simply in their hearts, believed that the French colony in Canada must suffer a like fate.

Frontenac's strategy assumed that the English colonies were a coherent group; there was no point, therefore, in trying to split them. Actually,
he brought them together. Instead of playing on the notorious intercolonial squabbles and differences of opinion, he managed to unite them in
several attempts to assault Quebec itself. While that unity often faltered,
particularly as Frontenac's successors modified his policy, it never lapsed
entirely, and established an important precedent of colonial unity of
effort.

In the short term, then, Frontenac's strategy failed—the English colonies rallied against the French and threw hard counterpunches against
Quebec itself. In the long term it was perilous—the conviction that nothing other than complete victory over the French in North America was
acceptable took root among English colonial leaders. In the medium term,
however, over a period of decades, Frontenac's raiding strategy succeeded.
French Canadian strokes against civilian targets in the late seventeenth
and early eighteenth centuries brought to a culmination a war of attrition
that did not cripple the English and Dutch, but did bring unbearable
pressure upon the Iroquois. The Five Nations, already stressed by illness
and long-standing wars with their Indian neighbors to the west and
north, found that even successful frontier warfare caused a drizzle of

casualties that they could not afford. The English and Dutch at Albany continued to supply them with guns and powder but provided nothing like the material support and effective leadership that the French did to their Indian clients. Promised expeditions against Canada collapsed, and the Iroquois found themselves bearing the brunt of war against the French and their Indian allies, including a campaign against the Onondaga villages led in person by the doughty seventy-six-year-old Frontenac in 1696. They were ready for a deal.

Frontenac's strategy helped buy New France decades of existence, despite the colony's innate weaknesses, which also, curiously, contributed to its strengths. The French did not seek to fill New France with settlers from Europe—and, indeed, for the average French peasant there was little to draw him to the frozen wilderness of Canada. Rather, France sought glory and profit for its leaders, souls for the Church, and strategic advantage for the king in its colony on the St. Lawrence. The English colonies, by way of contrast, developing with only fitful restraint from the English government at home, were filled with adventurers, speculators, and pioneers of all kinds. Although avarice characterized New France as much as it did the English colonies, it took a different form. Whereas French officials sought to carve out lucrative slices of the fur trade, Englishmen looked for land—tens of thousands of acres of it—which could only become profitable if developed and settled. The great disparity in numbers between Canada on the one hand and New England and New York on the other reflected the difference between a colony to which immigration ceased, effectively, by the end of the seventeenth century, and colonies that absorbed, and sought to absorb, waves of immigrants from England and beyond.

The Indians understood that the English sought to settle, whereas the French were content to trade, dominate, and convert. The Indians could cope with, indeed benefit from, the latter. The former meant, ultimately, their extinction as free peoples. Immediate rivalries and short-term interests could, of course, overcome this fundamental fact, but until English victory seemed so certain that accommodation looked better than confrontation, Indian self-interest indicated support for New France.

This fundamental consideration of interest does not by itself explain why the French did better with the Indians, for the most part, than did their English counterparts. Rather, superior French cultural understanding of and sympathy with the Indians, a more centrally controlled political system, and more effectively wielded military power played roles as well.[19] The French could wield the instruments of national power—war, trade, and propaganda—singly; the English were the creatures of multiple societies, lightly governed, often at cross purposes.

Frontenac's strategy required that the French beat the English in woodland diplomacy and warfare. They had two classes of leaders qualified to do that. The first were priests seeking to convert the Indians. The Jesuits—learned, pragmatic, dedicated—had plunged fearlessly into the forests of the New World at the very outset of the French experience in Canada, establishing a centrally coordinated influence on the Indians. The Crown and its representatives often mistrusted the "black robes," as the Indians called them, seeking to balance them with other clerical orders brought to the New World for that purpose, but they made use of them as well.

The second group, the military gentry of New France, was equally fitted to its task. Drawn in part from some of the leading families of France—which, of itself, undermines the notion that Canada was merely a backwater from the point of view of Paris—it found a home in the New World where its combination of martial vocation, diplomatic skill, and desire for glory would serve the interests of national policy. Soldier-trader-diplomats seduced the Iroquois from their English alliance with a mixture of courage, guile, and decisiveness. Take, for example, Louis-Thomas Chabert de Joncaire, captured by the Senecas and adopted by them, who became a trusted figure, an interlocutor for the Indians with the world of Quebec, and an effective agent in cutting off English access. To that end, he could negotiate as well as use more direct means when necessary. For example, after encountering an agent of the New York merchants in Iroquois country, Joncaire offered the unsuspecting New Yorker a convivial smoke. When the Englishman took out a knife to cut off a plug of tobacco, Joncaire generously held out his own, larger knife instead. The agent obligingly gave Joncaire his weapon—which the Frenchman promptly tossed into the underbrush while one of his aides brought a hatchet down on the man's skull.[20]

In the early eighteenth century, then, the competition between France and Britain for control of the New World became a far more even contest than a mere comparison of the numbers of inhabitants in the various colonies might suggest. Indeed, during the first half of the eighteenth century, it was the French, more than the English, who were aggressively, self-consciously, and successfully expanding their influence in Indian country. This effort took the form of expeditions exploring the Mississippi and laying claim to its shores and its tributaries, but it took more direct forms as well, as the French continued Frontenac's policy of placing themselves at the center of the Indian diplomatic system, and making themselves the brokers of peaceful relations among the tribes. They had no end of difficulties managing their turbulent, often mutually antagonistic clients, and they squabbled amongst themselves as only the isolated members of a small colony could, but they flourished.

Even after peace in Europe was signed in 1697 (the Peace of Ryswick), a kind of cold war in the New World persisted, as the French deftly combined a number of tools of influence and pressure to wean the Indians away from their English connection. As the English governor of New York wrote to the Board of Trade in 1699, "If a speedy and effectual course be not taken, we shall lose the Five Nations irrevocably, I foresee it plainly; the French never applied themselves so industriously as they do now, to debauch them from us; and we on our parts have nothing, nor do nothing to keep 'em in good humour and steady to us."[21] Richard Coote, Earl of Bellomont, like his predecessors and successors, had good reason to fear French Indian diplomacy.

The Nine Years' War from 1688 to 1697 had been fought out largely in Europe, where the protagonists were Louis XIV, king of France, and his great rivals, the Dutch and English, united under the leadership of William of Orange. It had been waged by sea and by land, in the Low Countries, in Germany, Catalonia, Ireland, and Italy as well as in Canada and the Caribbean. At its end the antagonists lapsed into a wary peace, brought about by financial exhaustion and stalemate; a Protestant Dutch king ruled the British isles and, for a time, peace returned to Europe. The war's end, however, in no way brought to an end the contest in North America. Far from it: The French pursued their diplomacy with the Iroquois, who having suffered exhaustion in their decades-long struggle with Canada, had received precious little support from the English.

The representatives of the English government in the colonies did not take an optimistic view of their predicament vis-à-vis the same Indians, particularly if they should lose control of the exhausted and demoralized

Iroquois. Bellomont had come to have a high regard for the martial qualities of the frustrated and increasingly suspicious Five Nations. Indeed, he warned his London superiors, if they swung to the French side they could "drive us quite out of this Continent." The Indians "laugh at the English and French for exposing their bodies in fight, and call 'em fools," and he had come to the painful conclusion that Indian skill at woodland warfare made them an indispensable ally in the contest between France and England. Now, he believed, the Indians despised the British, who had failed to maintain a corps of soldiers competent in woodland warfare, sending instead "raw men ... who by being unacquainted with the Indian way of fighting, contracted such a dread of 'em, that they proved cowardly.[22]

Bellomont realized that the colonies had not mastered the art of woodland warfare because they could not keep local men on the frontier long enough to do so. Nor were the regulars sent to the colonies in small numbers any better—"a parcel of the vilest fellows that ever wore the King's livery, the very scum of the army in Ireland and several Irish papists amongst 'em who have stirr'd up a general mutiny among the soldiers ... I have three fourths of the soldiers prisoners, and will try some of 'em tomorrow, and I am apt to believe we shall hang or shoot ten or a dozen of 'em."[23] Bellomont, an Anglo-Irish nobleman greedy for land and riches, had hoped to reestablish his fortunes in North America, but he attempted to serve larger interests as well. By the end of his tenure, he saw those interests in the greatest jeopardy.

---

*I gather up again all your hatchets ... which I place with mine
in a pit so deep that no one can take them*

While the English struggled to maintain themselves on the frontier, Frontenac's successor took an extraordinarily bold tack—nothing less than an attempt to solve the diplomatic dilemma from which Canada had suffered for decades. Already in September 1700 the Iroquois had signed a treaty with the French in which they regained prisoners and secured the right to sell furs at Fort Frontenac at the same price as in Montreal. Building on this success, in 1701 Governor Louis-Hector de Callières, Denon-ville's former subordinate, decided to strive for a general peace amongst the Indian tribes of Canada and the West with one another and with the French.

Callières, a scion of the French aristocracy and professional soldier, had served with distinction as governor of Montreal in the 1680s. His biographer describes him as having "the sense of discipline and the habit of command of the career soldier, an inflated feeling of self-importance, and a cantankerous disposition that was not improved by recurring attacks of gout."[24] As with many an acidic soldier before and since, these traits may have had something to do with the predicament in which he had found himself. He had had a trying time defending the outlying set-tlements of Montreal against the Iroquois who had ravaged settlements and slaughtered their inhabitants. He had helped mastermind Denon-ville's 1687 expedition against the Iroquois and had drawn up the abortive plan for an assault on Albany and New York. Suspicious of Iroquois motives, he had disapproved of Frontenac's overtures to them and advo-cated Frontenac's final campaign, which had destroyed their villages, in 1696. Upon becoming acting governor general following Frontenac's death in 1698, and later as governor of the entire colony, Callières continued a hard line with the Iroquois, who, pressed by their neighbors in the west, exhausted by war, and abandoned by the English in the aftermath of the European peace in 1697, sued for peace. Callières shrewdly made of this overture (complete with the return of thirteen French prisoners) a larger diplomatic stroke in Indian country—possibly the most successful ever. In July of 1700 he announced that a year later he would host a great assembly that would ratify a larger peace. In July 1701, the delegates began to arrive.

Under the eyes of several thousand spectators, the delegates—some thirteen hundred in all, from more than thirty tribes—came to Montreal. Among them were two hundred Iroquois, from all the tribes with the sole exception of the Mohawks, whose hostility to the French was deep to the point of immutability. Dressed in face paint, feathers, and robes, exchang-ing belts of wampum and other gifts, the best orators of each nation spoke. The conference opened on July 23, 1701, with condolence rituals, as the grand chief of the Senecas, Tekanoet, stood in a canoe and shed tears for the dead. Louis-Thomas Chabert de Joncaire then escorted the eighty-year-old chief to the grand council. There Indian delegates from across North America, Abenakis, Micmacs, Hurons, Potawatomis, Winnebagos, and many others joined them, thirty-nine sovereign nations in all, outnumbering the entire French population of Montreal. The treaty reflected years of patient French diplomacy, as well as the product of missions by the Indians themselves to Montreal and Quebec. The terms of the French version of the treaty were vague ("I gather up again all your hatchets, and all your other instruments of war, which I place with mine in a pit so deep that no one can take them back to disturb the tranquility that I have re-established among my children, and I recommend to you when you meet to treat each other as brothers, and make arrangements for the hunt together . . .") but the achievements were real.[25]

The Peace of Montreal—the greatest diplomatic event in North America until that point, and for many decades thereafter—established a peace that extended from what are now the Maritime Provinces of Canada, through New York, all the way west to what is now Illinois. It brought peace to the area around Montreal, allowing French farmers to till the land in relative tranquility, and it meant that the fur trade between Indian country and New France would proceed apace, even as the French government attempted to reduce the oversupply of beaver that had flooded the French market. While it did not remove all disputes between the French and the Iroquois, and in particular the Mohawks, who remained implacably hostile to the French, it allowed the government in Quebec to begin an expansion to the west that seemed for a time to make it likely that England and France would have to divide North America with France getting the larger share. In ensuing decades French outposts in the Great Lakes region attracted much of the fur trade to Canada, ensuring a stream of revenue for a colony that even so was never financially self-sufficient and was always vulnerable to abandonment by a French government that did not see it as a valuable economic investment, but rather as a strategic check to English expansion. The treaty established as well a core relationship between French and Indians, who already sensed the threat from the more dynamic English populations of the coast. Ironically, peace also created a minor problem for the French, because the uneasy truce among the Indians meant that those of the West could now gain access to Albany and the superior (and cheaper) English trade goods to be found there via the Iroquois middlemen with whom they were nominally at peace.

Callières had few illusions about the reliability of his settlement with the Iroquois, although it proved far more durable than he may have expected. In a move shrewder than Frontenac's, he tamped down raids on the New York frontier, fearing to reestablish the Anglo-Dutch alliance with the Iroquois, while continuing Frontenac's policy of waging low-level war along the New England frontier by supporting Abenaki raids there. This policy of selective warfare against the English colonies persisted through the War of the Spanish Succession at the beginning of the eighteenth century.

———— •—•—• ————

This handful of men with their conduct will in time,
if not prevented, ruin us all

English officials watched the "debauching of our Indians," as they called it, with increasing despair. Lord Bellomont died, exhausted and dispirited, in March 1701, his attention to Indian affairs distracted by the need to cope with the extreme bitterness of New York politics, and his curious business involvement with the legendary Captain Kidd. Others, however, pursued his line of strategic thinking.

Robert Livingston, a shrewd businessman and politician, one of New York's chief experts on Indian affairs and one of the few Britons (Scots, to be strictly truthful) to penetrate the close Dutch merchant class of Albany, saw clearly the solution to the combination of French diplomatic agility, Indian skill at forest warfare, and the apparently hopeless weakness of colonial militias. "The only way to secure the Northern part of America and the fishery there, would be the taking of Canada, which might be done with less charge to the Crown than has been lately expended at one French island." [26] A few frigates, a bomb ketch, and a regiment of regular troops sailing up the St. Lawrence, he thought, combined with a thrust down the Champlain corridor, would enable the English to evict the French from Canada. Were this solution—direct, violent, and conventional—not adopted, he warned, "the French will otherwise in time grow so formidable, by settling behind all the English Plantations and keeping a constant communication and correspondence with

Mississippi, that they will, by the forts and settlements they erect in the heart of the country, be enabled to infest our plantations by daily incursions upon them who lie scattered to and fro without any force to cover them." Nor could the English simply turn their back on the frontier. Were farms and outlying settlements to become untenable in the course of war, Livingston predicted, refugees would flee to towns along the coast, leaving the colonies unable to feed themselves. Strategies of frontier defense would fail, he insisted. He advocated instead a robust offensive into the heart of Canada, and the elimination of all French rule in North America.

When war broke out again in Europe (the War of the Spanish Succession, 1701–13, or Queen Anne's War, as it was known in the colonies), the strategic logics of both sides remained intact. The new French governor of Canada, Marquis Philippe de Rigaud de Vaudreuil, also continued the strategy of Frontenac as modified by Callières. He left the New York border in peace, for fear of reigniting Iroquois hostility, while inciting Indian raids on other frontiers as a way of keeping the English pinned down and, no less important, of keeping up an enmity between the Abenaki and New England. This policy succeeded in one way: Massachusetts, New Hampshire, and Maine suffered during this war.

Perhaps the most infamous of the successors to the Schenectady massacre was the raid on the English town of Deerfield, Massachusetts. A band of 250 French and Indians departed Chambly on the Richelieu River, south of Montreal, and, following the Great Warpath route, reached Deerfield on February 29, 1704, where, after a hard fight, they killed fifty of the residents and captured a hundred more.[27] The target of the raid did not lie along the Great Warpath, but the route of its raiders did, hugging the eastern shores of Lake Champlain and exploiting the water routes into western Massachusetts. As with most war parties, it consisted of a mixed group of Indians, including Iroquois Mohawks from Caughnawaga as well as Hurons and Abenakis, stiffened with French colonial troops and Canadian militia, and led by French Canadian officers of the gentry class. As in the case of the Schenectady raid, these parties were far larger than a normal Indian raiding band of ten or thirty and required considerably more elaborate logistical planning and preparation. They were also far more deadly in their effects, both material and psychological.

English government officials despaired of the ability of the colonists to mobilize their forces against the continuing French and Indian threat. Colonel Robert Quary, visiting the other colonies after leaving New York at the end of 1707, reported back from Connecticut that "this is a very populous country, able to raise ten thousand effective men, and yet would never assist their neighbors in defending the frontiers from the public enemy nor secure their own from the insults of the enemy who hath destroyed whole towns and carried away the inhabitants for want of a regulated government and militia."[28] Quary continued:

> I have often represented to your Honors the unhappy circumstances of her Majesty's Provinces on North America, who are ruined in their trade, harassed and destroyed by a handful of people, for the French are not more than three thousand effective men in all the parts of Canada, and Port Royal, whereas the Queen hath more than eighty thousand men in her several Provinces, which are able to eat up the French, and yet this handful of men with their conduct will in time, if not prevented, ruin us all.[29]

He had put his finger on the strategic puzzle: With inferior resources, the French were nonetheless winning the contest for North America.

One more major colonial figure saw matters exactly the same way, and launched the last major assault on Quebec via the Champlain valley for half a century. Samuel Vetch, a Scottish soldier become trader with Indians and French alike, proposed a "glorious enterprise"—nothing less than the conquest of Quebec itself. Coming to England in 1706 to make his case, he convinced British authorities of its practicality and assured himself the rank of colonel and the prospect of becoming governor of Canada should he succeed in conquering it. In a powerfully written memorandum, "Canada Surveyed," Vetch laid out a comprehensive picture of Canada's geography, population, and vulnerabilities, based on his own travels there as a merchant. He, too, marveled that Britain, with all its naval power, "should so tamely allow such a troublesome neighbor as the French, not only to sit down peaceably aside them, but with a handful of people vastly dispersed to possess a country of four thousand miles extent, quite encompassing and hemming in betwixt them and the sea, all the British Empire upon the said Continent of America."[30]

According to Vetch's plan, an expedition of English troops and New

England volunteers—perhaps twenty-five hundred in all—would assault Quebec and Montreal via the sea route, up the St. Lawrence. At the same time, a column of fifteen hundred colonial troops would attack north along the Champlain valley. The idea of a pincer attack along the two main waterways into the French Canadian heartland was appealing, but the challenges were formidable. The English would have to sail a British fleet up the St. Lawrence to besiege Quebec, while building a supply system in the wilderness that could support the advance of a large colonial force along the Champlain valley, sustaining colonial cooperation in the face of political disunion and the problems of sickness and indiscipline that always plagued colonial forces. The 1709 invasion plan collapsed, despite the muster of colonial troops assembled from New York and New England on Lake Champlain under Vetch's inspiration and leadership. The British ministry, in a moment of strategic fecklessness, decided not to send a fleet to the New World after all.[31]

A subsequent, exclusively naval assault on Quebec, under Admiral Sir Hovenden Walker, collapsed, too. This time the fleet arrived, and promptly. When it sailed from Boston on July 30, 1711, it included nine ships of the line, two bomb vessels, and sixty other vessels carrying six thousand British regulars—the largest force London had ever sent to North America. Inept navigation and the tricky rocks and shoals of the St. Lawrence soon brought the expedition to grief, however, when eight ships ran aground and foundered. Two hundred passengers and crew survived the wrecks and made it to the shelter of the forests, but over eight hundred soldiers and a hundred sailors drowned, their bodies washing up in heaps on the shore. The commanders of the ground forces were willing to press on, despite the dismal sight, but Walker lost his nerve and decided to give up the attempt.[32]

The failure of these campaigns further reduced English fortunes. The Iroquois continued to fear the consequences of permanent enmity with the French, while wishing to maintain their relationships with the traders of Albany. The French were assiduous in courting them, while working to extend their influence to the west, with tribes now willing to maintain peaceful relations with the Iroquois so long as the latter tolerated their trade with the merchants of Albany.

The formal conclusion of peace in Europe at Utrecht in 1713 gave the British much: not only recognition of the Protestant succession in

England and confirmation of the permanent separation of the Crowns of France and Spain, but much in the way of colonial possessions. In the Mediterranean, Spain ceded Gibraltar and Minorca, as well as the lucrative *asiento*, or contract for supplying Spanish America with slaves. Nova Scotia—Acadia as the French had called it—had fallen to the British, who, with Vetch as governor, held down a French peasant population with a couple of small garrisons. The British retained it, together with Newfoundland and Hudson Bay territory, but the French kept Canada, and held on to Isle Royale (Cape Breton Island), where they constructed the massive fortress city of Louisbourg as a naval and trading base to keep open the St. Lawrence and harass the New England trade.

Nor did peace in Europe mean tranquility along the frontier, for the proxy war continued. Dummer's War, for example, between 1722 and 1725, emerged out of Abenaki unwillingness to accept English rule in northern Maine. Behind it, however, lay French support and the perpetuation of Frontenac's raiding strategy. Under the guidance of a Jesuit priest, Sébastien Rale, who had established a mission at Norridgewock on the Kennebec River in 1694, the Abenakis traded with the English, but remained allied with the French. The talented Rale, author of a meticulous dictionary of the Abenaki language and much loved by the tribes he had proselytized, was also an agent of the French government, maintaining a close connection with Governor Vaudreuil. In July of 1722 Governor Shute of Massachusetts declared war, and colonial expeditions attacked the Indians and their French priest. Rale died in murky circumstances—a fair fight according to the New Englanders, a treacherous assassination during a negotiation according to the French—and the victorious Puritans joyfully carried his scalp off to Boston. But the Abenaki Indians of New England, driven from their homes farther south by the "Bostonnais," were not so easily discouraged, and attempted, though with less success than the Iroquois, to balance their economic dependence on the English with their preference for and support from the French.[33]

Peace in the New World thus did not resemble peace in the Old. During war a robust covert trade between the English colonies and New France might continue while pitched battles took place along the frontier; during peace, incitement of the horrors of frontier warfare accompanied polite diplomacy, solicitous regard for some captives, and nominal tranquility. Suspicious English officials believed that the French did better in peacetime with the Iroquois than during times of declared war, because they were more easily able to sell large quantities of firearms that might otherwise be intercepted by the Royal Navy. Missionaries worked on the religious and cultural disposition of the Indians, and French emissaries applied the arts of diplomacy that the English knew they sorely lacked.

In the years following the Peace of Utrecht, New France grew slowly in population, but more rapidly in power and military strength. The War of the Austrian Succession, from 1740 to 1748 (King George's War in the colonies), saw another flare of hostilities along the Great War-path, as the rising Anglo-Irish lord of the Mohawk valley, William John-son, assembled Mohawk raiding parties to attack the French, and the Canadians retaliated with renewed raids on Albany and Schenectady. In scale the hostilities in America were a pale shadow of those in Europe, with the one remarkable exception of the seizure of the French fortress city of Louisbourg on Cape Breton Island by an expedition of New Englanders supported by a British fleet. The Peace of Aix-la-Chapelle, which returned Louisbourg to the French, outraged the colonists, par-ticularly in New England, who brooded over this betrayal, as they saw it, of their interests.

Meanwhile, the French expanded their influence across the continent, building forts in the West. Their explorers roamed the Mississippi south, and the *coureurs du bois*, the traders who lived with the Indians, continued the profitable trade of their predecessors, bringing pelts to the colorful societies that grew up around such outposts as Fort Frontenac, Detroit, Michilimackinac, and Fort Niagara. There, watchful garrisons and the colonial *troupes de la marine* provided security and, at the king's expense, cheap goods to keep the Indians away from rival English posts such as Oswego on Lake Ontario.

On the Great Warpath the French pushed farther south. In 1730 Jean-Louis de la Corne de Chaptes, a French aristocrat who like many of his fellows combined a robust business career in the Indian fur trade with extensive woodland military service, proposed the construction of a fort at what is now Crown Point to contain the English who might otherwise press northward to Montreal.[34] The governor of Canada strongly endorsed the idea. In 1734 workmen and soldiers began to build Fort St. Frédéric, whose ruins are still visible today. After three years of construc-tion they had produced a four-story citadel and a dozen other buildings surrounded by an external wall with six bastions—the total about an acre in extent.[35] It was a small site in absolute terms, garrisoned by no more than a hundred soldiers plus families, but self-sufficient enough, with cows and vegetable gardens, and even a windmill for grinding grain, and superbly located as a base for operations against New England and New York—and, indeed, raiding parties against New Hampshire and Massachusetts departed from Fort St. Frédéric, which the English claimed, however ineffectually, as belonging to them. La Corne's son, La Corne St. Luc, a gifted woodland leader of Canadians and Indian war parties, began making good use of the raiding base that his father's foresight had created.

Peter Kalm, an inquisitive Swedish man of science, described the life of this southernmost outpost of French power on the Great Warpath as he observed it on his remarkable trip through the colonies in 1748–49. He had journeyed north from New York, through a dreary wasteland of burned out homesteads and farms, and was relieved to reach this oasis of European civilization. He praised the gracious hospitality of the governor of Fort St. Frédéric, Captain Paul-Louis Dazemard de Lusignan, a fifty-year-old Canadian soldier, "a man of learning and great politeness."[36] But Kalm also witnessed something else. On July 5, a "bloodcurdling outcry" interrupted a comfortable dinner with Lusignan. Coming to the window Kalm saw six Indians paddling a canoe to shore opposite the fort. With them in the canoe was a miserable nine-year-old boy, and in the bow of the canoe a long pole from which dangled a bloody scalp. It belonged to the boy's father, whom they had found and slain as he worked in the field with his son. The Indians, bedecked in the dead man's clothes, danced with the scalp, informing the French that they intended to take the boy and have him "marry one of their relations so that he might become one of them."

Lusignan "did not think it advisable to exasperate them," so, although it was a time of peace, he merely sent the Indians and their captive on to Montreal with provisions for their journey. It was a prudent act, which did not turn out too badly for the boy—the governor of Montreal shipped him back to New York. But it was one more incident of the war along the Great Warpath that never really ended despite nominal peace. Six decades after its conception, as modified and refined by his successors, Frontenac's strategy of pinning the English down by chronic, brutal frontier raiding remained intact and seemed to be succeeding. The English had not yet mustered the resources or found the strategy to bring about their desired, unlimited response—the extirpation of French rule in North America. But Frontenac had, unwittingly, given birth to an enduring American notion about war. His Anglo-American opponents had concluded that war was not a game of political advantage and statecraft, to be suspended from time to time by diplomacy and treaties, but rather a brutal struggle, to be resolved by complete, crushing, and definitive victory. That legacy lasted after Schenectady was rebuilt, and the tale of the massacre had been long forgotten.

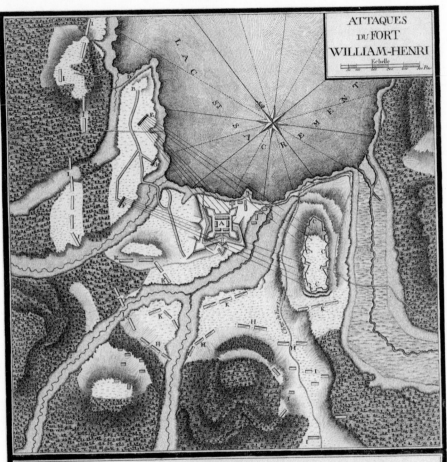

ATTAQUES
du FORT
WILLIAM-HENRI
Echelle

LAC ST SACREMENT

ATTAQUES DU FORT WILLIAM-HENRI
en Amérique
, par les troupes françaises aux ordres du Marquis de Montcalm.
Prise de ce fort le 7 Août 1757.

Renvois.

A. Fort William-Henri. B. Ouverture des tranchées la nuit du 4 au 5 Août.
C. Camp retranché, que les anglais allèrent occuper lors de l'arrivée des français.
D. Baie, où les français débarquèrent leur artillerie. E. Batterie de huit
canons & d'un mortier. F. Batterie de dix canons & d'un mortier. G. Batterie
de six pièces, dont on ne fit aucun usage. H. Position de M.ʳ de Levi
pendant l'investissement du fort. I. Position des troupes durant le siège.
K. Leur position après la prise pendant la demolition des retranchemens
faits par les anglais. ▬ Troupes sauvages.

C. P. S. C. M.

The siege of Fort William Henry. *Reproduced by permission of the
Society of the Cincinnati, Washington, D.C.*

CHAPTER TWO

Fort William Henry, 1757

The Americans are in general the dirtiest most contemptible
cowardly dogs that you can conceive

The Seven Years' War—what Americans sometimes call the French and Indian War—broke out in North America in the way so many wars do, as a result of a combination of deliberate but risky diplomatic and military moves, catalyzed by accidents and rooted in what Thucydides described as the origins of all wars, fear, honor, and interest. The immediate flashpoint occurred along the banks of the Ohio River. When Governor Robert Dinwiddie of Virginia sent a twenty-one-year-old George Washington first to ascertain French intentions in the West (in 1753) and then to forestall them at the Forks of the Ohio (in the spring and summer of 1754), neither had any thought of igniting a world war. But that is what happened, when Washington first ambushed a French party, killing its leader, and in turn found itself besieged, and forced to surrender, at Fort Necessity.[1]

But although George Washington had lit the match, many others had piled up the fuel for the conflagration. By the early 1750s the British government had quietly resolved to push the French out of the way west of the Appalachians, dispatching over a thousand regulars in two regiments under General Edward Braddock, the first overall commander in North America, to begin dismantling the system of French forts that threatened to hem the English colonies in. And even as they negotiated with the French, British statesmen had ordered the Royal Navy to pounce on a French convoy to North America, doing so on June 10, 1755, just as Braddock began his ill-fated march to Fort Duquesne, near present-day Pittsburgh.[2] Braddock's march culminated with the spectacular destruction of his force on July 9, 1755, at the hands of inferior numbers of Canadians and French-led Indians—a defeat from which George Washington, accompanying the hapless general, barely escaped. The French, not without reason, viewed the attack on Fort Duquesne and, no less, the botched attack on the convoy as a perfidious act of aggression in what was officially a time of peace.

The war that exploded that summer in North America spread during the next year across the globe and dealt with issues that had nothing to do with colonies, most notably the rivalry between Prussia and Austria-Hungary, aided by Russia, and British anxiety for Hanover, home of the royal house. The stakes were large enough in Europe, but in North America they were larger still—nothing less than the survival of New France on the one hand, or (as the colonists saw it) the permanent containment of the English colonies on the Atlantic seaboard on the other.

For well over half a century France and Great Britain had grappled for North American dominion. Despite the overwhelming numbers of the British colonies, the French were in no mood tamely to acquiesce to English probes into Ohio, or anywhere else in North America, for that matter.[3] In 1748 Louis XV had sacrificed the victories of the Maréchal de Saxe in Europe in order to obtain the restoration of the fortress city of Louisbourg on bleak Cape Breton Island. A succession of able French governors had strengthened Canada's defenses, improved the drill and equipment of its militia, and begun constructing forts to thwart and contain the British colonies of the Atlantic seaboard.

As throughout its history, French Canada relied on a combination of diplomatic and military skill to compensate for the meagerness of its population—barely five thousand Frenchmen had emigrated to Canada between 1713 and 1756, and on the eve of the Seven Years' War the total population probably numbered no more than eighty thousand. But it was

a thriving colony now, whose economy included not only agriculture, fishing, sealing, and the production of raw materials from the forests (tar, for
example), but a small shipbuilding industry as well. To the very end, Canada never paid its way as a colony, but some Frenchmen saw its potential
nonetheless.[4]

The French government was unwilling to sink unlimited funds into
the construction of outposts that yielded no substantial revenue and consumed scarce resources of money and men. But the statesmen of Paris
realized that Canada offered real strategic benefits, even though this fur-
producing colony consumed rather than generated revenue, and the sugar
islands of the West Indies were infinitely more lucrative. Canada had
other attractions that made it worth fighting for.

In the near term, Canada distracted and pinned down disproportionate English resources, which might otherwise be thrown against France.
It helped sustain the French fishing presence on the Great Banks of the
Atlantic, important both as a source of food and as a nursery for sailors
to man the French navy. In the longer term, it might, if united with the
infant settlements of Louisiana, grow into a much more powerful dominion, which could, in turn, contest British dominance of the Caribbean
and claim the real wealth produced there by the sugar islands. Canada
was not worth a vast investment of resources, then, particularly if the
Royal Navy could disrupt or even sever communications between France
and North America in a global war, but it was worth enough to merit the
dispatch of a small, efficient army under a capable commander, and that
is precisely what France did.

Neither London nor Paris viewed the war in North America as central to the broader conflict between them, but neither was prepared to
cede the fight. Both sent to the colonies relatively small but nonetheless
effective forces of regular troops to undertake war against their competi-
tor. In both cases, these commanders came into conflict with local officials
and faced the acute—in some cases, well-nigh insurmountable—challenge of adapting European modes of warfare to local circumstances, particularly those of the Great Warpath.

French forces in the New World consisted of full-time colonial troops,
militia, and regular soldiers dispatched from France.[5] The most important
of these were the *troupes de la marine*, controlled by the Ministry of the
Marine rather than the Ministry of War. Organized in independent com-

panies of approximately fifty men each, these men garrisoned Louisbourg and Louisiana (twenty and twenty-one companies, respectively), with another thirty companies in Canada as of 1756. Unlike regular regiments in which officers could, as was the custom of the time, purchase commissions, the *troupes de la marine* were manned by officers selected and promoted on the basis of merit. Service as officers in these units proved highly desirable for members of the Canadian gentry, so that by the time of the Seven Years' War the officer corps consisted of Canadians, while the enlisted ranks came from metropolitan France. These officers, who made the irregular war of the woodlands their particular specialty, with their soldiers accustomed to regular and bush warfare alike, accounted for many of the debacles suffered by English forces in the ensuing war.

Far more numerous—some thirteen thousand or more, compared to some fifteen hundred colonial regulars in Canada proper—were the Canadian militia. They consisted of all the men between fifteen and sixty in each parish, and served without pay; like their English counterparts they lacked the discipline for a stand-up, European-style fight in open terrain. But they were hardy, at home in the woods, and accustomed, after more than a century of Indian fighting, to bearing arms in defense of their homes. The product of a semifeudal society, they were more docile than their New England counterparts, or rather, more accepting of the authority of local seigneur and parish priest. When not fighting, they could serve to move supplies and maintain roads as well, being skilled in handling boats and the wielding of axes. They were thus a brand of part-time soldier comparable to their English opponents, but operating under a more centralized and therefore more effective authority.

The French regular units came from the French army, thereby creating a bureaucratic problem, because the colonies fell under the Ministry of Marine. But accepting the need of seconding the units to the Marine, in 1754 the Ministry of War sent to Canada six battalions from the regiments of La Reine, Artois, Bourgogne, Languedoc, Guyenne, and Béarn, followed in 1756 by battalions from the regiments of La Sarre and Royal Roussillon, and finally two more from the regiment of Berry. Of these ten battalions, numbering in total less than six thousand men, two went to Louisbourg, already garrisoned by two other battalions, for a grand total of twelve. Setting aside that fortress city (nominally, some twenty-four hundred regulars and a thousand *troupes de la marine* before the inevitable losses to disease and accident), one may estimate, therefore, that the French had at their disposal for the defense of Canada something less than five thousand regulars. These were good soldiers under officers able enough at European warfare, but without any qualities that distinguished them from their British counterparts.

British forces in North America consisted of regulars, provincial troops, and militia, all of which expanded tremendously during the war. Until 1754 regular British forces had consisted chiefly of the garrison of Nova Scotia, three understrength regiments. Plans to recruit two more regiments locally had lapsed, although the scheme was revived once war began, and two other regiments were sent with the ill-fated General Edward Braddock on his disastrous march to Fort Duquesne. As the war progressed, much larger regular forces were dispatched, and others created from scratch. *44Th 48Th*

The provincial (full-time colonial) troops and militia, however, proved collectively less effective than their Canadian counterparts. The colonies had, for decades past, been accustomed to raising their own units for major expeditions, and indeed one such had, miraculously enough, taken Louisbourg in 1745. But the provincials never achieved the quality of the *troupes de la marine*. Raised and released annually, officered not by regulars but by men from their own colonies, indifferently disciplined, prone to desertion, homesickness, and the more fatal diseases associated with the throwing together of rural populations under camp conditions exacerbated by poor hygiene, they were despised by the British, who used them chiefly on the lines of communications. "The lowest dregs of the People," said one general; "a proud, indolent, ignorant self sufficient set." Brigadier James Wolfe, who became perhaps the most famous of British commanders in North America, declared that, "the Americans are in general the dirtiest most contemptible cowardly dogs that you can conceive. There is no depending on them in action. They fall down dead in their own dirt and desert by battalions, officers and all. Such rascals as those are rather an encumbrance than any real strength to an army." [6]

For their part, the provincials were infuriated by the rule that any regular officer in effect outranked a provincial, and by the contempt that the British did not hesitate to display. [7] The British, and perhaps members of the aristocratic elite more generally, could not understand the societies that molded the provincials. They were more democratic, often electing their officers from the local elite; religious (at least in the case of the New Englanders), reflecting their roots in Puritan England; and they conceived their obligations in contractual terms.[8] These were antipathies that persisted well beyond the Seven Years' War and played no small role in shaping British perceptions of the American military capacity through the Revolution.

The American colonial militia, which served as a pool of recruits for the provincials, shared many of their characteristics. They were more poorly disciplined than the Canadian militia, were officered by election rather than appointment, and also rejected the notion that they could be routinely sent beyond their colonies or used for extended periods. Thus, although the colonies were so much more populous than New France— Massachusetts alone, with a population of 188,000 in 1750, had double that of Canada, and the combined total was almost 1.2 million—the military instruments at hand were weaker. Moreover, not all of that 1.2 million felt itself directly engaged in the war. The New England colonies, including Massachusetts, New Hampshire, and Connecticut, did, but colonies like New Jersey, with more than 70,000 people, had less to do with the war; and even large states that had turbulent frontiers, such as Pennsylvania, with 120,000, and Virginia with more than 230,000, found it difficult, for internal political reasons, to mobilize substantial forces and commit them to the conflict.

Some statesmen attempted to coordinate colonial defense—Benjamin Franklin, for example, who managed to arrange a convention of New England, New York, and Pennsylvania and Maryland in Albany, at the English terminus of the Great Warpath, in 1754. But internal divisions were difficult to overcome. Thus, although the raw strength of the English colonies was great, their political unity was negligible, and the capability of the British government to direct their efforts questionable. There had been no single British political or military authority in the colonies between the end of the seventeenth century and the arrival of General Edward Braddock in April 1755.

When the war began the British were also at a disadvantage in dealing with the Indians. General Braddock, upon arriving in North America, appointed a single commissioner to deal with the northern Indians. This was the first, and not entirely successful British effort to create a single Indian policy that could mirror that of the French in Canada. There was a lot of ground to make up. By 1754 a century of French policy, mixing force, strategic trade, religious conversion, and adroit diplomacy, had succeeded in completing the work started by land-hungry American settlers—the alienation of Indian loyalty or even neutrality toward the British Crown. In the West, the strong measures of the governors of Quebec had reasserted French influence in the Ohio and Mississippi valleys, and had chased off many of the English traders. The western Indians were, by and large, ready to join in French war parties for all the usual reasons Indians usually fought.

Only along the Great Warpath was there some uncertainty, where the Iroquois, internally divided, barely recovered from the demographic collapse of the late seventeenth and very early eighteenth centuries, remained disposed to the English. Or rather, where some of the Iroquois did: The region's Mohawks remained fairly reliable, but the other nations, to greater or lesser degree, were open to neutrality between French and English, or even support for Onontio, as they called the king of France. Torn between ancestral hatred of the French and fear of the land-greedy English, between the immediate reality of French power and the long-term loom of English numbers, and the religious tension between Catholic and Protestant converts, the Iroquois tried to find a middle path that would allow them to survive the great conflict. The war produced the calamity of Iroquois fighting Iroquois, as the western nations (the Senecas, most notably) tilted to the French, joining the Christianized Iroquois of Caughnawaga in fighting for France.

The counterpoise to expanding French influence lay chiefly with one remarkable man, William Johnson, in his own right a force worth a small army.[9] Born in Ireland in 1715, he began acting as agent for his uncle, a naval officer (later vice admiral), Sir Peter Warren, and in 1738 came to America to oversee Warren's properties in the Mohawk valley. With his uncle's capital and his own native wit and energy, he became a wealthy and powerful man, trading goods with the Indians and bringing English farm surpluses to market. His shops supplied traders with goods, undercutting the Dutch firms of Albany, which loathed him. Traveling with the Mohawks, learning their language, and bedding their women, he became a power in the land, colonel of the frontier militia at the end of King George's War. In 1755 the commander in chief in North America, Edward Braddock, wisely appointed him to manage relations with the Six

Nations. In 1756 Johnson became the superintendent of northern Indians, whom he exploited and protected in roughly equal measure. An odd feudal lord in the midst of a germinating democracy, Johnson was able to mediate among his Indian, German, and English clients. Uniquely, he could maintain the connection to the Iroquois even as all of their incentives appeared to point toward defection from the English cause. This was critical, because to lose the Iroquois would be to completely expose the frontier regions of New York and New England, which provincials and militia could not adequately protect.

Material resources, then, favored the British in the long run; but with respect to efficiency, a compact strategic position, centralization of administration, and superior relations with the allies who counted, the Indians, the French had the upper hand.

In this, as in all wars, the supreme political and military commanders mattered greatly. In 1755 at the head of New France stood two men: Pierre Rigaud de Vaudreuil de Cavaignal, and the Baron Jean-Armand Dieskau. Vaudreuil, the governor general of New France, had been born in Quebec in 1698 to a distinguished father, the colony's governor from 1703 to 1725.[10] He had served in the colonial regulars and the colonial administration, aiding his talented father and participating in wilderness exploration and diplomacy. After successful service as governor of Louisiana, where he played Indians off against one another and the British and developed the fledgling economy, he finally achieved his lifelong dream of becoming governor general of New France, sailing from Brest in May 1755 with Dieskau and the French army and narrowly missing a British naval ambush. He had spent two anxious years in France between appointments, watching as war with Britain had brewed a world away.

Vaudreuil was, unlike the British generals sent to command in the New World, a native of the continent, a Canadian, a loyal servant of the French Crown, no doubt, but someone for whom the welfare of the colony was a matter of upbringing and heartfelt loyalty. He adhered to Frontenac's strategic conception: The English colonies could not be conquered, but by using colonial regulars and Indians to ravage enemy frontiers and launching preemptive attacks on English bases, New France could pin the enemy down, stalemate him, and wait for favorable developments in other theaters of war to bring the conflict to a favorable conclusion. Fussy but courtly, aggressive in war and politically adroit in the handling of the

Indians and the Canadian *habitants*, he was as good a political leader as Canada could hope for. And, moreover, he combined political and military authority, at least for the first part of the war.

His military counterpart, Baron Dieskau, had been a protégé of the finest soldier of the age, Maréchal de Saxe, and had served as the military governor of Brest.[11] But when he arrived in Quebec in June 1755 he had little time to devise his own strategic plans, little knowledge of Canada, and in any case, had instructions to support Governor Vaudreuil. Neither man had much time to do more than prepare to parry the initial British assaults.

After Braddock's death, command in North America had descended suddenly upon the governor of Massachusetts, William Shirley. He had been the motive force in raising the expedition to take Louisbourg in 1745 and helped negotiate the Treaty of Aix-la-Chapelle at its conclusion. Returning to Massachusetts in 1753, he held to his imperial ambitions for Britain and pushed for the abortive Albany Plan of union in the face of the French and Indian threat. His martial ambitions, however, ran aground on colonial rivalries, his own indifferent skill as a commander, and the blundering of the provincial armies. His plan of 1755 for coordinated attacks on the French forts at Niagara, Fort St. Frédéric (Crown Point), and the Bay of Fundy had strategic merit. The way to deny the French the advantage of mobility and interior lines was to launch a simultaneous attack on many fronts, much the way the American Confederacy later succumbed to blockade and simultaneous offensives in West and East in 1864–65. Shirley intended to lead one thrust personally—to Oswego—but he also envisaged a powerful blow along the Lake Champlain route. As is often the case, however, a good strategic concept was one thing—the ability to implement it, something very different.

———•◆•———

The troops are in the best disposition possible,
and panting only for the attack

In the war that had now begun in North America, the Great Warpath had a central role to play—the map alone indicated that. From the French point of view it was the most direct, and potentially the most lethal,

approach to the Canadian core, the other two routes being the St.
Lawrence—guarded, for now, by the fortress city of Louisbourg and the
sheer difficulty of its navigation by a large fleet—and the Lake Ontario
route, which was more roundabout and lay through territory inhabited by
unfriendly Indians. Shirley had understood this, and urged William Johnson to seize a position at the southern end of Lake George to serve as a
base for operations northward.

William Johnson accepted the Massachusetts governor's plan, and
although he had his doubts about Shirley (who was attempting to orches-
trate a simultaneous offensive against Fort Niagara), did his best to carry
it out, despite friction with both Shirley and the governor of New York,
James de Lancey. Johnson's army of some thirty-five hundred men from
New England and New York was supported by three hundred Indians led
by the venerable Mohawk Chief Hendrick (Theyanoguin), brought in by
Johnson's influence. The provincial army was originally intended to
advance on Crown Point, taking Fort St. Frédéric, a lunge of almost fifty
miles through the wilderness. In the best case that would prove an ambitious objective for an army composed almost entirely of provincial troops.

Johnson first concentrated his force at the southern end of the Great
Carrying Place, the expanse of land between the Hudson and Lake St.
Sacrement (Lake George). His base was the newly built Fort Edward on
the Hudson. By the end of August 1755 the intelligence reports from
Johnson's Indians were dispiriting in the extreme. The French were alert
at Fort St. Frédéric; six thousand French troops had reportedly landed in
Quebec; the governor of Montreal had boasted that Canada would throw
eight thousand regulars and militia, plus Indians, at the advancing provincials; the French were fortifying Ticonderoga.[12] Johnson called a council of war of his senior subordinates. They approved a further advance,
but insisted that more assistance from the colonies was necessary and
suggested that as an immediate measure it made sense to build a fortified
camp at the southern end of Lake George—what would eventually
became known as Fort William Henry (or later, Fort George).

By early September 1755, Johnson and his army had constructed their
camp. But he soon found himself immersed in the wretched business of
sustaining an ill-disciplined force of quarrelsome provincials in the forests
of upstate New York. His base of supply lay fourteen miles in the rear at

Fort Edward, the road there a wilderness track recently hewn out of the forests. Indian raiders hovered on his flanks, and scouts—at least, those who returned with scalps still on their heads—reported the coming and going of boats and men at the new French camp at Ticonderoga, an outpost that would have to be taken before any thought could be had of moving on Fort St. Frédéric. Consolidating the position on Lake George proved challenge enough; by the beginning of September there could be little thought of getting as far as Crown Point in this season. Johnson was by experience, abilities, and temperament many things—a woodland entrepreneur, an adept at Indian politics, a feudal lord—but not a general. The burdens of command weighed heavily upon him: his unruly troops, the looming French attack, the turbulent politics of the Iroquois, and to cap it all, his growing suspicions of his chief, whom he saw in the darkest colors. Governor Shirley, he wrote the Board of Trade, "is and will be my inveterate Enemy; that the whole weight of his power, his influence, his craft, and abilities, will be exerted to blast my character." [13]

Johnson's fears (of the French at any rate) rested on reality. Vaudreuil, who had had the opportunity of perusing the late General Braddock's papers, taken from the mangled remains of the dead general's column, had learned of planned British offensives against Forts Frontenac, Niagara, and St. Frédéric. This last he viewed as the most serious threat. Until this point he had thought of ordering a blow at the British outpost at Oswego on Lake Ontario: Now he ordered Baron Dieskau to abandon that project and throw Johnson's army back. [14]

The supremely self-confident Dieskau did not object. He agreed with Vaudreuil that Johnson's force would, if left unmolested, advance as far as Montreal; he also believed that he had the better army. "The troops are in the best disposition possible, and panting only for the attack." His only fear was that the enemy "will beat a retreat on learning that we are on the march." [15] Dieskau had under him a force of fifteen hundred regulars, a thousand militia, and some five or six hundred Indians led by Captain La Corne St. Luc of the *troupes de la marine*, son of the de la Corne who had conceived the idea of building Fort St. Frédéric. Dieskau chose to leave a substantial garrison at Ticonderoga, deciding to attack Johnson's position with an elite force composed of two hundred regulars and some thirteen hundred militia and Indians—perhaps fifteen hundred in all. Leaving so many regular troops behind was his first mistake. The militia and Indians would fight well in the woods, but had neither the discipline nor the temperament to storm a fortified position.

With his relatively small force Dieskau planned to land some distance from the fortified camp at the southern end of Lake St. Sacrement. He would then bypass it and attack the more weakly held Fort Edward fourteen miles in the rear. Should he succeed, he would thereby bag two garrisons at a stroke, as Johnson's men would face the certain prospect of starvation once Dieskau had cut the supply line to Fort Edward. Dieskau, who had experienced much irregular warfare in Europe, was willing to risk an unorthodox blow, leaving Johnson's camp in his rear while attacking the Irishman's base on the Hudson.

The ensuing Battle of Lake George on September 8 was the product of blunders on both sides. Dieskau swung around Johnson's camp and approached Fort Edward, but then his Indians quailed (with reason) at the thought of assaulting a fortified position armed with cannon. Dieskau—like many French commanders before and after—had to defer to the native warriors and so doubled back toward Johnson's camp on Lake George. There he seized another opportunity. Johnson, learning of the French advance on Fort Edward, had first thought of sending five hundred men to burn the French boats while dispatching a like number to relieve Fort Edward. His Indians (and the native Americans seem to have had better judgment than either commander) sensibly objected to this dispersal of forces, so Johnson sent a column of a thousand colonists and Mohawks marching out to the relief of Fort Edward.

Despite the Mohawks' presence, the Anglo-American column wandered into a hasty ambush set by Dieskau—although the French commander ever after believed that some of his own Indians had tipped off the Iroquois in the English column. The ambush nonetheless turned into a rout, and the French pursued the fleeing colonials, killing the Mohawk chief, Hendrick, and dispersing the English.[16] Overconfidence impaired Dieskau's good sense. Approaching the fortified camp, he led a rush on the Anglo-American camp at Lake George with his tiny force of regulars backed by that minority of the Indians and militia who were brave, or foolish, enough to join him. The attack failed. Thrice wounded, Dieskau was captured, and the battle ended in stalemate outside the improvised

walls of Johnson's armed camp. Vaudreuil, who had given Dieskau exact-
ing (not to say excessively detailed) instructions, was appalled that the
general had made such a botch of it.

The season of large-scale campaigning ended as the cold winds of
autumn blew off the lakes. In that dismal late fall of 1755, Johnson,
wounded in the battle, harried and distressed by colonial troops marching back to their homes, had at least avoided disaster. He began the construction of a permanent fortification to replace the camp, along lines
drawn by the one regular officer in his contingent, engineer Captain William Eyre. This in itself represented a political success in coping with the
New Englanders, who were not interested in investing in hard labor for
the benefit of New York, as they saw it, and who had already labored hard
to build Fort Edward on the Hudson. Wary of European-style fortifications that would require large garrisons, they preferred palisades, vulnerable to artillery, no doubt, but easily burned and abandoned if that became
necessary.[17] Still, Eyre had a way with the provincials, and some, including
a young captain from Massachusetts, Jeduthan Baldwin, worked conscientiously to fulfill his design.

Johnson thus had his way—more or less. By late November 1755 Eyre
had designed and built the earthenwork structure known as Fort William
Henry in the approved European manner, an uneven rectangle with four
bastions, the walls thirty feet thick, boxed in by pine logs. But the work
was hard, and the army ill-equipped and disinclined to accept authority.
"The Fort I find goes on all things considered pretty well [but] there are
many difficulties to combat against, from that averseness to labour, and
the want of due subordination which I very early found to be the capital
sins of the army. I have made war against them by every method within
the extent of my power and abilities, but to me at least, they are inevitable."[18] Wounded, ill, and made sicker by the eighteenth-century treat-
ments of bleeding, blistering, and purging, Johnson complained in
October that his orders had been "daily and notoriously violated." Despite
urging from an increasingly peremptory Governor Shirley to attack
French forces at the junction of Lakes George and Champlain, he and his
council of war declined to do so that autumn. Johnson had trouble enough
managing the perilous line of supply to Fort Edward and the rancorous
enmity between New Yorkers and New Englanders in his camp. By the

end of the fall he turned over command of his shrinking army and the fort to Major General John Winslow, a Massachusetts soldier who had a long history of service in the militia and the provincial troops.

The two sides now settled into a kind of eighteenth-century version of trench warfare, albeit on an extended scale: the British finishing Fort William Henry and the French constructing a fort at Ticonderoga, or Carillon, as they called it. Both forward fortifications rested on a chain of installations stretching back—in the French case down the Champlain valley through Fort St. Frédéric to St. Johns, Chambly, and Montreal; in the British case to Fort Edward on the Hudson and Albany. The intervening thirty miles between Forts William Henry and Carillon became a no-man's-land, criss-crossed in all four seasons by raiding parties and scouts, on foot and in canoe.

While the Anglo-Americans hunkered down at the southern end of Lake George, the French consolidated their new position on Lake Champlain. In September 1755, possibly even before hearing about Dieskau's failure, Governor Vaudreuil had ordered the construction of a new fort, Carillon, on the Ticonderoga peninsula. Carillon offered the French some advantages that the small fort at Crown Point, Fort St. Frédéric, a dozen miles to the north, lacked. Although Fort St. Frédéric commanded the narrows of Lake Champlain, it was a small structure, lacking heavy artillery or the fortifications upon which to emplace them, and was surrounded by high ground, which would prove fatal in the event of a siege. To make the place truly secure would involve construction on a massive scale, likely to yield a fort too large to be adequately garrisoned by New France's few regulars. Besides, like Chambly further north, Fort St. Frédéric was a base for raiding parties and small convoys, not a fortress built to withstand siege. Its design—a square outerwork with a multistory keep—was relatively primitive by the standards of contemporary fortification.

The Carillon site, poised on a small appendix of elevated land sticking into Champlain and only three miles from Lake George (to which it was joined by a river), was more convenient for launching operations along either body of water.[19] Although it was dominated by the heights of Carillon, perhaps half a mile northwest of the fort itself, that area could be covered by field fortifications; the looming mountain known as Sugar Loaf, or Mount Defiance, was not yet seen as a potential menace. Carillon could delay a large-scale attack from the south or serve as a launching point for attacks in that direction along either lake.

In the spring of 1756, the cast of senior military leaders changed on both sides. To replace the wounded Dieskau (now interned in England, after three months' hospitable captivity in America), the king appointed a new commander of his forces in Canada, the Marquis Louis Joseph de Montcalm.[20] The new leader was a forty-three-year-old soldier who after twenty years of active military service had retired to a country estate in 1753. But in March 1756 he received the appointment to the rank of major general (*maréchal de camp*) and was sent to New France, there to support Governor Vaudreuil. It was a subordination this testy officer found difficult to bear. Arriving in Quebec after a five-week voyage across the Atlantic, he soon traveled to Oswego, where Vaudreuil had begun a siege against the English trading outpost. Montcalm, "extremely vain, determined to have his own way in all things, critical of everything that did not conform to his preconceived ideas and of anyone who failed to agree with him completely, and possessed of a savage tongue that he could not curb," was headed for a rocky relationship with the intrusive, micromanaging, entrepenurial Canadian governor.[21]

In theory, Montcalm reported to Vaudreuil. In practice, the marquis sent a stream of missives to friends at court complaining of the incompetence of the governor and the ineffectiveness of the Canadians. What lay underneath was not merely the typical tension between political and military authority—inherent in all wars save those conducted by a military dictator—but the tension between Canadian and French outlooks on war.

Montcalm, the regular soldier, came to New France determined to maintain the standards and discipline of his little army, including the social status of its officers. He deplored their habit of romancing Canadian girls, for example: "I have found our officers inclined to contract bad marriages," he wrote home in 1757.[22] In a memorandum to battalion commanders in his little expeditionary force, he instructed them to keep soldiers disciplined, to keep them apart from the population, and to adhere to the highest standards of formal drill. The troops should be kept separate from the Indians and (per the orders of Governor Vaudreuil) prohibited from drinking with them or selling arms to them.

More important, to the extent possible, Montcalm intended to fight a

European war on American soil, conducting conventional campaigns in which the Indians and Canadians would serve as adjuncts to his regulars. A strategic pessimist, he did not believe that Canada could long withstand a concerted British onslaught, and he certainly knew that from the point of view of France, the New World was a strategic sideshow. Commanding a compact, efficient, conventional force, Montcalm preferred the defensive on ground of his own choosing; he disdained raiding war and thought most of the French Canadian officers parochial, not very bright, and not particularly competent.

His nominal superior and rival, Vaudreuil, favored an aggressive use of the army. With this force—unprecedented in size for Canada, small though it was relative to the ultimate British opposition—he could implement Frontenac's strategy of keeping the British preoccupied with raiding warfare on the frontiers, but on a much grander scale than had been possible sixty years before. The French army could use the interior lines of Canada—the river and lake systems running west to east and north to south—to land a blow in one sector and then another, thereby holding at bay a much larger but more dispersed English force. Vaudreuil consistently saw opportunities for operational offensives against English forward bases, which had not been possible in previous colonial conflicts.

Montcalm, by contrast, favored improving the defensive position of the colony by strengthening the fortifications of both its core (particularly around Quebec) and its extremities—including those at the southern end of Lake Champlain. Being a professional soldier, he followed orders, but he had few hopes of success. Often, one felt, his preference was to lose honorably, even gloriously, to forces that would overwhelm his, rather than hazard them on what seemed to him harebrained raids into the wilderness. Disdaining the *troupes de la marine*, the Indians, and the Canadian militia, each in different ways, he sought to preserve his core of regular soldiers as long as possible, intending to fight set-piece battles, then retreat in good order until the inevitable end came, ideally with dignity.

Along the Great Warpath, 1756 was a year of stalemate. Following Shirley's instructions, Winslow assembled a large provincial force for the attack northward that Johnson had never attempted. But in July 1756 a new British supreme military commander, John Campbell, Earl of Loudoun, arrived in New York to replace Shirley. The fifty-one-year-old Scot, who had helped suppress the Highland uprising of 1745, did not place the same importance on the Great Warpath route as had Shirley, preferring to concentrate forces instead on the seizure of Louisbourg. And like British commanders before and after, he found himself at odds with colonial governors and troops.

A new northern front commander replacing Winslow, General Daniel Webb, arrived just before Loudoun in June 1756, but hesitated to go as far north as Albany until Loudoun's second in command, Major General James Abercromby, had also shown up. Throughout the summer of 1756, the British dithered. As for Montcalm, upon arriving in Quebec he declared his preference for standing on the defensive along the Great Warpath. He conceived of Carillon as the first of a series of positions from which he might delay advancing British forces. He reported to the minister of war at the end of August 1756 that the English had continued to strengthen Fort William Henry, while the French did the same at Ticonderoga, and at two small entrenched camps along the portage from Lake George to Lake Champlain. "Our design was to give them battle or to stop them at the portage of the Fall," he wrote, clearly preferring a defensive fight if possible, in wooded country where the Canadians and Indians could best support the French regulars against what was expected to be the main English thrust.[23] Goaded by Vaudreuil, however, Montcalm did launch an offensive westward, taking Fort Oswego on Lake Ontario. As for the Anglo-American army along the Great Warpath, a smallpox epidemic and unfounded scares of a French attack completed what divided and changing command and western defeat had wrought, and the proposed Great Warpath offensive of 1756 dissipated into futility. Fort William Henry itself remained, however, a solid base for further operations, the provincial troops there being reinforced by regulars and colonial rangers.

Vaudreuil remained focused on the Great Warpath, arguing for a preemptive strike against the English attack on that line that he felt must come sooner or later. By late fall 1756, he had concluded that the most desirable stroke in the coming year would be the destruction of Fort George (William Henry) and Fort Lydius (Fort Edward, the French name being that of a Dutch trader who once established a post there). Vaudreuil reasoned that Louisbourg guarded the St. Lawrence route, and he believed he could make an adequate defense of Quebec itself, even if a British fleet penetrated there. Oswego had fallen to the French, which meant that the chain of forts in the west was, for the time, secure. This left the Great Warpath.

As a first stroke, in February 1757 he ordered a daring winter raid of 1,500 men—250 volunteers from the regulars, 300 *troupes de la marine*, 650 Canadian militia, and 300 Indians under his brother, Pierre Rigaud de Vaudreuil (known as Rigaud)—against Fort William Henry. The raiders did not take the fort—an alert garrison of regulars and colonial rangers beat them off—but they burned boats, outbuildings, and firewood with a view to disrupting arrangements for an English offensive on the lake in the spring.[24] Montcalm's chief interest in his report back to Paris on this episode, however, was to make the point that his men were just as tough as the Canadians in enduring such a winter march, and to criticize Rigaud, a tough fifty-two-year-old bushfighter who had actually led remarkably well.[25] The civilian and military leaders of Canada were increasingly at loggerheads.

———•◦•———

We shall have no more to apprehend from the enemy on the frontier

Encouraged by this limited success, Vaudreuil insisted that the first major campaign of the 1757 season should consist of an attack on Fort William Henry, in order to prevent the long-feared main thrust north along the Great Warpath to Montreal. A large offensive action would, Vaudreuil believed, also keep the Indians active on the French side, and he feared leaving them unemployed. He guessed shrewdly that a successful French attack would yield a harvest of English supplies piled up in abundance at Fort William Henry and Fort Edward.[26] And although he disliked Montcalm, he had confidence in his abilities. With the eight thousand regulars, *troupes de la marine*, Canadian militia, and Indians he could put at Montcalm's disposal, Vaudreuil expected a success after which "we shall have no more to apprehend from the enemy on the frontier."

By June 1, 1757, Vaudreuil was pressing Montcalm for a summer attack on William Henry, and in his methodical way Montcalm complied, grudgingly accepting the large numbers of Indian allies that Vaudreuil's woodland diplomacy soon brought in. On July 12, Montcalm assembled his largest force yet—the eight thousand men Vaudreuil had promised, consisting of three thousand regulars in seven regiments, nearly as many Canadian militia organized by brigades named after their leaders and reinforced by small units of the *troupes de la Marine*, two hundred artillerists and engineers, and under the loose supervision of Captain La Corne St. Luc, eighteen hundred Indians, identified as "domiciliated" and from the "upper country."[27] Among the former were not only several hundred Abenakis, but 360 Iroquois—a number that reveals just what inroads the French had made into the Indian tribes most reliably pro-English in the past. Interestingly, the French returns from the expedition identify each group of Indians with the officers attached to them, including missionaries, interpreters, and Canadian aristocrats. The Indians from the "upper country" (*Pays d'en Haut*) were more numerous—almost a thousand in all—and had fewer Frenchmen associated with them.

Even allowing for the garrisons Montcalm would have to leave to operate and protect his line of supply going back to Carillon and thence to Montreal, the French commander could bring to bear over five thousand fighting men, in addition to the Indians, against Fort William Henry. It was as powerful a force as had ever been assembled in this remote part of the world.

Fort William Henry was now under the command of a conscientious regular officer, Lieutenant Colonel George Monro. The garrison consisted of regulars and provincials, nervously anticipating an attack from the north—a few scouts had brought back prisoners who confirmed as much. With most of his boats destroyed in Rigaud's winter raid, Monro could not deploy and sustain a large force to defend forward on Lake George, and anyway he was, as he well knew, outnumbered. A council of war wisely concluded as well that the Anglo-Americans could not oppose a French landing force at the water's edge; Indian war parties could easily land elsewhere and take the defenders in the rear. Instead, Monro and his men would have to defend the fort's perimeter, withstand the likely siege, and hope for a relief column from Fort Edward. There was a further problem. The fort could only house about five hundred defenders. The rest would have to be concentrated in an entrenched camp near the fort, but outside it, on a height of ground flanked, and in large measure secured, by swamps on either side.

Leaving Montreal on July 12, Montcalm arrived at Carillon six days later. His scouts did their work well, reconnoitering enemy positions, taking prisoners, and, no less important, denying the English knowledge of French plans by creating an invisible barrier of fear around Fort William Henry that few men dared to cross. Late that month a thirty-eight-year-old lieutenant in the colonial regulars, Joseph Marin de la Malgue, led a party of several hundred men down the lake, scouting out Fort Edward and William Henry, ambushed several smaller English patrols, returning with thirty-two scalps and a prisoner—although, as one French officer sourly noted, the Indians "know how to make two or even three out of one" scalp, so the number of dead Englishmen was probably half that many.[28] On July 24 a more serious skirmish occurred as the French jumped two dozen English boats at Sabbath Day Point. The Canadians and Indians in canoes inflicted 160 dead and took a similar number of prisoners. Montcalm, in the first of a series of clashes with his temperamental allies, with difficulty persuaded them to dispatch the prisoners to Montreal. Two days later he negotiated a continuation of the campaign with the Indians. One of his aides, Captain Louis Antoine de Bougainville, reflected, ruefully, on the need to keep the Indians in agreement with their European allies: "For these independent people whose assistance is purely voluntary, require to be consulted; everything must be communicated to them, and their opinions and caprices are oftentimes a law for us."[29]

The brilliant young Bougainville (not yet thirty) may have understood the problem better than his superior officer, which was not surprising, for he was the broader man. He had already written a two-volume work on calculus and was a member of the Royal Society in London; ahead of him lay a career as a naval officer, an explorer, and the scientific mastermind of Napoleon's expedition to Egypt. He had had no combat experience until the previous summer, but impressed even the demanding Marquis with his coolness under fire. Unlike Montcalm, he understood the importance of irregular warfare, even though he shared many of his commander's feelings about both the militia and the Indians.

As the French forces gathered at Carillon throughout July, and as their raiding parties isolated the fort and terrified its garrison, Monro's superior, Brigadier General Daniel Webb, watched anxiously from Fort Edward. Webb had had a typical military career, entering the British army in 1721 as an ensign in the Foot Guards; he had seen combat in Europe and had made a name as a conscientious administrator as well. In 1756 the Duke of Cumberland had sent him out to North America as the third in command after Loudoun and James Abercromby. His first mission, in the summer of 1756, had been a disaster, as he abandoned the job of marching to the relief of Oswego, falling back in a state of confusion compounded by hypochondria to New York, where Loudoun left him in command when the latter went to Halifax to supervise the siege of Louisbourg—itself another failure.

Webb spent June and most of July at Fort Edward, only traveling the fourteen miles to William Henry for a council of war on July 25, hastening back to the rear on the twenty-eighth at news that the French had finally begun to move. Only at this point did he send requests for militia to the governors of New England and New York, while keeping most of his garrison of thirty-four hundred hunkered down at Fort Edward. The militia flocked there, but Webb neither withdrew the garrison from William Henry nor attempted to relieve it.

On the last day of July 1757, Montcalm sent an advance guard of two thousand men down the western side of Lake George under the command of François-Gaston de Lévis, a Gascon of limited means and abundant talent. A brave and experienced soldier, he had established a solid reputation over more than two decades of soldiering. Impecunious but able, he was induced by the generous pay of the second in command of regular forces in Canada to accept an appointment to New France. He distinguished himself not only for his military ability, but for a certain diplomatic skill in managing two feuding superiors, Montcalm and Vaudreuil, who retained their regard for him to the end of the war. He first organized the artillery and transport for the William Henry expedition, and then while Montcalm assembled the rest of his army at the head of the lake, took charge of the van. While he and his men began operations in the vicinity of the fort, the main French army, poorly supplied with horse and oxen to assist the labor, laboriously portaged Montcalm's artillery (thirty-one guns, two large and ten small mortars, and three howitzers with thirty-five tons of ammunition) and supplies from Lake Champlain to the northern end of Lake George, reembarking in 250 bateaux for the journey south.[30] On August 2 this force rendezvoused at Great Sandy Bay, several miles from Fort William Henry, and then landed half a mile from the fort. In the meanwhile the vanguard and the Indians under Lévis had cut the road south to Fort Edward, opposite the entrenched camp. Fort William Henry was now surrounded.

While the French artillery laboriously moved into position, the Indians began the siege by killing over a hundred troops outside the walls and taking four prisoners, who informed Montcalm that the garrison numbered five hundred in the fort itself, and perhaps nine hundred in the entrenched camp outside it. What now ensued was the typical pattern of siege warfare, a carefully orchestrated and highly predictable routine of setting up batteries, digging approach trenches that would zigzag their way closer to the fort, a preliminary bombardment, and then either a successful assault or, more likely, surrender. It was a highly scientific style of warfare whose template any regular soldier would understand. The first batteries were emplaced six hundred yards or more from the fort; the second set of batteries less than four hundred yards, while the final trenches were dug at an angle to the fort's guns, into the fort's vegetable gardens, bringing the French front lines two hundred yards from the fort.

Even as French engineers began the investment of the fort, however, trouble was brewing between Montcalm and his Indian allies. On August 4, shortly after landing, Montcalm complained of the Indians' habit of spending time sniping at the English when what he needed was scouting; the Indians, for their part, complained of being neglected by Montcalm. And the Indians rendered a considerable service to the French general: They discovered a letter from General Webb's aide de camp on the body of a dead messenger. Webb, the aide had written to the commander of Fort William Henry, "has ordered me to acquaint you that he does not think it prudent (as you know his strength at this place) to attempt a junction or to assist you."[31] The dismal letter urged Monro to seek favorable terms of capitulation after putting up such resistance as he could. The letter was a powerful psychological weapon in the hands of the French commander, and he played it carefully. After a preliminary bombardment of several hours on August 7, Montcalm sent Bougainville to the fort under flag of truce, bringing with him the bloodstained document in order to shatter the garrison's morale.

The stubborn Monro did not quit, however. By the night of August 7, the French had completed two batteries, including several eighteen-pounder cannon firing solid shot and four howitzers and mortars capable of firing explosive shells into the crumbling structure of Fort William Henry. Indeed, these shells, flying in a high trajectory over the walls of the fort, did more damage than those battering the walls. Unbeknownst to Monro, Webb had changed his mind, and was now more willing to contemplate a relief of the fort, as the militia—summoned not much more than a week earlier—had arrived, and the defenses of Fort Edward had been put in order. Webb sent a new message conveying this change of heart, and his willingness to march, but it never reached Monro. The French constructed a third battery on August 8, and on the ninth, after a predawn meeting, the officers of the fort decided that they had had enough. At seven in the morning, Colonel Monro hoisted the white flag.

He received generous terms. The twenty-two hundred men of the garrison (more than Montcalm had realized) would march out carrying arms and baggage and would be allowed one small cannon as a token of respect for the resistance they had put up. They would be expected to observe an eighteen-month parole and would be exchanged for French prisoners. This meant that the prisoners would be sent back to Anglo-American lines, having taken a solemn oath not to bear arms until properly exchanged. Although Montcalm might have preferred to take the entire force as prisoners back to Canada, he realized that the colony, already on the edge of subsistence, could not afford to feed another two thousand mouths indefinitely. Besides, he had grave forebodings about the ability of the French to contain the "barbarity of the savages" if he were to take the prisoners north.[32] Montcalm warned Monro's emissary that the Indian chiefs would have to approve the terms. Apparently, they did so.

At noon the French took possession of the fort and entrenched camp. They discovered a rich haul: thirty-six artillery pieces with ample shot, shell, and powder, three thousand barrels of flour or pork; twenty-two hundred prisoners, and all at a cost of barely fifty men killed and wounded. Although the Indians plundered some of the possessions of the English in the entrenched camp, Montcalm was able to prevent disorder and immediately dispatched Captain Bougainville with a message describing his successes to Governor Vaudreuil in Montreal. He had, perhaps against his own expectations, achieved a complete, cheap, and staggering victory.

*The capitulation has unfortunately suffered some
infraction on the part of the Indians*

The challenge of getting two thousand disarmed and paroled prisoners
out of the fort and safely to Fort Edward remained. Under the cover of
darkness in the small hours of August 10, 1757, some two hundred French
guards—surely an insufficient number—prepared to escort the English
there. This plan was most likely conceived by Monro, with the approval
of Montcalm, in the hopes of avoiding Indian attacks.[33] La Corne and
other officers attached to the Indians insisted later that they had warned
that it would be a mistake for the English to slip out before daylight,
thereby angering the Indians, who would feel that an attempt had been
made to deceive them.[34]

If so, La Corne judged correctly. The Indians, angry at what they
viewed as a European conspiracy to protect the English, entered the camp,
killing seventeen wounded men left behind under French protection. The
Indians began kidnapping some blacks, women, and provincial soldiers—
possibly believing that only British soldiers were protected by the agreement to which they had not been a party. Worse was to come. The route
taken by the departing prisoners led through the Indian camp, and word
soon spread among the Indians about the scalping of the wounded in the
entrenched camp. Chaos set in. Groups of Indians plundered the prisoners, carried some off, tomahawked and scalped others. The French and
some of the prisoners fought back, but the column was long and the
escorts too few.

The numbers killed were surprisingly small—sixty-nine, according to
the most reliable modern account, although some estimates are more
than twice as high, with almost two hundred being carried off as prisoners. Montcalm reported personally intervening to stop the killing and the
pillage, saying that he ordered two chiefs from each Indian group to
accompany the English on their departure from the fort.[35] He had also
ordered La Corne and the others to escort the English. Whether either of
these orders had been given, or implemented, and what, if anything the
chiefs and French officers did to maintain order remains unclear.

Montcalm, furious though he was at the Indians, disavowed responsibility for their actions. He blamed the prisoners for not having disposed of all the rum in the camp before they left, which allowed the Indians to become drunk and uncontrollable. He had the nerve to tell the supreme English commander in the colonies, Lord Loudoun, that had the garrison "been willing to march out with more order and not taken fright at our Indians, which emboldened the latter," the column would have escaped serious injury.[36]

Montcalm found himself loathing the Indians and dismissing the English, who, he thought, should have been grateful to him for having exposed himself "much more to save them from the fury of the Indians than to capture their fort."[37] He and his staff had fretted at the problem of managing the unruly aboriginals throughout that summer, watching in helpless fury as western Indians, in particular, drifted into the French camp, clamored for gifts and drink, took a scalp or two, and wandered off. "No way to hold them; they had made a coup, and besides they lacked everything, no blankets, no deerskins, except very bad ones, no leggings, no vermilion. Those who send to the army Indians who lack everything, should come and command them themselves," wrote Bougainville even before the siege began.[38]

At the same time Montcalm and the governor of New France found new reasons to despise each other. Montcalm was delighted by his victory: "It procures us a heap of provisions for the subsistence of six thousand men for six weeks, some thirty pieces of artillery, [and] more ammunition than we have employed at a siege."[39] He had lost fewer than sixty men killed or wounded. To be sure, "the capitulation has unfortunately suffered some infraction on the part of the Indians. But what would be an infraction in Europe, cannot be so regarded in America, and I have written with firmness to General Webb and to Lord Loudoun on the subject, so as to deprive them of all excuse for not observing the terms on a slight pretense."

Vaudreuil took a different view—not of the massacre, to which he was indifferent, but of the lost opportunity to smash the English. On August 7 he urged Montcalm to capitalize on his victory and destroy the English supply base at Fort Edward. "Should we fail to reduce Fort Lydius this year, we may give it up, as we shall never again have such a fine opportunity. Indeed, General Lawdon [Loudoun] and all the regulars will occupy it next campaign, and then, far from it being in our power to assume the offensive, we shall be constrained to confine ourselves to the defensive."[40] The destruction of Fort Edward would throw the British and the Americans back all the way to Albany and delay any thrust along the Great Warpath by at least a year, maybe longer.

Montcalm refused, citing the thousands of militia now appearing, the need to send the Canadian militia back to bring in the harvest (Vaudreuil declared that it would be better to accept shortages of food this winter than to let Fort Edward remain intact), and the departure of the Indian allies.[41] The general razed William Henry, sent back the Canadians, withdrew to Carillon, and returned to Montreal by the end of August. He had gained a solid success and glory; he saw no opportunity missed, and certainly no military honor stained. He cited the words of the intendant of Canada (the civilian official responsible for the routine administration of the colony), François Bigot, to the effect that to have taken Fort Edward would have been to lose the harvest. "I could not have subsisted our army on Lake St. Sacrement after the month of August," he quoted Bigot as saying.[42] Whether the timorous Webb and the notoriously undisciplined militia at Fort Edward would have withstood the onslaught of the French, and whether the army might have subsisted for quite some time on its captured spoils, however, remain two unanswered questions.

The siege of Fort William Henry was a conventional operation of war executed in the European manner in the American wilderness. Montcalm was justly proud of his little army's accomplishment, its near-bloodless victory, its efficiency, and its indisputable success. The siege was the kind of fight he searched for in North America: a clean battle, fought by European norms. He did not try to exploit it, but, rather, deemed it a neat little success. As for the slaughter of prisoners, he accepted no responsibility, writing to Webb and Loudoun, in nearly identical language, that the honorable capitulation won by Colonel Monro's "gallant defense," would have been flawless had the English not provided rum to the Indians, and if the Indians, in turn, had "not supposed they had reason to complain of some ill treatment."[43] Montcalm was content, and his conscience clear, although, in some corner of his mind, he allowed that an "infraction" had indeed occurred. His aide de camp was more candid in his diary: "A great misfortune which we dreaded has happened. Apparently the capitulation is violated and all Europe will oblige us to justify ourselves."[44] Nor were the sufferings of the captives inconsequential, including scenes of forced cannibalism as well as torture.

The siege itself had had all the features of Enlightenment-age warfare—an orderly approach march, careful reconnaissance, siege, formal negotiations leading to surrender, honors for an enemy who had put up a brave fight but had not provoked the extremity of an assault that would have allowed for no quarter to be given. Parole was a common practice in European warfare, and continued in North America through the Civil War, when, for example, the 12,500 men of the Harper's Ferry garrison who surrendered to Stonewall Jackson in September 1862 meekly signed pledges not to fight until properly exchanged and then were sent on their way. It was a civilized way of dealing with prisoners in an age where the likely forms of confinement for prisoners—hulks or jails, or cramped open-air camps—were likely to prove as lethal as any field of combat.

But this was no European battlefield. To drive in the enemy's scouts and to secure information, Montcalm relied on his Indian allies: nearly eighteen hundred warriors from nearly forty nations, divided into two groups—those familiar with the French and to some extent under their control, and those from the *Pays d'en Haut*, with fewer French representatives among them, whose interests were very different from his. The Indians aiding the French army in its contest for North America were not fighting for national interest, or in fulfillment of oaths of obedience, or for money. They were not even, in most cases, fighting directly for their homes or their ways of life, other than in the indirect sense of having a foreboding about what the swelling English-controlled white presence meant for their long-term future. Rather they fought for glory, "counting coup," and to some extent for prisoners and loot. The Indians of the West, in particular, wished to return to their homes with tangible evidence of their prowess— which meant, in most cases, scalps swinging from their belts. For the Indians closer to the English frontier, revenge was undoubtedly a lure as well. In neither case would Indian motivation, and the Indian war culture, match the kind of rational, purposive use of force that, framed by a formal and decorative etiquette, constituted Montcalm's military culture.

The very notion of parole must have seemed bizarre, indeed, incomprehensible to the Indians. Tribes at war with one another did not have formal exchanges in which one treated enemy commanders as if they were respected guests come to visit under only slightly embarrassing circumstances, and enemy warriors as respected adversaries whose word to refrain from fighting until properly exchanged could be trusted. Prisoners were trophies, potential adoptees, sources of brutal entertainment, perhaps valuable sources of ransom, but not this. It is not surprising that the Indians, already at odds with Montcalm, who had attempted to direct them to forms of warfare alien to their ways, believing themselves cheated of their due rewards for hazardous duty, and perhaps inflamed by alcohol, were in a dangerous mood. When their suspicions received fuel in the form of an attempt to steal a march on them in the early morning darkness, it is no wonder that they ignited. When the force available to protect the prisoners was so small, it is even less wonder that the flames spread fast.

In some ways what is remarkable is how limited the slaughter was, which is why even the term "massacre" is questionable. There were not the coldblooded mass executions of Malmédy or the Katyn Forest, or even the casual brutality of the Bataan Death March; it was, rather, the assertion of norms of indigenous warfare in the midst of chaos, inebriation, and a clumsy attempt to outwit forest warriors. From the point of view of two and a half centuries' distance and a broader understanding of the ethnography of war, perhaps this was no massacre, at least in our sense. But although this may be the case, the reverberations of the events continued well after the horrors of those hot, brilliant days on Lake George ended.

For as inaccurate and inflammatory as the reports of the events at Fort William Henry were, they mattered. Some fairly cool accounts of the events did reach the newspapers: the *London Chronicle*, for example, reprinting a letter from New York dated August 27, 1757, recorded that "immediately on the surrender, an English officer heard the Indian chief violently accuse the French general with being false and a liar to them; that he had promised them the plunder of the English, and they would have it." The report made it clear that the number of casualties was unknown, and "that after the first fury of plundering the Indians stopped their hands of a sudden, and the French recovered many out of their hands whom they were carrying off." [45]

More typical was the report in the *Boston Gazette* quoting a letter from Albany of August 15. "The French, immediately after the capitulation, most perfidiously let their *Indian bloodhounds* loose upon our people. The throats of most, if not all the women were cut, their bellies ripped open, their bowels torn out and thrown upon the faces of their dead and dying bodies; and 'tis said that all the women were murdered in one way or another: that the children were taken by the heels and their brains beat out against trees or stones and not one of them survived." The outraged author called for revenge. He declared that it might be hard for English-men to kill prisoners suing for mercy, but asked, "will it not be strictly just, and absolutely necessary . . . to make some severe examples of our inhu-man enemies when they fall into our hands?" [46]

From the contemporary American and English points of view, this had indeed been a massacre. For Americans, this was another manifestation of the barbarity of the Indians and the malice of the French; for the English, it was an unconscionable violation of the laws of war. As a piece of propa-ganda, the infamy of the Fort William Henry massacre served admirably to mobilize the northern colonies against their traditional enemies.

Having imported European norms of warfare to the New World, English and French commanders struggled with an effort to impose them. Those norms were not necessarily gentler than those of the Indians and the colonists—they included, for example, savage forms of discipline including flogging and summary execution, and provided, under some circumstances, for garrisons to be denied quarter should they persist in a pointless defense. [47] But the massacre at Fort William Henry was some-thing different, and, to English and American eyes, particularly reprehen-sible. It was a violation of the norms of warfare, because, after all, the garrison had been granted surrender on honorable terms. And it pro-vided yet another manifestation of the ferocity of the native population, a larger demonstration of the horrors felt along a frontier in which indi-vidual families and small communities feared the raiding party and the scalping knife more, even, than disease or the afflictions of nature.

Warfare in the New World partook in large measure of European modes and norms. At a deeper level, not only European modes of fight-ing, but the aristocratic spirit that informed European understandings of officer culture took root here as well, and indeed survives to this day. At the same time, the New World, in part because of the intersection of the cultures composing it—European, Indian, and the new American (including Canadian)—and in part because of the physical circumstances in which war took place, challenged those norms. This had begun long before. Half a century earlier Cotton Mather had shrewdly observed of the Schenectady raiders that they were "French, with Indians, being half one, half t'other, half Indianized French, and half Frenchified Indians."[48] This is not a bad description of, among others, La Corne St. Luc.

European soldiers found themselves accepting savage acts that they would have rejected in Europe, as when Amherst himself later proposed infecting the Indians with smallpox. Indian warfare had never recognized the punctilio of European military manners; the freedom and equality of life in the wilderness or on its edge, including the denaturing of French aristocrats in the woodlands where they had settled, made English and French colonists willing to do what seemed practical, and avenge what appeared vicious, even if doing so meant stepping beyond the rules of war.

The lures of practicality and savagery, present whenever men wage war, came closer to the surface in America, even as a European military sensibility tried to enforce the old rules in new circumstances. Small wonder, then, that the American way of war in later years would show itself similarly ambivalent, adhering to international conventions in both the legal and customary sense, and then resorting to ruthless means when that appeared necessary. A century later, the same soldiers who agreeably paroled one another in the Maryland campaign of 1862 were willing to burn populations out of their homes in 1864; nearly a century after that, the same airmen who conceived of bombing strategies relying on the precision targeting of industry devised the most thorough means of annihilating cities ever applied. In 2011 a liberal American president had no compunction about ordering raiders into an allied country to kill, not capture, the architect of the September 11, 2001, terror attacks. The Navy SEALs who shot Osama bin Laden reported his death using as code for the founder of Al Qaeda the name of an Indian chieftain. Once again, the ruthless norms of frontier warfare trumped whatever compunctions international law and custom might have created.

It would never be the American way to take artistic satisfaction in elegant rituals of surrender in the European manner. Honor mattered, but victory mattered more. American military culture thus became a self-contradictory hybrid of form, restraint, and etiquette, on the one hand, improvisation, raw energy, and unwillingness to accept limits on the other. The story of Fort William Henry is a part of the explanation why.

CHAPTER THREE

The Battle on Snowshoes, 1758

I now thought it most prudent to retreat

After three hard years of frontier warfare, Major Robert Rogers, like most experienced soldiers before and since, knew a bad mission when he saw it. The twenty-six-year-old Rogers had lived most of his life in New Hampshire, serving as a teenager in two scouting companies along the frontier during King George's War—a war whose lesser events included the destruction of the family farm by Indians from St. Francis. In the 1750s he lived the life of a trapper and trader, reenlisting as soon as the French and Indian War broke out, and leading two dozen men into New Hampshire service, where he came to the attention of William Johnson. "I believe him to be as brave and honest a man as any I have equal knowledge of," Johnson wrote, declaring him "superior to most, inferior to none of his rank in these troops."[1] Since then Rogers had patrolled and raided in the Lake George/Lake Champlain region with his own unit of rangers—highly paid provincial troops, accompanied by regular volunteers, who scouted and harried the French and Indians, and were in turn spied on and ambushed by them.

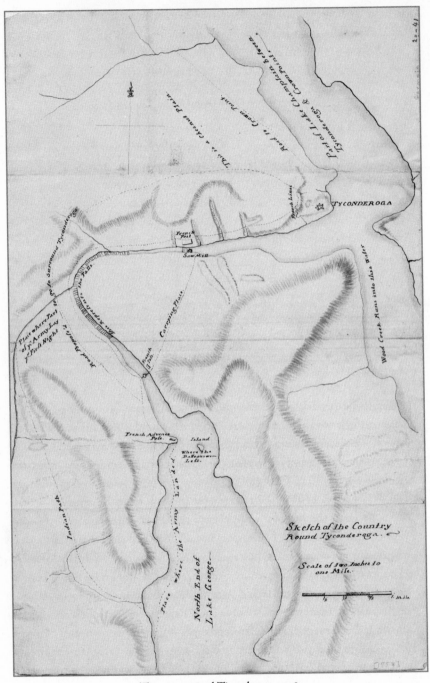

The area around Ticonderoga, 1758.
By permission, William L. Clements Library, University of Michigan

The mission he had been given by Lieutenant Colonel William Haviland in March 1758 was a reconnaissance in force to Fort Carillon, ordered as a follow-on operation to a scout that had been conducted by a company of Connecticut provincial troops under Captain Israel Putnam. Rogers was initially supposed to have four hundred men with him but, for reasons that remained unclear, Haviland, who commanded at Fort Edward, allowed him fewer than half as many. Worse, news of the proposed raid had spread through the camp. When one of Putnam's men deserted to the French, and after Indians had nabbed a servant of one of the camp sutlers, Rogers had good reason to fear that the mission had been compromised. Of Haviland's order to launch the reconnaissance with too small a force and after the mission had been compromised, he later wrote, "I must confess it appeared to me (ignorant and unskilled as I then was in politics and the art of war) incomprehensible."[2]

Haviland was having none of the twenty-seven-year-old provincial major's hesitations. The forty-year-old English lieutenant colonel, a highly competent but very much by-the-book regular in the British army, had clashed with Rogers before—most recently about some rangers blazing away on a hunting party near Fort Edward. Later Haviland had had two rangers flogged for stealing rum from the redcoats. On that occasion Rogers' men had rioted and cut down the whipping post. Haviland was furious, sneering at Rogers' warning that his men would desert if flogged. "I answered it would be better they were all gone than have such a riotous sort of people, but if he would catch me one that attempted it, I would endeavour to have him hanged as an example."[3] The two men detested each other.

A soldier Rogers was, however, so on March 10, 1758, he dutifully led some 180 men from his small island base on the Hudson adjacent to Fort Edward on the scout.[4] His men included English volunteers as well as provincials, all wrapped in layers of linen and woolen clothing to stay warm, for they could light no fires that might give their position away to the enemy. From Fort Edward to the ruins of Fort William Henry at the head of Lake George was a day's march. Once there, Rogers carefully sent out scouts some three miles ahead of the main body; finding no enemies, he camped, sending out more parties.

On the twelfth his band sighted a dog on the frozen lake, which caused Rogers to suspect an ambush by Indians, the canine's likely masters. He decided to move to Sabbath Day Point, a peninsula protruding into the lake on the western side, and wait until nightfall to avoid detection. Scouts equipped with small spyglasses continued to reconnoiter, and the rest of the force moved forward after nightfall, some fifteen men picking their way ahead as an advance guard, some moving on the frozen lake itself, using the skates that they habitually carried with them, others flanking on the left or western shore of the lake. As the column crept forward in the dark, and some eight miles before the French forward outpost at the northern end of Lake George, one of his scouts on skates returned with a report of campfires on the eastern shore.

Rogers ordered his men to squat on the ice while he pondered his next move.[5] Upon reflection he decided to move all of his force to the shelter of the woods on the western side of the narrow lake. There he deposited the hand-sleighs his men had dragged and the packs they had carried and deployed them for an attack, only to discover that the supposed campfires were the phosphorescent glow of rotten wood. The tension of impending action eased. "We returned to our packs, and there lay the remainder of the night without fire."[6]

Following a council of war the next morning, March 13, Rogers decided to continue to move on the western shore by snowshoes, avoiding the lake, bypassing the French camp that served as the listening post of Fort Carillon at the northern end of this water approach to the French fort. Halting at noon to rest and allowing the French in the fort to complete their daily patrols undisturbed, the rangers planned to set their ambushes by night for the next day. They were looking for a good position between Carillon and the French outpost on Lake George, where they could intercept small groups of Frenchmen moving between the main fort and the outpost. Rogers did not know, however, that half a dozen Abenaki Indians on a scout had come across his tracks and his campsite and, evading the rangers, had hastened to Carillon to raise the alarm. An impulsive band of Indians swarmed out of the fort led by a Canadian officer hoping to control them; half an hour later, a more formidable Canadian officer, Levrault de Langis, led out a larger group of two hundred bolstered by a few dozen Canadians and Frenchmen.

In the afternoon's failing light, however, Rogers' scouts saw only the first party of nearly one hundred Indians loping toward them from Ticonderoga. The rangers immediately dropped their packs and prepared for battle. Deploying lengthwise across a narrow depression between a mountain on the right, and a rivulet on the left, Rogers divided his men into two groups; they set a hasty ambush. At 4:00 P.M. the Indians walked into it. The Indians, sensing something was wrong, hesitated at the last moment, and a ranger fired his musket a few seconds too early. But the trap worked. A blast of gunfire, and the French and Indians were routed. Most of Rogers' small force pursued the fleeing enemy while the rest paused to take scalps and plunder the dead.

Charging with knife and tomahawk, for many had not had time to reload, the rangers noticed their enemy pausing and returning fire. And then the second, much stronger French force of two hundred Indians and Canadians hit them. Losing some fifty men in the initial shock of this encounter, Rogers and his force retreated to the east, up the mountain face, hoping to work their way back to the northern end of Lake George. By Rogers' account they repulsed the enemy several times, until their position was in danger of being turned by what he estimated as several hundred Indians on their right. "I now thought it most prudent to retreat, and bring off with me as many of my party as I possibly could," Rogers recalled later.[7]

To prevent his force from being surrounded, Rogers sent out two flanking parties, with eighteen and fifteen men respectively, to his right and left. The fight was close, within twenty yards, and went on for an hour and a half. The retreating rangers could hear the screams of their wounded comrades being tortured to death by the Indians as the surviving rangers conducted their awkward retreat, clumping up hill on the wood-and-sinew snowshoes that made all movement slow and clumsy. The rangers had to reload their muskets carefully because when damp their firearms were no more than clubs attached to metal tubes. Even when in good order these weapons could only fire a single shot every twenty seconds at a bounding tomahawk-wielding Indian in war paint. The flank party on the right, eighteen men under Lieutenant William Hendrick Phillips, became detached from the main group and was surrounded. After a shouted conversation with Rogers, Phillips surrendered. The remaining men fought with the determination of those who could expect no quarter from an enemy who had chosen to scalp the wounded before killing them rather than after.

As the long shadows fell under the trees Rogers and his men followed the guidance he had always given in the event of disaster—disperse and rendezvous at a fixed point, in this case, the place where they had cached their sleds on Lake George. Some made it back with their leader, reaching Lake George at nightfall, and retreating the next day in the direction of Fort Edward. Others became detached, two English officers and five men stumbling into Fort Carillon four days after the battle, exhausted and starving. Although in the lore of the North Country Rogers is supposed to have escaped the pursuing French and Indians by sliding down a several-hundred-foot-high rock face—Rogers Rock, as it is still known—the more prosaic truth would appear to be that the Fort Carillon party simply stopped pursuing.[8] As Montcalm reported back to Paris: "[Rogers] has been utterly defeated; our Indians would not give any quarter; they have brought back one hundred and forty-six scalps; they retained only three prisoners to furnish *live letters to their father*."[9] Having suffered much from Rogers and his men, the Indians had no inclination to preserve their lives. Three captives—what the Indians called "live letters"—would provide their "father,"—Vaudreuil, as much intelligence as he needed.

On March 14, Rogers and the remnants of his party marched up the lake and rendezvoused with Captain John Stark six miles north of the remains of Fort William Henry. The next day they staggered back into Fort Edward. Rogers put the best possible face on the debacle: The enemy, instead of numbering three hundred, became in his account a force twice or thrice that size; the enemy's losses a comforting 150 dead and as many wounded.

Oddly enough, "The Battle on Snowshoes" became part of the lore of Rogers and his men—a defeat, perhaps, but somehow the legend of Rogers' slide down the rock, war whoops ringing in the air, atoned in the popular imagination for a catastrophic defeat. The elite scouts of the English army had lost 125 men, by Rogers' count, almost two-thirds of a considerable raiding party, in one fight. Nor had they inflicted anything like the damage Rogers claimed. Instead of having suffered nearly three hundred killed and wounded, the French reported a loss of two Europeans seriously wounded, four Indians killed, and sixteen wounded. The battle had been, purely and simply, a debacle.[10]

Our Indians would not give any quarter

By March 1758 the tide in North America had turned in favor of the British and the American colonists, although this may not have yet become fully apparent to the contestants. The British now had larger regular forces in North America, and were sending more, while the colonies were raising more provincial units. The British had, as well, more able commanders than in the past, who were building on the foundation laid by the Earl of Loudoun. Expeditions against Fort Duquesne, Louisbourg, and even along the Great Warpath were in the planning stages. Some in the British high command had toyed with the idea of a four-thousand-man raid on Carillon during the winter, but it proved too ambitious a plan for implementation. For the moment, however, on that central front, in the no-man's-land between Fort Edward and Fort Carillon, the stalemate remained, a setting for scores of small but brutal fights of which the Battle on Snowshoes was but one.

Great battles, Winston Churchill once wrote, "are the principal milestones of secular history," not merely affecting campaigns but shaping moods and atmospheres." Large set-piece battles frame most military history, including the French and Indian War. Sieges such as that of Fort William Henry, even very large woodland fights such as the Battle of the Monongahela in which General Braddock lost his life, and certainly the culminating battle on the Plains of Abraham helped decide the war.

Most wars, however, contain parallel campaigns, one of which consists of a completely different kind of fighting than the big battles—the wars of raid, ambuscade, and intelligence gathering. In the wars for North America these battles continued through the seasons, unlike conventional campaigning, and followed different rules. By the mid and late eighteenth century the armies of Europe, and above all the French and the English, had reached high standards of skill and discipline for fights that involved the massing of forces in linear formations and open fields, or in siege warfare. This, by way of contrast, was a war of dispersed and moving groups, operating often either in or very near forests. It was not a war of armies—what military theorists would later call the operational level of war—but of small fights that might, or might not, collectively amount to much.

European armies had experienced irregular warfare in their colonies and on the periphery of Europe, most notably in the borderlands between Austria and the Ottoman Empire. They had, moreover, long understood the importance of troops who could skirmish in advance of large formations, seize key points like villages or bridges, and scout. But the challenge in North America was different. The forest—a grimly threatening and uncanny environment for a European peasant—was exceptionally suited to stealthy movement. "Skulking warfare," the English called Indian tactics, and this was surely a good place to skulk.

The stakes were larger than in Europe too. In an area of long, lonely distances, poor roads, and river and lake lines of communication with very little in the way of populated areas, supply lines were uniquely vulnerable to disruption by raiding parties. And there was a psychological dimension, too. The now long-standing French strategy of employing the Indians to attack frontier settlements imposed upon harried English commanders the need to make some provision for their protection. Woodland fighting had been integral to French policy for more than six decades.

Raiding warfare, then, though known in the Old World, was quite different and considerably more important in the New. On the American side the most famous name was that of the commander at the Battle on Snowshoes, Robert Rogers.[12] He had had his share of successes. On Christmas Eve 1757, for example, he had led a winter scout of Fort Carillon in the course of which he slaughtered all but three of the cattle upon which the French garrison relied for fresh meat. To add insult to injury, he had left a note for the commandant at Carillon, attached the head of one of the cattle—"an ill-timed and very low piece of braggadocio," one French officer sniffed.[13]

The myth of Rogers' rangers—silent men in green uniform, moving through the woods to reconnoiter, raid, and scout—has, over decades and centuries, captured the imagination of historians, novelists, and even filmmakers. (Alas, even the green uniforms are at least partly imaginary; they were probably clad in a motley variety of clothing.)[14] Soldiers, too: One of the most famous units in the United States Army, the Seventy-fifth Ranger Regiment, claims Rogers' unit in its lineage.

The truth, however, is that despite the legend, despite Rogers' undeniable skill as a woodland leader, and despite the heroism of so many of his officers and men, the rangers were, by and large, inferior to their opponents. Throughout the French and Indian War raiding parties of French and Indians ranged south as far as Albany. With one or two notable exceptions, Rogers and his men prowled the outskirts of Carillon and Fort St. Frédéric, but did not haunt the suburbs of Montreal, or sever the supply lines of French forces along the front lines of the war for North America. The French garrison at Carillon found Rogers an annoyance and an embarrassment, but not a serious threat to their survival.

Irregular forces, particularly those that are the stuff of legend, rarely actually accomplish all that their publicists (including themselves) promise. The famed Lawrence of Arabia did not drive the Turks from Arabia, or even cause the surrender of a single major Turkish garrison. Something similar might be said of Tito's partisans in Yugoslavia during World War II. But the issue here goes beyond the difference between historical reputation and actual accomplishment. There were, no doubt, plenty of successful scouts by Rogers and his men, but more typical was an engagement like the rangers' first battle on snowshoes, which uncannily foreshadowed the second. On January 21, 1757, the rangers pounced on several French sleighs on the ice of Lake Champlain, and as happened in March 1758, they were counter-ambushed, losing thirty killed, wounded, or taken prisoner out of seventy-four engaged.[15] To the very end of the French and Indian War, Rogers and his men were often worsted in the small war of ambuscade and skirmish, and often right near the bases from which they operated.

Rogers himself was not to blame for this unhappy record. Almost all of his superiors—including, eventually, the overall British commander in North America, General Jeffery Amherst—viewed him as an outstanding commander, and his unit became a nursery of future American military leaders. His counterparts in the same line of work fared no better, indeed worse. British officers, despising their services, often used them only to terrorize civilians rather than beat the French and Indians.

The answer must be found chiefly on the other side, not so much in the inferiority of Rogers' men, but in the superiority of their opponents. These were a combination of French officers and a few regular *troupes de la marine*, some Canadian militia, large numbers of Indians, and most important of all, Canadian-born French officers who were the most important element in the mix. Consider the careers of three Canadian officers who, at one time or another during the war, sparred with Rogers along the Great Warpath.

Born in 1719 the son of a French officer, Joseph Marin de la Malgue began his frontier career at the age of thirteen, when he accompanied his father in exploring the *Pays d'en Haut*.[16] By the age of twenty-one he was negotiating agreements with the Sioux in the vicinity of what is now Green Bay, Wisconsin. His trading and diplomatic career was, as was the case with so many members of the Canadian nobility, interspersed with fighting. In 1745 he traveled across the continent to join in the fight at the very tip of what is now Nova Scotia, in the siege of Louisbourg. It was, in fact, Marin who brought back word that August that the fortress city had fallen. After marrying a relative of the future governor of France in 1745, he joined a raid led by his father that destroyed Saratoga (now Schuyler-ville), New York, returning to Acadia in 1746 to conduct guerrilla war against the English. Returning in 1749 to the West Marin made peace between Sioux and Ojibwas and furthered French trading interests in what is now Minnesota—all the while holding the humble rank of ensign in the colonial troops. From 1756 to 1758 he raided the area around Fort William Henry, the Connecticut River, and Albany, getting the best of Rogers and his men in several skirmishes, and then led raids on the Pennsylvania frontier before being captured by British forces at the end of the war near Fort Niagara.

Marin's career bears a strong resemblance to that of Rogers' opposite number at the Battle on Snowshoes, Jean-Baptiste Levrault de Langis Montegron. Langis was a thirty-five-year-old ensign who, like Marin, came from a military family—his father and older brothers had also been colonial regulars. He led scouting parties throughout the North Country, including the outskirts of Fort Edward, where with a band of a hundred Indians he ambushed fifty woodcutters, killing twenty and capturing half a dozen more. Serving under Marin, he raided the English lines of communication between Fort George (the old Fort William Henry) and Fort Edward.[17]

More astounding yet was the career of the most interesting Canadian warrior chief of them all, La Corne St. Luc. Born in 1711, he came from a large family, and like many a French gentleman made his fortune trading furs in the West, including what is now Michigan, Ontario, and Wisconsin. He ended up a wealthy man, and one of the largest slaveowners in Canada. Fluent in four or five Indian languages, he moved easily among Indian tribes, West and East. He had led warrior bands of 150 to 200 from Fort St. Frédéric during King George's War. It was not until 1755, however, that he made the rank of captain in the colonial regulars. Like his Indian associates he took scalps, and for his achievements received the Croix de St. Louis, the French monarchy's equivalent of Napoleon's *legion d'honneur*. He had led Montcalm's Indian auxiliaries at Fort William Henry, and in the lore of New England bore a large share of responsibility for the atrocities committed there.

The careers of Marin, Langis, and La Corne, like those of other French Canadian military leaders, help explain French domination of the woodland fight, for these were European leaders who made the Indians effective collectively for a larger military purpose. As individual warriors the Indians excelled. Their culture valued courage, patience, and daring. Having lived their entire lives in the woods, they were utterly at home there. Many of their militarily relevant skills resulted from their hunting way of life—the ability to move silently through the woods, to follow trails, to survive using the materials of the forest for food, transportation, and shelter. The qualities that such a life required—patience in stalking, ability to endure prolonged periods of discomfort and hunger—were also invaluable in this kind of warfare. But the Indians were also, to European eyes, fickle, easily discouraged by what seemed to the white men relatively minor losses, often motivated by aims different from those of the English and French, and prone to internal rivalries and squabbling, all accentuated by a keen sense of personal honor just as strong as, though different from, that of any Old World aristocrat. Franco-Indian war parties, and certainly the larger ones, did not usually consist of a single tribe. They were, rather, made up of groups of Indians from differing tribes, some of which had considerable antipathy to one another.

A sprinkling of Canadian militia and perhaps a few regulars could provide some solidity to the Indian war band. The Canadian *habitant,* in particular, though not as good a woodsman as the native, was nonetheless far more skilled in woodcraft than his Old World counterpart. As undisciplined as the Canadian militia might be, they were still far more amenable to the direction of officers than the Indians. Far better were the hardened regulars of the *troupe de la marine*. But indispensable to the mix was the Canadian aristocrat, a type with no real counterpart in the American colonies. The Marins, Langises, and La Cornes came from the gentry of France, but their families had taken root in Canada, and their identities were tied up with that of New France. They had inherited an ethos of service to the Crown and, above all, of military endeavor, which made it natural for a thirteen-year-old boy to plunge into the wilderness with his father the officer—and for him, in turn, at the end of his life to take his son to the far corners of Africa in the service of the king.

These were not men who had given their lives to chivalry. Some made fortunes in the wilderness trading furs for European goods; their economic and military lives were inextricably intertwined. Their lives, spent very largely with the Indians, meant that they mastered not only the ways of the woods but Indian culture, or rather cultures. It was not so much that they had developed particularly close relationships with any one tribe (although some did). Marin's Indian contacts ranged from the Sioux of the West to the Micmacs of Nova Scotia, nations speaking mutually unintelligible languages. But these Canadian officers, by virtue of their lives and travels in Indian country, had learned to be diplomats as well, brokering agreements, leading war bands composed of Indians from different (sometimes mutually hostile) tribes and clans. As practical anthropologists of the Indian world they moved easily within it; as gentry they commanded deference from the Canadian peasantry, who, if considerably more independent than their Norman counterparts in the Old World, nonetheless respected their social superiors.

Their military careers were part of their lives, but these officers did not, seemingly, care overmuch about the external marks of success and progress. Langis was an ensign at age thirty-seven, when a luckier or wealthier soldier might have been a colonel or better. It probably made little difference to him and his peers. Operating as they did independently and in command of their own units of whatever size, formal hierarchy meant little—no sprig of the French aristocracy freshly arrived from Paris would give himself airs when on a woodland raiding party led by such a man. And within the small, tight world of New France, reputation counted far more than rank, which is why when Montcalm ordered a scout from Carillon in the summer of 1758 officers of considerably more senior rank volunteered to serve under a lowly ensign.

There were no real counterparts to the Canadian warrior gentry in the American colonies. There were British gentlemen on the make, and plenty of them, but they were chiefly interested in the acquisition of land and the building up of estates. The Briton who comes closest to the Canadian model was William Johnson, the semifeudal baron of the Mohawk valley. But Johnson's military career was a side pursuit, and he himself knew that it was not his strength. He remained, ultimately, of the white man's world, preoccupied by its interests and politics. Much of his energy was taken up feuding with English colonial rivals, and in the end, his chief aim was the development of his manor and estates. Johnson was an important figure on the frontier, but he was unique.

There were Indian traders, but they were overwhelmingly focused on making money; they engaged in warfare on occasion but it was not their inherited vocation. There were rugged frontiersmen like Rogers, but they, too, were in peacetime focused on regular pursuits, chiefly farming or frontier trade. Because the British regular army presence in America was inconsiderable until the Seven Years' War, there was no class of officers who were at ease in the woods. And although they proselytized the Indians, the clergy of the colonies were more inclined to denounce native Americans as imps of the devil than to seek to live among them and learn their ways, let alone manage or lead them.

Religion cemented the French hold on the Indians. French priests mastered Indian languages and cultures and tolerated divergences from the formal practices of the Church. Catholicism was an easier faith for the Indians to adopt (or, more accurately, incorporate into their own complex belief systems) than the unyielding faith of New England's Protestants, whose efforts at converting the Indian were either half-hearted and ineffective or, as in the case of Eleazar Wheelock's Indian school, which became Dartmouth College, part of a larger attempt at acculturation that the Indians resisted. Perhaps for the same reason that Catholicism was able to establish itself among other animist and pagan peoples by wisely incorporating some of their beliefs, rituals, and icons, and turning a blind eye to others, the Church seems to have had an easier time of it than the Protestants. Perhaps, too, the mysteries and rites of Catholicism, in contrast with the stark simplicity of Puritan worship, helped; conversely, the dependence of Protestant belief on mastery of the Bible surely created another barrier to Indians who had had no previous experience of a written language, and who would have to learn a faith resting on a text in a foreign tongue.

Thus, a peculiar French military-aristocratic caste grew and flourished in the New World, and rooted there. The few who returned to France after the English conquest of Canada rarely had an easy time of it: They had found their home across the Atlantic. For the last fifty years of its existence New France owed her survival, in large part, to the ability of this tiny group—a few hundred men, if that—to implement the raiding strategy Frontenac had set in motion more than half a century before.

——•◆•——

The peculiar tactics of a strange enemy in a strange country

The English could not afford to ignore the superiority in woodland warfare of the Canadian-led and -reinforced Indian bands. Even in the mid–eighteenth century, when the frontier had advanced inland, and when physical survival was no longer in question—when, in fact, the issue was whether the French could survive English onslaughts, and not the other way around—political and military imperatives forced English and American leaders to respond.

Frontier warfare, not unlike terrorism today, had a broader popular audience that magnified its importance in the politics of the time. Spectacular raids like that on Schenectady in 1690 or Deerfield in 1704 had been widely reported in the colonies, and the cruelties inflicted on civilian populations were a source of anger and horror. The same was true of the massacre at Fort William Henry in 1757. As the English colonies became increasingly representative and open societies, in which royal governors depended on local legislatures for funds and support, one could not ignore the frontier, or suggest that local militias would have to bear the burden of defense. Nor could the English—unlike the French—exercise satisfactory control over where colonists settled. The vast migration of speculators and farmers had begun, and it was a tide that the governments of the time lacked the means, and usually the desire, to stop. Something had to be done to protect the frontier, and even if the measures adopted were often inadequate, there had to be a response.

British commanders in the Seven Years' War realized, almost imme-diately, that their preferred strategy—simultaneous thrusts against New France in the West (specifically, against Fort Duquesne at the Forks of the Ohio and Oswego on Lake Ontario) down the Champlain valley, and up the St. Lawrence—required some ability to meet an irregular opponent on its own terms. Woodland warriors were indispensable. Without them, armies could not acquire intelligence about the enemy and deny him the ability to strike at their own, exposed lines of supply in the woods and on lakes. British commanders despaired at the gap between what the enemy knew about them, and what they knew about him. "They have every intel-ligence the people can learn from appearances, or by another means; and this intelligence goes from all places," complained the Earl of Loudoun to William Pitt in June 1757.[18] Indeed, a scan of French records shows that the French commanders, including Montcalm, were well informed about which English units and commanders opposed them, although (as often happens with military intelligence) they exaggerated the actual numbers in arms against them. Some of that intelligence was gathered by spies, but much of it resulted from the continuous scouting conducted by French-led parties and the interrogation of the prisoners they took. Without sim-ilar units that could penetrate a screen of Indian raiding parties, the British were blind.

A lack of woodland-crafty troops meant not only ignorance of the enemy but inevitable defeat in the forest. Braddock's shocking defeat in 1755 had illustrated the British problem. His column had substantially outnumbered the Franco-Indian force opposite them, which consisted of perhaps 250 French and Canadians and something over 600 Indians.[19] He was no fool: He had, he thought, taken the proper precautions of sending out advance and flanking parties on his march. The former included a small group of Indians under William Johnson's deputy, George Croghan, and the latter some British light infantry and American soldiers. The firefight that ensued had calamitous results not simply because of the ambush itself, but because Braddock's army, most defi-nitely including its commander, were unable to fight competently in the woodland environment.[20]

If the British could win the war by storming the citadel at Quebec with a conventional army and doing nothing else, they could defeat the French without mastering the arts of wilderness warfare. But such a campaign would be hazardous in the extreme, depending not merely on the navigation of the St. Lawrence, but on the ability to throw a substantial army ashore, sustain it, and complete the siege of a fortified city in the short campaigning window assured by a wintry climate. Instead, British strategy called for a concerted, multithrust campaign against Canada. And such advances would require operations in the forests not just during one campaigning season, but over several. For armies to survive such campaigns the British needed woodland warriors of their own.

Indians, in quantity, were not to be had, at least not until the war had decisively swung in favor of the British. Some Indians sided with the English—the Mohican Indians of Stockbridge, for example, who figured in Rogers' rangers, and who, after similarly siding with the Americans during the Revolution, were deported to Wisconsin as a reward for their pains. The Mohawks remained largely pro-English, and in the complicated diplomacy of the frontier some other tribes, clans, or subclans would, for various reasons, work with the subjects of King George. But for the most part, the Indians were either warily neutral, or, understandably, pro-French.

The great mass of American militia and provincial troops offered no solution either. The militia were notoriously prickly about going beyond their local areas—in 1757 Governor Pownall of Massachusetts, for example, told Pitt that he had attempted to send a force from there to relieve General Webb at Fort William Henry, but that some of the militia had refused to go beyond the boundaries of the colony.[21] Provincial troops were, in theory, easier to use, but usually poorly disciplined, sticklers for their contractual rights, and, in point of fact, no better in the woods than the English regulars. Most of the colonial soldiers were farmers, not woodland trappers, and although they might be familiar with musket and axe, they could not be assumed to have the woodcraft possessed in abundance by their enemies.

The creation of ranger units composed of American volunteers proved only a partial solution to the British problem. Far more expensive than regular or provincial troops, the good units were few. Even Rogers' results were mixed; under inferior commanders they were no better than any other provincial troops. Like all special units then and since, they proved unruly in garrison, as the Whipping Post Mutiny revealed. The best, like all elite units, were inclined to play fast and loose with formal discipline, to look down their noses at strait-laced regulars, and, in general, to make themselves obnoxious to conventional soldiers. These warmly reciprocated the rangers' animosity. When General Thomas Gage took command in Albany in February 1759, he made use of the opportunity to undermine and denigrate them. "You will find them not very alert in obeying orders, especially when at a distance and at home," he wrote Major General Jeffery Amherst.[22] Gage exploited one of the most galling features of Anglo-American relations, the discrepancy in rank, ordering that the rangers, who "certainly have no rank in the Army," should not be allowed to give orders to regular officers in their midst. Rogers' friction with Lieutenant Colonel Haviland at Fort Edward was entirely typical, even though the more enterprising junior British officers made it a point to go out on patrols with the rangers to learn their craft.

Ranger units would ever be too small and specialized for tasks such as building and protecting wilderness roads or conducting large assaults on substantial enemy camps—the equivalent of Rigaud's daring winter raid on Fort William Henry in the winter of 1757, for example. And British officers, like regular soldiers throughout history, desired the benefits of irregular raiders and scouts, yet wanted them subject to normal discipline. If a large supply of elite rangers could not be found, or if they would not meet the requirements of the new situation, there were two other possibilities: the creation of specialized light infantry as part of the regular forces, and the raising of hybrid units, composed of men who could function well in the woods, but who would be subject to regular forms of organization and discipline. The British tried both.

The development of light infantry in the British army is generally traced to the Seven Years' War in North America.[23] In normal European-style warfare, the job of the infantry was to deliver mass fire from closely packed lines at short range—forty or fifty yards, or less. The skills they required were, above all, the discipline that would turn men into automatons who could load, fire, and move under the stress of combat; who could perform the complicated parade ground formations that could turn column to line, and line to column; who, when ordered, would fix bayonet and charge in good order. But in Europe by the Seven Years' War military commanders and theorists had discovered the need for soldiers who could act as skirmishers, seizing villages, for example, a cloud of fighters who could probe an enemy position, delay his advance, harass his flanks.

Such troops would fight in a rather different manner, in more open formations (perhaps not even in formations as generally understood), engaging more in aimed fire and less in the rippling volleys of line warfare, and
with much greater independence for junior officers and even individual
soldiers than was the norm in European warfare.

In Europe such units were often light cavalry (often known as Hus-
sars) or were recruited from gamekeepers and hunting populations (and
hence known as *chasseurs* or *jägers*—"hunters"), or consisted of soldiers
from the troubled borderlands of the Ottoman Empire.[24] In North America, however, and particularly along the Great Warpath, light cavalry had
little to offer. The problem was not merely the lack of open ground suitable for charges, but the problem of feeding an animal that required a
regular diet of forty pounds of fodder a day, and that, unlike a man, would
weaken, sicken, and even die if deprived of his rations for any length of
time. The physical environment of the northern colonies along the frontier simply could not provide that food, and the logistical demands attendant on bringing it to the front would have been too severe. Consequently,
the environment demanded a much larger and more elaborate light infantry establishment than anything the British had known to this point.

The pioneer in this service was George Augustus, Lord Howe. Howe,
aged thirty-four, in command of the Fifty-fifth of Foot, decided to learn
the methods of woodland warfare by accompanying the rangers, and
adopting many of their methods.[25] Having gone patrolling with Rogers,
he began training regulars to imitate the rangers. He modified the regulars' uniform, trimming off the tails of coats that could get entangled in
the brush, cutting the long hair characteristic of the day, browning the
barrels of muskets whose gleam would give away their position to a waiting enemy. With others, including Rogers' mortal enemy Thomas Gage,
he formed light infantry companies, the beginning of a practice that eventually put one such light infantry company in each regiment. Normal
practice became that of grouping together light infantry companies for
special missions, and then redistributing them to their parent regiments
afterward.[26]

Howe influenced the raising not merely of individual companies but
of regiments of light infantry, the Eightieth and later the Eighty-fifth and
Ninetieth, which entered the British line in 1759. But light infantry
required both officers and men suitable for this service, and the regular

British army had few of those in North America at the height of the Seven Years' War. Moreover, Howe's successor as the leading light infantry officer, Thomas Gage, had neither his charisma as a leader nor his abilities as a tactical commander. And light infantry, though better suited for woodland warfare than the regulars, remained only partly competent at it.

There was one more solution open to the British, raising units of men ready, by virtue of their previous backgrounds, to serve as woodland soldiers. Following Braddock's defeat the British government received a proposal to raise four battalions of provincial (that is, American) soldiers, led by British and foreign officers. This was the origin of the Royal American Regiment, subsequently the Sixtieth of Foot, today's Rifle Regiment or Royal Green Jackets of the British army.[27] The idea was to recruit Americans and foreign Protestants, particularly woodsmen from Germany and Switzerland, many of whom had recently immigrated to the United States. The regiment was created at the very end of 1755, and immediately began recruiting in Pennsylvania and elsewhere in North America.[28]

The commanders of the battalions thus raised were remarkable Swiss-born officers, most notably Henri Bouquet and Frédéric Haldimand, both of whom made names for themselves as frontier commanders in North America. Other officers who served with the Royal Americans became equally prominent. Two regiments of provincial troops, absorbed as the Fiftieth and Fifty-first regiments into the British army, were amalgamated into the Royal Americans as well. These soldiers, together with Germans from Pennsylvania and frontiersmen from New York and Albany, made up the rank and file.[29]

The four battalions of the Sixtieth served throughout the colonies during the Seven Years' War; they were at Fort Edward and Saratoga along the Great Warpath; they were in Pennsylvania; and they served at the siege of Louisbourg. One battalion of the Sixtieth took part in the battle of the Plains of Abraham outside Quebec—and, more than a century later, the Sixtieth was still there when the British garrisons left Canada in 1871. The Royal Americans, however, were only one regiment, albeit a large one, in the British establishment, and neither they, nor the light infantry, nor the rangers fully managed to match the French and Indians at the tactical level of forest warfare.

But they did not have to. Together, the combination of rangers, light infantry, and the Royal Americans gave the English and Americans not dominance in woodland warfare, but enough capability to survive in it—and to bring the weight of their numbers to bear. Anglo-American resources were adequate to allow the superior forces Pitt was sending to North America to deliver the blows that could finish off the French. The various light forces the British empire assembled were able to protect the lines of supply to their armies concentrating on Canada, provide adequate intelligence, contain the damage of French and Indian raiders, and even land a few sharp counterpunches. That was sufficient for the task.

Rogers Rules of Ranging

Quite apart from his myth, however, Rogers left a larger legacy to the American way of war: the rendering into system of what had been art. In 1765 he published his *Journals*, "an account of several excursions he made under the Generals who commanded upon the Continent of North America, during the late War." [30] He included in that work a short treatise on ranging warfare that he had written for his men when he had first ranged his unit. Reading it one sees a document astonishingly similar to today's Field Manual 7-8, *Infantry Rifle Platoon and Squad*, of the United States Army. [31]

Rogers' rules of ranging are, like any good field manual, the embodiment of tactical common sense. [32] "If your number be small, march in a single file, keeping at such a distance from each other as to prevent one shot from killing two men," or, "If the enemy is so superior that you are in danger of being surrounded by them, let the whole body disperse, and every one take a different road to the place of rendezvous appointed for that evening, which must every morning be ordered and fixed for the evening ensuing"—very much the same as the field manual's guidance that a patrol leader must "consider the use and locations of rally points. A rally point is a place designated by the leader where the platoon moves to reassemble and reorganize if it becomes dispersed." A second lieutenant today learns what Rogers taught two and a half centuries ago.

Rogers was undoubtedly a natural genius, of a sort, at woodland warfare—audacious, woodcrafty, and rugged. His men came of similar stock. But he relied not simply on his or his men's untrained instincts or accumulated experience, as the French could with their Indians, but on rules and practices that could be formally communicated, standard operating procedures that could be conveyed and reinforced in training. Rogers' short manual—a pamphlet, really—on patrolling codified common sense and the painful lessons of experience. It represents an important evolution in the history of military thought and practice, because it attempted to render the art of woodland fighting into something teachable and transmittable as military doctrine, a general way of approaching problems to be adapted to circumstances. And, indeed, Rogers told his readers that "there are, however, a thousand occurrences and circumstances which may happen, that will make it necessary, in some measure to depart from" these rules.

Rogers had invented doctrine for small-unit tactics—and it is a tribute to both the military yearning for a lineage and the soundness of the principles involved that the United States Army's Ranger school at Fort Benning, Georgia, still issues a card with "Rogers Rules of Ranging." That card, reproduced as Appendix D to Field Manual 7-8, reads as follows:

———— ◆ ————

Standing Orders, Rogers' Rangers

1. Don't forget nothing.

2. Have your musket clean as a whistle, hatchet scoured, sixty rounds powder and ball, and be ready to march at a minute's warning.

3. When you're on the march, act the way you would if you was sneaking up on a deer. See the enemy first.

4. Tell the truth about what you see and what you do. There is an army depending on us for correct information. You can lie all you please when you tell other folks about the Rangers, but don't never lie to a Ranger or officer.

5. Don't never take a chance you don't have to.

6. When we're on the march we march single file, far enough apart so one shot can't go through two men.

7. If we strike swamps, or soft ground, we spread out abreast, so it's hard to track us.

8. When we march, we keep moving till dark, so as to give the enemy the least possible chance at us.

9. When we camp, half the party stays awake while the other half sleeps.

10. If we take prisoners, we keep 'em separate till we have had time to examine them, so they can't cook up a story between 'em.

11. Don't ever march home the same way. Take a different route so you won't be ambushed.

12. No matter whether we travel in big parties or little ones, each party has to keep a scout 20 yards ahead, 20 yards on each flank, and 20 yards in the rear so the main body can't be surprised and wiped out.

13. Every night you'll be told where to meet if surrounded by a superior force.

14. Don't sit down to eat without posting sentries.

15. Don't sleep beyond dawn. Dawn's when the French and Indians attack.

16. Don't cross a river by a regular ford.

17. If somebody's trailing you, make a circle, come back onto your own tracks, and ambush the folks that aim to ambush you.

18. Don't stand up when the enemy's coming against you. Kneel down, lie down, hide behind a tree.

19. Let the enemy come till he's almost close enough to touch. Then let him have it and jump out and finish him up with your hatchet.

The source for this list seems, almost certainly, to be not Rogers' original guide, but the fictional rendition of it in Kenneth Roberts's 1937 novel about Rogers, *Northwest Passage*, in which the dyspeptic Sergeant McNott is preparing two new recruits for the raid on St. Francis that capped Rogers' activities in the French and Indian War.[33]

Until the middle nineteenth century, armies did rather little tactical training, but a great deal of drilling: Officers and sergeants sought to habituate their men to regular, precise movements so that they could perform maneuvers that were essentially the same on parade ground and battlefield. At the small-unit level—say, companies of fifty soldiers—tactics did not really exist: It was the job of soldiers to form lines and on order fire at the enemies in front of them. For the rangers, however, this was not the case. They fought in very small units, and their leaders were expected to make decisions similar in kind to those being made by American sergeants and captains in Iraq or Afghanistan 250 years later. Their soldiers used the tactics of fire and movement, and required skills in stealthy advance, reconnoitering, and retreat. In a firefight like the Battle on Snowshoes, junior leaders had to control small, often dispersed groups of soldiers and coordinate their activities with a larger unit. By contrast, the chief job of an infantry lieutenant in Europe was to show courage while men dropped all around him.

Here was a new enterprise: taking intelligent and independent civilians and teaching them warlike skills that they would have to use and adapt in an unfamiliar environment. The other fighting men of the eighteenth century were, for the most part, either life-long warriors like the native Americans, or the drilled, often brutalized members of the European peasantry or lower class of artisans, turned into serviceable machines by a harsh discipline. That is why Lieutenant Colonel Haviland—a decent man, friend of political philosopher Edmund Burke—found the rangers' aversion to flogging so outrageous. Rogers' rangers, on the other hand, were the forerunners of the infantrymen of a much later age, citizen soldiers molded by carefully conceived systems of military thought intended to guide practice but not dictate it, disciplined, yes, but not beaten into mechanical docility.

Today, an elite United States infantry regiment claims Rogers' rangers as its lineage. Rogers' men, however, resembled far more the citizen soldiers who won American wars in the nineteenth and twentieth centuries.

The real legacy of Rogers' rangers belongs to the average soldiers who fought independently, cannily, and tenaciously under competent sergeants and junior officers not because such was their natural aptitude, or even because of the cause for which they fought, but because of the army that had trained them, and indirectly, the society that had produced them.[34] The Battle on Snowshoes decided little—nothing, in fact. But it reveals a great deal about the system that produces American soldiers to the present day.

CHAPTER FOUR

Fort Carillon, 1758

This has been a most Bloody Fight[1]

The Forty-second of Foot, the Scottish Highlands regiment known as the Black Watch, has had many a bad day in its glorious and sanguinary past: It formed a square at Waterloo; slogged through the mud and squalor of the Somme and Passchendaele; made a fighting retreat at Dunkirk; took part in the victory of El Alamein; landed at Normandy on D-Day; won its 151st battle honor in the Korean War; and liberated Basra in 2003. But perhaps its worst day was on July 8, 1758, at the fort that the French called Carillon, and the British, following the Indian name, Ticonderoga.

The regiment, formed less than twenty years before, in 1739, out of a collection of independent companies of loyal Scottish Highlanders whose job it was to keep their more contumacious cousins in Britain's north under some kind of control, had taken their places in the march of the largest army seen in North America, some seventeen thousand strong, moving northward on Lake George. They were part of four columns of boats, screened by a corps of batteaumen, rangers, and light infantry, followed in turn by artillery and supply vessels. Their officers had read them

PLAN DU FORT CARILLON
Echelle

ATTAQUES DES RETRANCHEMENS DEVANT LE FORT CARILLON
en Amérique
par les anglais commandés par le général Abercrombie contre les français
aux ordres du Marquis de Montcalm le 8 Juillet 1758.

Renvois.

A Le fort Carillon. B Retranchemens, que les français ont commencé à faire le 7 Juillet
au matin. C Camp de l'armée française, où elle se rendit le 6 & resta sous les armes pendant
la nuit du 7 au 8. Le 8 à la pointe du jour elle prit la position D en ordre de bataille derrière les
retranchemens. E Les grénadiers & les piquets pour reserve derrière chaque bataillon. F Colonnes des
anglais, qui attaquent les retranchemens à midi & demie. G Pelotons de troupes legéres & provincia-
les fusillant entre ces colonnes. H Les canadiens sortent du retranchement, & attaquent une colonne
anglaise en flanc. I Chaloupes des anglais, qui parurent pendant l'attaque, & furent repoussées par
l'artillerie du fort. K Retraite des colonnes anglaises dans leur premier camp près des moulins à scier
vers sept heures du soir; leur troupes legéres couvrirent cette retraite par leur feu prolongé jusques
dans la nuit. L Position des français après la retraite des anglais. M Batteries redoutes &
retranchemens, que les français établerent après le combat.

C.P.S.C.M.

The British assault on Fort Carillon, 1758. Reproduced by permission of the
Society of the Cincinnati, Washington, D.C.

the Articles of War in Gaelic as well as English (which many of the soldiers did not understand), and the pipers played as they rowed the weary miles to Sabbath Day Point two-thirds of the way down the lake.[2] The regiment had arrived in North America in the summer of 1756. Three of its companies remained in the rear at Fort Edward and in New York, but the other ten, one thousand strong, had embarked on their first American campaign. Like most Europeans new to this continent, the officers and men were bemused by the flora and fauna of the wilderness. Captain James Murray described to his brother killing rattlesnakes "about four feet long and as thick as the small of one's leg," and although their meat was "insipid" and its smell "exactly like a goat, ranker if possible," he noted that "they make the richest and best soup that can be which I eat of and like much."[3] Events soon drove thoughts of rattlesnake soup out of Captain Murray's head.

After a successful and largely unopposed landing at the north of Lake George on July 6, the Highlanders had joined in the approach march to the French position at Ticonderoga; they did not take part in the skirmish that routed French outposts at the cost of the van's commander, Lord George Howe. But on the eighth they flung themselves at the right of the French line on the Heights of Carillon—the rather grandiosely named hillocks about three-quarters of a mile to the northwest of the fort there. Here, the Highlanders, like their comrades along the line, attempted repeatedly to storm a dense abatis—layers of trees (oaks and chestnuts, in all likelihood) cut down, their tops facing outward, their branches interwoven, backed by a breastwork manned by French troops. Three times their commander ordered them to withdraw, and three times they ignored him, one officer of the Fifty-fifth marveling that the Black Watch "appeared like roaring lions breaking from their chains."[4] Canadian militia and colonial infantry attacked their flank, but the Scots brushed them off and continued to plunge into the dense growth. They got close to the French soldiers, barely visible in the greenery and smoke, who manned firing positions and picked them off, the Frenchmen passing loaded muskets to the marksmen on the wall. Some of the Highlanders even crossed over the barrier, but the French reserves, held for such a moment, counterattacked, and bayoneted the few who did.[5]

The Highlanders' casualties, killed and wounded, included almost all of their officers, and a grand total of 647 out of one thousand men, almost

two-thirds of the initial strength. Reverend John Cleaveland, a chaplain
to a battalion of Massachusetts provincials, marveled at the debacle. "The
conduct is thought to be marvelous strange," he said of the headlong
assaults launched without artillery preparation against this position
impregnable to infantry equipped only with musket and bayonet (and,
for the Highlanders, broadswords). But the good reverend was even more
surprised and, indeed, disgusted when, the next day, the demoralized
army, the largest thus far assembled in North America and still vastly
larger than the French garrison, meekly retreated to Fort George, the base
situated near, and partly on the ruins of Fort William Henry.

A general invasion of Canada at the very root

The assault on Fort Carillon was the one unsuccessful part of the decisive
swing of the war against New France. The new strategy was a set of simultaneous offensives aimed at isolating the core of Quebec from France and
overwhelming the French with forces composed of large numbers of regulars. It represented "a general invasion of Canada at the very root"[6] and
involved a change of command as well.

The shift in British strategy is usually attributed to one man—William Pitt, who in November 1756 became secretary of state for the southern department (basically, most of the world outside Europe) following a
set of defeats that had weakened the Newcastle Ministry, including the
fall of Minorca to the French. Often ill, but energetic, Pitt infused the
British war effort with new vigor. Skeptical of British commitments to
fight in Germany, he advocated pouring vast sums of money into subsi-
dies to Frederick of Prussia, while turning the efforts of the Royal Navy
and the army overseas, to Africa, the Caribbean, India, and North America. He had begun this process in North America on the penultimate day
of 1757 by recalling the commander in chief, John Campbell, fourth Earl
of Loudoun, promoting Loudoun's number two in his place. Pitt, however, denied Major General James Abercromby the plenipotentiary powers assigned his predecessor. Instead, he ordered his senior military
commanders in North America to correspond directly with him: A strong

civilian hand was now felt in the conduct of the war. Behind the change of command was a shift in resources. By 1758 the British had twenty-three battalions of regulars in North America, and reinforcements and replacements continued to flow in. Eventually some twenty-three thousand regulars were sent to or recruited in North America, a remarkable contrast with the regulars sent from France to Canada, who numbered scarcely a quarter that number.[7]

Pitt sketched out for Abercromby the new British approach to the war in North America.[8] The king, his first minister said, had decided to commit fourteen thousand troops under the command of Major General Jeffery Amherst to the siege of Louisbourg, the great fortress city and naval base at the northern end of what is now Nova Scotia that was vital to French America but separate from it. After arranging for the efficient deployment of that force, he directed, Abercromby was to invade Canada by way of Crown Point, seizing Montreal. Pitt stressed the importance of securing the support of the governors of the northern provinces. He went on to appoint Brigadier John Forbes to command an expedition against Fort Duquesne, expelling the French from Pennsylvania and redeeming the disaster of Braddock's defeat in its vicinity in 1755.

Abercromby was enjoined to raise as many rangers as possible, sending at least six hundred to support the forces besieging Louisbourg. In parallel, Pitt had written to the governors of Massachusetts, New Hampshire, Connecticut, Rhode Island, New York, and New Jersey urging them to raise at least twenty thousand men to support the expedition to Crown Point. The king would provide arms, ammunition, tents, and provisions, asking of the provinces the clothing and pay of the troops.[9] Pitt aimed to cut off Canada's extremities—Louisbourg, her forward positions on Lake Champlain, Fort Duquesne—and then strike at her heart, the cities of Montreal and Quebec and the narrow belt of villages and towns along the 125 miles that separated them. At last, the British strategic concept first sketched at the beginning of the eighteenth century was coming to fruition. With confidence in their own resources, if only they could be mobilized, the British statesmen were determined to destroy New France, and in the most direct way possible.

The mood in Paris was far less resolute. Louis xv and his court faced two questions: what expense was Canada worth, and what, practically, could be done? The colony had never made money, but the humiliation of losing Canada meant a great deal to French statesmen. The loss of a naval presence in the North Atlantic that would flow from a complete collapse would mean the death blow to France's fisheries on the western side of the North Atlantic. On the positive side of the ledger, a continuing struggle would tie down British forces that would otherwise make mischief elsewhere. The practicalities, however, made for greater trouble.

Of these, the two greatest and interrelated problems stemmed from the British naval challenge to France's sea lines of communication to Canada, and feeding the soldiers stationed there. French ships in small numbers could, and did, get through to Quebec and Montreal up the St. Lawrence, almost until the colony's demise in 1760. In May 1759 fifteen transports and two frigates made it through to the colony with four hundred recruits and six thousand tons of food.[10] But these were modest, almost furtive efforts, and in constant jeopardy. British naval dominance, pronounced at the beginning of the war, grew throughout it. In 1755, the Royal Navy had 117 ships of the line and 74 cruisers (frigates, for the most part), versus 57 and 31 for the French. Five years later, the British had added 18 ships of the line and 26 cruisers, while the French had lost 3 ships of the line and added only 6 cruisers.[11] But this does not fully capture the decay of French naval power and the growth of a Royal Navy that doubled its manpower even as it won victories against the outnumbered French fleet.[12] The added aggressiveness of Royal Navy commanders following the salutary example of the execution of the hapless Admiral Byng on his own quarterdeck on March 14, 1757, amplified the effect of this material superiority.

No less problematic was the question of supplying the colony. Canada had a far more precarious agricultural base than the English colonies: Every spring and summer food shortages loomed, particularly after a year with a bad harvest. By April 1758, the bread ration in Quebec had been reduced to a couple of ounces a day, and horse had become a feature of Canadian cuisine.[13] Even had the French court been willing to go to the expense, effort, and hazard of sending a few thousand more soldiers to Canada, how would it feed them, without still more vulnerable convoys of food ships? The French chose an unsatisfactory solution: to provide modest reinforcements to Montcalm and equally modest supplies to the colony, hoping to recoup any losses in the New World with victories in the Old.

In Canada, the mood was one of quiet desperation, which led, however, to very different conclusions in its divided high command. Montcalm, increasingly pessimistic, favored concentrating his scanty regulars near the colony's core and fighting defensive battles. Governor Vaudreuil, on the other hand, clung to the traditional Canadian strategy of forward defense from wilderness forts, and extensive raiding. As the campaigning season of 1758 began, he had devised a plan to attack Schenectady—again—with a force of four hundred French troops drawn from Montcalm's scanty force of regulars, four hundred Canadian militia, and as many as a thousand Indians under the veteran François-Gaston de Lévis, Montcalm's extremely capable deputy, and Vaudreuil's no less experienced brother Rigaud, leader of the midwinter raid on Fort William Henry in 1757.

Vaudreuil's concept was to inflict spectacular devastation on the frontier and achieve two objectives at once. The colonial forces Pitt was busily raising (and which the French knew about) would find themselves dispatched by anxious governors and assemblies to garrison the frontier, rather than support a British invasion of Canada. And, in addition, the Indians (to whose psychology Vaudreuil was keenly sensitive) would be impressed at this demonstration of French prowess. Montcalm, who ever since the Fort William Henry massacre had viewed the Indians with particular distaste and contempt, sneered at the governor's schemes.

Thus, it was with divided councils that Canada awaited what a difficult new year would bring.

———◆———

A very good Second man anywhere

The new commander in chief in New York, James Abercromby, was a steady Scots soldier, the son of a laird, and formerly the commander of the Royal Scots, the First of Foot. The *Dictionary of National Biography* takes a dim view of his previous career during the War of Austrian Succession: "Corpulent, lethargic, and unambitious, he avoided responsibility in all these duties."[14] Lord Loudoun, whom he replaced in 1758, described him as "a good Officer, and a very good Second man anywhere."[15] His French opponents may have judged him best. Montcalm's brilliant young chief of staff, Louis Antoine de Bougainville, wrote of him shortly before the battle at Ticonderoga: "a man of more courage than resolution . . . age has lessened in him the fire necessary for the execution of great undertakings. . . . He expresses himself with difficulty, talks little, writes better than he speaks."[16] Testimony here to the shrewdness of Bougainville's judgment, but also to the excellence of French intelligence, which combined careful scrutiny of American and English newspapers and interrogation of prisoners and deserters with more traditional forms of espionage.

Abercromby had secured a place in North America through his connections with the Duke of Newcastle and Loudoun, who brought him over when he replaced Governor William Shirley as the overall commander in North America. Abercromby seems, in truth, to be just what Loudoun described—a conscientious number two, who now, unfortunately for all concerned, had become number one. For the moment, however, the magnitude of resources that the British were pouring into the fight for Canada concealed his deficiencies. The first major move against France in North America had come in late February 1758, when a fleet of twenty-three ships of the line and eighteen frigates had sailed from Britain for Halifax, Nova Scotia. They arrived at nearly the same time in May that a meager resupply convoy of eight French ships crept up the St. Lawrence to rescue Quebec from the brink of starvation. On June 8 the British fleet, with 150 transports and nearly fourteen thousand men under Jeffery Amherst, began landings in the vicinity of the fortress city of Louisbourg at the tip of what is now Cape Breton Island.

By late May, provincial and British troops had also begun massing at Albany for Abercromby's thrust up the Great Warpath. The logistical effort was immense: In mid-June ten thousand muskets and camp gear for four thousand men arrived in New York from Britain, allowing the equipping of a large provincial force. A thousand bateaux and two hundred whaleboats had assembled at Lake George, under the able command of Lieutenant Colonel John Bradstreet, a professional soldier born in Nova Scotia of an English officer and a French Acadian mother. To Bradstreet goes the credit for the efficient equipment and movement of the entire army, and a warlike drive that reflected a competence well beyond the moving of troops and materiel.

Abercromby's force consisted of eight battalions of regulars (two from the Sixtieth of Foot, the Royal Americans raised in the colonies) with 44 pieces of artillery, some 5,800 men or more.[17] Seventeen smaller regiments of provincials—mainly from Massachusetts, Connecticut, and New York, with some units from Rhode Island, New Hampshire, and New Jersey, plus seven companies of rangers (two of them Stockbridge Indians), 1,600 batteaumen, and 400 Indians under Sir William Johnson made up another 11,775, for a grand total of 17,600.

On June 19, several regiments of regulars, New Jersey provincials, and rangers had reoccupied the site of Fort William Henry and begun building a new base there, Fort George. By the end of June, thousands of provincial troops had gathered the vast quantities of supplies the army needed, and their transportation, including a thousand bateaux and several hundred whaleboats.[18] Artillery, ammunition, and tentage poured into the site of the massacre of the previous year.

French patrols observed this massing of forces. Thirty-five-year-old ensign de Langis—who had vanquished Rogers at the Battle on Snowshoes—reconnoitered the buildup with a force of 178 troops from Carillon on July 4. The French had already begun making dispositions. On the last day of June, Montcalm had arrived at Carillon; for once he and Governor Vaudreuil agreed that here was the most menaced point in the outerworks of New France. Vaudreuil canceled the planned raid down the Mohawk valley to Schenectady and ordered the Chevalier Lévis with his four hundred picked regulars to march to the aid of Montcalm in the defense of Carillon.

Eight battalions of French troops, almost all of the regulars available to the French commander, now assembled at Carillon, supported by a handful of *troupes de la marine* and Canadian militia. Of some forty-two hundred French soldiers, more than 90 percent were regulars from Europe; the Indians were virtually absent. Montcalm would make his stand with the regulars of his army—the hard core of European veterans whom he trusted. Like many a coalition commander before and since, he may have felt some relief at being able to do so without troublesome allies.

He made his choice well aware that he was up against forces vastly superior in numbers and equipment. The eight British battalions opposite him had, in some cases, more than twice as many soldiers as their French opposite numbers. The total Anglo-American force outnumbered the French by a bit more than four to one. As for the fort itself, designed to hold four hundred troops at most, Montcalm despised it as a poorly built specimen of corrupt Canadian jobbery, designed by an inept relative of Vaudreuil, dominated by high ground, barely defensible.

On July 5, Abercromby embarked at the southern end of Lake George and moved north, more than a thousand boats dotting the waters of Lake George, as appalled French and Canadian scouts watched their movements from the concealment of the shore. It would be difficult not to believe that Carillon was doomed, and with it, Montcalm's irreplaceable little army and indeed, New France.

Montcalm faced a choice: to hold to Carillon, or attempt to block the British at the northern end of Lake George.[19] Here, forest and steep hills dominate the limited landing grounds, not much more than a half mile wide, where an army could land and approach Ticonderoga. It might well have made sense to fight there, at the water's edge. Montcalm, however, decided to leave three battalions at the head of the portage road on Lake George and to pull his remaining force back to Fort Carillon, where some of his men began felling trees and creating breastworks on the heights three-quarters of a mile from the fort on July 5. On that day, the British flotilla moved some twenty-five miles down Lake George to Sabbath Day Point, where it camped—and, craftily, reembarked at midnight, hoping to avoid detection by the French. By the next morning they reached the north end of Lake George. Montcalm, apprised of the British approach, withdrew his three battalions and the scouting forces that had shadowed the advancing army. He did, however, leave one detachment at the northern end of the lake, which on the morning of July 6 also withdrew in the face of Abercromby's van.

The Chute River, some three and a half miles in length, flows from Lake George to Champlain creating five falls, providing the force to power a sawmill that the French had built perhaps a mile and a half from the fort. The Chute has one large bulge toward the north; cutting across the base of that bulge, to its south, was a portage road for wagons to carry goods, and even boats, from Lake George to Lake Champlain. Several small streams fed into the river from the north and west, most notably Trout, or Bernetz, Brook (scene of the Battle on Snowshoes). At the time of the battle, paths ran along the Chute, and from Lake George to Trout Brook. Carillon itself was oriented southeast, on a peninsula at the junction of the Chute, with Lake Champlain to the north and its continuation in Wood Creek to the south. A mile south of Fort Carillon, and separated from the peninsula by the mouth of the Chute, looms what the French called Rattlesnake Mountain, which the English subsequently called Mount Defiance, a steep, nine-hundred-foot-high wooded mountain overlooking the fort.

The British army had landed at the northern end of Lake George without opposition—a hopeful sign. In an effort to outflank the French, whom they believed to be present but withdrawing to Ticonderoga, Lord Howe, Abercromby's second in command, led one of four columns that he dispatched through the woods, west of the river. Rogers' rangers had already picked their way close to the Chute, past where it intersected Trout Brook. That afternoon, around four o'clock, Montcalm's rear guard, commanded by Captain Trépezec with some 350 men, including 250 regulars and about 100 colonial troops—no Indians—had withdrawn before the advancing British, hoping to make a westerly circuit around them. Trépezec's unit lost its bearings but finally blundered into Trout Brook and began moving along it southerly to the intersection with the Chute, from where it could find its way back to Carillon. As it did so, it stumbled into a detachment of the First Connecticut sent to reinforce the rangers, and a firefight began.

Here the absence of the Indians told. The French force had the worst of it and was effectively annihilated, as a Massachusetts regiment from one of the columns moved to the sound of the guns and caught the French, already pressed by the combined Connecticut troops and rangers, in the flank. Captain Trépezec was mortally wounded, and only fifty of his men made it back, the remaining three hundred being killed or captured in a confused forest fight. The British and Americans had suffered a third as many losses, but one more grievous than all the rest: Lord George Howe, the brilliant and well-loved thirty-three-year-old second in command, had fallen to a musket ball—French, possibly, or friendly fire from a panicky Connecticut soldier.[20]

Lord Howe's death demoralized the army. His fall deprived it of a commander who grasped the nature of woodland warfare, who got on with the Americans, and who seems to have carried the burden of tactical planning for the operation. His loss outweighed a tactical success that the Anglo-Americans, so used to defeat in the woods, barely recognized as such. The rattled British advanced; the anxious French withdrew to Carillon, and Montcalm's men redoubled their feverish labors fortifying the heights there.

— • ✦ • —

Abundance of time to mow us down like a field of corn

They would have to wait one more day. On the seventh of July, Abercromby convened an early morning council of war, at which Colonel John Bradstreet, whose sixteen hundred river boatmen had done such a competent job of leading the army north, begged to be allowed to march directly up the portage road that cut across the loop of the Chute. Abercromby seems reluctantly to have agreed to this suggestion. The fact that a logistician would have to ask for, and would then receive, such a role says something about senior leadership under Abercromby. It raises the first of many questions about his newly appointed second in command, General Thomas Gage, whose own Eightieth Regiment of light infantry had been formed to serve as the army's forward units, diminishing thereby its reliance on rangers and Indians. Gage, throughout the campaign and the battle, was notable chiefly by his absence.

Others, however, took the initiative, for later that morning Bradstreet led a large column of over four thousand men, composed of regulars, provincials, and rangers, up the direct, more obvious, but from the French point of view, more defensible route, the portage road. He secured the sawmill, where late in the afternoon the commanding general and his staff arrived and settled in. Abercromby thereupon ordered a reconnaissance of the French position by his engineer, Lieutenant Matthew Clerk, and Captain James Abercrombie, a thrusting young officer (possibly related to the commanding general) who had spent time with Rogers and his men. With an escort from Captain John Stark's rangers, the two men climbed Mount Defiance and spied out the French position.[21]

Clerk was standing in for his superior, John Montrésor, who was ill and had been detached to manage the supply depot at Fort George. Because Clerk died of wounds shortly after the battle, and hence could not defend himself, he subsequently received much undeserved blame for what ensued. From today's Mount Defiance, a mile away, he could see French soldiers building their fortified lines on the Heights of Carillon, three-quarters of a mile from the fort. But the thickness of the vegetation and the fact that the French were deliberately incorporating living trees into the abatis made the position look far less impressive than it really was. Indeed, the French had begun the defensive line only two days earlier, and had just begun working on it in earnest, but it was no less formidable for all that. Clerk reported to Abercromby, suggesting that after another scout the following morning, he find a location for an artillery battery to be placed at the foot of Mount Defiance, which could enfilade the French line from the south, and facilitate, thereby, an attack on it.

By the next day, the morning of July 8, the French had, by strenuous exertions, laid out in front of Ticonderoga two lines: a thinly manned and hastily constructed breastwork of logs as a picket line, to keep enemy scouts at bay and to give warning of an attack, and the main line of resistance, a much stronger wall of logs in front of which lay the felled trees and saplings, interwoven and lashed together. This dense field fortification, 150 feet in depth, was virtually impassable to infantry. The British knew that a defensive line lay before them, but underestimated the strength of the French position. While Lieutenant Clerk prepared to move an artillery battery—a substantial undertaking involving the construction of rafts to float down the Chute—another group of officers, including Bradstreet, Captain Abercrombie, and a "foreign engineer," probably a French Huguenot named Charles Rivez, conducted another reconnaissance of the French lines.[22] This was even less informative than that of the afternoon before, because it went no farther than the first French line, the thinly manned, improvised breastwork the French had intelligently put out *in front* of the main abatis to thwart just such a reconnaissance.

Abercromby convened a council of war from which provincial officers were excluded: He decided to attack (or perhaps let others push him into the decision). Having sent off the newly arrived Sir William Johnson and his four hundred Indians—probably to cover the artillery battery being emplaced at the base of Mount Defiance—the British army lined up for the assault.[23] A line of skirmishers consisting of rangers, bateaumen, and

light infantry would go first, followed by the New York and Massachusetts provincial regiments, with the British regiments, organized in three
small brigades of two or three battalions each, in the third line to deliver
the main blow, the Connecticut and New Jersey regiments serving as a
reserve or rear guard in case of lurking Indian or Canadian raiders.

Around noon the rangers encountered the first French line, and from
it they drove off the enemy's pickets. Meanwhile, Lieutenant Clerk and
his artillery battery, which was supposed to cover the assault, floated
down to the mouth of the Chute River at around two in the afternoon,
perhaps earlier. In keeping with the mishaps of the day, they steered to the
left of a mudbank in the river, rather than to the right, and thereby came
within close range of Fort Ticonderoga's artillery. The French guns
opened up, sinking several of the boats and forcing the remainder to flee.
Indeed, the French salvo may have been misinterpreted by British commanders as the signal for *their* assaults, setting the conditions for the
debacle that ensued.

In any event, the New Yorkers on the left of the British line, who had
brushed through the French picket line, mistakenly thinking that they
had breached the main French position, cheered. Hearing their cheers
and the cannon fire, on the right General Haviland (Rogers' irascible former superior) launched the main assault. From 1:30 P.M. to 7:00 P.M. a
confused wave of British assaults crashed into the main French position,
British regiments bearing the brunt, assisted, here and there, by provincial units.

Lieutenant William Grant of the Black Watch described these direct
assaults into the eighteenth-century equivalent of the barbed-wire entan-
glements of World War I:

> We laboured under unsurmountable difficulties: the enemy's breastwork
> was about nine or ten feet high, upon the top of which they had plenty
> of wall-pieces [swivel guns and large-caliber muskets] fixed, and well
> lined on the side with small arms. But the difficult access to their lines
> was what gave them a fatal advantage over us: they took care to cut down
> monstrous large fir and oak trees, &c., which covered all the ground from
> the foot of the breastwork, about the distance of a cannon shot every way
> in their front. This not only broke our ranks, and made it impossible for
> us to keep our order, but put it entirely out of our power to advance

briskly; which gave the enemy abundance of time to mow us down like a field of corn, with their wall pieces and small arms, before we fired a single shot, being ordered to receive the enemy's fire, and march with shouldered arms until we came up close to their breastwork.[24]

Meanwhile, even as the assaults on the French left and center ebbed, the Forty-second of Foot launched its furious assaults on the French right, gaining the walls of the French position only to be repulsed. By seven o'clock at night the gunfire died down, and the Anglo-American army withdrew, covered by the light infantry. The butcher's bill was grim, although its actual size is a matter of some dispute, since the French buried some 800 men, while others were recovered by the British. The best estimate seems to be some 1,000 killed and 1,500 wounded on the British side, 70 or 80 percent of them regulars. The French had lost far fewer—perhaps 100 killed and fewer than 300 wounded. But this meant that when the disaster of Trépezec's force was added to the total, Montcalm had suffered 13 percent casualties, Abercromby a little more, perhaps 15 percent.[25]

Abercromby decided to withdraw to the Lake George beachhead. For the moment he left a thin line of pickets observing the battlefield as his shattered regiments regrouped. But, as one veteran of the retreat recalled, "Word came that the French were going down to the lake, to cut off our retreat and take our bateaux, in consequence of which the army was rallied about midnight or after and ordered to march to the lake to secure our retreat and boats, in a dismal dark night, through a thick pine swamp." The pickets fired a hasty volley at the French soldiers who, in the way of eighteenth-century warfare, were rifling the pockets of the dead and wounded strewn across the abatis, and scurried off.[26]

On the ninth the French recovered the English wounded who had lain on the field overnight, buried the dead, and refurbished and strengthened their entrenchments, preparing to weather another assault. It never came. When volunteers went out to reconnoiter the enemy position they found that the encampment at the sawmill was empty. A further reconnaissance on the tenth scoured the area between the sawmill and the northern end of Lake George but found only the detritus of an army beating a hasty retreat. Abercromby's army had, not to put too fine a point on it, fled the field.

It had been a sad botch of a battle. Howe's unlucky death was an ill fortune of war, and Clerk's inadequate reconnaissance on the seventh may simply have reflected the limits of what a man could see from a mile off in the wooded terrain. Abercromby's subordinates, with the exception of Bradstreet, did not serve him well. But there is little doubt that Abercromby had no grip on his own army. "The eagerness of the Troops for the Attack was the loss of that Day & nothing Else," was the judgment of Captain Abercrombie, and he captured thereby a fundamental truth—even if his own perception of the weakness of the French line in the second reconnaissance, that of the morning of the eighth, played some role in bringing on the debacle.[27] The army was in a curious state on July 8—alarmed by the death of Howe, yet eager to charge straight ahead, brush aside the enemy's entrenchments, and finish the job in the kind of close-quarters bayonet assault that they understood far better than woodland skirmishing.

Abercromby, like all defeated generals, had his excuses, not all of them implausible. In a letter to a relative written in mid-August, six weeks after the battle, he made them.[28] French reinforcements were on the way (true—Rigaud de Vaudreuil showed up with the rest of the force intended for the Schenectady raid, some three thousand Canadians and Indians in total, by July 13). That force might indeed have wreaked havoc on the tenuous British supply lines and rear areas. To have brought up the siege artillery for a deliberate attack would have been the work of a week, and besides, the scouting parties had said that the enemy's lines could be stormed. As for the retreat, Abercromby pled his losses in officers and men (indeed, the British regiments had lost many of their officers) and disparaged the provincial soldiers as panicky and unreliable—"Their Officers, with a very few Exceptions, are worse than their Men." "Considering that we had not then 4000 Regulars fit for Duty, and those too unofficer'd" he was, he almost seemed to say, in effect outnumbered. "I had but a nominal army," he said.

But Abercromby's real failure—compounded by catastrophic losses in officers—was an inability to impose his will on his army. He wrote plaintively of the attack, "And it was what the whole Officers and Troops earnestly wished for," as if those wishes, rather than a commander's intentions, had a legitimate role in shaping his decisions. And in the end, his miserable confession that "my Health and constitution is greatly impair'd within these five Months,—the great Fatigue of my body," he allowed, being surpassed only by his "extreme Anxiety" of mind. The collapse of his own morale is indicated by his willingness to let his most able subordinate, Colonel John Bradstreet, depart on an expedition against Fort Frontenac only five days after the failed assault—thereby depriving himself of the subordinate and soldiers who might have made possible a second strike at Carillon.

Abercromby was no physical coward, accompanying the Highlanders to the front as he did. But as a general, he had failed. He did not get artillery in place in time to support the attack, did not control the launching of the initial attack or rein in the fruitless frontal assaults once it had become apparent that the French had constructed a far more formidable position than he had anticipated. He then allowed the army to withdraw precipitously when, after all, he still outnumbered the enemy by three or four to one. His subordinates subsequently turned against him. Gage, with the aggressive and much disliked founder of the Royal Americans, James Prevost, wrote his hapless commander insinuating letters of advice, including, on July 29, the suggestion that Abercromby at least keep a book that copied the orders given to each of his subordinates so that he could keep track of his own instructions.[29] These letters, and the fact that Prevost and Gage—who comes across as a minor Iago of British camp life—slyly sent copies of them to the Duke of Cumberland, son of George II, captain-general of the British army and the bloody victor of Culloden against Scottish rebels in 1745, suggest, first, that Abercromby's own subordinates had written him off after having failed adequately to support him in battle, and second, that the basic administrative machinery of the army could not cope with the strain of the summer campaign. And, indeed, the fragile logistical systems of any eighteenth-century army would have strained to sustain a renewed advance toward Carillon.

There were further humiliations in store. Three weeks after the battle, on July 28, the ubiquitous La Corne St. Luc, with several hundred Indians and Canadians, pounced on a two-hundred-man supply convoy moving between Fort Edward and Fort George at the southern end of Lake George. "His detachment took III scalps and 80 prisoners," and after smashing barrels of wine and rum, killing the oxen, and plundering the rest he returned to Carillon.[30] The dispirited Anglo-American camp hummed with reports of La Corne's brutalities: a pregnant woman disemboweled, and the head of a four-year-old boy stuck on a pole at the woman's head.[31] His own casualties were one Iroquois dead and three wounded.[32] Governor Vaudreuil, however, was delighted by the raid, if not the accompanying mayhem, and both he and Montcalm recommended that the king make him a chevalier of the Croix de St. Louis as a reward.

Fort Carillon is worth nothing

Viewed from one perspective, the fall of Ticonderoga would have made remarkably little difference one way or another. As long as Montcalm could keep his army intact, even if Abercromby had taken the fort, it is unlikely that Montreal would have fallen in 1758. There were other points along the Great Warpath where the French could have delayed a British advance until autumnal weather made the prospects chilling in more than one sense. The British had no warships on Lake Champlain, which meant that even the tiny French flotilla (a supply schooner and three poorly constructed xebecs, lateen-rigged Mediterranean vessels under Jean d'Olabaratz, a fisherman turned corsair) would pose a real obstacle until he could build his own fleet. Moreover, so great a force as Abercromby had would have been as much impediment as advantage in an extended march north. Simply feeding it would have been a monstrous task. Nor was he the kind of commander to make a daring dash of a hundred miles or more with the idea of bringing the war to a close at the end of one campaigning season.

A lot of blood had been shed, of course. But the British did not lack for replacements, while the French most certainly did. While Abercromby and his men were licking their wounds at the southern end of Lake George, on July 26, barely two weeks after the defeat at Carillon, Louisbourg fell to the combined British naval and land forces that had efficiently smashed fortifications and a French squadron in the harbor alike. Louisbourg, now in British hands, would serve as the launching point for the decisive campaign of the war, Brigadier James Wolfe's attack on Quebec. And part of Abercromby's army did some good. Bradstreet took three thousand men—colonials, chiefly—to Lake Ontario, and on August 27 he took Fort Frontenac, today's Kingston, Ontario. The capture of French supplies there, the destruction of the French naval flotilla on the lake, and the reduction of the fort opened up another route into the French colony, damaging French prestige with the Indians and helping cut Montreal off from the western parts of North America. It was a brilliant and consequential action.

The debacle at Ticonderoga, however, did matter, in both the short and the longer terms; it mattered as many battles do, in what it did to individual commanders, how it shaped reputations, and the symbols that it created. Abercromby, well-meaning incompetent, suffered the inevitable consequence of relief later that year, though not complete disgrace. He was promoted to lieutenant general and, in 1772, to general, although no one was foolish enough to give him command of anything again. From a safe perch in Parliament he spent his retirement railing against the Americans and urging the government to take a firm hand with them during the troubles of the 1760s and 1770s. What happened to his opponent was far more interesting.

One might think that Montcalm would have been elated at his success at Fort Ticonderoga. Far from it. Later that summer he ordered the building of a large cross on the battlefield, inscribed with a Latin verse composed by Bougainville attributing victory to God alone. In less reverential moments, however, he knew that he had won considerable personal glory from this success. As a good soldier, however, he could guess that his opponents would not give him another such opportunity to "mow them down like corn." Like a Confederate who had beaten back a Union assault in the Wilderness in 1864, or a German soldier on the Eastern Front in 1944, he knew that the success was no more than a temporary respite; that the enemy would come at him again, with greater numbers, better equipment, and no less determination, while his own side dwindled in number, physical strength, and eventually will to fight. He knew, moreover, that as his chief of staff, Louis Antoine de Bougainville, wrote, in the run-up to the battle a precipice had opened at his feet. Had the British taken the fort by siege or by portaging boats to Lake Champlain, he would have had to withdraw, first to Fort St. Frédéric at Crown Point, and then back to Canada altogether.[33] It felt like a close-run thing.

Not being a strategically minded soldier, Montcalm did not comfort himself with the theoretical consolation that he was fulfilling a useful function merely by delaying the inevitable, or holding the enemy in play until victories in Europe could help restore the balance in the New World. And unlike the Confederate or the German, he did not have the emotional solace of fighting for a homeland. He fought, instead, for a colony in a howling wilderness, settled largely by people he disliked or could not understand, and at the mercy (or so he thought) of corrupt, scheming, and incompetent civilian leaders. On July 12, four days after the battle, he wrote to Marshal Belle Isle, the French minister of war:

> For myself, I do not ask you any other than to procure me the King's leave to return. My health suffers, my purse is exhausted. At the end of the year I shall owe the treasurer of the Colony ten thousand crowns (*écus*). And more than all, the trouble and contradictions I experience; the impossibility in which I am placed of doing good and preventing evil, determine me earnestly to pray his Majesty to grant me this favor, the only one I ambition.[34]

For Montcalm, the outpost he had defended so gloriously was hardly worth it. He had André Doreil, the commissary of war (in effect the deputy quartermaster general of the colony, responsible for the care and feeding of French regular troops), write to Belle Isle later that July that "Fort Carillon is worth nothing and costs the King as much as Brisack [presumably the town of Neuf-Brisach, a masterpiece of French military engineering in Alsace]." Carillon, Doreil went on, was constructed by "an ignoramus," related to Governor Vaudreuil, "whose fortune 'twas desirous to make and who has made it.... Ineptness, intrigue, lies, cupidity, will in a short time destroy this Colony, which costs the King so dearly."[35]

The victory at Carillon actually exacerbated the long-simmering quarrel between Montcalm and Vaudreuil, who immediately exhorted his general to exploit the victory and take the offensive. As Montcalm sourly reported, "Since the night of the eighth, the Marquis de Vaudreuil, full of *advantageous ideas*, which experience in war and knowledge of a frontier he has never seen, would soon make him lay aside, does not cease writing to me."[36]

Vaudreuil, for his part, gave as good as he got, and in the documents we find his paragraph by paragraph rebuttal of Montcalm's account of how the Battle of Ticonderoga had unfolded.[37] In particular, he staunchly defended himself against the charge of having diverted sixteen hundred men to the Schenectady raid, making the case for that enterprise while acknowledging the need to cancel it in order to support Montcalm. He continued to fret, with reason, about Montcalm's contempt for both the Canadians and the Indians. Meanwhile, Canada's Indian allies, indispensable to the defense of the colony, complained bitterly about Montcalm's treatment of them.

Vaudreuil's brother Rigaud had arrived at Carillon three days after the battle, on July 11, followed by more Canadian militia on the thirteenth. From this moment the bad blood between Canadian and Indian on the one hand and French general on the other only got worse. Bougainville, Montcalm's chief of staff, found the Canadians' compliments on the victory "more forced than sincere," and immediately began complaining about Indian pilfering from the regulars. The Canadians who led the Indians, he wrote, were "vile souls, mercenaries, cruel men, who are occupied only in retaining their control over the Indians, from which they draw a great profit in countenancing all their vices and even in furnishing the means of satisfying them."[38] And as for the reinforcements, why, clearly, Bougainville believed, Vaudreuil had sent them so that he could report back to Paris that he had encouraged Montcalm to exploit his victory and provided the resources to do so, but that the general failed. "The dirty trick of the year," the chief of staff snapped.[39]

Feelings on the other side were no less strong. Meeting with Vaudreuil on July 30, a delegation of various Indian tribes described their conversation with Montcalm when they arrived after the great battle:

> We took the earliest opportunity to tell him that we were greatly mortified in not having shared his victory. He answered us curtly: You are come at a time when I have no further need of you. Are you come only to behold dead bodies? Go behind the fort, you will find some. I have no need of you to kill any English. We withdrew from his quarters to consult together.
>
> The next day we were to bid him good morning; we asked him leave to go on the Lydius road [the original name for Fort Edward]. He struck his table saying: F. . . . ! you shall not go. Go to the devil, if you are not satisfied.
>
> Father. We did not require an interpreter to understand these words. We immediately told him that we were surprised at his anger without having given him any provocation. The council was not long; we each returned home.

Montcalm, presumably realizing that it was unwise to leave himself without any Indians to screen his front, asked Lévis, who got on far better with them, to persuade some of the outraged chiefs to stay. But the chiefs' wounded pride was not assuaged. After making their complaints to Governor Vaudreuil they concluded ominously:

> We came for comfort to you, Father, and to warn you that our men are so disgusted that they will never consent to go where M. de Montcalm will command. Therefore, Father, make your arrangements accordingly.[40]

The truth was probably captured by the often-maligned intendant of New France, the corrupt François Bigot, in a latter to the minister of marine later that summer:

> The Marquis de Montcalm and the Marquis de Vaudreuil are both necessary parties for the preservation and defense of Canada. The former has made himself known as a good General and a man of vast detail, smart and active, zealous for the service. The latter does what he pleases with the Indian Nations and the Canadians, and he is thoroughly conversant with the nature of the fighting in this country; he also knows how to turn to advantage the terror which the English have of the Indians. As I am equally attached to both, I should live on the best terms with them, but I doubt if they will do the same.[41]

Bigot, who had charge of virtually all civil affairs in Canada, made a goodly bit of money on the side, in keeping with eighteenth-century norms, but was no fool.

As occasionally happens in war, ego, personal antipathy, and strategic disagreements made a toxic brew. This became clear throughout the late summer and autumn of 1758 as the two leaders fought a battle of memoranda to one another and to the authorities in France. Montcalm dismissed Vaudreuil's preferred strategy of aggressive raiding of the English colonies and a vigorous forward defense of the colony as "petty means, petty ideas, petty councils." "It is no longer the time when a few scalps, or the burning of a few houses is any advantage." The war, he believed, had completely changed its character, and there was nothing for it but to pull French and Canadian forces to the very core of New France, namely,

Montreal and Quebec—which, however, he believed to be doomed in any event. Vaudreuil argued that to forsake the forward posts of Carillon and Fort St. Frédéric (Crown Point) would be to lose the support of the local Indians and to sacrifice the only commodity that could save Canada—time.

The high command in Paris turned down Montcalm's request to be relieved. Instead he received a promotion to the rank of lieutenant general in October 1758, possibly to reward him for success, possibly to motivate him to fight to the bitter end. More important, he gained control of all the forces in the colony, allowing him to escape, or at least thwart, Vaudreuil's nominal supervision. In letters back home in April of 1759, Montcalm told Marshal Belle Isle frankly that "Canada will be taken this campaign, and assuredly during the next, if there be not some unforeseen good luck, a powerful diversion by sea against the English colonies, or some gross blunders on the part of the enemy." [42] It is not just defeated generals who can suffer the psychological effects of battle. In Montcalm's case a particular kind of victory actually reinforced some of his worst characteristics—his pessimism, his inability to work with his Canadian counterparts, his contempt for militia and Indians, and his preference for glory rather than modest strategic accomplishment.

Now war is established here on the European basis

Thus Bougainville after the victory at Ticonderoga. But the conclusion that he drew from this—that "it is no longer a matter of making a raid, but conquering or being conquered"—was both an opportunity to sneer at Vaudreuil and the Canadians, who (Bougainville declared) thought they understood war but did not, and an occasion for disheartening reflection. He and his beloved commander knew the forces arrayed against them—they could read the force lists in the American newspapers—and they drew the inevitable conclusions. They expected the campaign of 1759 to seal the fate of Quebec.

Pitt moved swiftly to sack Abercromby, replacing him with Major General Jeffery Amherst. A forty-two-year-old regular, Amherst had known war for fifteen years before coming to North America, becoming popular with the Americans, more popular perhaps than he deserved. In truth, he did not particularly care for either America or Americans, but that did not matter at this juncture.[43] He had served as a quartermaster in Germany, was careful, methodical, uninspired, and, in a war that would be decided by weight of numbers and ample logistics, probably the right man for the job. He handed the direct assault on Quebec via the St. Lawrence over to his deputy, Brigadier James Wolfe: He placed himself at what he conceived to be the decisive point, the Great Warpath route.

Once again, in the late spring and early summer of 1759, British and provincial forces massed, and once again launched a methodical approach on Carillon.[44] Six battalions of regulars and nine of provincials marched north, accompanied once again by Bradstreet's bateaumen, rangers, and some Mohawk Indians. Amherst drilled his men in conventional tactics: "As the enemy have very few regular troops to oppose us, and no yelling of Indians, or fire of Canadians, can possibly withstand two ranks, if the men are silent, attentive, and obedient to their officers."[45] On June 20, the British forces marched out of their northernmost strong position, Fort Edward, eighteen miles by wilderness road southeast of Lake George. Several regiments were put to work building two posts to secure the line of communication, and for the next month the army toiled near the ruins of the old Fort William Henry, laying out roads and the fort and creating a logistical hub, massing provisions, loading whaleboats and bateaux, and constructing a floating artillery battery known as a radeau—an odd, seven-sided gunboat. Their mood was good: Intelligence arrived from prisoners who had escaped from Quebec that the enemy was short of provisions and bracing himself for three thrusts—at Quebec from the recently captured French base at Louisbourg, at Montreal from the direction of the Great Lakes, and toward the same city via Ticonderoga, Crown Point, and Chambly on Lake Champlain. But the dangers remained, as a careless party of eighteen New Jersey provincials on Lake George found out on July 2. Six dead and scalped, two wounded and escaped, six missing just outside the camp: The rangers and light infantry went in fruitless hot pursuit.

On July 21 the sergeants roused their men at two o'clock in the morning; by 9:00 A.M. the vast flotilla began moving slowly north. In front again was a screen of Lieutenant Colonel Gage's Eightieth Regiment;

behind them were arrayed four columns, each consisting of two boats abreast, the righthand column (the one most likely to encounter the French) consisting of the cream of the British forces: rangers, light infantry, and grenadiers. An armed sloop brought up the rear. The slow-moving force spent the night on the lake, and at daybreak landed at its northern end. They encountered only a handful of French soldiers and Indians serving as a rear guard: The rangers took a few prisoners and killed and scalped the rest. On the twenty-third the army closed in on the lines of last year's battle.

Amherst had his men bring up the artillery, a siege train including eight howitzers and thirteen mortars capable of hurling explosive shells eight, ten, or even thirteen inches in diameter.[46] Yet even as the prodigious labor of hauling up the artillery began, scouts on nearby Mount Defiance noticed that the French seemed to be preparing their boats for an evacuation. At the same time, the French opened up a continuous artillery fire from the fort, inflicting a few casualties, including the deputy adjutant general, cut in two by a cannonball. It soon became apparent that the French were deliberately ruining their own guns by the incessant fire. On the night of July 26, two deserters came into the camp and told Amherst that the French had evacuated the fort, leaving a burning fuse to the powder magazine. He offered the renegades one hundred guineas—a staggering sum of money—to show a party where it was so that it could be extinguished, but they refused, and at eleven o'clock at night a jagged flame lit the summer night over the peninsula of Carillon. The fort was shattered by the explosion, but five light infantrymen dashed into the burning, smoking wreck and snatched from the ruin the French colors as a trophy.

A week later, Amherst advanced twelve miles north to Crown Point, where the French similarly blew up and abandoned Fort St. Frédéric on July 31. Here he stopped, ordering his engineer to begin laying out a new and massive fort. Where nature oriented Ticonderoga southward, as a base for operations into New York from Canada, Crown Point was just the reverse. Lake Champlain was narrow here, too, but this was a convenient place from which to control access to both it and Lake George. Suspecting that French Canada might survive this war, and needing to keep his army occupied while he prepared for his next move, he ordered the construction of a massive fort, several times the size of the ruined Fort Carillon.

This Post secures entirely all his Majesty's Dominions that are behind it from the Inroads of the Enemy and the scalping parties that have infested the whole Country, and it will give great peace and quiet to the King's Subjects who will now settle in their habitations from this to New York.[47]

The British army settled in here, Amherst troubled by reports of four small French vessels on Lake Champlain. The British hauled boats across to Lake Champlain, and when they had built gunboats, and a couple of warships—a sloop and a brig that outgunned the French xebecs—were ready, began a slow advance north toward Montreal. After cutting off the tiny French flotilla near Isle aux Noix up the Richelieu River just north of Lake Champlain, on October 18 Amherst learned of the fall of Quebec. There was a touch of frost in the air, but more worrisome to his mind was the possibility that a large French force, untethered from Quebec, would turn on him. "This will of course bring Mons de Vaudreuil & the whole Army to Montreal," he decided, "so that I shall decline my intended operations & get back to Crown Point."[48] In line with this inglorious deduction, he retreated there.

Despite the anticlimactic campaign along the Champlain corridor— all it really consisted of was a few skirmishes and a well-executed retreat conducted by the French commander, François-Charles de Bourlamaque—1759, the "year of miracles," saw, very nearly, the completion of the work of the destruction of New France. James Wolfe had sailed up the St. Lawrence, and after a protracted campaign that ruined the farmers and civilian population of Quebec, finally lured Montcalm out of the walls of a ruined city for the climactic battle on September 13.

Montcalm's contempt for Canadian means of making war—"hunting excursions," as he called them—his vindication at Carillon, and his profound pessimism about New France's prospects led him to conduct a conventional defense of Quebec.[49] He seems almost deliberately to have chosen death in a desperate, doomed, but glorious sally from the fortifications, to fight an unequal battle on the Plains of Abraham outside the city's wall, rather than continue a canny defense of Canada's citadel. Had Montcalm simply withdrawn to Quebec's walls after failing to block British general James Wolfe's ascent of the cliffs to the Plains of Abraham, his opponent, already fearing the approaching weather and the possibility of being trapped by ice, would have had to withdraw. And had Montcalm been able to motivate and make effective use of the Canadian militia who were, in fact, fighting for their homes, he might have managed at least a draw in that unnecessary battle in the open. Instead, he chose a fight in the open field in which he threw the burden of the fighting on his ragged regulars, who broke after barely twenty minutes of battle.

Wolfe and Montcalm received mortal wounds that secured their reputations for a long time. It would take over a century before historians would realize just how grave some of their mistakes were. But the fall of Quebec did not quite settle the issue of the war. There was little hope for New France, but its grim defenders were not quite ready to give up yet. The remnants of the French and Canadian forces retreated to Montreal, where they prepared one last thrust, drawing on the dwindling resources of a dying colony.

In the early spring of 1760 Chevalier François de Lévis, Montcalm's successor, led a force of some seven thousand French soldiers, Canadian militia, and Indians—an amalgam that he, unlike Montcalm, could manage—in a counterattack on Quebec. Curiously, his opponent, Brigadier James Murray, made the same mistake Montcalm had made: He came out of the city to fight. The French won the last battle in a campaign that culminated in calamity. At the Battle of Sainte Foy, not far from the city walls, on April 28, 1760, Lévis inflicted a bloody defeat on a British force a bit over half the size of his own. Some eleven hundred British soldiers were killed and wounded, versus some eight hundred French, and the former withdrew from the field into the walled city. Lévis maintained a siege until, in May, British ships, rather than the hoped-for French fleet, appeared in the St. Lawrence. Events a world away, most notably the decisive defeat of a French fleet of twenty-one ships of the line at Quiberon Bay on November 20, 1759, had shattered French hopes of relieving Quebec.

The war for Canada ended a year after the fall of Quebec, as three British armies under Amherst converged at Montreal and forced the colony's surrender. The British commander allowed generous terms of surrender: The militia, for example, to be allowed to return home unmolested; the civilian and military leaders of the colony to be conveyed to Great Britain with their papers and household goods; regular and colonial troops and their families to receive similar treatment; freedom of religion guaranteed to the population; rights of trade similar to those of British subjects, and more.[50]

One item, however, Amherst declined: a ritual surrender, with all the honors of war—the defeated garrison marching out with drums beating, six cannon to accompany them, military salutes and all the demonstration of regard of one professional warrior for another that European military ceremony could muster. Instead, he severely informed the French, their forces would simply lay down their arms and be replaced by the British, who would march in and take their places. It was the final payback for the massacre at Fort William Henry, and for what he described as the "cruel and barbarous war" the French had waged against the English.[51]

It was a stunning insult to the forty-one-year-old Lévis, who furiously demanded that Governor Vaudreuil break off the negotiations and accept the consequences of British forces storming the last remaining citadel of New France. Vaudreuil, knowing the slaughter and rapine that would ensue, refused; Lévis then proposed withdrawing the French units to the Ile Sainte Hélène, there to die in battle or by self-imposed starvation, rather than in dishonor. Vaudreuil refused again, ordering Lévis to surrender, which he grudgingly did, after burning the regimental flags to deny the English trophies won in an ignoble triumph, and refusing to dine with the victor as custom demanded.

New France had succumbed to overwhelming numbers and British naval superiority, but the former was not necessarily decisive, nor the latter predetermined. In the two final battles of New France, the Plains of Abraham and Sainte Foy, the French actually outnumbered their opponents. Even with the resources and naval conditions that obtained in 1759–60, there was nothing inevitable about the acrimonious disputes between Vaudreuil and Montcalm, or the latter's seeming determination to lose gloriously surrounded by Frenchmen, rather than protract the war with an adroit harnessing of Canadians and Indians together with the regulars.

The French and Indian War, as Americans would afterward call it, was no more than one theater in the much larger global conflict, known as the Seven Years' War, whose outcome was far from certain. Americans reasonably, if in the event unjustly, apprehended that Britain would again trade large swathes of the frozen north for small, lucrative sugar islands in the West Indies. At the end of the day even the fall of Quebec was not determinative: The deal the European powers would cut at the end of the war was, which is why pamphleteers spoke up before the final peace was made. Benjamin Franklin, skilled in the use of satire to make a political point, gave, among other facetious reasons for handing Canada back to France:

> What tho' the blood of thousands of unarmed English farmers, surprised and assassinated in their fields; of harmless women and children murdered in their beds; doth at length call for vengeance;—what tho' the Canadian measure of iniquity be full, and if ever any country did, that country now certainly does, deserve the judgment of *extirpation*;—yet let not us be the executioners of Divine justice;—it will look as if Englishmen were revengeful.[52]

There was a debate in London about whether it would be better to keep Guadeloupe and let France have a truncated Canada in return, severed from the West by English control of the Ohio valley and the western lakes.[53] In the end, British statesmen declined to make the trade, and a new strategic chapter opened in North America.

———•◆•———

The Gibraltar of North America

The French victory at Carillon shaped Montcalm's attitude and the conduct of his final campaign in 1759. As for the British and Americans, their debacle at Fort Carillon in 1758 had its largest consequences not on strategy, but on individuals and states of mind. The greatest effect on the British side may even have come before the disastrous attacks had properly begun. The death of George Augustus Lord Howe not only deprived the British army of a capable leader of light infantry. It cost a future king one of the few competent British generals who could also establish rapport with, and win the admiration of, colonial soldiers. The province of Massachusetts paid for a monument to Howe at Westminster Abbey after the war. When the Crown attempted to hold on to the same province in 1775 it had to turn to Major General Thomas Gage—the missing second in command at Ticonderoga in 1758, who undermined after battle the commander he had failed to support during it, who previously failed as leader of General Edward Braddock's vanguard in 1755, who schemed against Robert Rogers and subsequently blocked Colonel John Bradstreet's promotions to higher posts.[54] There were few better choices available.

British commanders, who by and large shared Montcalm's disdain for part-time soldiers, never really got to see what fighting material they had at their disposal in the shape of American soldiers. There were exceptions: the highly competent Lieutenant Colonel William Eyre, builder (and briefly commander) of Fort William Henry, who commanded the Forty-fourth Regiment at Ticonderoga, said in a letter to a friend, "I must confess the Colony Troops behaved extremely Well were in great Spirits & was Willing to do Any thing they Were desired," but he was in a minority.[55] Far more common were the attitudes reflected in Abercromby's efforts to deflect blame after the battle, or those compiled by Douglas Leach from various British commanders speaking of the provincials: "Their sloth and ignorance is not to be described," "mostly vagabonds," "absolutely undependable," "obstinate and ungovernable," "cowards they are; soldiers they are not."[56] The feelings were warmly reciprocated.

The view that in the final destruction of Canada provincial units played little role, that the key battles of Louisbourg and the Plains of Abraham took place with negligible visible American participation, is true, though only partly true. Amherst's eventual advance to Montreal and Bradstreet's capture of Fort Frontenac depended in large part on the participation of colonial troops, and the labor of an essentially colonial supply system. And up to a third of Wolfe's troops were, in fact, American recruits in British units.[57]

But there is another and in some ways more important side to this story. We sometimes marvel at the audacity of the revolutionary generation in taking on the global superpower of 1775. Consider, however, what American leaders—many of whom had fought under British command—knew about the quality of British leadership. Abercromby's failure at Ticonderoga merely reinforced an image of incompetence that had already taken root, and had been reinforced by other episodes, including Braddock's defeat in 1755 and General Webb's timid failure to lift the siege of Fort William Henry. There had been some considerable successes, too—the reduction of the fortress city of Louisbourg in the same year as the Carillon debacle, for instance. But the men of Massachusetts and Maine had taken Louisbourg in 1745 without a British regular army (although with the indispensable support of the Royal Navy), only to see that nest of privateers (as New Englanders conceived it) traded off to the French in a spirit of indifference to American security needs.

Lord George Howe had been an exception in his regard for the provincial soldiers under his command and their respect for him. For their part, the American soldiers serving under British command, including Amherst's, were appalled at the harshness of the military regimen under which they lived. Robert Webster, a sergeant in Fitch's Fourth Connecticut Regiment, served under Amherst from April through November 1759. His diary—much of it written at Crown Point, where he labored on the fortifications—is a grim tale of deserters being hanged, or receiving floggings of five hundred or even a thousand lashes, virtual death sentences.[58] The Great Warpath campaigns exposed American officers to British condescension and American soldiers to British brutality; the assault on Carillon in 1758 exposed British incompetence. The former stoked resentment, the latter inspired a certain degree of confidence.

The summer 1758 campaign along the Great Warpath also helped train a generation of American officers who could build and lead armies to fight for American independence. The patriot armies of the American Revolution imitated the British army in many ways—copying many of its organizational forms, although from the outset, particularly with regard to discipline, they made changes. Seventeen years after Carillon, veterans of that blundering fight encountered one another again, but now on opposing sides.

In June 1775 General Thomas Gage was the British commander in Boston, indeed, the British commander in chief in North America. Underneath him were other officers who had served at Carillon, such as the former aide-de-camp of the hapless Abercromby of Carillon, now Colonel James Abercrombie, as well as William Howe, brother of George Howe, who had fallen there. Opposite them were men who had served with Rogers—Israel Putnam and John Stark, among others. Again, on June 17, 1775, there was a frontal assault, perhaps the most famous frontal assault received by American forces in history, at Breed's and Bunker

Hills on June 17, 1775. The consequences were the mirror of Ticonderoga: The assaults succeeded, but the British took the hills at the cost of more than a thousand killed and wounded, among them Abercrombie, who died leading his grenadiers. Unlike the case in 1758, however, the defenders came away encouraged by what they had achieved. British generalship gained no luster from the attack, or operational or strategic advantage from it.

It was easy for British politicians and generals, in the years after 1760, to dismiss the backbreaking labor of the American soldiers who had done some of the fighting, and most of the road and fortress building, the rowing and hauling, that made the Great Warpath a clear road to Montreal. Yet in the 1750s along the Great Warpath, Americans learned much. They learned the basics of how to raise, equip, and discipline battalions of infantry; they learned light infantry and ranging tactics; and perhaps most important of all, they learned how to organize, move, and sustain substantial forces, even in the wilderness. A wealthy Dutch American New Yorker, Philip Schuyler, worked in the commissariat service of the northern army—good preparation for his later role as commander of the northern army against the British during the critical years of 1776–77. Unwittingly, along the Great Warpath and elsewhere the British army had trained its opponents in the next great American war.

These experiences lingered, so when the time came to fortify Boston, New York, or Philadelphia, the Americans were surprisingly ready. On more than one occasion during the struggle for American independence, the British were stunned by the speed with which the Americans could build fortifications, roads, and fleets, and by their ability to sustain forces, however awkwardly or inefficiently, in a howling wilderness. When in 1776 the Americans had to fortify the Ticonderoga complex, including Mount Independence across the lake, they turned to their own rough and ready engineer, Jeduthan Baldwin of Massachusetts. He had learned his trade from then major William Eyre, building Fort William Henry in 1755.

The crisis lay in the future. In the immediate aftermath of the fall of French Canada, peace came to the Warpath. The remains of Amherst's army continued the drudgery of building Crown Point, a fortress that lacked a strategic purpose after the French surrendered Canada. Settlers, including veterans of the Carillon campaign receiving compensation in the form of land grants, moved into the valley. But even as an ancient quarrel had finally ended, another was already brewing. Scarcely a decade separated the Peace of Paris in 1763 and the first explosions of a new and even more consequential war, which would lead to American independence.

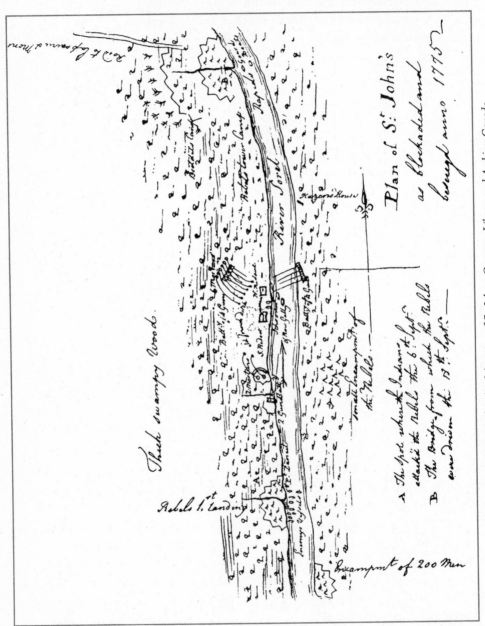

A contemporary British sketch of the siege of St. Johns. *Courtesy, Library and Archives Canada*

CHAPTER FIVE

St. Johns, 1775

―――◆◆◆―――

So I sit down to write to a few friends by way of farewell

―――◆◆◆―――

Understandably, Benjamin Franklin expected to die on this trip. At age seventy, ill, rheumatic, and exhausted, he had agreed to undertake an arduous journey from Philadelphia to Montreal, as the Continental Congress had requested. The purpose was to redeem, if possible, what looked to be the failing invasion of Canada that had begun with bright hopes less than a year earlier. It was now mid-April 1776, and after the rigors of travel in the bleak North Country April, he and his party had paused to take advantage of the hospitality of Major General Philip Schuyler, the American commander of the northern theater of war. But this was only Saratoga: Ahead lay the lakes, still chock-a-block with ice, and, as if to remind him that winter had not quite loosened its grip, six inches of snow had fallen only three days before. He had taken up the pen to respond to a letter from his friend, Josiah Quincy, grieving over the loss of his brilliant young son Josiah Quincy, Jr., a friend and associate of John Adams, who had died of tuberculosis just as he returned from Britain with valuable intelligence. "I begin to apprehend that I have undertaken a fatigue that at my time of life may prove too much for me, so I sit down to write a few friends by way of farewell," Franklin wrote.[1]

The old men's letters, however, dealt less with Quincy's bereavement or Franklin's mortality than with the prospects of American separation from Great Britain. Quincy had asked why the Continental Congress had proven so reluctant to decide for independence. Franklin responded, "The novelty of the thing deters some, the doubt of success others, the vain hope of reconciliation many." Still, the old fox counted on British blunders to carry the country to independence. "But our enemies take continually every proper measure to remove these obstacles, and their endeavors are attended with success, since every day furnishes us with new causes of increasing enmity, and new reasons for wishing an eternal separation."

The Continental Congress had appointed Franklin, one of the Revolution's indispensable men, to a Committee of Secret Correspondence that managed the diplomacy (and much of the intelligence work) of the embryonic country. This urgent mission to lead a commission to investigate and help manage the faltering invasion of Quebec, however, took precedence even over those tasks. Franklin had three companions in addition to servants. Samuel Chase, a militant known as the "Maryland Demosthenes," later convinced the Maryland assembly to reverse its vote opposing independence, and then rode one hundred miles in two days to sign the Declaration of Independence. Charles Carroll, another Marylander, subsequently became the only Catholic to sign the Declaration, and the last of the signers to die (in 1832). Carroll's cousin, John—a Catholic priest fluent in French, joined to help win over the suspicious Canadian *habitants*. All three men were thirty years or more Franklin's junior.

For a time, it had looked as though all of North America, including Canada, might join in the revolt against the British throne. That had been the high hope with which American forces had moved north the previous spring. But since the end of 1775 all had gone awry—a dreadful repulse at Quebec at the very end of the year had cost the American commander, General Richard Montgomery, his life, and left his able deputy, Colonel Benedict Arnold, wounded. The Americans feared the imminent arrival of a British fleet to relieve the siege of the capital of Canada, bringing with it a British army that would drive the ragged, sickening rebels before them, and possibly invade the colonies from the north. Given the changes in leadership in the American forces, their precarious financing, the delicate politics of working with the French Canadians and the small community of English merchants, Congress had deemed it expedient to send a small group of its ablest men to inspect the situation on the ground and revive American prospects if they could. Hence the difficult journey of Franklin and his colleagues along the Great Warpath.

The commissioners had toiled north, inspecting one half-finished defensive position after another. On April 2, they had started their trip up the Hudson from New York City, a city anxious with rumors of impending British attack. John Carroll found it not "the gay, polite place it used to be esteemed," but "almost a desert, unless for the troops."[2] They stopped at the only fortification blocking the Hudson between New York and Albany, Fort Constitution, across from West Point. "There is not one gunner or artillery man in the fort. Nothing but pork, beef, and flour, no vegetables; no barrack master. The minute men work about six hours in the day, and that with great reluctance," Franklin gloomily observed.[3] After hard going for another ten days they paused at Saratoga (today's Schuylerville), where he wrote his letter to Josiah Quincy.

Despite his forebodings, Franklin did not die. After recovering some of his strength while gratefully accepting Schuyler's hospitality for a week, he and the other commissioners pushed on, inspecting more crumbling fortifications as they did so—Fort Edward on the Hudson, Fort George at the southern end of the lake of that name, Ticonderoga, Crown Point—all, to differing degrees, "in a ruinous condition," as Charles Carroll noted in his journal.[4] They journeyed in bateaux along the lake, crossing the border and inspecting the old French lines at Isle aux Noix, and finally, on April 29, 1776, they arrived at Montreal, greeted by (now) Brigadier General Arnold, artillery salutes, and "a genteel company of ladies and gentlemen." Their hosts escorted them to the home of Mr. Thomas Walker, a wealthy Montreal merchant and justice of the peace. Walker, a ringleader of the pro-American faction in Canada, had tangled repeatedly with the military government of Quebec ever since arriving there in 1763. His animus against the British military—which included denying billeted troops bedding, firewood, and kitchen facilities—may explain why, in December 1764, twenty men (probably from the local garrison) invaded his house, beat him severely, and cut off one of his ears. Thence forward, the Crown had in him an inveterate enemy, and, from 1775, the invading

Americans, an invaluable source of information and support. He and his wife now welcomed the visiting commissioners to their large and comfortable home.

A final, if lesser ordeal awaited the weary commissioners, who yearned for rest from their exhausting trip. "After drinking tea, and sitting some time, we went to an elegant supper, which was followed with the singing of the ladies," John Carroll politely recalled. It would have been rather more agreeable "if we had not been so much fatigued with our journey."[5] But there was no time to waste. The next day the commissioners began to see if they could recover something of what had once promised to be a glorious, and a likely, opportunity to drive Great Britain from the shores of her American colonies.

———————

You have been conquered into liberty

The war of American independence began not only with the fighting at Lexington and Concord in April 1775, but also with a spectacular act of attempted subversion—the attempt to make Canada the fourteenth colony to revolt against Great Britain. Almost as soon as the clumsily gathering colonies had begun to organize themselves as a loose collection of states, they decided to undermine and if necessary overthrow the government headquartered in Quebec. And in what seemed to many Englishmen an act of exceptional gall, they did so in the name of liberty, after denouncing the British government for having granted privileges to French Canada that, after all, merely allowed that colony to continue much as it had under Louis xv.

In this strange story, the Great Warpath played a very large part. After the Seven Years' War, the British government decided, for a number of reasons, to maintain a substantial standing force in the American colonies.[6] From this decision, a subsequent effort to reassert British prerogatives (particularly with regard to taxes) in America, and from the Quebec Act of 1774, arose the immediate causes of the American Revolution. This last piece of ill-timed legislation played a particularly important role in feeding the fears of the colonists.

The conquest of Canada in 1760, and the ratification of that conquest by the Treaty of Paris in 1763, had left Great Britain with a new and vexing problem of imperial management. What should it do with the hardy Canadians, French-speaking and Catholic, who showed little inclination to leave the homes they had wrested from the wilderness?[7] The negligible emigration of Englishmen or colonists to Canada—some merchants to Montreal and Quebec, but no influx of settlers—compounded the demographic problem. Quebec's military governors decided early on to make generous accommodations to the religious and legal systems of New France—in effect, to keep intact most of the structures of the French colony, save only allegiance to the Crown.

Dawdling for years, the British government inched its way to the formalizing of this arrangement. With exquisitely bad timing, in 1774 it completed the process by passing the Quebec Act. Three provisions of the legislation stood out. The act expanded the territory of Quebec to include much of the Indian Reserve, territories in what is now Wisconsin, Illinois, Michigan, Indiana, and Ohio. In addition, it not only tolerated the Catholic religion, it eliminated the old oath of allegiance, which referred to the Protestant faith. Finally, the act provided for the application of French civil law in private matters, while retaining the English common law for public administration. These three features of the act infuriated Americans already inclined to suspect the worst of the British government. They saw a plot to hem in their natural expansion to the west; as a deeply Protestant people they worried about the expansion of an authoritarian Catholic faith and a betrayal of their own; and they interpreted the resumption of French law in Quebec as a precedent for depriving other British subjects of the rights of trial by jury.

When the first Continental Congress met in September 1774 to consider British pressure on Boston, it discussed a document known as the Suffolk Resolves, drawn up by a convention in Suffolk County, which included Boston, in Massachusetts. The Resolves recalled the ancient Puritan grievance with the British government, "which of old persecuted, scourged, and exiled our fugitive parents from their native shores, now pursues us, their guiltless children, with unrelenting severity," and included a list of grievances, not least among them the "late act of parliament for establishing the Roman Catholic religion and the French laws in that extensive country, now called Canada." This the delegates deemed "dangerous in an extreme degree to the Protestant religion and to the civil rights and liberties of all America; and, therefore, as men and Protestant Christians, we are indispensably obliged to take all proper measures for our security."[8]

As the Congress deliberated its way to responses to the so-called Intolerable Acts that had effectively suspended the government of Massachusetts, closed the port of Boston, and crippled the local courts, the Congress wrote to the people of Great Britain on October 21, 1774. In addition to their other complaints, they deplored the Quebec Act for establishing Catholicism (rather than tolerating it), depriving the people in Canada "of a right to an assembly, trials by jury and the English laws in civil cases," and for expanding the borders of Canada. Here and throughout, the Congress determined to reach public opinion of all kinds—in Great Britain, but also, as it soon transpired, in Canada.

Five days after its address to the people of Great Britain, Congress issued a lengthy letter to the inhabitants of the province of Quebec, a document subsequently translated into French and printed for general distribution up north. It began with a tribute to Canadian mettle: "When the fortune of war, after a gallant and glorious resistance, had incorporated you with the body of English subjects, we rejoiced in the truly valuable addition, both on our own and your account; expecting, as courage and generosity are naturally united, our brave enemies would become our hearty friends."[9] The writers of the pamphlet urged upon the Canadians the merits of habeas corpus, protection of property, and trial by jury; mindful of the religious antagonisms in play, they avowed the transcendent importance of freedom of religion. And combining promise and menace they concluded:

> You have been conquered into liberty, if you act as you ought. This work is not of man. You are a small people, compared to those who with open arms invite you into a fellowship. A moment's reflection should convince you which will be most for your interest and happiness, to have all the rest of North-America your unalterable friends, or your inveterate enemies. The injuries of Boston have roused and associated every colony, from Nova-Scotia to Georgia. Your province is the only link wanting, to complete the bright and strong chain of union.[10]

In the early days of the American Revolution a powerful notion had already taken root: that the best way to avert a threat was to forestall it by democratic subversion backed by force. On the one hand, these revolutionaries—who did not, quite yet, think of themselves as such, though the idea lay not far below the surface—believed that they had an essentially conservative cause, to protect their rights as Englishmen. On the other hand, to protect these rights they employed arguments both universal in nature and advantageous to their cause. They wielded simultaneously the lure of freedom and no small amount of threat should their targets refuse to take the offer of liberty. It took time, however, for Congress to make the move implied by the letter to the inhabitants of Canada, namely, invasion.

Keep them in awe

From the fall of Montreal in 1760 through the outbreak of the Revolution fifteen years later, the Great Warpath had served as a corridor for movement between New England and Canada. The area became modestly more settled, particularly as former soldiers took up land grants offered in reward for service. A new problem arose in the shape of a fierce intercolonial dispute. Unrelated to the tumults of Boston in the early 1770s, bands of settlers, including the turbulent gang known as the Green Mountain Boys, had swarmed into the area known as the Hampshire Grants—the unsettled region west of the Connecticut River now chiefly in Vermont. The long-suffering lieutenant governor of New York, Cadwallader Colden, deplored "this body of lawless men," who, no longer restrained by fear of the French and Indians, were defying law and government and seizing land reserved for veterans of the previous war.[11] For their part, the Green Mountain Boys claimed, with some justice, that these lands belonged to them by right of grants from Governor Benning Wentworth of New Hampshire.

A British garrison in the area might contain these unruly frontiersmen and put psychological pressure, if nothing more, on the restive New

England colonies. In the 1760s and early 1770s a residual British military presence in the region had in fact continued. The great fortress of Crown Point, constructed at Amherst's orders before it was clear that Canada would remain under British control, and, twelve miles to its south, Fort Ticonderoga, had modest garrisons that kept an eye on vast quantities of artillery and lesser amounts of other military stores. In the spring of 1773, however, a fire had destroyed the powder magazine and earthworks of Crown Point. A May 1774 survey by Captain John Montrésor, the British engineer, gloomily concluded that "the conflagration of the late fort has rendered it an amazing useless mass of earth only." Fort Ticonderoga, blown up by the French as they evacuated in 1759, was not much better: "Its ruinous situation is such that it would require more to repair it than the constructing of a new fort."[12]

In 1774, the year before the Revolution began, the motive of imperial control became more pressing, as relations worsened between mother country and colonists. Canada's acting governor, Major General Frédéric Haldimand, and the Earl of Dartmouth (the secretary of state for American affairs) corresponded about rebuilding Crown Point, but neither could manage the substantial diversion of resources, human, financial, and material, to accomplish it during the short New York spring and summer. In May 1774, even as Parliament was acting to close the port of Boston and in effect annul the charter of Massachusetts, the commander in Canada, Haldimand, wrote to this effect:

> I intend to suggest to him [Lieutenant General Thomas Gage, commander in chief in North America] the propriety of having a couple of regiments drawn from Canada to station them at Crown Point under the pretext of rebuilding that fort, which from its situation not only secures the communication with Canada but also opens an easy access to the back settlements of the northern colonies and may keep them in awe should any of them be rash enough to incline to acts of open force and violence.[13]

Those last lines deserve particular emphasis. Haldimand was one of the shrewdest of King George's generals. One of the Swiss officers recruited to stand up the Sixtieth of Foot, the Royal Americans, he had participated in the disastrous assault on Fort Ticonderoga in 1758, had afterward commanded at Fort Edward, where he had supervised Rogers' rangers, and had spent the 1760s and 1770s serving on the frontier, in Florida and in Canada. Fifty-six years old in 1774, he saw the utility of having positions of strength along the Great Warpath to contain and to menace the American colonies. But what exactly did it mean to keep the rebellious colonists "in awe"? It would mean threatening interruption of their commerce, possibly, or even a march inland from the forts. Conceivably as well (and this would have occurred to anyone who had lived through the 1750s in New England) it would mean turning loose the dispossessed, resentful, and increasingly fearful Indians on the still-isolated American woodland settlements. Yet such a measure would in itself enrage and further embitter colonists in no mood to defer to royal authority.

In the event, however, General Gage had his hands full attempting to pacify Boston and its environs, and as violence spread in 1775 he drew off troops from Canada for that purpose. Dartmouth had notified Haldimand in a letter as early as February 1774 that the king had decided to reduce the rebellious colonies to "dependence."[14] Since it would take time to amass troops in Britain, the occupation of Boston, the seat of the rebellion, took precedence, and this in turn meant that Canada would have no troops to spare to strengthen its grip on Lake Champlain.

But Haldimand's concept echoed through British strategic deliberations during the fifteen months from the Boston Tea Party in December 1773 to the battles of Lexington and Concord in April 1775. British strategists, who knew the Great Warpath from previous experience, saw it as a series of points of leverage against their rebellious subjects. The Americans, for their part, viewed it as an avenue by which they might be attacked—or along which they might attack themselves, thrusting northward to complete the work of eliminating British rule in North America.

By early 1775 a mood of anxiety pervaded the Great Warpath, each side beginning to prepare, however reluctantly, for war. In Canada, the newly returned governor, Major General Sir Guy Carleton, wrote uneasily about the problem of maintaining British rule in Canada. At age fifty-one he, too, had served in the Royal Americans, had fought at Quebec, in Europe, and in Cuba, but had spent the years since 1768 as governor of Canada. Saturnine and cutting in manner, he had pressed hard for the

Quebec Act. Despite a dour and forbidding personality, however, he had established rapport with the French elite of Canada and understood the value of tolerance and clemency—even, on occasion, to rebels.

Carleton now proposed raising a battalion or two of regular Canadian troops officered by the gentry, thereby tying the latter to the Crown. In the Canadian militia—so formidable under the French—he placed less reliance. Were they to be called up and used against the New Englanders, "It would give an appearance of truth to our sons of sedition, at this very moment busily employed instilling into their minds that the [Quebec] Act was passed merely to serve the present purposes of government and in the full intention of ruling over them with all the despotism of their ancient masters."[15]

One of these "sons of sedition" was a thirty-year-old Yale-educated lawyer and politician from Massachusetts named John Brown, who had been sent north by a committee of Boston patriots in February 1775 to see if he could stir up a Canadian revolt. In April 1775 Carleton received reports that Brown had addressed the small community of English merchants in Montreal, a group out of sympathy with the Quebec Act, and well-disposed to the Boston rebels. Brown had reportedly combined the usual denunciations of tyrannical rule with threats to the Canadians, "assuring them that if a man of them should dare to take up arms and act against the Bostonians thirty thousand of them will march into Canada and lay waste the whole country."[16] Brown's cover as a horse dealer for this subversive mission had been compromised by his failure to buy a single quadruped during a two-month stay in the province.

Meanwhile, the mood among American colonists was apprehensive in the extreme. One sharp observer of North American affairs was a bilingual Scot, Hugh Finlay, who had come to Canada to make his fortune through trade and land deals after the Peace of Paris in 1763. Having discovered government service as a supplementary route to wealth, he had managed to be made surveyor of the post roads in North America. His conscientious inspection trip through the Lake Champlain country at this time revealed much about the unsettled mood of local opinion. He reported back to his brother, "When I was on my way from Skenesboro I found the whole country in expectation of a body of Indians and Canadians. A man stopped me and asked me if I was from Canada and whether the Canadians were far advanced on their march." He continued:

On Lake Champlain an ignorant poor settler was lamenting the fate of New England. Bishops were to be sent over, Presbyterians were to be persecuted and a tenth of everything they possessed was to go towards the maintenance of the enemies of the Kirk—that Popery was to prevail and the righteous Dissenters were to be crushed.[17]

Anxiety, then, on both sides. And as one explosion flashed out in the Massachusetts towns of Lexington and Concord in April 1775, another fuse had been lit up north.

Come out of there, you damned old rat!

As he headed north on his subversive mission in the winter of 1775, John Brown had seen the decrepit forts at Ticonderoga and Crown Point and thought them ripe for the seizing. So, too, did another, far more colorful character. Ethan Allen, born in Connecticut, had tried his hand (successfully) at running an iron foundry; his personal aggressiveness, however, and peculiar brand of deism—a belief in Nature's God—alienated the devout Protestants of the communities in which he briefly lived. In 1770 this philosophical autodidact and masterful political agitator moved to the Green Mountains of today's Vermont, and (in addition to hunting) took up the cause of the squatters in the Hampshire Grants. He founded the Green Mountain Boys in 1771 and used a combination of agitation and intimidation just short of lethal violence against the authorities of New York, who claimed the area. For Allen, Fort Ticonderoga seemed like a promising target for the kind of rough-and-tumble politics that he favored. Soon the Green Mountain Boys were meeting at their favorite gathering spot, the Catamount Tavern in Bennington—named after the stuffed wildcat mounted on a pole facing the despised New Yorkers—to plot the enterprise. They were doing so that May when another band of Americans with a similar idea showed up: sixteen Connecticut men, reinforced with two score more from Massachusetts. John Brown joined later. A small group of prominent Connecticut political leaders, acting unofficially, had launched their small detachment on this enterprise. By the beginning of May the Vermonters and New England men had gathered and were ready to move.

To add further confusion to the mix, another outsized personality also in his early thirties showed up on the scene: Benedict Arnold, a resident of Connecticut but acting on behalf of Massachusetts. Arnold had volunteered for service as a boy in the French and Indian War, deserting after a brief sojourn at Fort William Henry to return to his dying mother's bedside. In the years before the Revolution he made a comfortable living as a sea captain and trader traveling between Canada and the West Indies. As a consequence, he viewed with scorn His Majesty's efforts to extract revenue from what the British considered smuggling and he understood as free enterprise. A short, stocky, fiery-tempered man, in 1774 he had joined the Governor's Footguards of New Haven, and elected captain by men who knew a leader when they saw one, led them north on word of the fights at Lexington and Concord, helping himself to the powder and shot of the town arsenal (without authorization) on the way.

Arnold knew Canada, remembered the ruined state of Ticonderoga and Crown Point, and knew something else as well: some one hundred artillery pieces and a dozen mortars remained there. Although not a trained soldier, he knew that here lay an invaluable resource for the American army forming in Cambridge, and for the siege of Boston soon to come. He and his men had arrived in Boston five days after the fights at Lexington and Concord, but he saw an opportunity to gain the glory that he craved. On April 30, 1775, he put his case to the Massachusetts Committee of Safety, the eleven-man body charged with the military security of the colony. Of the defenses of Ticonderoga he declared, "The place could not hold out an hour against a vigorous onset."[18] The Massachusetts men, despite some reservations about infringing on New York territory, saw the force of his argument. On May 3 they gave him a commission as colonel and authority to raise four hundred men, appoint their officers, and take the fort; they had already authorized him to requisition the ammunition and horses he would need, plus one hundred pounds in expenses. Not willing to wait for his men to gather, Arnold, having dispersed two trusted captains to recruit men in western Massachusetts, rode hard up north. He got to Castleton only to find the last of Allen's band departing, but he immediately declared that as the only formally commissioned member of the party—a colonel to boot—he should be placed in command. He went in hot pursuit of Allen, the rear guard of grumbling Green Mountain Boys following suspiciously in his wake.

Thus, in May 1775, we have the following expedition leaving Castleton (now in the state of Vermont) for Fort Ticonderoga. In the lead, amateur philosopher and theologian, frontier politician, and accomplished rough-neck Ethan Allen with two hundred anarchical Green Mountain Boys; Benedict Arnold, ambitious, masterful, hot-tempered, imperious, and for the moment, without followers; and a subversive lawyer, John Brown, who had known Arnold in New Haven and disliked him, accompanying a deeply indebted, boastful, vindictive tavern keeper commanding the Pitts-field, Massachusetts militia, Colonel (his own, informal appellation) James Easton. This was an unlikely band of brothers. But Allen (who had decided to give himself the title colonel as well) behaved with surprising restraint when Arnold finally linked up with the column. Arnold had the organiza-tional skills the expedition needed and, for whatever it was worth, some kind of official imprimatur in what might otherwise be seen (if unsuccess-ful) as mere banditry. But Allen had the political smarts to box Arnold in, and exercised them. Although subsequent accounts differed, Allen seems to have offered, and Arnold to have accepted, a joint command.

On May 9 the patriots finally reached the shore of Lake Champlain, and that night, after various mishaps—someone had neglected to assem-ble the boats to get across—landed some eighty men on the New York shore as day broke. With Allen and Arnold in the van, and as Allen's con-siderably steadier cousin Seth Warner ferried more troops across the lake, the small band crept along to the southern side of the fort. Brushing past a startled sentry, they plunged inside. According to Allen, another sentry thrust with a bayonet at the leader of the Green Mountain Boys, who knocked him down and then demanded to know where the commander of the fort slept. There, in Allen's own immortal rendering, the patriot leader demanded that the shocked captain surrender, "In the name of the great Jehovah and the Continental Congress."

More reliable accounts suggest that Allen actually said, "Come out of there, you damned old rat!"[19] The surprised British captain had no choice but to yield the fort—his forty-four men and some two dozen depen-dents were in no position to put up a fight. Allen and Arnold kept their prisoners safe from physical abuse, but the Green Mountain Boys showed themselves more interested in plunder and pillage than in securing the outpost. Ninety gallons of rum split among roughly that many men, in particular, made for a glorious drunk, which soon commenced. Allen hastily penned a triumphant report to the Massachusetts Congress that omitted mention of Benedict Arnold, but did manage a glowing report of the assault: "The soldiery behaved with such resistless fury, that they so terrified the King's Troops that they durst not fire on their assailants, and our soldiery was agreeably disappointed." [20] Arnold, on the same day, wrote furiously to the Committee of Safety, "There is here at present near one hundred men, who are in the greatest confusion and anarchy, destroying and plundering private property, committing every enormity, and paying no attention to publick service." [21] He conceded that Allen was a "proper man to head his own wild people," but pointed out, correctly, that the head of the Green Mountain Boys had little notion of military discipline or order.

Arnold, meanwhile, quarreled with Easton, who, during the assault spent time in the rear fiddling with supposedly damp powder in his musket. The fiery leader without followers became convinced that the militia leader was a coward. Harsh words followed, and a challenge to a duel, which Easton declined. Arnold then publicly administered a set of kicks to the timorous innkeeper (who wore a cutlass and carried a pair of pistols at the time), earning him one of those determined enemies who dogged him henceforth. [22] Easton, who had skills as a writer of poison pen letters that he lacked as a warrior, began traducing Arnold in missives back to Congress.

While Allen's patriotic hooligans guzzled, looted, and in twos and threes drifted back to their homesteads across Lake Champlain, however, Arnold and Allen succeeded in securing, albeit weakly, the Great Warpath itself. Allen had sent a detachment to Skenesborough (today's Whitehall) at the very southern end of Lake Champlain, where it turns into Wood Creek. There lay the estate of Philip Skene, a wealthy veteran of the Seven Years' War, who had established a thriving sawmill, an iron forge, and a small community of tenants. Skene had fought at Ticonderoga in 1758 and again in 1759, but after a distinguished part in the siege of Havana decided to become a landowner in New York, and to his fifty thousand acres and several hundred tenants had added the lieutenant governorship of Ticonderoga and Crown Point during a trip to London in 1775. Arrested as a British official in June 1775 as he got off the ship in Philadelphia, he was not present when Allen's men attacked his settlement.

After a brief standoff the rebels took not only the estate, but a schooner moored there, and sailed it to Ticonderoga. Renamed *Liberty*, it became the first American warship on the lake. Allen's men—landsmen all—handed it over to one of Arnold's friends and subordinates, who had providentially shown up with fifty men at Skenesborough en route to join his superior at Ticonderoga. At the same time, Seth Warner had taken fifty Green Mountain Boys to Crown Point and taken that outpost from its ten caretakers. Warner, a laconic, muscular, six-foot-two woodsman, had a gravity and steadiness that Allen lacked, and that made him a natural military leader.

With Arnold's men finally arriving as Allen's men drifted home, the balance between the commanders shifted. Good skipper that he was, Arnold soon imposed something approaching military order and discipline. His nautical mind had instantly perceived the importance of achieving maritime superiority on Lake Champlain. The only armed British vessel on the lake was the sloop *Betsey*, a supply vessel, which he had hoped to seize at Ticonderoga. Discovering that she lay instead beyond the northern end of the lake, at the Richelieu River port of St. Johns, he seized the initiative. With fifty men, he took the schooner *Liberty*, fitted it out with four small guns and six swivel pieces, and sailed north accompanied by two bateaux on May 14. The wind failed just short of the border, but Arnold shifted thirty-five men into the two bateaux, and, at six in the morning on Thursday May 18, fell on the defenders of St. Johns—a dozen soldiers guarding the decrepit French works there. He captured them, and then seized the sloop from its caretaker crew of seven. Discovering nine bateaux at the dock, he destroyed four and carried off the other five, plus a pair of artillery pieces.[23] His prisoners, who had heard of the events at Ticonderoga, but had failed to take precautions lest a similar fate befall them, informed him that a relief column was marching to St. Johns. Arnold departed three hours after the briskly conducted raid had begun, and before British reinforcements arrived.

It was a brilliant, bloodless victory. It was also, however, an attack on Canada, and hence an aggressive act of war, and hence different from what had been, arguably, the defensive battles of Lexington and Concord. Arnold had displayed the qualities that made him "the most brilliant soldier of the Revolution," as words etched in a stone monument later described him. He saw both an operational necessity (maritime superiority on the lakes) and a fleeting opportunity (the combination of the seizure of the *Liberty* and the lag until the British could send reinforcements); he acted decisively, and fast, and when one plan failed he replaced it with another. And, unlike many commanders before and since, he knew when to quit.

Ethan Allen, by contrast, was a commander who did not know when to quit. Perhaps ruminating on a lost opportunity for glory, he had begun rowing north on Lake Champlain with his remaining one hundred Green Mountain Boys and scanty provisions. Arnold explained to his ebullient colleague that an attempt to seize St. Johns, rather than raid it, would likely fail, but Allen insisted. Arnold reluctantly gave him and his men supplies: Allen landed across the river from St. Johns and woke to the dismaying prospect of two hundred newly arrived British troops formed up a short distance away and opening fire on his outnumbered band. He beat a hasty and inglorious retreat.[24]

We, for our parts, are determined to live free,
or not at all

Allen's and Arnold's escapades disconcerted many in Congress who still hoped to restore some kind of relationship with Great Britain. Both men passionately advocated an invasion of Canada, even as they fell out with each other. Quite apart from expanding the united colonies by adding Canada to the thirteen rebellious provinces, the seizure of Canada followed by a similar upheaval in Nova Scotia would deny the British the bases they would need to invade and subjugate America. Invasion made strategic sense.

But the two leaders temporarily lost their leading roles in this debate. Brown and Easton, now inveterate enemies of Arnold, began vilifying him to Congress and the Massachusetts assembly, leading to Arnold's eventual recall. And, as Arnold began writing his report to Congress while in Albany en route back he learned of his wife's death; he hurried home to care for his three sons. Allen, meanwhile, had asked to have the Green Mountain Boys made a part of the Continental Army with himself at their head. The stolid farmers composing the committees of public safety in the Hampshire Grants, however, wisely decided on Seth Warner as a steadier leader. Nothing daunted, the spirited Allen cheerfully returned to the army as an unattached force of nature.

Arnold and Allen had stepped temporarily offstage, but as often happens in war, their successes took on lives of their own. The fall of Ticonderoga and Crown Point, and Arnold's successful raid on St. Johns and squelching of Philip Skene's loyalist settlement at the southern end of Lake Champlain, opened up opportunities. On May 18, 1775, John Brown reported back to Congress on the seizure of Ticonderoga and his own mission of espionage and subversion in Canada. He passed along rumors of the British recruiting Indians to fall on the settlements in the back country, and he used a chilling name that evoked horrors of an earlier war: "The conductors of this grand expedition are to be Monsieur *St. Luke le Corne*, the villain who let loose the *Indians* on the prisoners at Fort *William Henry*, and one of his associates."[25]

On the other hand, Brown and others continued to report widespread disaffection with British rule in Canada. Congress concluded that the war of subversion should continue, and to that end, in the closing days of May, Congress appointed a committee of three of its shrewdest members— John Jay, Samuel Adams, and Silas Deane—to compose a second letter to the "oppressed inhabitants of Canada," appealing to their fears of their British masters:

> You are liable by their edicts to be transported into foreign countries to fight Battles in which you have no interest, and to spill your blood in conflicts from which neither honor nor emolument can be derived: Nay, the enjoyment of your very religion, on the present system, depends on a legislature in which you have no share, and over which you have no control, and your priests are exposed to expulsion, banishment, and ruin, whenever their wealth and possessions furnish sufficient temptation.[26]

"We, for our parts, are determined to live free, or not at all," the document concluded, and Congress ordered it translated into French and distributed in Canada.

Having done this, however, Congress hesitated, unsure whether to launch an army to complete the task begun with such apparent ease. Indeed, on June 1, Congress decided that "no expedition or incursion ought to be undertaken or made, by any colony or body of colonists, against or into Canada." The records suggest that some in Congress simply hesitated to take an irrevocable step: Lexington and Concord had been acts of self-defense. To invade another colony was quite a different matter. Some, too, undoubtedly feared that an armed incursion into Canada would meet resistance from the same Canadians who, after all, had long viewed the men of New York and New England as implacable religious as well as national foes. And Congress found itself preoccupied with the raising of an army, the establishing of its organization and internal laws, and, not least, the selection of its commander in chief. Having chosen George Washington for that task on June 16, 1775, however, and having convinced itself that the British were preparing to launch a force to retake Fort Ticonderoga and Crown Point, its mood changed. A few days after appointing the new commander in chief, Congress had given Washington four major generals, one of whom, Philip Schuyler, would command the northern theater of war.

Schuyler, a tall, austere, aloof, immaculately dressed Dutch American North Country aristocrat, had served with Colonel John Bradstreet in the French war: he understood logistics. He also had considerable experience of Indian diplomacy and an unquenchable commitment to American independence. Congress authorized him, first, to inquire into the situation on the Great Warpath, including the attitudes of the Canadians and the Indians, and then to seize St. Johns and Montreal "if he finds it practicable & not disagreeable to the Canadians."[27] Congress thus left the momentous decision to Schuyler. He favored the invasion, and decided that a rebel army would advance up the Great Warpath to St. Johns, Montreal, and then Quebec. His superior and, soon, friend George Washington agreed with the decision, but added a further element to it.

Mulling over matters during August, in September 1775 the new commander in chief conceived of an original scheme: to couple the main advance up Lake Champlain with an attack via Canada's back door. Washington would send some one thousand troops directly against Quebec via the difficult, but practicable, Kennebec River route through Maine. This force would either take Quebec directly by assault or provide a useful diversion as Schuyler's main force attacked north via St. Johns and Montreal. To lead it he picked his most audacious and capable sub-ordinate—Benedict Arnold. Both Schuyler and Arnold, he knew, under-stood "the absolute Necessity of preserving the Friendship of the Canadians," and he urged them to maintain "a strict Discipline & punc-tual Payment for all Necessaries brought to our Camp." [28] He directed Arnold on September 14 to "check by every Motive of Duty, and Fear of Punishment every Attempt to Plunder or insult any of the Inhabitants of Canada," and he authorized the use of the death penalty to that end. In words that captured the ideology of independence, as well as the prudent measures needed to achieve it, Washington directed that the invading armies must

> avoid all Disrespect or Contempt of the Religion of the Country and its Ceremonies—Prudence, Policy and a true Christian Spirit will lead us to look with Compassion upon their Errors without insulting them—While we are Contending for our own Liberty, we should be very cau-tious of violating the Rights of Conscience in others; ever considering that God alone is the Judge of the Hearts of Men and to him only in this Case they are answerable. [29]

Congress, the commander in chief, and the commanders in the field understood that this was to be a subversive invasion, in which the army would seek to win over a foreign population composed of their tradi-tional enemies, mistrusted on religious grounds, and adhering to tradi-tions alien to their own. It was, thus, doubly bold, in propelling substantial forces through the wilderness in a *coup de main* aimed at forestalling Brit-ish reinforcements to Canada, and in seeking to win over a people so alien to themselves. Thus, in the fall of 1775, the second wave of operations along the Great Warpath began.

Meanwhile the British were reeling from setbacks across North America—the collapse of royal governments throughout the colonies during that turbulent spring, the fierce fighting at Lexington and Con-cord in April, the loss of Fort Ticonderoga and Crown Point in May, and finally the Pyrrhic victory at Bunker Hill in June. The Earl of Dartmouth, secretary of state for the colonies and the man for now most concerned with restoring order in North America, was appalled to learn of the fall of Ticonderoga and Crown Point, which were "particularly painful to me."[30] On the ground matters looked even worse. Throughout early June Canada's governor, Major General Sir Guy Carleton, expressed his alarm to the distant authorities in London. On June 7 he observed that he had barely six hundred rank and file fit for duty, and no armed vessels. The French militia system had fallen apart, "and the minds of the people poisoned by the same hypocrisy and lies practiced with so much success in the other provinces and which their emissaries and friends here have spread abroad with great art and diligence."[31] Carleton regretted the introduction of habeas corpus and the English criminal code, because "these laws, now used as arms against the state, require more public virtue and greater fidelity to their prince than is generally to be met with amongst the set of people here." The gentry he thought he could count on—they had risen against Allen during his sortie against St. Johns. But neither the Canadian peasants nor the Indians had shown any appetite for engaging the American invaders.

By June 1775 the British commanders in North America knew that, as their commander in chief, Lieutenant General Thomas Gage, warned, "war is likely to become general," and that the Great Warpath would be a major theater of operations. Gage began laying plans for a much larger campaign, which would include at least three armies, one each in Boston and New York, and a third corps, including regulars, Canadians, and Indians, operating on Lake Champlain. After Bunker Hill Gage gloomily admitted that "the rebels are not the despicable rabble too many have supposed them to be."[32] Carleton had come to a similar conclusion and called for an army of ten or twelve thousand men to operate from Canada against New England.

At the same time, authorities in England, operating with information from late May, had begun conceiving on their own a massive escalation of violence in North America. They contemplated not only the raising of a vast force, to include hired troops from abroad as well as British regulars, but the use of Indians. As early as July 25, Dartmouth wrote to the unofficial successor of Sir William Johnson (who, unfortunately for the British cause, had died in 1774) urging him to induce the Six Nations "to take up the hatchet against His Majesty's rebellious subjects in America."[33] The rebels had forced Guy Johnson, one of Sir William's relatives, as well as Sir William's only legitimate son, John, from their homes in the Mohawk valley, but the two men had maintained their ties to the Iroquois—who, however, were uneasy about getting involved in a white man's fight. The beginnings of a massive deployment to Quebec from Great Britain, orders (quietly blocked by Carleton for now) to rouse the Indians, and a substantial American invasion were all in the works. The next campaign along the Great Warpath promised something far more lethal than the shambolic, if consequential victories of the late spring of 1775.

Englishmen fighting against Englishmen, French against French and Indians of the same Tribe against each other

In late June 1775 the Congress appointed Richard Montgomery, a short, pockmarked, thirty-eight-year-old Irishman, as a brigadier general. Like so many in this war, he had soldiered along the Great Warpath before, serving under Jeffery Amherst as a junior officer in the Seventeenth Regiment. He had taken part in the seizure of Ticonderoga and Crown Point in 1759, and the climactic 1760 siege of Montreal—the town he was to attack now, fifteen years later. Thwarted in his professional ambitions, for he lacked political patronage, and disheartened by Britain's policy in North America, Montgomery sold his commission and moved to New York in late 1772 or early 1773. There he met and married into the distinguished Livingston family and found himself propelled into politics and, unsurprisingly, military service. Washington ordered him north as second in command to Philip Schuyler.[34]

Schuyler and Montgomery made an excellent team, the latter taking field command when rheumatism and other ailments incapacitated the older man. Schuyler arrived at Ticonderoga in mid-July 1775; Montgomery showed up a month later. Meanwhile, John Brown had conducted another espionage mission to Canada, bringing back the valuable information that the British had two nearly complete gunboats built at St. Johns. Mustering their forces—some twelve hundred men from Connecticut and New York—the two generals moved north, rendezvousing on September 4 at the Isle La Motte, at the northern end of Lake Champlain.

Governor Carleton faced a desperate decision: how to deploy the meager forces under his command to prevent an invasion? He now had barely 750 regulars in all of Canada, plus some unreliable English and French militia, the scarcely more constant Indians (whom the Americans had made every effort, as the British put it, to "debauch"), and a scattering of sailors, workmen, and artillerymen. Reinforcements from Britain would not arrive any time soon, but he could hope to raise further forces from the enterprising Colonel Allan Maclean's Royal Highland Emigrants (veterans, many of them Scots, of the Seven Years' War), loyal Canadians, English volunteers, and the Indians, whom Guy Johnson was actively propagandizing.

Still, he had to make do with the scanty forces available to him, and he decided to concentrate three-quarters of them—chiefly soldiers of the Royal Fusiliers (Seventh Regiment) and the Twenty-sixth Regiment, plus some volunteers, artillerymen, and soldiers of the Royal Highland Emigrants—at St. Johns along the Richelieu River. This left barely two hundred regulars for Montreal, Quebec, and lesser outposts.[35] Located on the Richelieu River perhaps two-thirds of the way to Montreal from the American border, St. Johns lay midway between two old French forts— Isle aux Noix, an island in the Richelieu River, and Chambly, the last old French outpost before Montreal. Unlike either location, however, St. Johns had a naval shipyard, which now harbored, in addition to the boats being built, the *Royal Savage*, a two-masted schooner that, with twelve small cannon (eight four-pounders and four six-pounders) plus ten swivels, posed a serious threat to the American *Enterprise* (the sloop Arnold had captured at St. Johns, with twelve four-pounders and ten swivels) and the small schooner taken at Skenesboro, *Liberty* (four four-pounders, four two-pounders).

The old French fort had, like all earth and log structures, decayed rapidly following the war, and there was no time to replace it properly. But since July, the British had done the next-best thing, enclosing some of the key structures (houses and sheds) in two well-constructed earthen redoubts, one 250 feet long and 200 feet wide, another some 600 feet to the north slightly larger. Around each of the two fortifications they had dug an eight-foot-wide, seven-foot-deep ditch lined with chevaux-de-frise, logs with sharp stakes embedded in them. A trench shielded on either side by log palisades linked the two redoubts, which boasted some forty artillery pieces among them. A very stubborn Scot, Major Charles Preston of the Twenty-sixth, commanded. Carleton had left Chambly, Montreal, and Quebec itself thinly guarded, and as yet had no idea of the second, potentially more lethal thrust that would come directly at Quebec via the Kennebec.

Montgomery effectively took command of the American expedition: Schuyler, wracked by illness, went back to Ticonderoga to do what he did best, managing the army's complicated logistics, which demanded not only an eye for detail (supplies had to alternate between water and road movement, a difficult operation to choreograph) but skill in dealing with fractious contractors. An initial American sortie on September 10 to cut communications between St. Johns and Chambly failed, but Montgomery persisted. He fell back to Isle aux Noix in preparation for a far more regular assault. As he did so, he sent out Ethan Allen and John Brown to raise Canadians to fight the British. On the 17th, Brown, who had now become a militia major, raided British supply lines from Chambly north of the isolated town. It was Allen, however, who characteristically claimed great success, reporting back on September 20: "You may rely on it that I shall join you in about three days, with five hundred or more *Canadian* volunteers. I could raise one or two thousand in a week's time, but will first visit the Army with a less number, and if necessary will go again recruiting. Those that used to be enemies to our cause come cap in hand to me; and I swear by the *Lord* I can raise three times the number of our Army in *Canada*, provided you continue the siege."[36] Allen again succumbed to an intoxicating vision of glory. On September 24 he had assembled perhaps two hundred followers, mostly Canadians, and moved north. All but eighty quietly slipped away on the march to Montreal, but then Allen happened upon John Brown with two hundred of his own Canadians on the southern shore of the St. Lawrence, opposite the city. With nine thousand inhabitants, Montreal had only sixty regulars to defend it. The temptation of taking Montreal before Montgomery had seized St. Johns got the better of Allen. Having rounded up thirty Americans, his eighty Canadians in tow, and with a promise of support from John Brown, Allen crossed the river north of the city in a miscellaneous collection of boats. Brown, however, in an omission never satisfactorily explained, did not show up, and after a brief panic in the city, Carleton rallied over three hundred militia and regulars to take on the invaders.

Allen and his men soon surrendered. According to another of the possibly apocryphal but always entertaining legends that surrounded Allen, a pair of Indians tried to kill the Vermonter. He fended them off by seizing a small British officer, whirling him around as a kind of human shield until rescued. After an unpleasant scene with Carleton's deputy, Brigadier General Richard Prescott, who had a short way with rebels, Allen found himself bundled off in chains to Great Britain.[37]

In the midst of this, the devil himself made an appearance. Montreal's most notorious resident, none other than La Corne St. Luc himself, now offered to cut a deal with the invading Americans.[38] The French partisan had fought to the bitter end against the invading English, commanding the Indians at the last battle of Canada (a French victory), at Sainte Foy just outside Quebec in 1760. In September 1761 he had taken a British offer of free transportation back to France on board the *Auguste*, a rickety ship nearly set on fire three times by a careless cook as it sailed down the St. Lawrence. A storm blew up; sails tore and masts shattered; the ship foundered on the remote Cape Breton Island shore. His brother and nephews drowned; his own two sons slipped out of his hands as he handed them into the ship's boat and were swept away. He and six others staggered ashore, and after doing what they could to bury those of the 114 crew and passengers who had perished and washed up on to the beach, he found some local Indians, with whom he left his companions, and then began a fifteen-hundred-mile trek to Quebec in the dead of winter.[39] He made it.

Fate had kept him in Canada, so, naturally, he continued to conspire against the British until it became clear that the Peace of Paris had given them the country, at which point he married off his daughter to a Scot and proceeded to ingratiate himself with the new order—until the Americans arrived. Montgomery, with misgivings, agreed to a negotiation. In the meanwhile, however, La Corne, having taken note of the repulse of Ethan Allen's sally, promptly handed Montgomery's letter to Sir Guy Carleton. The governor, an upright and a suspicious man, probably despairing of figuring out where the old French warhound's attachments really lay, burned it and brushed him off.

Meanwhile, Montgomery's army had begun to sicken—six hundred ill, the general gloomily reported—and the mixed collection of New Yorkers, Connecticut troops, Green Mountain Boys, and some New

Hampshiremen eyed one another with considerable intracolonial suspicion. Nonetheless, Montgomery rallied his men. He neutralized the *Royal Savage* by laying a boom across the river and constructing a battery at Isle aux Noix, thus preventing the British ship from sailing into Lake Champlain and attacking the American line of communications. He maneuvered five hundred of his men northwest of St. Johns, cutting it off from supplies at Chambly, and he began the tedious work of preparing a proper siege of St. Johns.

The Americans now had St. Johns surrounded, although not sealed off. The British still sent out patrols. On one occasion they picked up an Indian and none other than Moses Hazen, owner of one of the houses protected by the redoubts. A former member of Rogers' rangers and veteran of the capture of Quebec, Hazen had settled in Canada after the war. "The Indian who was taken was buffeted by our Indians and sent back. Mr. Hazen and Mr. Tucker who were found with the Rebels (though indeed without Arms) were kept prisoners in the Forts." [40] The Americans had arrested Hazen once as a British spy, or rather informer, which he had been; he had switched sides and now paid the penalty. Major Preston mused after the siege, "In this Affair, as there have since been throughout the Campaign in Canada there were Englishmen fighting against Englishmen, French against French and Indians of the same Tribe against each other." [41] Deserters went in both directions, and neither side quite knew who stood where. The war of American independence was often a civil war, riddled with ambiguous and shifting loyalties.

The Americans peppered the garrison with fire, finally sinking *Royal Savage* at the dock, but their batteries were distant from the fort, their aim poor, their discipline wretched. The garrison hung on. A drunken Indian came into the fort and reported good news (accurate)—Allen's defeat at Montreal—and bad news (inaccurate), "four thousand Canadians being in arms against us." The regulars sent the "Wildman" on his way, and then "we had our daily little Cannonade & 17 Shells burst amongst us in the Evening, without hurting any one." [42] The Americans brought up a heavy mortar to hurl thirteen-inch explosive shells at the redoubts. September passed and October wore on. Cold, driving rain, and sleet made the regulars and Canadians acutely miserable; some crowded for warmth in the cellars of the shattered buildings; others found the stench of their unwashed, diarrhea-ridden comrades too much to take in such close quarters, and braved the cold and midnight wake-up shells fired by the rebels, sleeping outdoors or walking about until morning. The houses in the redoubts were soon reduced to heaps of boards, shattered glass, and broken bricks. Wine and spirits ran out, and finally, the garrison had eight days of two-thirds rations left, salt pork and flour.

Chambly yielded to the rebels on October 18, but still the St. Johns garrison hung on, Preston noting bitterly that no message from Carleton ever came through to the fort. Carleton made one attempt with his militia and small body of regulars to relieve the fort, on October 31, but encountered three hundred Green Mountain Boys under Seth Warner at Longueil on the outskirts of Montreal. Outnumbered but well led, Warner's men beat off the cautious probe, and Carleton retreated. On November 3, finally, Preston surrendered. He had no high opinion of his enemies, who, he thought, using proper siege techniques of zig-zagging trenches, might soon have reduced the redoubts to rubble. The grim Scottish soldier had not merely displayed tremendous endurance. By his nearly two months of resistance he had derailed the American invasion of Canada. Montgomery's army had sickened; Allen's failed escapade had restored British spirits; and the Americans had begun to wear out their welcome in part because they had also begun to run out of hard money with which to pay the *habitants* for supplies.

Throughout the siege the Americans and British had waged a struggle for influence on both the Canadians and Indians. Carleton's able lieutenant governor had noted with alarm that the rebels had been "sending out some parties and many emissaries to debauch the minds of the Canadians and Indians, in which they have proved too successful, and for which they were too well-prepared by the cabals and intrigues of these last two years."[43] Hugh Finlay, writing from Quebec, was no less depressed, writing to his superior in London that the Indians "have made their peace with the provincials and are returning to their homes. The rebels have nothing to fear from the Canadians [either], nine in ten are in their interests and heartily wish them success."[44]

The Americans had waged an active war of subversion, abetted, the British believed, by what Finlay called "the lower class of the British subjects" who had convinced the Canadians of:

what they called English liberty—few of them understanding what they undertook to explain, they implanted a spirit of licentiousness in the minds of the new subjects and the consequence is that they have changed their former obedient and obliging behavior for a disrespectful and insolent carriage toward their superiors. "Are we not" say they "British subjects? Is not the poorest *habitant* among us a man? Our *seigneur* is no more." It is very perceptible that they conceive English liberty to consist in a right to say and do what they please.[45]

The translated pamphlets and the lure of a world without taxes and *seigneurs* appealed to the Canadians, while the Indians hesitated: They remained dangerous, but they understood their own long-term vulnerability to the vastly more numerous colonists very well.

Carleton, however, often derided by some of his subordinates—abler but narrower fighting men—had practiced his own, conservative counterinsurgency campaign with considerable political skill. He mobilized the groups in Canada most sympathetic to British rule: loyal settlers, Indians, veterans, the *seigneurs*, and the clergy. The democratic infection threatened the latter two groups considerably, and more than a few of the gentry sputtered in outrage when the Canadian militia refused to muster under their orders. Cleverly, the *habitants* insisted to British authorities that they would gladly fight on their behalf, but only under proper British officers—who, they well knew, were too few to lead the militia. But some of the gentry retained influence, and the clergy did as well. The latter could exercise negative control, by refusing to read the widely disseminated American letters and proclamations to their largely illiterate flocks. And they could take harsher measures, including refusing confession or even Christian burial to those who did not hew to the Church and share its leaders' adherence to the Crown.[46] For his part, Carleton used leniency—he held back the Indians, much to the anger of his more hotheaded subordinates, and refrained from counterproductive violence. But he also gave local agitators, including Thomas Walker in Montreal, the choice between exile and imprisonment—and gladly gave Walker the latter when he refused to leave.

Despite his army's failing health, Montgomery lost little time in moving on Montreal after his victory at St. Johns, departing in a snowstorm on November 6 and taking the city, abandoned by its defenders, on November 13. British forces fell back. On that very night, Arnold and his men, who had made an epic journey through the Maine wilderness, crossed the St. Lawrence opposite Quebec. But Colonel Allan Maclean had beaten him to it, arriving in the city with a small but invaluable core of regulars scarcely thirty-six hours before. Maclean, a fifty-year-old former rebel himself (one of the Scottish veterans of Culloden, pardoned and brought into the British army), had raised the Royal Highland Emigrants. He, too, was no stranger to the Great Warpath, having served in the Royal Americans in 1758 at Ticonderoga, and like Preston, he brought to America a full measure of stubborn Scottish courage.

British forces withdrew to Quebec. An American battery posted on the banks of the St. Lawrence River bluffed a small flotilla under General Prescott, Ethan Allen's brutal captor, into an ignominious surrender on November 17. Carleton had himself slipped past American sentinels in a whaleboat the day before, arriving at the besieged city of Quebec on November 19. From here, however, his fortunes brightened. With Maclean and Lieutenant Governor Cramahé he cobbled together a patchwork garrison—70 regulars of the Royal Fusiliers, 230 Royal Highland Emigrants, several hundred each of marines, British, and Canadian militia, 400 sailors, and others—1,600 in all. They outnumbered Arnold nearly three to one, and boasted over one hundred artillery pieces on the wall, but bided, for now, within the walls.[47] Carleton expelled all who would not fight in defense of the city, refused any communication with the enemy, and hunkered down for a winter siege.

By early December, Montgomery and Arnold had united their forces opposite the walls of Quebec. At this point however, the exhausted American armies, still outnumbered by those they besieged, faced not only Carleton's force, but an impending deadline: the expiry of the enlistment of many of their soldiers. In a desperate effort in the early morning of December 31, they attempted to storm the city. It was a disaster: Montgomery was killed and Arnold shot in the leg. Wounded as he was, Arnold—barely—kept a grip on the demoralized remnants of the two expeditions throughout the winter, continued the siege with a tiny force, and awaited reinforcements. But there could be no mistaking this for anything other than a debacle, and barring some collapse in British morale or a spectacularly daring assault, the Americans would eventually have to retreat.

A noble train of artillery

Even as the rebel armies prepared their doomed New Year's Eve assault on Quebec city, however, the invasion of Canada along the Great War-path had yielded something tangible, as the result of the exertions of a tall, stout, cheerful, twenty-five-year-old bookseller by the name of Henry Knox.[48] Knox, whose bookshop had serviced the English officers sta-tioned in Boston, had devoured works on artillery tactics and served with some distinction in the Boston militia. John Adams recommended him to Washington to serve as chief of the Continental Army's artillery. The dif-ficulty, of course, was that the army besieging the British in Boston had no artillery to speak of.

Knox hit on the same solution that had occurred to Arnold: the artil-lery strewn around the ruined fortresses of Ticonderoga and Crown Point. Winning Washington's approval, he pressed north with his brother William, leaving in mid-November and arriving at Fort Ticonderoga on December 6. En route he stopped overnight at Fort George at the south-ern end of Lake George, where he shared a room with John André, an elegant, brilliant young British lieutenant recently captured at Chambly with other soldiers of the Royal Fusiliers (the Seventh Regiment) headed south before a prisoner exchange. The two young men soon discovered a common interest in literature as well as the finer points of military theory. Knox and André spent the night in animated and convivial conversation about books and war.[49]

Knox assembled a forty-two-sledge convoy to carry fifty-nine pieces of artillery, including guns, howitzers, and mortars from Crown Point and Ticonderoga, to Washington's army besieging Boston. The challenge was to haul some sixty tons of ordnance over three hundred miles to Cambridge. Knox wrote to Washington that he hoped in two weeks "to be able to present your Excellency, a noble train of artillery," but it took a month and a half to do so.

Knox, working with Schuyler's support, brought together soldiers and local contractors to carry the great guns south to Lake George. An eleven-year-old boy, helping his father manage the wagons they had rented to the army, described driving past the site of old Fort William Henry. "We were approaching the bloody pond and the scene of some terrible slaughters. My imagination peopled every bush with ghosts."[50] But if ghosts still haunted the massacre site, they had blessed the enterprise. The convoy proceeded south to Glen Falls, Saratoga, and Albany, before reaching the Massachusetts border. There, Knox headed east through the Berkshires, through Westfield, Springfield, Worcester, Framingham, and ultimately, to Cambridge. It was a herculean task. Guns crashed through soft ice or bogged down in three-foot-deep snow; meanwhile Knox alternated between riding ahead of the convoy to arrange shelter, food, replacement horses or oxen, and teamsters to manage them and coordinating the delicate process of recovering sunken guns along the way. Curious and helpful villagers, through motives patriotic and mercenary, helped out, remarking on what they termed "big shooting irons" and requesting the pleasing ceremony of a salute from the largest cannon. The militia companies of western Massachusetts turned out, too. Knox noted wryly, after being introduced to their numerous leaders, "what a pity it is that our soldiers are not as numerous as our officers."[51]

By the end of January 1776 they had arrived in Cambridge, and Washington now had the tools to bring to an end the siege of Boston, crammed with almost as many British soldiers and Tories as inhabitants. In early March, feinting from the town of Roxbury at the narrow neck of land that led to Boston from the mainland, he simultaneously moved the guns of "the noble train" to Dorchester Heights, southeast of Roxbury, where they would command not only the town but the harbor. Painstakingly, Washington's men moved the artillery into position, after an audacious, covert overnight occupation of Dorchester Heights. "The rebels have done more in one night than my whole army may have done in a month," the British commander, Sir William Howe, admitted.[52] Once the Americans had positioned the guns behind improvised fortifications—the ground being too frozen for digging—the British must either land troops to storm the position, risking a repetition of the Bunker Hill debacle, or evacuate Boston. A storm thwarted a plan for the former, so good sense indicated the latter, with the result that March 17 became known thenceforth in Boston as Evacuation Day. The depressed loyalists sailing away with the British Army included Thomas Flucker, former secretary of the province, and his wife, Hannah. They had deplored their daughter Lucy's match with one Henry Knox, a mere tradesman, whom they doubted would amount to much, and who had revealed such unsuspected and unwelcome talents. They never saw rebellious daughter and deeply disliked son-in-law again.

The final consummation of our wishes

It was in a state of high anxiety, then, that Congress had sent its commission led by Benjamin Franklin north in March 1776 to see if it could make subversive war succeed. "You are, with all convenient despatch, to repair to *Canada*, and make known to the people of that country the wishes and intentions of the Congress with respect to them." [53] The commissioners would teach the Canadians how to handle the freedom into which they had been conquered. They would explain representative democracy, as well as the operation of Committees of Safety to keep an eye on the enemies of freedom. They would expose the tyrannical designs of Parliament, and play on their fears, their desire for glory, and their self-interest so that they would "aspire to a portion of that power by which they are ruled, and not . . . remain the mere spoils and prey of conquerors and lords." [54] The commissioners were to offer the Canadians membership in the united colonies on the same terms as any other colony. In addition to settling all disputes between the American armies and the Canadians, "You are to establish a free press," the instruction continued, adding with no evident sense of irony, "and . . . give directions for the frequent publication of such pieces as may be of service to the cause of the United Colonies."

Arriving in Montreal six weeks later, however, the commissioners soon realized that the army in Canada, under its new commander, Major General John Thomas, could not hope to hold the country. Thomas—an able and experienced veteran of the first conquest of Montreal in 1760 who had placed Knox's artillery on Dorchester Heights—reached Que-

bec on May 1 to replace Arnold, and he wrote the newly arrived commissioners that he had discovered barely half of the nineteen hundred men
there fit for service, the rest down with smallpox. Hundreds of enlistments had expired, and there was scant gunpowder and provisions for
only six days. Subversion, furthermore, had failed: The Canadians, as
Carleton had cynically but accurately observed when the tide had flowed
in a different direction, sided with whomever seemed strongest.[55]

On May 6, 1776, the besieged inhabitants of Quebec, short of rations
but eagerly expectant of a rescue, saw a ship sailing up the St. Lawrence:
It proved to be HMS *Surprise*, the first of two frigates in the van of the
long-awaited British reinforcements. Two hundred soldiers and marines
tromped off the ship. Carleton immediately took them, mustered six
hundred of the garrison, and ordered a deliberate advance from the walls
of Quebec. They encountered no resistance. The rebel army "had retreated
in the utmost hurry and confusion, leaving all their provisions, artillery
and ammunition and baggage behind, in much the same way as the
French had raised the siege sixteen years before; and thus we got a complete victory without bloodshed," as Hugh Finlay noted with pleasure in
his diary.[56]

Franklin and his fellow commissioners realized that the venture had
failed despite Congress's best efforts (John Hancock and his associates
had continued to send a steady stream of troops and such money as they
had up north). Two days after reaching Montreal they reported that "the
small pox is in the army," noting uneasily that "General Thomas has unfortunately never had it."[57] They described for Hancock "the general apprehension, that we shall be driven out of the Province as soon as the King's
troops can arrive." On May 6, the day the *Surprise* sailed up the St. Lawrence to Quebec, Franklin gloomily explained a key reason why the
Americans had lost the battle for Canadian hearts and minds:

> the want of money frequently constrains the Commanders to have
> recourse to violences in providing the army with carriages, and other
> conveniences, which indispose and irritate the minds of the people. We
> have reason to conclude that the change of sentiments, which we under-
> stand has taken place in this colony, is owing to the above mentioned
> cause, and to other arbitrary proceedings.

He and his colleagues saw no choice but "to withdraw our army and for-tify the passes on the lakes to prevent the enemy, and the Canadians, if so inclined, from making irruptions into and depredations on our fron-tiers."[58] Congress reluctantly agreed, and on May 22, 1776, ordered Schuy-ler to concentrate on "the protection and assistance of our Canadian friends, and the securing so much of that country as may prevent any communication between our enemies and the Indians." The politicians in Philadelphia envisioned a retreat to Isle aux Noix or beyond, to Ticon-deroga. The details of fortifications, building a fleet on Lake Champlain, carving out roads, they left to Schuyler, but they did order the commis-sioners to audit the books, restore order and discipline, and punish the guilty, to avert a worse disaster.[59]

Franklin, whose health had worsened again at Montreal, did not lin-ger to accomplish these tasks, heading south before his younger col-leagues. Accompanied by the Catholic priest, John Carroll, who nursed the ailing statesman, he managed to get back to Saratoga by the end of May 1776. His other traveling companions were less congenial than the kindly priest. Thomas Walker and his wife had hosted Franklin and his colleagues in Montreal: They had now become refugees, since as a leading local rebel he would be marked for reprisal by the advancing British. The embittered Walkers spent most of the journey toward Saratoga "taunting our conduct in Canada," to the point that the ill and disappointed Frank-lin could barely bring himself to speak to them. Franklin wrote to his fel-low commissioners Samuel Chase and Charles Carroll, who had remained in Canada to manage matters as best they could, "I think they both have excellent talents at making themselves enemies, and I believe, live where they will, they will never be long without them." However sore his bones, Franklin's sense of humor remained intact.[60]

As he wended his way back to Philadelphia, Franklin may not have wasted much time ruminating about lost opportunities. But it is nonethe-less worth assessing the strategic judgment of all those who launched the Canadian venture. The British had, no doubt, secured the allegiance of much of the Canadian gentry and priesthood; the *habitants*, however, had proven quite willing to come to terms with the invading Americans. The anxiety of Carleton, Lieutenant Governor Cramahé, and other intelligent observers about the disloyalty of the Canadian peasantry suggests that as long as the Americans held the upper hand militarily, they could hold the province.

The twin invasions of Canada came close to success, particularly in the fall of 1775. Had St. Johns fallen sooner, Montgomery and Arnold would have linked up in mid-November, not early December. Had this happened, had Montgomery managed to bag Maclean and his small column before they got to Quebec, had the politically indispensable Carleton been killed or captured, had Arnold's column had somewhat better luck (an incompetent subordinate abandoned him, taking a third of his men and the expedition's supplies on the way up), it is likely that Quebec would have fallen to a *coup de main* before the winter. The British fleet would have arrived in the spring, but the reconquest of a well-fortified city, defended by commanders the caliber of Arnold and Montgomery, would not have been trivial, and would have required a substantial campaign lasting many weeks. And a complete occupation of the province of Quebec might have led more Canadians and Indians to throw their lot in with the Americans. The campaigns of 1776 would have looked very different. In a more distant future, the question of whether Quebec would fly a British or an American flag would have been more open.

By the spring of 1776, however, such opportunities were remote. Even when he set off in April, Franklin may have intuited that the commission could not redeem the Canadian adventure. But it had served at least one large purpose, nudging the other colonies to make the final, irrevocable step toward independence from Great Britain. By ratifying in its instructions to the commissioners the objective of overthrowing British rule in Canada, Congress had tacitly transformed a war for the rights of Englishmen into a war of independence. John Adams later described the drafting of the instructions to the commissioners going to Canada as "one step more towards our great object, a general recommendation to the States to institute governments."[61] Describing Congress's recommendation to the people of Canada that they create a representative government and unite with the other colonies, he noted that a substantial minority argued against the instructions "with great zeal." Congress's final decision he described as "strong proof of the real determination of a majority of Congress to go with us to the final consummation of our wishes"—true and irrevocable independence from Great Britain.

The operations against Ticonderoga and Crown Point arose in part

from the spontaneous initiative of ambitious, driven leaders in their thirties like Allen and Arnold; in part to prevent British coercion of the colonies from outposts in the back country; and in part because the
opportunity easily to secure the vast stores of artillery weakly guarded at
Ticonderoga and Crown Point appealed to political and military leaders
confronting a swelling British army in Boston. But the leaders of the Revolution turned these forces and objectives into something larger and
more ambitious: the overthrow of the government of Canada, and the
uniting of that colony with the others to form a common front against
Great Britain.

The abortive invasion of Canada combined, in a distinctively American way, idealism and calculating *realpolitik*. The invaders sincerely advocated representative government and individual liberty, while manipulating
local beliefs, brazenly attacking a neighbor in order to secure the fundamental and perilous decision for independence. In years to come, Americans in many other places—from Mexico to the Philippines, Vietnam to
Iraq—would behave similarly, waging wars for liberty and interest, conquering others into freedom, and as in Canada, with mixed motives and
uncertain outcomes.

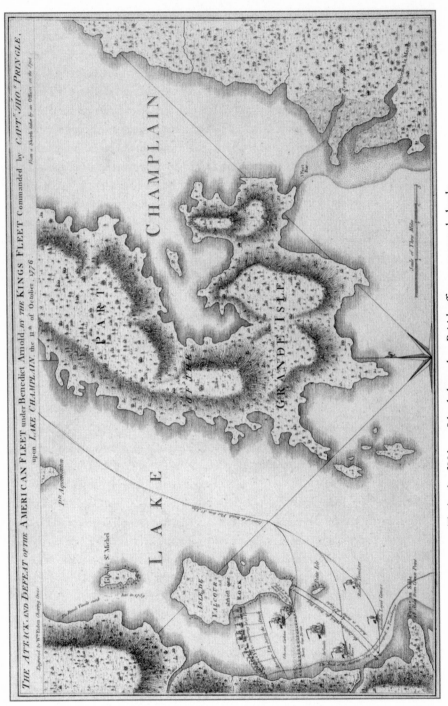

The battle of Valcour Island, drawn by a British officer present at the battle.
Reproduced by permission of the Society of the Cincinnati, Washington, D.C.

CHAPTER SIX

Valcour Island, 1776

We should suppress all signs of triumph on the occasion

Colonel Jeduthan Baldwin, chief engineer of the American fortifications at Mount Independence and Fort Ticonderoga, finally thought a bit better of his men. They "work with life and spirits this day which shows a determined resolution to defend the place to the last extremity." They had better, he knew, for the day before, on October 13, 1776, Baldwin had learned of the shattering defeat suffered by the American fleet on Lake Champlain. The refugees from isolated farms came stumbling into Ticonderoga, "a melancholy sight," Baldwin recorded in his journal, "but we may expect a more melancholy scene tomorrow."[1] Indeed he could. The succeeding days brought grim sights, as the few battle-mangled ships that had survived the wreck of Benedict Arnold's flotilla and the paroled American soldiers, including Arnold's deputy, Brigadier General David Waterbury, hustled to the rear.

Conscientious New Englander that he was, Baldwin reacted to disaster by working harder. A forty-four-year-old farmer, not a soldier, he was, nonetheless, a veteran. In 1756 he had helped that highly competent (and procolonial) engineer Captain William Eyre lay out Fort William Henry, which seems to be where he learned the rudiments of the military trade he now practiced. He led a militia company, and participated in scouts with Robert Rogers around Crown Point. Once, he recalled in his journal, he and his comrades had come across nine men "all stripped shot scalped and cut in the most dreadful manner." When the Revolution began, Baldwin, now a prosperous citizen of Brookfield, Massachusetts, helped lay out the fortifications around Boston, lost his brother in the Battle of Bunker Hill, and then went north to the army in Canada. He had earned the confidence of his commanders, and was now the senior American in the Continental Army's minuscule engineer corps, which consisted chiefly of European professionals.

Baldwin and his men did not have long to wait for the appearance of the victorious British fleet. On October 17, 1776, it arrived at Crown Point twelve miles north of Ticonderoga and Mount Independence, under the command of Sir Guy Carleton. The peninsula and ruined fortifications suddenly sprouted orderly rows of white tents, as thousands of British soldiers and hired German troops stretched their legs following the cramped voyage south. British patrols probed—birchbark canoes slipping along the lake, a boat or two driven off Fort Ticonderoga by a fire, Indian war parties pouncing on the few soldiers or civilians foolish or unlucky enough to have strayed outside the lines, capturing a couple, killing and scalping a few others. On October 28 a major in one of the Pennsylvania regiments observed fourteen flat-bottom boats crossing from east to west; rumor had it that the enemy had landed three thousand men. But, like Colonel Baldwin, he thought the rebel army was ready for a fight. "Never were men in a better disposition to end the quarrel by conquest or death,"[2] he wrote his wife, in one of a series of letters more given to disparaging New Englanders ("a set of dirty, low, griping, cowardly rascals") than patriotic chest thumping.[3]

By this point, however, a pensive Carleton had decided to call it quits. An assault against the works Baldwin had constructed did not look promising, and besides, he had only the vanguard of his army with him—he would need to bring up the full force, a matter of at least a couple of weeks. He would not even attempt to hold his forward base, Crown Point, over the winter. "The severe season is approaching very fast," he told Major General Sir William Howe, now commanding in New York. The

Americans had, in their usual thorough way, demolished what they could at Crown Point, and the British lacked material as well as time to build barracks and storehouses for a garrison there.[4] Carleton hoped that he had at least diverted some troops from the operations at Long Island and New York City; he had, also, of course, expelled the rebels from Canada and now nearly obliterated their fleet.

Unlike others in the British camp, however, Carleton took little pleasure in such triumphs, writing back to his considerably more enthusiastic deputy, Major General John Burgyone, "This success cannot be deemed less than a complete victory; but considering it was obtained over the kings subjects, that, which in other circumstances ought to be a proper cause of public rejoicing, is, in these, a matter only of great concern." To the disgust of the ambitious, and not overly loyal, Burgoyne, who craved smashing victories over the rebels, he advised, "We should suppress all signs of triumph on the occasion."[5] On November 2, to the relief both of British soldiers feeling the cold autumn winds on the lake and looking apprehensively at the snow on the mountaintops, and of the rebel troops bracing themselves for a climactic battle, the British fleet sailed back north to winter quarters. The first British invasion from Canada had ended.

⸻ ◆ ⸻

By thus bringing on a general Distress,
create a general Disposition to Submission.

The victorious British army and fleet that paused before the fortifications of Ticonderoga and Mount Independence in that frosty autumn owed their existence to the energy of the new director of the American War, Lord George Germain. A year earlier, in November 1775, he had replaced the indolent Earl of Dartmouth as the secretary of state for the American Department. An energetic sixty years of age, tall, heavyset, blue-eyed, he had been a lifelong friend of James Wolfe, the conqueror of Quebec, and he was determined to defeat the Americans. Charges of disobedience at the Battle of Minden during the Seven Years' War had dogged him, brave and competent soldier though he had been for years. He had been dismissed from the army and after requesting a court-martial to clear his name, narrowly escaped the death penalty. These experiences left this proud, forceful man a stubborn, hardworking loner.

Germain did not believe it possible or desirable to reconquer America inch by inch. But he did believe in the quick administration of heavy, stunning blows to demoralize the rebel leadership, restore the morale of loyal subjects, and convince waverers that the war could only end in reunion—albeit on modified terms—between Britain and America. He moved swiftly, shifting commanders, pouring resources into the conflict, and transforming British strategy.

Lieutenant General Thomas Gage, whose record had been so dubious at Ticonderoga in 1758, had during the spring of 1775 given the British government the debacles of Lexington, Concord, and Bunker Hill. His reputation in ruins, he sailed for home that October. King George III confided supreme command in North America to General William Howe and his brother Admiral Richard Howe, brothers of the much-loved commander of light troops, Lord George Howe, who had fallen in the fatal skirmish before Ticonderoga in 1758. As peace commissioners they could offer generous terms and easy pardons, but behind them would sail an expeditionary force that would convince the Americans that resistance was pointless. That winter of 1775, Major General John Burgoyne, who had been one of Gage's deputies, also sailed home, to sell the ministry on a new strategy.

Burgoyne, a dashing cavalryman, parliamentarian, and playwright, was nothing if not ambitious—in his schemes and for his career. He made the case that the British government should reposition Gage's army, now besieged in Boston, moving it to New York, whence it would push up the Hudson. Simultaneously, the British would launch another army from Canada, southward along the Great Warpath. The two armies would link up in the vicinity of Albany, thus encircling New England. Most British commanders agreed with the basic idea.

By occupying the water route between Quebec and New York, the British expected substantially to isolate the source of the revolutionary infection in New England. Not only could British riverine and naval forces operating along the Hudson interdict the movement of supplies between north and south: A series of outposts in the back country could provide launching pads for Indian attacks on the rebellious colonies (tying down local forces, much as the French had done in previous wars) and create rallying points for the beleaguered loyalists, whom British authorities believed to be numerous. Smashing the Continental Army, as it hoped to do, the main British army could then help restore loyal governments. "It was expected," noted the officials in London:

> that not only Canada would be recovered, but a communication opened with the King's Forces on the Side of the Atlantic; and by that means place the Rebel Army between two Fires. That by harassing the western Frontiers of the Rebel provinces, the Inhabitants who now supplied their Troops with provisions, would be forced to fly to them for protection, and, instead of relieving, increase their Difficulties of finding Subsistence.

From this flowed the British theory of victory: "By thus bringing on a general Distress, create a general Disposition to Submission."[6]

This was a far from unreasonable plan. In the last quarter of the eighteenth century, unlike the twentieth, there was no presumption that sooner or later colonies must become self-governing, independent countries—the reverse, in fact. The American Revolution began as an anticolonial revolt. Only in the twentieth century and after did the word "empire" acquire connotations of defensiveness, overextension, and preordained doom. As the colonial empires of Europe disintegrated, observers assumed that they inevitably must do so: The only questions were those of pace, cost, and consequence. Not so eighteenth-century Great Britain, an empire still on the rise, led by men to whom rebellion—in itself, an effort to create a new, North American empire—was merely a challenge to be beaten down.

The first order of business, though, must be the rescue of Carleton at Quebec. The governor's desperate messages, sent in mid-November 1775, arrived in London six weeks later, on Christmas Day 1775, and Germain acted swiftly in response.[7] By early January 1776 he had decided to send ten thousand troops to Canada, led by an advance party of several warships and transports bringing a preliminary relief to the city.[8] It was this force, led by the frigate *Surprise* and small ship of the line *Isis*, that relieved the besieged city on May 6. Following behind them sailed a mass of reinforcements second only to that being sent to General William Howe for operations against New York. In February, Germain wrote to Carleton that the second wave of forces headed his way, which would sail by the end of March, would include eight regiments of infantry plus artillery under Major General Burgoyne; five thousand hired German troops would go as well, some three thousand of them also in March. Germain ordered Burgoyne to reinforce Carleton if Quebec still held; to retake the city if it had surrendered and replace the governor if he had fallen.

By the end of March London knew of the failure of the rebel assault on Quebec on December 31, and Germain wrote Howe urging Burgoyne's pincer movement. For his part, Howe, under the guns that Henry Knox had brought from the Great Warpath to Dorchester Heights, departed Boston on March 17, sailing with his troops and Loyalist refugees to Halifax, before regrouping for his assault on New York, a protracted affair that would take until the summer of 1776 and beyond to consummate.

That May, Carleton immediately used the modest reinforcements and the larger psychological effect of the relief of Quebec to disperse the rebel army. He knew, as did the weak, sickened rebels, that the two warships were but the precursor to a massive, indeed, extraordinary pulse of power hurled toward North America by the rulers of Great Britain. And he fully expected to use the army—larger than that which James Wolfe had brought to the Plains of Abraham less than twenty years before, further reinforced with locally recruited Canadians, loyalists, and Indians—to expel the rebels from Canada and to pursue them down Lake Champlain to the Hudson.

• • •

I therefore put the best face on matters and
betrayed no marks of fear

As 1776 began, the Americans still hoped to hold on to Canada, even after the failure of the assaults on Quebec city in the waning days of 1775. Arnold, wounded though he was, with only seven hundred troops near Quebec still maintained a siege of that place, whose garrison outnumbered his tiny army. His subordinates wished to pull back from the city, but he believed that that would have a devastating impact on the morale

...hold at the beginning of April. Toiling through the ...arrived in Montreal at the end of that month. He ...d a dismal situation: no preparations to defend the city, ...d, no hard currency, inadequate forces, troops leaving as ...listments expired. When he reached Quebec, relieving the ...Wooster a day before HMS *Surprise* appeared, he found an ...eplorable situation: Of the nineteen hundred men there ...were fit for duty. Thomas supervised the retreat as best he ...a different disaster struck: At the end of May he caught small-pox...on June 2, he died.

...arleton's forces steadily advanced and American forces tumbled up ...t. Lawrence to Montreal, they suffered one failure after another. Another incompetent, a Pennsylvanian this time, Brigadier General William Thompson, promoted to that rank over the objections of Washington, commanded the army's rear guard. Advised by the congressional commissioners to block the advancing British (who by the beginning of June had received five of the promised eight British regiments, plus some of the Germans), he decided to outflank the advancing British at the town of Three Rivers, northeast of Montreal and the junction of the St. Lawrence and the Richelieu River. On June 2 the Americans crossed the river to attack the British; the British sailed up the St. Lawrence behind them, cutting off their retreat. On June 8, although outnumbering the enemy by two to one, the Americans suffered another ignominious defeat, wandering into swamps and losing some three hundred men killed, wounded, or captured—among the last group was General Thompson himself.

Congress sent more troops and new commanders north. Brigadier General John Sullivan went next. Washington liked the bumptious, aggressive New Hampshire lawyer turned soldier even if he had doubts about his steadiness. He described Sullivan to John Hancock as "active, spirited, and zealously attached to the cause." But his "foibles" included "a little tincture of vanity," "an over desire of being popular, which now and then leads him into some embarrassments."[12] Sullivan's political acuity and military abilities did not, alas, quite match his aggressiveness and high self-opinion. On June 6, a day after taking command, he reported back to Washington that he had "no doubt of the general attachment of the Canadians." He expressed splendid, if delusional, confidence that "I

of the Canadians. "I therefore pu

no marks of fear." Still, he told Wa

troops to take and hold Quebec.[9]

Arnold of the importance the America

"To whomsoever it belongs, in their

turn."[10]

Throughout the winter and spring Washi

to reinforce the American army in Canada.

Wooster, a sixty-five-year-old veteran of the

1745, and of the campaigns against Ticonderoga

Indian War a decade later, commanded in Montrea

the convalescing Arnold before Quebec—an unfortu

was old, prejudiced against Catholics, incapable of en

and, though plucky, tactically incompetent. In a letter fr

the end of May 1776, Charles Carroll and Samuel Chase

commission told the president of Congress, John Hancoc

found Wooster, "in our opinion totally unfit to command your

conduct the War." The damage, however, had been done.[11] Disc

the army, never strong, had crumbled under Wooster, leading to the

laging of the increasingly resentful local population.

Arnold, now in command at Montreal, was the only competent

mander the Americans had in Canada. In April 1776 he had po

detachment of his forces at the Cedars, some twenty-eight miles

west of Montreal, to block British-led Indian forces from taki

Americans in the rear. Colonel Timothy Bedel of New Hampshire

manded four hundred men in a strongly fortified position. Learni

the approach of an enemy force, Bedel handed command over to his

ber two, Isaac Butterfield, and departed posthaste for Montreal

Arnold's inexpressible fury, Butterfield promptly surrendered to s

forty British regulars and two hundred Indians. Arnold pressed for

court-martial of both men, who were subsequently cashiered for cow

ice and incompetence, and who thereafter joined Arnold's growing ros

of inveterate enemies.

Washington sent Brigadier General John Thomas, the capable v

eran who had supervised the movement of artillery to Dorchest

Heights—to take command of the army in Canada. "General Thoma

will take the burthen off your shoulders," Washington informed the limp may venture to assure you and the Congress that I can in a few days reduce the army to order and with the assistance of a kind Providence put a new face to our affairs" and, indeed, move again on Quebec.

A week in command, and the defeat at Three Rivers, sobered Sullivan up, or rather, plunged him into despair. "I think only of a glorious death or victory obtained against superior numbers."[13] In the interim he had discovered the reality: the power of the British army, and the near total decrepitude of his own forces. He had to strain himself to the limit to prevent a complete collapse of the army but, following what he believed to be congressional wishes, he determined to retain a foothold in Canada, making a stand at the town of Sorel, at the junction of the Richelieu and St. Lawrence. And, indeed, at the end of May another congressional committee appointed to advise Washington and other senior commanders on Canadian strategy had insisted that "the Congress are fully convinced of the absolute necessity of keeping the possession of that country, and that they expect the forces in that department will contest every foot of the ground with the enemies to these colonies."[14]

Congress's desire to maintain an unyielding defense of Canada compounded the calamities of the American forces. This wish did not take the form of an unambiguous order to die in place, but neither could an American general ignore it. Although congressional sentiment did not comport with the facts on the ground, it nonetheless exercised a powerful influence on Sullivan, the last American commander in Canada. On June 10, Arnold, now directing what remained of the rear guard, pleaded with him to liquidate the Canadian commitment:

> Shall we sacrifice the few men we have by endeavoring to keep possession of a small part of the country which can be of little or no service to us? The junction of the Canadians with the Colonies—an object which brought us into this country—is now at an end. Let us quit them, and secure our own country before it is too late. There will be more honor in making a safe retreat than hazarding a battle against such superiority, which will doubtless be attended with the loss of men, artillery, etc. and the only pass to our country. These arguments are not urged by fear for my personal safety: I am content to be the last man who quits this country, and fall, so that my country may rise. But let us not fall together.[15]

Sullivan stubbornly delayed—and, as Arnold predicted, the American army soon found itself bypassed by a British fleet that occupied Montreal and began to march overland towards St. Johns. The Americans retreated to that port in the nick of time, and there, on June 18, a council of war finally prevailed upon Sullivan to order a retreat first to Isle aux Noix, and then southward. Arnold, accompanied by Colonel Baldwin, supervised the torching of all the public buildings of St. Johns and the destruction of what remained of the American supplies. Together, the two men left in the last bateau—after Arnold had calmly stripped saddle and bridle from his horse, and shot it to deny him to the enemy.[16] The American adventure in Canada was over.

———— • • • ————

The small pox! The small pox! What shall we do with it?" [17]

Bad luck, inadequate funds, wretched leadership (Arnold and Montgomery excepted), and indiscipline had undermined the American invasion of Canada. So, too, had determined British resistance, Germain's prompt reinforcements, and the leadership of Carleton and his chief subordinates. But an utterly inhuman enemy did as much to defeat the invasion as any material factor: *Variola major*, the smallpox.[18] This excruciating disease, which ravaged North American Indians in their encounters with the Europeans, hit epidemic proportions during the Revolution. A week or two after infection, the first symptoms set in—fever, aches, nausea, and malaise. These flulike symptoms gave way to sores in mouth, throat, and nose, and from there ghastly suffering began—acutely painful pustules, bleeding from all orifices, dehydration, a hideous merging of scabbing eruptions, secondary infections, a loathsome stench, and, in many cases, death. Many eighteenth-century authorities viewed inoculation with considerable suspicion; unlike vaccination (introduced at the end of the eighteenth century using cowpox), this involved taking material from the pustules of a smallpox sufferer and inserting them into incisions in the patient's skin. The result might be a nonlethal, but still acutely miserable form of the disease or, for many unfortunates, simply the full-blown thing.

The widely spread out Americans had had less exposure to smallpox than their European counterparts. When Americans from different parts of the country assembled in close and unhygienic quarters, that is, in military camps, they created a situation ripe for epidemic. Conditions for a smallpox outbreak were ideal in the army besieging Quebec.[19] Exhausted, weak, and shut in by the cold weather, the soldiers of Arnold's and Montgomery's small armies soon succumbed to the contagion in December 1775. Arnold, ever the active commander, issued sensible commands to quarantine and hospitalize soldiers with *Variola*, but to little avail, and the northern army had to cope with a disease that crippled the army just as British reinforcements could be expected to arrive.

When Jeduthan Baldwin arrived at Sorel in mid-May 1776 on his way north to serve as engineer to the northern army, he took the advice from multiple quarters to "take the small pox," and did so, in the company of several senior officers. A week after the inoculation, on May 23, he reported in his diary severe headache and body pains, and a loss of appetite that lasted a week. By June 1 he counted forty pox marks on his face; by the fifth he had broken out all over, and suffered from "an extreme fire and itching [that] made me very uncomfortable." He took the usual remedy—induced vomiting. As the army retreated to Chambly on the eleventh he was "weak and covered with the scales of the Pox and unfit to travel." Not until June 15—a month after the initial inoculation, and three weeks after the first disabling symptoms—do we find him functioning effectively again, supervising the burning of public buildings at St. Johns as the army retreated out of Canada.

This retreating, ragged, starved, lousy, thievish, pockey army

Throughout these calamities, Major General Philip Schuyler, wearing himself out maintaining the logistical support of the northern army (and conducting active Indian diplomacy on the side), did not despair. He sharply told Sullivan in a letter of June 20, "I cannot by any means approve that you should 'think only of a glorious death or a victory obtained against superior numbers' . . . the evacuation of Canada will certainly be attended with many disagreeable ends, but will not mean the total destruction of our Army and a consequent loss of the country."[20] Schuyler knew that the Americans had two assets: naval command of Lake Champlain and strong positions at the southern end of the lake. To reinforce the former, Schuyler had already begun a modest naval construction program at the very southern end of Lake Champlain, at Skenesborough, and had peppered Washington with requests for saws, cordage, and all the other necessities of shipbuilding.

Arnold, however, provided the animating force for the construction of a fleet to reinforce the handful of armed vessels that he had seized the previous year. He had, in fact, barely left Canada before he began laying out to Schuyler and Washington the kind of effort needed. In particular, Arnold told Washington, the northern army would need not just materiel, but men who knew how to handle it. He called for three hundred carpenters, including at least fifty who had taken part in the construction of row galleys for the defense of Philadelphia, for these he believed the best vessels to build for the American fleet on Lake Champlain. Arnold knew that the British would soon build their own fleet on the lake and warned that they would succeed "unless every nerve on our part is strained to exceed them in a naval armament."[21]

Arnold's and Schuyler's urgent pleas to Washington and to Congress came at a delicate time. Once the British had evacuated Boston in March, Washington had moved the Continental Army to New York, the obvious target for Howe's reinforced army. Philadelphia, another obvious target, also required assistance. Despite this, Washington sent off some units to strengthen the northern army, including some of the seafaring men from Connecticut regiments. And, almost as consequentially, he and Congress had decided to change the command in the north once again. At the end of June, he sent Major General Horatio Gates north to take command of the army in Canada. Gates, of modest birth, had risen in the British army to the rank of major, and was wounded serving alongside General Edward Braddock at the debacle on the Monongahela in 1755. At war's end, he settled in England where, his military career seemingly blocked, he sold his commission in 1772 and moved to Virginia. Along the way, and probably as a result of his professional disappointments, he had wrestled with alcohol and debt, and became increasingly radical, a democrat by conviction, or at least resentment. He had served Washington well in organizing the army around Boston and was a natural choice to pull together the remnants of the Canadian army.

Gates arrived at Fort Ticonderoga to find an army ill ("the camp had more the appearance of a general hospital than an army formed to oppose the invasion of a successful and enterprising enemy"), riven with colonial animosities, and, on top of it all, with a muddled command.[22] It probably helped that Sullivan soon left the army in a huff at being superseded by Gates, just in time to be captured by the British during the battles for New York. A British civilian who met Sullivan in captivity found him "remarkable neither for decency nor probity, but very much for a species of low chicane, in which the lawyers in general of this country are known to excel, and by which he himself has succeeded to his present eminence of situation."[23]

His successor, Gates, however, found himself discomfited as well. He had received orders to command the army in Canada, it being assumed that the forces in New York would remain under the command of Philip Schuyler. But when he arrived on the scene, the army had left Canada, and its remnants had been folded into Schuyler's forces. No army in Canada existed. The two men wrangled, more or less amicably, until Congress resolved the issue by putting Gates under Schuyler's orders, and although Gates seems to have winked at the stream of letters from politicians deploring Schuyler, he maintained a good working relationship with him. They began reassembling, disciplining, and organizing the army at the southern end of the Lake.

In early July, Colonel Jeduthan Baldwin, more or less recovered from the smallpox, had taken up his next task, laying out fortifications at Chimney Point, across the lake from Crown Point, the northernmost position of the retreating army. The ruined fortress lay at the tip of a peninsula running from south to north into the lake. Roughly two and a half miles long and one mile across, this finger of land is bounded on the west by Bulwagga Bay, and on the east by a narrow channel dominated by Chimney Point on what is now the Vermont side. On July 6 the new commander, Gates, appeared with Schuyler to inspect the works; Baldwin dined with the generals, and then accompanied them across the lake to Crown Point, where they convened a council of war on the next day.

The council of war that met at Crown Point on July 7 included Schuyler, Gates, Arnold, the unhappy Sullivan, and Baron Friederich von

Woedtke, one of the early foreign volunteers eager to make their fame and possibly fortune fighting for the Americans. (A twenty-six-year-old Prussian officer, Woedtke had received the rank of brigadier general, accompanied Franklin north to Canada, and was by now noted chiefly for his consistent inebriation.) The generals agreed that the army could not make a stand at Crown Point—the area was too extensive, the risk of the enemy forcing the passage or, by landing in Bulwagga Bay, cutting the army off from its line of retreat too great. Instead, the Americans would hold Crown Point only as an advanced post, and withdraw twelve miles south, to Fort Ticonderoga and the parallel mountain on the eastern side of the strait, soon to be named Mount Independence in view of that momentous event.

Baldwin, presumably accustomed by now to the vagaries of commanders changing their minds, learned that his efforts at Chimney Point were for nought. He received a new set of instructions: Lay out fortifications on Mount Independence and build a road from there that would enable the militia of New England to come to the relief of the Ticonderoga/ Mount Independence complex when the enemy attacked. Dutifully he did so, in the rain and mud, for it was a wet July, with indifferent laborers and inadequate tools. Ten days after the work had begun he returned to his quarters and discovered that someone had pried open his clothes chest, stealing his hat, cloak, jackets, breeches, and compass. Something snapped: He asked Sullivan (still his nominal superior) to be relieved, "as I am heartily tired of this retreating, ragged, starved, lousy, thievish, pockey army in this unhealthy country." [24]

———————•◆•———————

Prodigies of labour

Fortunately, Horatio Gates talked Baldwin out of the fit of temper, and by the end of July the engineer had command over the entire Mount Independence site, supervising carpenters, smiths, armorers, rope and wheel makers, sawyers, and shingle makers. The army had found a solid spot on which to rest, difficult for the enemy to outflank, or so Schuyler and Gates believed, and close to the new enterprise: the naval base at

Skenesborough where, at the end of July, Gates put Arnold in command of the shipbuilding enterprise, which had lagged badly.

The Americans knew that before too long a hostile fleet would, as they said, "pay them a visit." As Arnold had foreseen, the British, for their part, had come well prepared to build their own fleet on Lake Champlain. They faced one insuperable obstacle: the rapids of the Richelieu, which meant that they could not sail vessels from the St. Lawrence directly onto the lake. Moreover, Arnold and Baldwin had thoroughly demolished the dockyard of St. Johns, the necessary naval base; it would need to be reestablished.

But Germain's foresight, and British naval power, could counterbalance much of this deficiency. At first the British attempted to haul two schooners launched in Quebec (*Maria* and *Carleton*) overland to St. Johns. They bogged down and had to be disassembled. The British took apart the more important three-masted sloop of war *Inflexible* then on the stocks at Quebec, shipped its timbers up the St. Lawrence, and thence carried them to St. Johns, where workmen rebuilt the warship.[25] Between the fleet, the transports, and the naval dockyard at Quebec, the British possessed all the necessities for shipbuilding—the tools, cordage, pitch and oakum for caulking, and a uniform armament. Most important of all, they had an ample supply of carpenters and even a few shipwrights to build the ships, sailors to man them, and officers to command them— more than 650 prime seamen from the warships and transports lying off Quebec. But all this would take time. They would have to build a flotilla of gunboats (ten shipped in prefabricated kits from England, ten new built in Canada) and train soldiers to man them, and above all they needed to construct four hundred bateaux from scratch to carry the army south, once the St. Johns base was established. The commodore of the British fleet at Quebec would be proud of the "prodigies of labour" involved, noting with pride that *Inflexible* sailed less than a month after its keel was laid at the rebuilt St. Johns dockyard in early September. But to rebuild the dockyard, move the materials there, and construct the warships and transports ended up taking twice as long as the mere six weeks it had required to roust the invading Americans from Canada.[26]

For the moment, then, the Americans exercised a precarious command of the lake with the vessels that Arnold had captured the previous year (schooner *Liberty*, sloop *Enterprise*), the schooner *Royal Savage* captured by Montgomery at St. Johns, and the schooner *Revenge*, built at Ticonderoga. The ships were lightly armed, mainly with puny two- or four-pounder cannon and swivels, and indifferently manned with lands-men, but they would have been enough to slaughter an unescorted army of thousands of men attempting to travel the lake in crowded bateaux. To supplement this core of a fleet the Americans now built two kinds of ves-sels: gondolas (or gundelows, as they were sometimes called) and row gal-leys.

The gondolas had a single heavy gun in the bow (usually a twelve-pounder) and a lighter gun (usually a nine-pounder) on each side. Dou-ble-ended, with a single mast carrying two square sails and a jib, flat-bottomed and lacking freeboard or cover for its crew, the gondola was exposed, uncomfortable, and a miserable sailor unless the wind came directly aft. Its sweeps served as its usual means of propulsion, the forty-five-man crew attempting to push the lumbering vessel along the lake's cold, deep waters in the teeth of Champlain's northerly winds. The row galley, a type of craft building aplenty in Philadelphia for the defense of that city, had more promise. Longer (roughly seventy-two feet instead of fifty-three feet), it carried two lateen sails, better for sailing against the wind and easily handled by unskilled crews, and a heavier, but again, a mixed armament of nine guns—an eighteen-pounder in the bows, twelve-pounders in the stern, and three six-pounders on each side. The galleys were easier to handle, had more firepower, and offered better pro-tection for their somewhat larger crews.

The summer passed in feverish activity, which seemed to consist, for the Americans, of one frustration after another. One acidic observer was twenty-year-old Colonel John Trumbull, a talented Harvard-educated soldier, formerly an aide to George Washington, and a talented artist who painted some of the iconic pictures of the war of American independence. In mid-August he wrote to his father, the extremely active governor of Connecticut Jonathan Trumbull, "How we shall maintain our naval supe-riority I must confess myself much at a loss. 'Tis true we build a thing *called* a Gondola, perhaps as much as one in a week—but where is our rigging for them, where our guns?"[27] Naval carpenters were scarce, sailors even more so, since the robust privateering effort now under way in American ports offered considerably more lucrative employment. And both kinds of men were desperately needed in Philadelphia and New

York to construct and man the flotillas needed there. When the carpenters did arrive their high pay excited envy—mitigated, perhaps, by the fact that many subsequently fell ill with smallpox or the ague.

The generals were having a dismal time of it, too, but for other reasons. Schuyler, ill and worn out, suffered constant attack from New Englanders who loathed him. He wanted to resign, telling Washington that "suspicion and envy have followed me, from the moment I came to the command, I have experienced the most illiberal abuse, in many of the colonies, and even in the Army I commanded."²⁸ The New Englanders liked Gates more, but he was deeply pessimistic, declaring it "exceedingly doubtful if it will be in my power to be more than the wretched spectator of a ruined army," forlornly placing his hope in "Him who gives the Race to the Slow and the Battle to the Weak."²⁹ The best of them all, Arnold, was now being persecuted, perversely, by the court-martial he had requested for those responsible for the disaster of the Cedars. Command of the fleet he had built would at least get him away from his enemies, but to achieve that he had to overcome the exceedingly stubborn Jacobus Wynkoop, whom Gates had ordered him to replace in charge of the Lake Champlain squadron. Wynkoop was "resolved to go under command of no man," and went so far as to fire shots across the bows of ships moving under the orders of the new commander.³⁰ Exasperated beyond endurance, Gates ordered Arnold to arrest Wynkoop and send him under confinement for trial at Ticonderoga.

To top it all, a council of field-grade officers, mainly from New England, had protested the withdrawal from Crown Point to Ticonderoga, on the specious grounds that this would open the frontier to Indian and Tory raids. Copies of their letter had, intentionally, no doubt, reached Washington and Congress. Washington, ever politically sensitive, and unfamiliar with the indefensible layout of Crown Point, reprimanded Schuyler and Gates. "I must however express my sorrow at the resolution of your Council & wish, that it had never happened; as every body who speaks of it also does; & that the measure could yet be changed with propriety."³¹ Schuyler and Gates were outraged that their own officers had questioned their judgment (a further blow to discipline, as they pointedly observed to Washington), and at Washington's own advisers.

As for the opinion of Washington's officers in New York about the conduct of the northern army, Gates let loose his own broadside: "They,

Sir, having every ample supply at hand, make no allowance for the misfortunes & wants, of this Army; nor for the Delay & difficulty that Attends
the procuring every thing Necessary here."

> Had we a healthy army, four times the number of the enemy; our maga-
> zines full, our artillery complete, stores of every kind in profuse abun-
> dance, with vast & populous towns, and countries close at hand, to
> supply our wants; your Excellency would hear no complaints from this
> Army.[32]

Washington—at this point in late July 1776 contemplating a British army
occupying Staten Island and coiled to spring at Manhattan, a force that
by the time Gates's letter arrived, numbered something like thirty-two
thousand men—could be excused his anxiety. But the northern army had
some reason to feel isolated, ill-supported, and forgotten except in the
matter of reproaches. It is therefore not entirely surprising that the news
of America's declaration of independence did not even cause Jeduthan
Baldwin to discuss the matter in his journal. He did, however, mournfully
note that when one of the gondolas test-fired a mortar the "mortar split"
and barely missed killing the crew.

———•◆•———

The refuse of every regiment, and the Seamen few of them ever wet with Salt Water

Having energized the shipbuilding at Skenesborough, including pressing
the construction of the row galleys, Benedict Arnold found himself in
command of the American fleet. On August 7, 1776, Gates gave Arnold
his orders. His overriding mission would be "preventing the Enemy's
invasion of our Country. . . . It is a defensive War we are carrying on;
therefore, no wanton risqué, or unnecessary Display of the Power of the
Fleet, is at any Time to influence your Conduct."[33] But coupled with this
caution was an injunction that made such restraint difficult. "A resolute,
but judicious Defence of the Northern Entrance into this Side of the
Continent, is the momentous Part, which is committed to your Courage

and Abilities. I doubt not you will secure it from further invasion." Arnold's command required an unusual blend of prudence and audacity to follow these orders, menacing the British but not hazarding all unless it was absolutely necessary. And, sounding a note that would become familiar with Gates, the general modestly declared that "as I am entirely unacquainted with maritime Affairs, I shall not presume to give any Directions" about discipline.

Having shunted aside the previously mutinous but now abjectly contrite Wynkoop, at the end of August Arnold took the nucleus of the fleet north. He had few illusions about their chances, and in one of the few personally revealing dispatches he sent Gates he confessed that "when the Enemy drive us back to Ticonderoga, I have some thoughts of going to Congress, & begging leave to resign—do you think they will make me a Major General (*entre nous*)?"[34] The strain of campaigning and intrigue, compounded by Arnold's own formidable ambition, had revealed a crack in his character that would, in time, ruinously split it asunder. But he had every reason to feel disgruntled. A drunken young sot like Woedtke (now dead of exposure and alcohol abuse) had received a rank equal to his—for what? He had served under inferior commanders like Sullivan and Wooster, who, too blind to their own weaknesses and the enemy's abilities, or too timid to admit the realities of the position, had protracted the agonizing and inevitable withdrawal from Canada. Under him had served a string of cowards and fools—Easton, Bedel, Butterfield, and the list would only grow—who had slandered him in Philadelphia. He had been badly wounded; he had lost his wife and, very often, he found himself superseded by generals of far lesser ability. The strain of exhaustion, wounds, disappointment, loss, and thwarted ambition told on Arnold. And now, to cap it all, in early September 1776, on the verge of a major engagement with a far superior British force, he was falsely accused of the theft of public stores in Montreal by those he had himself accused. "I cannot but think it extremely cruel, when I have sacrificed my ease, health and great part of my private property in the cause of my country, to be calumniated as a robber and thief, at a time too when I have it not in my power to be heard in my own defense."[35] For a willful, passionate, domineering and supremely able man, it was almost too much to bear.

The task before him was far from simple. Gates had worded his orders cleverly: Arnold was to fight the enemy every step of the way—Congress and the fearful New England states demanded no less; but he was not to throw the fleet away for nothing. He would have to engage the enemy as far north as possible—but where and how? Since the arrival of the British army at St. Johns reliable intelligence had dwindled to a trickle. Lavishly funded Indian diplomacy conducted by William Johnson's son and nephew, John Johnson and Guy Johnson, had won the natives over. They, and the Canadians as well, would take the winning side in any conflict, and at the moment, the British looked like winners. A cloud of expert skirmishers and raiding parties surrounded St. Johns, and although a couple of brave American scouting parties got close, not all made it back. The local population, no longer in regular contact with the Americans, alienated by the rough occupation, and in any case apprehensively eager to resume good relations with the English, provided little information.

At the end of September, when Arnold's vessels were patrolling the northern end of the lake, the *Liberty*, off the Isle La Motte, spotted a Canadian who waved them in, asking to be taken off to provide information. The suspicious skipper had the sweeps out and had his crew cautiously move the ship in closer to shore, stern first, swivel guns loaded and fuses lit. The Frenchman suddenly ducked down—and several hundred regulars, Canadians, and Indians rose out of the brush along the shore and opened fire. A couple of blasts from the swivels and energetic handling of the sweeps prevented the enemy from overwhelming the American ship.[36] But Arnold concluded that individual American ships would henceforth run the risk of being swarmed by the birchbark canoes now mustering along the banks at the northern end of the lake. The fleet clustered together.

The few scouts who made it back with prisoners yielded little, but Arnold knew that the British were building furiously. "I am inclined to think, on comparing all accounts, that the enemy will soon have a considerable naval force."[37] Even if his forces could match the enemy in weight of metal and number of fighting ships (which he doubted), in all other respects he knew himself to be inferior. His fleet was understrength (he had roughly five hundred men, and estimated that he needed at least a hundred more) and most of those not up to the task. "We have but very indifferent men, in general," he wrote Gates, and most of those who were nominally seamen "know very little of the matter."[38] The soldiers designated as marines were "the refuse of every regiment, and the Seamen few of them ever wet with Salt Water."[39] Many of them had only their ragged summer uniforms: He pleaded with Gates for at least one coat or blanket per man.

Even in the summer, a cool breeze often blows across the lake. No September (and most definitely, no mid-October) pleasure boater on Lake Champlain would go out for a day trip without a windbreaker and a sweater. A modern reader might well reflect on what it would be like for a man to row and sail for weeks on end on the lake during these months, without anything other than worn shirt and pants, eating rancid salt pork and perhaps some hard biscuit. Consider further that the men doing this had, in some cases, already endured smallpox, or severe colds (the ague, in eighteenth-century parlance), and "the camp disorder" (dysentery). They either knew of or had seen firsthand the collapse of the American enterprise in Canada, and had but a dim opinion of their leaders there. They knew as well that assembling opposite them was an army composed of some of the finest infantry in Europe, and a fleet manned by the finest sailors, veterans of the Royal Navy. The shores of the lake teemed with Indians, tales of whose terror had haunted their youth. Arnold's men knew at this point that they were not particularly fine soldiers. As they wrestled with unfamiliar ropes and blistered their hands manning sweeps on their crudely built, inadequately kitted-out ships, they most certainly knew that they were barely competent sailors.

Arnold had to lead such men, and find a way to enable them to delay the flotilla building at St. Johns. He continued to plead for more supplies: "Rum as much as you please; Clothing, for at least half the men in the fleet who are naked; One hundred seamen (no land lubbers)" but with little hope.[40] He had not enough powder to train his men with live fire: Instead they ran the guns in and out, going through the motions of the loading, aiming, firing, clearing, and reloading. The fleet had enough ammunition for one fight, and then, perhaps, a desperate retreat.

Arnold did not know yet that the British fleet would outclass him quite as much as it did, though not for lack of trying, having sent out both scouts and Canadian spies, and he knew that at the very least it would be a naval force equal to his own in terms of weight of metal (a key measure of naval potential). He knew that in a fight on the open water the training and quality of crews would tell in favor of the British. His orders required that he defend north as far as possible, for as long as possible—but he also knew that to linger beyond a certain point was to risk the loss of his wretchedly clad and fed crews to exposure. Three or more weeks on the open water would be impossible. He knew that his task was to delay, and that beyond a certain point—mid-October, as he told Gates on the seventh of that month—the British were unlikely to attack. The rapidly deteriorating autumn weather would not only make the navigation of the lake difficult for British bateaux. Even if they succeeded in destroying the American fleet, they would face the daunting prospect of a siege or assault of the Ticonderoga/Mount Independence position as a North Country winter came howling in. The challenge was to find a place to position the fleet that would meet his multiple requirements. By mid-September, Arnold had picked a position to hold, and on the twenty-third he arrived there: Valcour Island.

⎯⎯⎯ ◆ ⎯⎯⎯

A strife of pigmies for the prize of a continent

The northern, and broadest part of Lake Champlain is divided in two by a peninsula and a chain of islands. The western half opens onto the Richelieu River, and thus formed the natural corridor for the British fleet. Opposite the very southern end of the largest of the islands, Grand Isle, just off the western shore lies Valcour, an oddly shaped, roughly oval island two miles from north to south and less than a mile wide, separated by less than two-thirds of a mile from the New York mainland.

Arnold anchored his fleet here, just south of a small peninsula on the island, Bluff Point. It was a position with numerous advantages. A fleet sailing southward up the lake would not detect the American fleet until it was well past Valcour, unless it sent scouts all the way around the island. The small peninsula and the angle of the island itself would have screened the American fleet from view until a scouting vessel had sailed more than halfway down the channel between the island and the mainland. And the northern end of that channel would be hazardous for large ships, being blocked by a shoal squarely in the middle of the channel.

The prevailing winds, Arnold knew, came from the north. To attack him, therefore, an enemy would have to beat back against the wind, entering the confined space between Valcour and the western shore. His vessels, anchored in a concave arc, could concentrate their fire as the enemy attempted to come to grips. It was a brilliantly chosen position to maximize his men's chances against a more numerous and technically superior foe. To camouflage his ships and shield his men against snipers (and perhaps to give them some cover from the wind), he had them lash saplings to the bulwarks of the boats. In this posture, awaiting either a British attack or a date so late that he could safely retreat down to Buttonmould Bay on the eastern shore of Champlain about thirteen miles north of Crown Point, he held.

Arnold might, of course, have chosen to withdraw, or (as his second in command, David Waterbury, preferred) conduct a fighting retreat down the lake. But the former would have violated his orders from Gates and the intention behind them. And the latter would expose the force to combat on the open water, where the British advantages would tell far more clearly. Perhaps most important, at this point it was simply psychologically impossible for the American high command to have built a fleet and not used it against the enemy. After a spring and summer of continual defeat and retreat, and aware now as well of the debacle on Long Island, the Americans had to put up a fight. And although as we have seen, Arnold knew when a fight was pointless, he was hardly the man to avoid combat.

The situation was worse than he knew. The British fleet that sailed from St. Johns could hurl twice the weight of metal that Arnold's fleet could. Leading it was *Inflexible,* a ship-rigged sloop of war mounting eighteen twelve-pounders, supported by schooners *Maria* and *Carleton* with fourteen and twelve six-pounders each, a captured gondola with seven nine-pounders, the ungainly radeau *Thunderer* (a kind of floating battery) with six twenty-four-pounders, six twelve-pounders, and two howitzers, supported by some twenty gunboats with one heavy gun each, and several dozen long boats. The heart of the fleet were the ship and the two schooners, each of which could maneuver effectively, but the British had also trained artillerymen to handle the gunboats competently.[41] Arnold had three row galleys (*Congress,* under his command, *Washington,* under Waterbury, now his subordinate, and *Trumbull*), eight gondolas, the schooners *Royal Savage* and *Revenge,* sloop *Enterprise,* and cutter *Lee.* By the standards of the time, the opposing fleets were negligible collections of miscellaneous ships, manned by some five hundred Americans, and a rather larger number of British sailors backed by the advance elements of the army of invasion. What lay before them, however, was what America's great naval theorist Alfred Thayer Mahan later described as "a strife of pigmies for the prize of a continent."[42]

With the main vessels of the fleet complete, the British finally left St. Johns on October 5, cautiously looking for the Americans. On the eleventh of October, as Arnold had expected, the British sailed past Valcour Island, detecting the Americans too late. Arnold sallied with the three row galleys and the *Royal Savage* to lure the British into the fire sack of his battle line. They came willingly enough. The galleys, with their lateen sails and sweeps, made it easily back into the line, but the *Royal Savage*, damaged by British shot, lacking oars and, perhaps, a competent crew, ran hard aground on a barely noticeable rock at the very tip of Valcour Island. The British eventually seized *Royal Savage*, despite the concentrated fire of the American fleet, boarded her, and held her against the fire of the American fleet until, finally, they set her afire and withdrew.

Meanwhile, schooner *Carleton* sailed into the teeth of the American fleet. Her skipper and his first mate went down, and the loss of a cable attached to her anchor—a spring in naval parlance—which held her in position, nearly lost the ship. At the last moment a midshipman by the name of Edward Pellew—later one of the most famous naval officers of the Napoleonic Wars—dashed out on the bowsprit and manhandled her jib so that she could turn and escape the American guns. The British gunboats kept up a steady drumfire of grapeshot against the Americans anchored with their broadsides to the enemy. Pointing bow first they made small targets, and their professional crews served their weapons well.

The loss of *Royal Savage* was a hard blow—it was the handiest of the American ships, and, moreover, contained Arnold's personal papers, all of which were lost. Other ships were badly battered, and gondola *Philadelphia* sank. In the hammering that went on that day the superior gunnery of the British told. Arnold's flagship, *Congress*, on which he had had to point most of the guns himself, took seven shots between wind and water. Other ships took a similar pounding. The British, on the other hand, lost only one gunboat, although a Hessian captain soberly reported later that the rebel fire had done more damage than they had realized: "Our ships were pretty well mended and patched up with boards and stoppers."[43] *Carleton* was out of the fight, but the other British ships, and most notably the *Inflexible*, which finally managed to deliver broadside after broadside of her well-aimed twelve-pounders, were perfectly fit to fight. More to the point, however, having fired off three-quarters of their ammunition, the Americans were in no position to continue the battle with any hope of success.

That evening, a somber council of war agreed that to continue the battle on the morrow would merely court disaster. Taking advantage of a heavy fog the next morning, the American fleet cut its cables and silently slipped past the British fleet, hugging the western shore as it did so. Carleton, furious at the sight of the empty Valcour bay the next morning, was further frustrated by a perverse wind that blew up from the south, delaying the pursuit. But on October 13 it shifted back into the north, and the reckoning now came for Arnold's fleet. On that day Carleton pursued and took two of the American ships, including row galley *Washington*, commanded by Arnold's deputy, General Waterbury. Carleton treated Waterbury with punctilious courtesy. On discovering that Waterbury had received his commission from the governor of Connecticut he held out his hand and said,

> General Waterbury, I am happy to take you by the hand, now that I see that you are not serving under a commission and orders of the rebel Congress, but of Governor Trumbull. You are acting under a legitimate and acknowledged authority. He is responsible for the abuse he has made of that authority. That which is a high crime in him, is but an error in you; it was your duty to obey him, your legitimate superior.[44]

Carleton was being shrewd as well as generous in giving Waterbury and his men their paroles, allowing them to go home after promising not to engage in fighting until properly exchanged. Colonel John Trumbull, son of the same Governor Trumbull who had commissioned the unfortunate Waterbury, greeted the paroled prisoners when they reached Ticonderoga. Then, realizing just how dangerous to the rebel cause British kindness could be, he promptly ordered the boats containing them prisoners moored under a battery at the fort, the prisoners not allowed to land, and suggested to Gates (who concurred) that the men should be hustled off to Skenesborough, where they could not infect the anxious garrison of Ticonderoga with tales of British humanity.

Arnold's fleet now scattered. The Americans had scuttled gondola *Providence* at their first stop at Schuyler Island, eight miles south of Valcour, following the escape from there; *New Jersey*, which had taken water, ran aground, and its crew abandoned the cutter *Lee* on the New York shore. Several of the ships made it to Crown Point: galley *Trumbull*, sloop *Enterprise* (Arnold's designated hospital ship), schooner *Revenge*, and gondola *New York*. That left Arnold with *Congress* and the four remaining gondolas. He made for a small bay some ten miles north of Crown Point and just south of Buttonmould Bay, on the eastern shore, figuring, correctly, that he could beat off an enemy who would have to attack him into the wind. Arnold handled his ship, which had borne the brunt of the rearguard action, brilliantly, fighting off three of the enemy. He beached his ships and—last man off, as usual—saw them burned to the waterline before leading his men on an arduous trek to Crown Point, narrowly missing an Indian ambush along the way. Upon arriving there, he quickly persuaded the commander at Crown Point, Colonel Thomas Hartley, to burn the buildings and withdraw to Ticonderoga with him. The next day, the British arrived, and although the Americans summoned the militia and braced themselves for an attack, it never came. Carleton, mindful of the change of seasons, and having with him only the advance brigade of his army (the rest of which, still sheltering at St. Johns, waited for the word to advance), wisely withdrew. The ferocious resistance put up by Arnold had made a decided impression, and the fortifications before Carleton teemed with eight thousand Americans, largely recovered from smallpox and apparently in a mood to fight.

If the British had finished with the weary Americans, however, their own side had not. With exquisite ill-timing, Congress had dispatched a commission to investigate the accounts of the northern army. Prudently, however, they decided not to visit a prospective battlefield during any unpleasantness: "Being informed by the General [Gates] of the great probability of our army being now attacked by the enemy, or that such an event might be hourly expected, we have concluded to wait here [Saratoga] until we shall have the pleasure of hearing from you."[45]

———◆·◆———

The most brilliant soldier of the Continental Army

Arnold, as ever, attracted more than his share of criticism after Valcour. Some charges were simply preposterous, including that he had left the wounded to die in the burning wrecks of *Congress* and the four gondolas.[46] In fact, he threatened to run through with his sword a gunner who abandoned a wounded officer—when *Congress* blew up, however, a corpse seems to have gone with it.[47] Less scurrilous, but no less damaging tactical criticism came, as it often does, from gentlemen the strength of whose opinion was in direct proportion to their distance from the fight. Richard Henry Lee, who had proposed independence to the Continental Congress in June, wrote to Thomas Jefferson on November 3:

> By every account from Lake Champlain we had reason to think ourselves in no danger on that water for this Campaign. Nor did Gen. Arnold seem to apprehend any until he was defeated by an enemy four times as strong as himself. This officer, fiery, hot, and impetuous, but without discretion, never thought of informing himself how the enemy went on, and he had no idea of retiring, when he saw them coming, though so much superior to his force.[48]

Gates did not share this view. Writing to Governor Trumbull of Connecticut on the twenty-second of October he declared, "It would have been happy for the United States had the gallant behaviour and steady good conduct of that excellent officer [Arnold] been supported by a fleet in any degree equal to the enemy's. As the case stands, though they boast a victory, they must respect the vanquished."[49] Gates, Schuyler, and Washington all approved Arnold's conduct of the fight, understanding as they did the odds against him. And of subsequent historians the most interesting judgment came from Alfred Thayer Mahan, the intellectual godfather of American sea power, who wrote over a century later. Mahan praised Arnold's conduct of the Valcour battle extravagantly. He pointed out that without the American fleet and the time it had bought, Ticonderoga would have fallen in September to the British, and then the effects would have been calamitous. In mid-September, after all, the British completed their occupation of New York City. The news of two such losses would have been devastating to patriot morale, and would almost surely have set the British up to complete the strategy of pincer movements meeting at Albany early in the next year.[50]

The building of the fleet forced an invaluable delay on the British invasion from Canada. Arnold could not have avoided contesting the British effort: His orders and the mood of the country (and above all Congress) demanded it. At the end of the day, the losses were slight by comparison with the far larger number of killed, wounded, and captured lost in fighting on Long Island and in the vicinity of New York City during the summer of 1776. Arnold lost 80 killed and wounded, plus some 110 captured and paroled; the British had 30 or 40 casualties and lost three small boats. By way of contrast the Battle of Brooklyn Heights on August 27 had cost the Americans at least 300 killed and 1,000 captured, plus many hundreds more wounded. More to the point, given superior British resources in ships, men, and naval stores, there was little hope of sustaining command of the lake without a fight. Quite apart from the opprobrium that would have attached to a mere withdrawal to Ticonderoga, what would the fleet have done there in the next season against so thoroughly superior a British force? As Mahan noted, it would have been "valueless, if buried in port." Geography alone would have bottled it up behind the fortifications of Ticonderoga and Mount Independence. As it was, the Americans had preserved the nucleus of a naval force that could do some small good in the confined waters around what must be the main line of resistance against a British attack, Fort Ticonderoga. Arnold's fleet had given the American cause the most valuable gift of all—time. He had denied the British what would have been a shocking bookend to their victories in the vicinity of New York, and he had set an example of remarkable courage, determination, and skill that exercised a usefully restraining effect on British generalship thereafter.

Benedict Arnold is the most disturbing figure in American military history, perhaps because he is one of its most extraordinary. From the moment that he appeared on the stage of the American war for independence, he dominated many of its early points of decision—seeing the opportunity at Ticonderoga, seizing the nucleus of a fleet on Champlain, successfully raiding the main British base at St. Johns, leading his men on a desperate wilderness march to Quebec, nearly taking the city, maintaining a siege there against all odds, making as much order out of the debacle that was the retreat from Canada as possible, building a fleet from nothing, and then fighting it with cunning as well as courage. In April 1777, at home on leave following these escapades, he repulsed a British raid on his native Connecticut, before returning to deflect a British invasion of the Mohawk valley by ruse and strategem, and then, having broken with Gates, leading the northern army to its two victories that culminated in the surrender of Burgoyne's army at Saratoga in October 1777.

The combination of Arnold's skills is staggering: He led on land and on the water, in siege and in the field, he had the talents to build a fleet and then fight it to the death. His men followed him willingly, indeed, eagerly: It was an impulsive gesture that led them to follow him, though he was technically no longer in command, in the final charge in which he took his second wound at the Battle of Saratoga in September 1777. His dispatches reveal no vainglory, but rather a combination of sobriety in judging his circumstances (think of his pleas with Sullivan to accelerate the inevitable withdrawal to Isle aux Noix and beyond), realism in assessing his prospects, and determination to do the best he could. In the years 1775–77 he fought his corner on offense as well as defense, and throughout sacrificed health, fortune, and family for a cause in which he believed.

Which is what made his ultimate treason so stunning, so appalling. When Washington arrived at West Point on September 24, 1780, and learned of Arnold's treason, he sank into a silent funk, emerging from it only to say, "Arnold has betrayed me. Whom can we trust now?" [51] Arnold's turn began sometime in 1779, when he was serving as military governor of Philadelphia after prolonged convalescence. It was a role for which he was miscast and where his instincts to protect former Tories from abuse came into conflict with those of the bare-knuckled patriots of the town. His second wife, Peggy Shippen, daughter of loyalists, almost certainly had something to do with it. He undoubtedly felt some measure of disgust at the conniving, profiteering, and low politics that drained him of the idealism that took him to war in the first place, even as he probably resorted to some corrupt practices to recover his own diminished fortune.

It had something to do with the morbid effects on a proud, prickly, passionate man of utter exhaustion and two debilitating wounds in the same leg, the second of which laid him up for six brooding months and left him crippled for life. It undoubtedly had something to do with the eighteenth-century culture of honor: He had been abused, traduced, and mistreated by colleagues, subordinates, and Congress. He successfully defended himself in a court-martial, in January 1780, but even then his own mentor, Washington, did not back him up when the politicians of Philadelphia came after him; Arnold did not forgive that. In August 1780 he angled for, and received, command of the vital fortifications at West Point, turning down the second-in-command position that Washington had urged upon him. He did so in order to betray it.

Given all that he suffered and endured, in leading his men, in fighting the enemy, and above all from his own side, given his exposure to hardball politics, incessant accusations of misconduct partly justified and mostly not, given his dismay at the protracted failures of Congress and democratic politicians, it should not be entirely surprising that Arnold's character snapped under the strain. No matter: His name will forever be a byword for the blackest treason.

But therein lay a problem. It became particularly acute in 1877 at the centennial of the American Revolution, as a triumphant country, not long past the deadliest threat to its existence since the Revolution, celebrated a century of independence. The small town of Schuylerville, home to the site where Burgoyne surrendered his army on October 17, 1777, took part with its own elaborate ceremony exactly one hundred years later, complete with orotund oratory, and, of course, a grand parade of veterans of the Civil War. Generals from that conflict were in abundance, as were the lingering descendants of some of the revolutionary veterans.

The ceremony focused on the laying of the foundation of a monument on the site where John Burgoyne surrendered his army to the soldiers and militiamen of Horatio Gates. The grandmaster of the Masons of the state of New York supervised the laying of the cornerstone, intoning the Masons' ritual questions and answers: "What is the jewel of your office?" "The level." "What does it teach?" "The equality of all men."[52] It took five years to complete the 155-foot-high obelisk, which had four gables for life-sized statues. Facing north stood Horatio Gates, who commanded at Saratoga; two other niches were occupied by Philip Schuyler and Daniel

Morgan, commander of the indispensable riflemen who won the first Battle of Saratoga. By design, facing south toward the battlefield stood, and still stands, an empty niche.

It was not the only such intentionally ambivalent memorial to Arnold. In the old cadet chapel at West Point, a tablet bore only his rank and his birth date; on the battlefield at Saratoga a few years after the Saratoga centennial John Watts De Peyster, former adjutant general of the New York militia, prolific historian, and wealthy citizen, put up a memorial that featured, on the one side, an inscription referring to the "most brilliant soldier of the Continental Army" without naming him, and on the other, only a wounded leg.

On that beautiful autumn day in 1877, one of the speakers, a politician by the name of Throckmorton, devoted an entire address to Arnold. Recounting in approving detail the English officers who cut Arnold dead after the Revolution, and expounding on the traitor's "blackened soul," the politician concluded:

> The niche can never really be vacant—empty to the sight—Benedict Arnold will fill it. There he will stand, pilloried before the gaze of centuries, ten thousand times more than if a figure of bronze met the eye with the word "traitor" stamped upon it. The designers of the monument leave that vacant niche from no fondness in contemplating the dark crime of the traitor, but because of the lesson it must forever teach.[53]

All well enough, no doubt, but one wonders how many of those present contemplated memories of treachery considerably more fresh. After all, many if not most of the grown men in the audience, enjoying the bands, the bunting, and the ceremony, if not the speeches, had borne arms in a far more recent and far bloodier struggle to maintain the Union that the revolutionary generation had created.

Horatio Seymour gave the keynote address before Throckmorton spoke. Seymour, a Democrat, had twice served as governor of New York, including during the Civil War, later running against Ulysses S. Grant for president and losing. He had reluctantly supported the war, but, as governor in 1863–64, he had opposed conscription, opposed giving soldiers the vote, and had attempted to conciliate the rioters following the bloody antidraft (and viciously anti-Negro) mayhem in New York City in 1863.

Seymour (who, of course, denounced Arnold) declared that the monument would not "foster sectional prejudices; every citizen of every state of this union will feel as he looks on it that he has a right to stand on this ground."[54] Like many politicians of his day, Seymour hoped to use the centennial of the Revolution to help reconcile North and South.

Arnold made, and makes, a convenient monster of treachery, because some other examples have always been too close, too painful, too disruptive to contemplate. Yet other military leaders of his caliber, who had contributed nothing—as he most certainly had—to the creation of the United States, did infinitely more to bring it to the edge of destruction. Following his treason Arnold conducted several short, tactically successful but strategically inconsequential raids in Connecticut and Virginia; his example rattled the American leadership, but had no impact on the war itself. By way of contrast, the deeds of Robert E. Lee, Stonewall Jackson, and many other Confederates brought the Union within a hairsbreadth of dissolution. When Arnold, a mere civilian, took up arms, he had no country to which he had sworn allegiance: the soldiers of the United States Army who doffed blue for gray uniforms most definitely had.

Arnold's treason stands out as a uniquely horrible deed, and he as an embodiment of treachery, only if one can force oneself to view the Civil War as something other than mere rebellion. If invested with enough horror, one can make his deed so utterly incomprehensible and irredeemable as to be beyond contemplation, debate, or mere reflection. The demonization of Arnold served a rhetorical purpose in a new United States struggling to establish its identity, and perhaps in a post–Civil War United States struggling to recover its unity.[55] But the price of Throckmortoning Arnold, as it were, is unwarrantably and unjustly to forget, or exculpate, the circumstances and individuals that drove him to betray his country, and to reduce a tragic figure to a mere caricature. Arnold long made a thoroughly useful and workable villain, but by using him as such, Americans avoided reflections that would be troubling, painful, and valuable in coming to terms with our past.

CHAPTER SEVEN

Hubbardton, 1777

─────◆◆◆─────

The most speedy junction of the two armies

─────◆◆◆─────

The first invasion of the United States from Canada had ended in October 1776 with the destruction of most of the American fleet following the Battle of Valcour Island, and the decision by Major General (and governor) Guy Carleton to withdraw his army to Canada, the season being too late for further campaigning. But Britain's fundamental strategic decision to cut the colonies in two by a thrust from Canada along Lake Champlain and the Hudson River corridor still stood. Indeed, from a remove of several thousand miles, Lord George Germain, architect of the American war, could not understand why Carleton had failed to advance that course of action by at least permanently occupying the southern end of Lake Champlain. On January 14, 1777, he wrote to General William Howe, commanding in New York, that "it was a great mortification to me to be informed that the army from Canada had thought it right to leave Crown Point unoccupied and repass the lake."[1] He made it clear to the senior general that he expected a different outcome in this next campaign.

Germain believed that Carleton had been dilatory. Ungraciously, he let

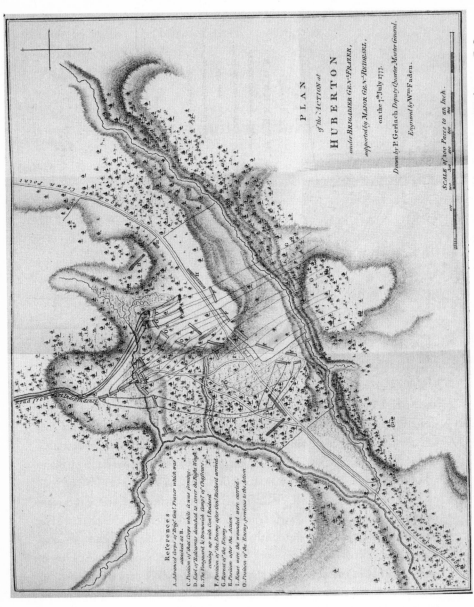

PLAN
of the ACTION at
HUBERTON
under BRIGADIER GENL FRAZER,
supported by MAJOR GENL REIDESEL,
on the 7th July 1777.

Drawn by P. Gerlach Deputy Quarter Master General.

Engraved by Wm Faden.

SCALE of 200 Paces to an Inch.

References

A. Advanced Corps of Brigt Genl Frazer which was
    attacked at B.
C. Position of that Corps while it was joining.
D. Earl of Balcarras detached to cover the Right Wing.
E. The Vanguard & Brunswick Corps of Chasseurs
    coming up with Genl Reidesel
F. Position of the Enemy after Genl Reidesel arrived.
G. Retreat of the Enemy.
H. Position after the Action.
I. Mount were the wounded were carried.
O. Position of the Enemy, previous to the Action.

A British map of the battle of Hubbardton. Reproduced by permission of the Society of the Cincinnati, Washington, D.C.

the touchy governor of Canada know as much, tartly suggesting that as a result of Carleton's terminating the campaign in early November "a very considerable number of the insurgents, finding their presence no longer necessary near Ticonderoga, immediately marched from thence and joined the rebel forces in the provinces of New York and Jersey." To make matters worse, Germain (incorrectly) opined, this reinforcement enabled Washington to launch the desperate counterattacks at Trenton and Princeton that broke the momentum of Howe's triumphant occupation of New Jersey during the fall of 1776.[2] For his part, Carleton seethed at this tactless and false accusation, and wrote long letters to Germain pointing out the quite remarkable accomplishments of 1776—the relief of Quebec, the expulsion of the Americans from Canada, the construction of a British fleet on Champlain, and the destruction of the American one there—and the impossibility of supplying an advanced base at Crown Point through a North American winter. He declared, in later letters, that Germain was animated by personal enmity toward him, and asked to be relieved of his command.[3]

In a prolonged exchange of mails—two months passed between the dispatch of one reproachful letter and its receipt by its freshly infuriated recipient—the two men bickered about what had been, and what might have been, accomplished the previous year. Germain had, in the meanwhile, decided to change not strategy so much as commanders in Canada. During the fall of 1776, Lieutenant General John Burgoyne had been supposed to command the British forces invading America from Canada, but had arrived too late to do so, and had chafed in the rear while Carleton conducted the campaign that destroyed the American fleet and brought the British to Ticonderoga. Now, however, Burgoyne sailed for America earlier in the year, leaving in March and arriving in May, with orders to take command of all British forces in the northern theater outside Canada.

Burgoyne had spent the winter in London, where he had written an extensive memorandum, "Thoughts for Conducting the War from the Side of Canada," which he submitted to Germain at the end of February.[4] Burgoyne may not have spent the winter intriguing against Carleton (who, in his dour and responsible way, spent the bleak months of December through April at his post of duty, in Canada). Clearly, however, he desired the command of the invading army in 1777, and was not beyond casually disparaging the previous campaign in order to get it.

Burgoyne was a gambler, a bon vivant, and a lighthearted playwright. But he was not the near incompetent often depicted, and although he expected to be able to defeat the Americans, driving on his own to Albany before joining up with, or at least supporting, Howe's operations from New York, he laid his plans carefully. He thought Ticonderoga capable of containing an American garrison of up to twelve thousand men. In his memorandum to Germain he soberly anticipated that the enemy "will take measures to block up the road from Ticonderoga to Albany by way of Skenesborough." Burgoyne anticipated a difficult campaign, but thought the effort manageable if the army had at its disposal eight thousand regulars, artillery, a corps of watermen, two thousand Canadians, and a thousand Indians. He did not require a supporting thrust up the Hudson by Howe in New York in order to break through the rebel armies, believing that he could get to Albany (an area rife with loyalists, he thought) on his own. But he did expect that the two armies would then operate jointly. For his part, Germain wrote to Carleton that "it is become highly necessary that the most speedy junction of the two armies should be effected," and that therefore he should provide Burgoyne all possible support, including arranging a diversionary operation along the Mohawk River by Colonel Barry St. Leger, with some seven hundred British, German, and loyalist troops, as well as a large force of Indians.[5] St. Leger, another veteran of the previous war, was reputed a capable backwoods leader.

British strategy for 1777 became a muddle, however, partly because of the difficulty of coordinating from London generals operating at opposite corners of the North American continent, and partly because of the willfulness of General William Howe. In New York, at the end of November 1776, Howe had originally proposed twin ten-thousand-man thrusts up the Hudson and at Boston from Rhode Island, while eight thousand soldiers chased Washington in New Jersey and an additional seven thousand garrisoned Rhode Island and New York. If these ventures succeeded, Howe believed, he could then swing the full force of his army against the American capital, Philadelphia. Before Germain could even respond to this plan, however, Howe changed his mind in favor of an earlier attack on Philadelphia, with only a minor effort up the Hudson. Still, at the end of the day, all of the British generals believed that Burgoyne could reach Albany on his own, without support from Howe. All believed as well—as did the American northern commander, Major

General Philip Schuyler—that he would find a sympathetic and support-ive populace when he arrived.

When Burgoyne arrived back in Canada in May 1777, Carleton swal-lowed his anger at being superseded in command of the field army and gave the younger man his full, if grudging, support. But Burgoyne had already begun to discover the difficulties his campaign would encounter. He did not get the number of troops he had requested, for one thing—but then, generals rarely do. Still, with a force of some 7,000 British and German troops as of July 1—3,700 British, 3,000 Germans, plus several hundred artillerymen—he had not done too badly.[6] The Canadians were a very dif-ferent matter. He had fewer than two hundred rather than the two thou-sand he had hoped for—and those were "awkward, ignorant, disinclined to the service, and spiritless."[7] Carleton sourly informed him that if the gov-ernment in London had expected much more, "it surely was not upon information proceeding from me." The governor blamed the indulgent gov-ernment the Canadians had experienced since 1760, and offered a grum-bling tribute to American subversion:"The American spirit of licentiousness and independence" had infected the *habitants*.[8] Burgoyne glumly agreed.

The lack of Canadian troops, and of large numbers of loyalists, augured worse for the campaign than Burgoyne realized. During the Seven Years' War, the British had used provincial troops to guard supply lines and perform the arduous construction activities—road and barrack building—upon which the army depended. They would need this service again. Moreover, the British remembered the Canadians' former skill in light infantry warfare, although they believed that the Indians, coupled with the excellent light infantry of the British and the Germans (includ-ing the riflemen of the *jäger* troops), could cope with the Americans in the woods. But the lack of competent second-rate troops chiefly meant that once Burgoyne's army took Crown Point and Ticonderoga he would have to waste invaluable regular troops constructing and maintaining his com-munications, losing strength and time to do so. In fact, the logistical chal-lenge was even worse than this. The new commissary general of Canada had warned that the army would need some four hundred horses for the artillery alone, and five hundred two-horse carts to supply the army on its march from the southern end of Lake Champlain to Albany. It never received half that many.[9]

If Burgoyne was disappointed in his Canadian and American allies, he found the Indians considerably more enthusiastic. But as he discovered, it was no small matter to have the advantage of their skill in woodland warfare without paying a corresponding set of penalties. Burgoyne had ambitious notions: He would use the Indians to intimidate the rebels without alienating the loyal population. His chief counselor in these matters was none other than La Corne St. Luc, veteran of decades of raids on the New England frontier, leader of the Indians at Fort William Henry in 1757, briefly friend of the Americans during their invasion of Canada in 1775, but now (for the moment, at any rate) firmly on the British side.

La Corne's views on the Americans had hardened after Montgomery's successor in command in Canada, General David Wooster, mistrusting the sixty-six-year-old Canadian (who had approached both sides in 1775), had shipped him off to Pennsylvania in 1776. There being no convincing evidence against La Corne, however, he had been released, after which, in April 1777, he had sought out the last royal governor of New York, William Tryon, and given him some characteristic advice. Turn the Indians loose against the "miserable rebels," he recommended. "Il faut brutalizer les affaires" ("we must brutalize the business"), he told the somewhat less bloodthirsty loyalist, who nonetheless passed the comments along to British authorities.[10] Burgoyne gladly asked La Corne (whom he described to Germain as "a Canadian gentleman of honor and parts") to manage the Indians.[11] The British general did reflect that the challenge would be to "keep up [the Indians'] terror and avoid their cruelty." La Corne probably kept to himself his assessment of the absurdity of that notion.[12]

Despite all of his difficulties, Burgoyne, ably supported by Carleton, mobilized his forces and from the seventeenth through the twentieth of June 1777 assembled his army at Cumberland Point, some five miles north of Valcour Island, and launched the second British invasion from Canada of the now independent United States of America.

———— ·•◆•· ————

This post has been too much neglected

However irksome the challenges for Burgoyne's army may have looked, they were mere inconveniences compared with the predicament of the

Americans at Ticonderoga and Crown Point. Very shortly after the with-drawal of Carleton's fleet in November 1776, much of the army had left Ticonderoga and Mount Independence for Albany and points south, accompanied by Horatio Gates and Benedict Arnold. Colonel Jeduthan Baldwin, the self-taught engineer who had constructed much of the fortifi-cations, took leave as well, departing on December 4 for a short visit home, to Brookfield, Massachusetts, which he reached two months later after dutifully checking in with headquarters in Cambridge, Massachusetts. After a week at home, the same sense of duty had him trudging back to Ticonderoga, arriving there on February 24, 1777, in a driving snowstorm.

That winter of 1776–77 at Ticonderoga was grim—as grim in its own way as the far more famous encampment at Valley Forge. The small gar-rison was under the competent command of Colonel Anthony Wayne, a short, fiery thirty-two-year-old who had served in the provincial assem-bly of Pennsylvania, but soon abandoned politics for his natural voca-tion—war. The troops consisted of a handful of regiments from New England and the middle colonies who loathed one another, a problem compounded by the sheer hardship of the winter. Over the years the gar-risons of Ticonderoga had stripped the immediate area around it of fire-wood, and it was a matter of "unexpressible concern" to the commander simply to get enough fuel to stave off the bitter North Country cold.[13] Morale had been none too high even as the British had approached dur-ing the previous campaign, a disconsolate General Gates telling his sullen garrison that "the General is very unhappy to see the want of that spirit, alertness, and industry so necessary for the immediate completion of the forts, and redoubt, prevail so shamefully in this army. The fleet have played a noble part, let it not be said hereafter, that the cause of all Amer-ica was injured by the supineness of the Northern Army."[14]

Supine or not, however, the northern army's numbers shrank swiftly once the British had withdrawn to Canada in November 1776. By the end of the month Colonel Wayne, commanding one regiment each from Con-necticut, Massachusetts, and New Jersey, plus three from his native Penn-sylvania, had some 2,450 rank and file on his books—of whom fewer than half, 1,100 in all, were fit for duty, with nearly as many sick and the rest on furlough or detachment.[15] Colonial antipathies made a miserable set of circumstances worse. When Wayne ordered the Third New Jersey from its barracks at Ticonderoga to the exposed hillside of Mount Independence, the troops suspected Pennsylvania prejudice against their state. And when the son of the colonel of the Sixth Massachusetts began mending the broken shoes of soldiers in his father's regiment, the Pennsylvania officers expressed their disgust at this undignified democratical spirit by sneers, followed, after a drinking bout, by smashing his workbench to pieces. A riot ensued in which some thirty or forty shots were exchanged between the soldiers involved.[16] Small wonder that in February 1777 Wayne was at his wit's end, writing to his commander, Philip Schuyler:

> I have not been able to prevail on the Eastern [New England] troops to stay one hour longer than the expiration of their time . . . I should esteem it as a particular favor if you could get me relieved—my health being much impaired. I have been necessitated to act as quartermaster, camp engineer, and commandant—and worried with wretches applying for discharges or furloughs—*as you used to be* until I am a mere skeleton. I am next to inform you that this post has been too much neglected— and I fear notwithstanding all the expense and trouble we have had last summer and this winter to render it tenable—it is left an easy prey to the enemy for want of proper supplies to maintain an Army in the spring . . . [17]

Schuyler could offer his subordinate little more than sympathy. The commander of the northern army expected a second British invasion to come in the summer—indeed, he had worried about large-scale raids during the winter of 1777 as well. The overall commander of American forces, George Washington, took a decidedly more sanguine view, however. He had few Continental troops to send north, so he urged the New England states, and Massachusetts and New Hampshire above all, to reinforce Ticonderoga, arguing, with some justice, that to send troops from other colonies would be to expose the garrison to "the prejudices and jealousies [that] have prevailed where those of different states have acted together."[18] As late as mid-June, just as Burgoyne had massed his flotilla, Washington told Schuyler that he remained convinced

> that if General Howe had not a certainty of a full reinforcement from England, part of the troops from Canada would be ordered around for that purpose. That the European reinforcement will be short or very late is beyond a doubt, and therefore the move from Canada more probable.[19]

Washington had his own problems. He had hung on during the winter of 1776–77 in New Jersey with barely twenty-five hundred men, the nub of an army, and by spring was feverishly gathering forces to counter Howe's next move. He believed that a substantial American force at Peekskill, some forty miles north of New York on the Hudson, but one hundred miles south of Albany, could block an attack from New York City up the Hudson, or reinforce Ticonderoga if it came to that. And he feared a thrust by Howe at Philadelphia. As he had told Schuyler earlier that spring, "The disaffection of Pennsylvania, which I fear is much beyond anything you have conceived, and the depression of the people of this state, render a strong support necessary to prevent a systematical submission—besides, the loss of Philadelphia would prove an irreparable injury, as we draw thence almost all our supplies."[20] "I cannot help thinking much too large a part of our force is directed to Ticonderoga,"[21] the worried commander in chief concluded.

On May 5 Washington sent Major General Arthur St. Clair north to replace the exhausted Anthony Wayne. He did this not out of consideration for Wayne, but rather to prepare for his own forthcoming campaign. Wayne was a Pennsylvanian, and Washington wanted him urgently to command Pennsylvania troops in the battle for Philadelphia. St. Clair, like Richard Montgomery, was a former British officer who had thrown his lot in with the Americans. In 1757, at age twenty, he had abandoned his medical studies in Edinburgh to join the Sixtieth—the Royal Americans—with whom he served at Louisbourg and Quebec. After the war, having married a wealthy Bostonian, he settled down in Pennsylvania, where he became a solid bulwark of the community. He had raised a Pennsylvania regiment in 1775, served with distinction at Trenton and Princeton, and by 1777 was one of five major generals, promoted ahead of the still seething Benedict Arnold. St. Clair arrived in mid-June, bringing in tow his eleven-year-old son, on the curious grounds that he needed to look after the lad's education—at a fort soon to be under siege.

As storm clouds gathered up north that summer, Washington held forces at Peekskill, but refused to send more to Ticonderoga. He had concluded that the fort could withstand Burgoyne without much help: "The garrison of Ticonderoga is sufficient to hold it against any attack."[22] Meanwhile, Schuyler kept writing to persuade his overconfident commander in chief that the forces at Ticonderoga were too weak to hold both sides of the lake. He enclosed a letter from the newly arrived St. Clair, warning that he could not "see the least prospect of our being able to defend the post unless the militia come in, and should the enemy protract their operations or invest us and content themselves with a simple blockade, we are infallibly ruined." [23]

On June 13, 1777, St. Clair took command of the defenses of a sprawling complex that included Mount Independence, the southern tongue of Lake Champlain, and Ticonderoga and its outworks. During the winter, dutiful Jeduthan Baldwin had worked mightily on his pet project of blocking the southern end of Lake Champlain by building a series of "cassoons" on the ice between Ticonderoga and Mount Independence. These were cribs of wood filled with stones built on the ice. When the ice melted (so the theory was), the structures would sink to the lake bottom, where, together with a large boom guarded by artillery batteries on either side, they would prevent the British fleet from sweeping down to Skenesborough. His men also labored at building blockhouses on Mount Independence, a practice that met with some considerable skepticism from Thaddeus Kosciuszko, a Polish engineer, who favored more orthodox field entrenchments. Kosciuszko had been part of the party that had climbed Mount Defiance the previous spring, and he believed it should be fortified. When he tried to suggest that Baldwin abandon the practice of building blockhouses and instead fortify the unprotected hill with extensive redoubts, he met with polite, but unyielding opposition. Fortunately, Baldwin let Kosciuszko work on constructing the floating bridge to Mount Independence, as well as some redoubts there. [24]

By the end of June, the American garrison at Ticonderoga, reinforced somewhat by replacements, consisted of some twenty-two hundred men scattered over two major positions, Fort Ticonderoga on the western side of the lake and Mount Independence on the eastern side. The previous summer, Wayne and Arnold had confirmed an uncomfortable suspicion raised by Colonel John Trumbull, son of the governor of Connecticut, namely, that artillery hauled up Mount Defiance—roughly a mile from the fort—could just range the Ticonderoga position. They had tested the proposition in two ways, by firing a cannon from the fort at the mountain (it landed halfway up, which meant that with the advantage of height, guns on the mountain could hit the fort) and by scrambling up it themselves. If Arnold, with a bad leg, could get up there, a determined enemy might as well. But neither Wayne nor his successor occupied Mount Defiance. Without a water source at the top, no substantial outpost could long sustain itself, and in any case, the garrison was thinly stretched as it was, because Ticonderoga included outposts up to a mile away from the fort proper, including the old French fortifications and an outpost on a hill called Mount Hope.

As Burgoyne's troops moved out of winter quarters and assembled at the northern end of the lake in late June, the Americans knew little of what was transpiring to their north. British maritime superiority on the lake, of course, ruled out reconnaissance by water. The Americans had a small contingent of rangers, ably led by Benjamin Whitcomb. The British had a particular vendetta against Whitcomb, who had unchivalrously picked off a British general in the woods the previous June. The standing orders issued after that event were that if "he or any of his party, or any other party of the same nature come within reach of our men, it is hoped they will not honor them with a soldier's death, if they can possibly avoid it, but reserve them for a due punishment, which can only be inflicted by the hangman." [25] In the event, the Indians and British and German light infantry prevented Whitcomb and his men from penetrating anywhere near the main body of the army. Indeed, on June 17, as they returned from a scout, one of the ranger parties was ambushed halfway between Crown Point and Ticonderoga by one of Burgoyne's Indian bands. [26] Thus, by June, when the British advance begun, the Americans knew something ugly impended, but could not be certain what.

St. Clair began his tour of duty on a depressed note. Upon arriving he immediately wrote to Schuyler, "If the enemy intend to attack us, I assure you, Sir, we are very ill prepared to receive them." [27] He had barely fifteen hundred Continental troops plus seven hundred militiamen from New Hampshire and Massachusetts. "We cannot increase our numbers by calling in the militia without ruin" because the garrison had only seven weeks of meat with which to feed itself. Even cartridge paper was in short supply.

On June 20 Schuyler came to Ticonderoga to see the position for himself and convened a council of war. In addition to himself and St. Clair, the chief members of the council were two other brigadiers and Brigadier General Matthias Alexis de Roche Fermoy, the commander on Mount Independence, one of a number of French generals commissioned by

Congress in the hopes that they would bring European expertise to a new army. Roche Fermoy seems, at best, to have made it to the rank of captain in the French army and, what was worse, had no command of English.

The generals agreed that Ticonderoga and Mount Independence lacked adequate numbers of troops to hold against a determined attack, but decided that "both posts ought, nevertheless, to be maintained as long as possible, consistent with the safety of the troops and stores," and that if confronted with the choice, St. Clair should withdraw to Mount Independence.[28] Schuyler appealed one more time to Washington for reinforcements, and meanwhile, the army did its best to finish the bridge and boom across the lake, complete the fortifications on Mount Independence, and brace for an attack.

If the Ticonderoga position had any hope at all, it lay in calling in the militia of the New England states. These men were only a few days away and highly motivated to appear, because they viewed Ticonderoga as a gateway to their own country. Yet St. Clair seemed strangely reluctant to summon them. He wrote to Schuyler on June 25 that:

> If the militia were called in, they might possibly enable us to keep possession, but I have not yet ventured upon that step, on account of the low state of our provisions, there not being more than thirty-five days meat for the troops now here, and the uncertainty in which we were with regard to the enemy's designs.[29]

St. Clair at this point declared that he had two thousand men, and needed four times as many to hold his position. That he would not call up reinforcements because he could not feed them meat was not entirely true (he was short of meat, but not out of it). He seemed to suggest that he would call up the militia, however, if he knew what the enemy were up to. But for much of this time he seemed not merely ignorant of British moves but confused about their intentions. St. Clair's letters to Schuyler at the end of June suggest that he did not believe the British had come in strength. Starting on the eighteenth he said, "I am at a loss to form a judgment of the designs of the enemy" on the twenty-fifth he said, "They are moving towards us, but whether in force or not I have not yet been able to discover."

What loomed throughout was St. Clair's depression at the thought of a real confrontation with the British. Periodically he bucked himself up by telling Schuyler, on June 30, for example, "My people are in the best disposition possible, and I have no doubt about giving a good account of the enemy, should they think proper to attack us."[30] But most of the time, even as he exhausted himself in inspecting his troops and urging on their activities, he prepared for defeat. He would call in the Berkshire and Vermont militia, he told Schuyler on June 25, but:

> This, however, is clear to me, that we shall be obliged to abandon this side, and then they will soon force the other from us; nor do I see that a retreat will in any shape be practicable. Everything, however, shall be done, that is possible, to frustrate the designs of the enemy; but what can be expected from troops ill armed, naked, and unaccoutred.[31]

The general was practically defeated before the battle had begun.

The enemy were abandoning Ticonderoga

As St. Clair fretted, Burgoyne deployed an elite advanced corps, followed by the bulk of the army in two divisions, or wings. Brigadier General Simon Fraser led the van, composed of light infantry and grenadiers plus the Twenty-fourth of Foot. Fraser, at age forty-eight, was an altogether superior officer of some thirty years' service. He, too, had served in the Sixtieth Regiment, the Royal Americans, and fought at Louisbourg and under Wolfe at Quebec; he had fought as well on the Continent, and in the American war had led his own Twenty-fourth Regiment and others in the campaign that drove the Americans out of Canada. Burgoyne's right wing, led by Major General William Phillips, a solid professional soldier with no previous American experience, consisted of two brigades of British troops. A brisk, slightly plump, and thoroughly professional thirty-eight-year-old German major general, Friederich Adolphus von Riedesel, led two brigades of Germans, plus a similar elite force of light infantry and grenadiers. Burgoyne told his men to expect the rebels to make extensive use of fortified places and "the strategems and enterprises of little war," against which the great remedy was "a reliance on the bayonet." The rebels, putting their reliance on entrenchments and sniping, would discover that "the onset of bayonets in the hands of the valiant is irresistible."[32] But for all this and similar bluster, Burgoyne and his men moved up the lake carefully: He had witnessed Bunker Hill in 1775, and knew that the bayonet could indeed succeed against entrenched rebels, but at a very high price in blood.

Fraser, as commander of the van, knew that he did not have a good understanding of the ground around Ticonderoga. But on June 18 his scouts brought in a particularly useful prisoner, James Macintosh, a soldier from the last war in the Seventy-eighth Regiment, a Highlands regiment in which Fraser had served. Macintosh lived a quarter of a mile from the American lines, and, with some coaxing from his erstwhile countryman and commander, provided him with a detailed account of the country around Ticonderoga. Fraser annotated the extensive interrogation report, noting, "It appears pretty evident that no time should be lost in moving a corps of the army towards the enemy for the purpose of investing lines cutting off their supplies & attacking their convoys."[33]

By July 1, leading elements of the advanced corps under Fraser had reached Three Mile Point, within sight of Fort Ticonderoga. St. Clair, at this juncture, managed to convince himself that the appearance of two ships, eighteen gunboats, and three sloops at his very doorstep, at Three Mile Point, "does not look like their being strong." Fraser dug in there, and on the evening of the second conferred with Burgoyne. As he did, St. Clair wrote to Schuyler, "I am still of opinion that the enemy have no great force here, but whether the whole of their army may as yet be come up I am not certain."

Burgoyne initially intended to have Riedesel's Germans cut off Mount Independence by moving down the east side of the lake—a bad idea, Fraser thought, since "they are a helpless kind of troops in woods" and would be exposed to getting cut off. Instead, he suggested, he could reconnoiter the Ticonderoga side with a view to beginning a more regular attack. By July 3, his troops had sealed off Fort Ticonderoga from its hinterland, seizing the abandoned American outpost at Mount Hope, a hill a mile and a half distant from the fort. In the meantime, Riedesel and his men had begun toiling through the woods on the eastern shore of the lake, hoping to cut off Mount Independence from Vermont, although the stream and marshes to the east of the mount impeded their movements.

Finally, St. Clair became seriously alarmed. On the third, American scouts took a prisoner from the Forty-seventh Regiment. They closeted him with an ample supply of rum and a fellow Scot who pretended to be a prisoner, but was, in fact, a plant placed there to wheedle secrets out of him. St. Clair learned the truth: The British and Germans had arrived in force, as two German deserters soon confirmed.[34] Finally, the American commander called in the Vermont militia, but too late. On the Fourth, Burgoyne, informed of a commotion in the rebel lines, authorized Fraser to push ahead. "You are to remember," Fraser wrote a friend, "that Burgoyne's great apprehension was, that the Rebel army would go off and the conquest would not have been sufficiently brilliant by a great number of prisoners, or a large quantity of stores."[35]

Drunken Indians spoiled a stealthy approach, but Fraser, supported by Burgoyne's second in command, Major General Phillips, soon took up a position some fifteen hundred yards from the old French lines. Fraser then sent a scouting party—some forty light infantry and a few Indians—to reconnoiter Sugar Loaf Hill, or Mount Defiance as the rebels called it. The scouts reported back at midnight on the fourth that they had reached the summit, and Fraser decided to take a look for himself, arriving at two in the afternoon on the fifth. "A sagacious Indian was so struck with the situation of this hill," Fraser recorded, "that he asked if the great father of the sun had created it lately, as in the various contests about possessing Ticonderoga, he wondered it never occurred to any person to occupy it before we did." Sagacious indeed, since neither the French nor the British in previous campaigns had thought of holding it, although some of the more perceptive Americans in 1776 had.

Fraser and his men moved swiftly. His engineer, Lieutenant William Twiss, organized the hauling of a pair of twelve-pounder artillery pieces to the top of the hill. The thirty-two-year-old Twiss, despite his junior rank, had already made a name for himself by organizing the yards for the construction of the British fleet on Lake Champlain. He acted quickly now: It required prodigious labor to hack a road through the thick underbrush and then arrange rope and tackle to lug the artillery pieces up the steep slopes, but Twiss accomplished the job in less than a day. The artillery would have been ready to open up on the evening of the sixth. At three o'clock in the morning, however, word came to Fraser from two deserters: "The enemy were abandoning Ticonderoga and the works on Mount Independence."[36]

As the vise had tightened around the Mount Independence/Ticonderoga complex, on July 5, St. Clair convened a second council of general officers—Roche Fermoy, Enoch Poor, John Patterson, and Colonel Warner Long. They had seen the British soldiers on Mount Defiance; they knew Riedesel and his men were probing toward Mount Independence; they knew they were completely cut off from Lake George by Fraser's men. The council decided on a withdrawal, declaring "a retreat ought to be undertaken as soon as possible, and that we shall be very fortunate to effect it."[37] They would march out by night.

Once again in his weary military career, Jeduthan Baldwin found himself summoned by his superiors—this time, at nine o'clock at night on the fifth—and told yet again of military misfortune and a change in plans. He was to evacuate all stores from Ticonderoga starting at two o'clock in the morning. St. Clair's plan was to send the sick from the hospital at Mount Independence by water, together with the stores, under escort from the few remaining ships of the American fleet, to Skenesborough. St. Clair would march the rest of the army over the floating bridge, across the lake. He would immediately abandon the Mount Independence position (despite the resolve of the June 20 council of war) and march down the road built the previous year to Castleton, linking up with the supplies and what was left of the fleet at Skenesborough a couple of days later.

St. Clair's hopes for an orderly withdrawal collapsed under mischance, panic, and incompetence. As the troops began marching in the dark hours of the morning of the sixth, a fire burst out at the cabin of Roche Fermoy, the commander on Mount Independence. Whether Roche Fermoy had misunderstood orders and was destroying his domicile to deny it to the enemy (as he subsequently claimed) or set fire to his own house in a drunken stupor (as was more widely believed), the blaze attracted the attention of the British. His officers subsequently petitioned to be removed from his command "as they can neither understand him, nor he them," which may have been the politest thing they could say about him.[38]

The retreat degenerated into confusion. The American soldiers ordered to hold the last battery on Mount Independence, covering the withdrawal, instead got roaringly drunk. The British gunboats made short work of Baldwin's bridge and its supporting boom—half an hour's work to cut through the labor of months—and the American commanders found themselves leading not a withdrawal, but a rout.

They certainly behaved with great gallantry [39]

Burgoyne, having taken Ticonderoga, pursued the rebels. The ships of the fleet occupied Skenesborough shortly after noon on July 6, taking or destroying the remnants of the American fleet on Lake Champlain.[40] The American army had now lost all of its supplies. Meanwhile, St. Clair attempted to make of the withdrawal on the military road from Mount Independence something more or less orderly. He needed to do so, for Burgoyne had ordered Fraser's advance guard to pursue the fleeing rebels.

Commanding the American rear guard was Seth Warner, a figure utterly different from St. Clair. Although the son of a doctor, he was far more a son of the woodlands than of the study, and in 1763, at age twenty, he had moved to the New Hampshire Grants, in what is now Vermont. The six-foot-two Warner joined the Green Mountain Boys, and despite a pleasant personality took a leading role in the campaign of intimidation waged against New Yorkers claiming to control Vermont—and was included, in March 1774, in the list of miscreants declared outlaws by the New York legislature. He had marched with Ethan Allen and Benedict Arnold to Ticonderoga, had taken Crown Point, and had been chosen by the Green Mountain Boys to replace Allen as their regimental commander in July 1776. He had fought with Montgomery in the invasion of Canada, beating off Carleton's attempt to relieve the siege of St. Johns.

To hold off the inevitable pursuit, St. Clair had initially posted Colonel Ebenezer Francis, commander of the Eleventh Massachusetts, with some 450 men of his own regiment and detachments from several others, to command the rear guard in the first stage of the withdrawal. Throughout the sixth the long column followed the military road that ran from Mount Independence to the main road to Castleton. At the hamlet of Hubbardton, however, St. Clair designated Warner, chief of the Green

Mountain Boys, as commander of a reinforced rear guard, which would include, in addition to his own and Francis's men, Colonel Nathan Hale (no relation to the spy) and the Second New Hampshire. The main body paused for several hours to rest and then moved on; at 4:00 P.M. Francis finally showed up, bringing along with him many of the sick whom St. Clair had charged him to protect. The three commanders—Warner, Francis, and Hale—conferred in an abandoned cabin. They decided, contrary to St. Clair's orders, to delay following the main body, joining up at Castleton, until the next morning.

They did so on several grounds. The rear guard had got word of a party of Indians and Tories that had swept through the area—as it turned out, a detachment that came south along the Vermont side of the lake several days earlier, but that the retreating Americans feared were the forerunners of the British pursuit. What mattered was that the Indians had made off with several townsmen and moved on in the direction of Castleton. For Warner in particular, the notion of leaving behind the few remaining settlers in the area, as well as sick or stragglers, was abhorrent: It meant consigning them to the Indians that Burgoyne had already whipped up against the Americans. Not much farther down the road— two and a half miles south, at Ransomvale—the militia had already encamped, blocking the road ahead. Besides, Hubbardton offered a strong position to defend. The military road from Mount Independence descended through a saddle in the hills down to a small, marshy brook; it then skirted Monument Hill, a long, dominating piece of ground running north to south. The Americans could hope to defend the brook, and if necessary fall back to the hill, behind the crest of which lay the road to Castleton.

Warner dispatched parties to bring in local settlers, and collecting the exhausted stragglers and sick in a camp at the base of Monument Hill, had his men lay obstacles behind Sucker Brook, while sending out pickets who could give the alarm if they saw British forces coming through the saddle between the hills down to the stream. He planned to withdraw early the next morning, but until then, as he thought, held a strong position.

The pursuit, led by Fraser, consisted of light infantry and grenadiers, augmented by two companies of his own Twenty-fourth Regiment, with some German troops following on behind. Riedesel, with a hand-picked force of 180 men, led these, with some 1,100 German troops following on. Fraser had had his own troubles getting started, as his men had plundered the abandoned American camp at Mount Independence, and the arrival of Riedesel—superior to him in rank—was a mixed blessing. But the German, whether from tact or because he knew that his heavily equipped men could not keep up with Fraser's light infantry, told Fraser to go on and that he would catch up. Fraser had set a murderous pace, some thirteen miles on the blazing hot first day, before starting out again around three in the morning on July 7.

Two hours later, at five in the morning, Fraser's Tory and Indian scouts encountered the American sentries at the saddle between the hills where the military road descended to Sucker Brook. A few shots shattered the morning stillness, alerting the American force, which had been preparing to move out to continue the retreat. Fraser paused, then sent scouts out to swing around the road, bypassing the first American encampment along the brook. The scouts, who probably climbed a steep hill, Mount Zion, to the south of the American position, could see that the American rear guard was now a lot stronger than previously thought. They estimated that it numbered over a thousand men. Torn between prudence, which suggested waiting for the Germans to come up, and an urgent desire to hit the Americans before they could escape, Fraser acquiesced to the request of Major Robert Grant, who had battlefield command of Fraser's own Twenty-fourth Regiment, to attack.

Grant led the advance guard down to Sucker Brook and paid the penalty for his rashness, falling with a score of his men as the Americans fired from behind the abbatis that they had laid down behind the brook. The British deployed from column into a line to outflank and assault the American position, and the Americans retreated up Monument Hill, where Warner, Francis, and Hale had been preparing to march down the road to Castleton that lay parallel to the hill's crest. By now Warner had received word from St. Clair of yet another disaster: The British had taken Skenesborough and destroyed what American warships remained there. St. Clair intended to retreat further to Rutland, rather than Castleton, in order to avoid pursuit.

The Americans had lined up in order of march on the Castleton road behind the crest of Monument Hill—Hale to the north, then Francis, and finally Warner on the southern end—when the British attack began.

Hale gave command of the New Hampshiremen to his number two and dashed down the slope to hustle the sick, wounded, and stragglers up Monument Hill from Sucker Brook, getting them away ahead of the advancing British. Warner, meanwhile, swung down the hill to attack the British on their right as they toiled up the slope. Fraser, reading the situation quickly, reacted by sending his light infantry and grenadiers further right, outflanking Warner in turn, and establishing a roadblock, cutting off the Americans' retreat southward to Castleton. The Americans, pressed by the attacking British, fell back to the east, behind the Castleton road to a log fence, with light infantry and grenadiers sweeping across their left, the rest of the British light infantry and advance guard advancing straight up the hill. A general battle ensued: Hale was overrun trying to rescue the sick and the wounded, Fraser's infantry pushed forward with loss up Monument Hill and toward the second American position along the log fence. Francis fell to a British volley. Fraser, commanding the British left, was attacked by Hale's men, who "began pretty briskly," as he later confided to a relative, just as Riedesel arrived.

The battle had gone on for over an hour when the Germans showed up at 8:30 A.M. Riedesel ordered his band to play—a clever touch of psychological warfare—and the Americans, who had put up a vigorous fight, fell back before German bayonets and the rifles of the *jägers*, the only rifle-armed troops at the battle. Warner, seeing the road to Castleton blocked, his position outflanked on both ends, and his men retreating, ordered them to disperse to the east and make their way to Manchester, over another hill line (Pittsford ridge), which the British ascended but did not cross.

It had been a bloody little fight. According to the best tally of casualties, the British lost 184 killed and wounded out of 850 engaged, and their German allies 24 out of 180—a total casualty rate of about 20 percent. The Americans, who had roughly the same number of troops, had suffered 137 killed and wounded, as well as some 234 prisoners taken, for a total casualty rate of 33 percent. The Americans had stood and fought, and fought well: The commander of Fraser's light infantry said later that "circumstanced as the enemy was, as an army very hard pressed in their retreat, they certainly behaved with great gallantry."

More to the point, he concurred with Fraser's judgment that further pursuit was impossible.[41] Burgoyne's deputy adjutant general later

Burgoyne, contrary to myth, had done what he could to reduce the encumbrances under which most eighteenth-century armies labored. Even so, it took until September 13 before he could assemble at his base on the Hudson the thirty days of provisions he thought he needed to continue the campaign. It was not even that the Americans had successfully attacked the line of communication—they had been routed shortly after Hubbardton in another engagement at Fort Anne. Rather, a supply line stretching from Canada to Crown Point, to Skenesborough, to Fort Edward on the Hudson required twice as many carts and twice as many bateaux as he had available to him. When his men finally arrived at Stillwater on the Hudson, they had been sadly diminished by the battles of Hubbardton and, much more so, Bennington (at which Burgoyne lost 200 killed and some 700 captured out of a total force of 1,400), disease, and the need to occupy Fort Ticonderoga with 900 men, around a fifth of his dwindling army. (An American raid on the fort on September 19 netted some prisoners, but failed to dislodge or even much to unnerve the garrison.)

Once again, Benedict Arnold appeared at the right time, and led the American army in two victories, first at Freeman's Farm on September 19, and more decisively at the Battle of Bemis Heights on October 7. On that date, having been driven to quit the army by an increasingly jealous Horatio Gates, he had been about to depart for Washington's army at Philadelphia. Preparing to depart, he heard the firing as the British launched a sortie. Without an official role in the army, he nonetheless rode to the sound of the guns, led his men in two successful charges, and took a bullet in his left leg. His horse reared from a mortal wound and came down on him, causing multiple fractures in the wounded leg. His men, frantically pulling the dead horse off him, asked where he had been hit. The same leg as at Quebec, he gasped, but he wished it had been his heart. Before passing out from pain he stopped his men from bayoneting the Hessian soldier who had shot him, saying that the man had merely done his duty.[48]

For long-suffering Jeduthan Baldwin, the memory of Saratoga was far sweeter. When Burgoyne finally surrendered on October 17, 1777, he wrote in his journal: "About eleven o'clock am the enemy laid down their arms and marched out through our Army the most agreeable sight that ever my eyes beheld." [49] Burgoyne's surrender to a vast American force, just under twenty thousand strong, marked a turning point in the Revolution. There was no concealing the magnitude of this loss: an entire army, including its commanders, taken prisoner, and a vital element in British strategy shattered. Saratoga made it possible for the French to openly declare war, where they had, until now, only quietly supported the Americans with munitions, money, and (unevenly) military experts. The French, torn between desire to avenge themselves on Great Britain, and fear of the many costs another great war would bring, had hesitated to fight openly until they had reasonable assurance that the Americans could win. [50] Now they had it.

By the time he surrendered Burgoyne claimed that he had barely 1,900 British troops and 1,600 Germans—3,500 in all, according to his own account (considerably more, according to contemporary historians, who estimate some 5,900 troops in all). [51] In any case, the British army of invasion was wiped out. Burgoyne spent the next years explaining how it had happened.

The Canadians had not wished to take part in this war—so much had been clear. The local loyalists provided useful intelligence, but Burgoyne pronounced himself frustrated by their seemingly contradictory reasons for fighting: "One man's views went to the profit which he was to enjoy when his corps should be complete; another's to the protection of the district in which he resided; a third was wholly intent upon revenge against his personal enemies; and all of them were repugnant even to an idea of subordination." [52] There were only a couple of exceptions that Burgoyne mentioned—a loyalist scout named Captain Justus Sherwood, a founding member of the Green Mountain Boys who had nonetheless remained true to the king, who had courageously slipped through American lines on several occasions. But in truth, Burgoyne never really understood or knew how to lead the Americans he thought he was liberating from the tyranny of Congress.

As for the Indians, the defeated commander later lamented the "caprice, the superstition, the self-interestedness of the Indian character" and sprinkled his comments on them with words like "depravity" and "ferocity." He reserved his harshest words for the Canadian Indian handlers he had so warmly praised at the beginning of the campaign.

I never doubted that their evil passions were fomented, and their defection completed by the cabals of the Canadian interpreters. Rapacity, self-
interest, and presumption are the characteristics of these men, with some
few exceptions. The acquisition of the Indian language has usually been
a certain fortune to a man with an artful head and a convenient conscience.[53]

This last observation was almost surely a reference to that old wolf La
Corne St. Luc, who, being no fool, had quietly slipped away from the
army before the final debacle. The Canadian aristocrat had his own reservations about Burgoyne, whom he described to Germain as brave but
slow and uncreative. The Indians disappeared, in part under the lash of
Burgoyne's rebukes over the McCrea killing, but mainly because, experienced as they were, they could smell defeat coming in the kind of battles
white men fought, and wished no part of it.

Burgoyne ended the campaign a bitter man, blaming Germain, Howe,
the Canadians, the Indians, the Tories, everyone but himself and his
troops. He sought a parliamentary inquiry, which, however, never completed its work, and while he attempted to clear his name, his army, supposed to return under parole to England, was held by Congress on a
technicality. The Convention Army, as it became known, was marched to
Massachusetts, then herded south, and melted away, soldiers dying of illness or escaping into the not altogether unfriendly back country, marrying local girls and becoming Americans. A few came home after the war.
While their erstwhile commander attempted vainly to clear his own
name, most simply vanished.

We shall never defend a Post, until we shoot a general

The eventual triumph of the Saratoga campaign, however, did not end the
controversy over the fall of Ticonderoga. At the time, it had a huge effect
on British as well as American morale. King George, upon hearing the
news, leaped up crying, "I have beat them! I have beat all the Americans!"

while American leaders were both despondent and furious.[54] John Adams wrote to his wife, Abigail, in mid-August:

> I think we shall never defend a Post, until we shoot a general. After that we shall defend posts, and this event in my opinion is not far off. No other fort will ever be evacuated without an enquiry, nor any officer come off without a court martial. We must trifle no more. We have suffered too many disgraces to pass unexpiated. Every disgrace must be wiped off.[55]

He was hardly alone. Reverend Thomas Allen had preached hellfire and brimstone to the garrison at Ticonderoga on July 5, warning that "our camp is filled with blasphemers and resounds with the language of the infernal regions." With a peculiarly grim New England satisfaction he later noted that shortly after he delivered this reproof to the assembled sinners, the garrison had to flee. "How are the mighty fallen and the weapons of war have perished." But, he went on late that summer, much depended on "the treatment of those five general officers who gave up Ticonderoga and those 175 Tory traitors taken in arms in the militia battle near Bennington. If these cannot be brought to justice, then am I ready to pronounce, what is in my opinion, the sad doom of these states; the end is come, your end is come, your destruction, death is nigh."[56]

A congressional committee recommended a court-martial of St. Clair, and after more than a year's delay, that took place. The charges contended that by June 20, a week after arriving at Ticonderoga, St. Clair should have made at least a tentative decision to hold or retreat. By June 24, the judge advocate prosecuting the case noted, St. Clair's scouts were telling him that the enemy was numerous, and yet the general only a day later informed Congress that he could not tell whether the enemy was in force. Drawing on the testimony of Jesse Leavenworth—a Connecticut man serving in the quartermaster corps—the prosecutor, as well as a congressional report, insisted that the work on fortifying Mount Independence was sluggish, that once small scouting parties had been rebuffed St. Clair failed to send out larger ones, and that by sending his eleven-year-old son off to Albany on June 29 he had already tacitly accepted the inevitability of the decision that he subsequently took on July 5, to withdraw from

Ticonderoga and Mount Independence as well. To St. Clair, a man with a prickly eighteenth-century sense of honor, the charges read in that courtroom must have crashed as loudly as any cannon shots—"neglect of duty . . . cowardice, treachery, incapacity as a general . . . inattention to the progress of the enemy . . . shamefully abandoning the posts of Ticonderoga and Mount Independence."[57]

The records of the court martial indicate that the real gravamen of the charge lay not so much in the fact of having to retreat at all, as in the timing of St. Clair's decisions, the execution of the withdrawal, and the failure to make a fight. And indeed—though the judge advocate did not make the case this way—these three elements were intertwined. As the records indicated, St. Clair had doubted his ability to hold on to his position from the very outset of his tenure at Ticonderoga. But he seemed to have been strangely unwilling even to think about, much less prepare for, a withdrawal, hence the hurried scenes of the late night of July 5 and early morning of the sixth.

St. Clair offered a more spirited defense in the courtroom than he had in the field. He shrewdly poured scorn on Leavenworth, the chief witness for the prosecution, whose testimony proved a distraction, given that the most damning elements in the indictment came from St. Clair's own dispatches. But the defeated general had a point. He had been told repeatedly that a full blown attack on Ticonderoga was unlikely; he ascribed this to Congress, but in truth, the erroneous judgment came chiefly from Washington, who had not sent two brigades of reinforcements north until early July, by which time they could not rescue the fort, although they did help rebuild the nucleus of the northern army. The council of war on June 20 had left a muddled picture, St. Clair insisted, and he had reason to think that it left him exposed no matter what course he chose. He had indeed sent out reconnaissance parties, only to find them overmatched by the Indians, and he made the entirely reasonable point that to send out larger parties would have done little good. Small numbers of men—three or four in some cases—would have a better chance of slipping through enemy lines, observing, and infiltrating back with useful information.

Above all, St. Clair knew—as did Burgoyne, as did John Adams and King George III, for that matter—that he occupied a post of extraordinary sensitivity. Mount Independence was arguably, from the narrowly military point of view, the more important position on the lake, although it was unlikely that it could hold long if the western side of the lake fell. Among other things, Mount Independence's water supply lay within cannon shot of the western side of the lake. But Ticonderoga, from the psychological point of view, mattered a great deal. The New England colonies saw it as the back door to their hinterlands, whence Indian raiders could once again set the borderlands aflame, as they had so often done in the wars with the French. And Abercromby's spectacular defeat twenty years before still resounded. In the imagination of politicians and common folk, the word "Ticonderoga" connoted a fortress of enormous strength. It had, after all, been held successfully against an army five times the size of its garrison, and many veterans of that assault could tell the tale of the fruitless, bloody assaults on its works. Burgoyne's large artillery train (for which he later received harsh criticism) resulted in large part from the need to prepare to blast through the field fortifications that the Americans had erected on the old French lines. And if Burgoyne himself wanted prisoners and booty, as Fraser intimated, the general also knew that the trophy of Ticonderoga itself was worth a great deal.

Small wonder, then, that St. Clair had hesitated to pull out of this position. Only three weeks after taking over a hopeless command he found himself besieged, outnumbered by more than two to one, facing an enemy whom he had been told would never approach in force. The wise, if painful choice, was to live to fight another day.

*Stung by the envenomed tongue of malice,
and pointed at by the finger of folly*

St. Clair's defense mixed reasonable argument, learned reference to retrograde movements by outnumbered armies, and maudlin self-pity. But he made at least one churlish as well as dishonest claim. In attempting to explain the loss of the army's supplies (and the remnants of the navy) at Skenesborough, he attempted to foist the blame onto Warner. It was a debacle, he confessed:

but not from any fault of mine. That was the only place to which they could have been removed; and had not my march been delayed, as has been shewn, by Colonel Warner's unfortunately taking upon himself to judge of and disobey his orders, I should have arrived at Skeensborough time enough to have protected the stores, and probably to have cut off that party of the enemy which pursued them.[58]

St. Clair had already heard that the British were at Skenesborough before Hubbardton, as we have seen. In fact, the British had arrived on the afternoon of July 6, the day before Warner's battle.

There was a clash of cultures here. St. Clair, by early training and temperament a professional soldier, clung doggedly to the letter of his orders, and moped about his reputation. Self-pity permeates the record: "Had I left Ticonderoga one week sooner, I should certainly have been hanged, and probably without the ceremony of a court-martial."[59] "I have been hung up to be stung by the envenomed tongue of malice, and pointed at by the finger of folly," he told a court sympathetic to his plight.[60] And St. Clair obliquely warned his congressional persecutors of what would happen were they to "stoop to hunt down an individual," bringing themselves thereby into contempt.

For St. Clair, and to some extent for the professional soldiers who subsequently studied him, the matter was clear. Congress had stuck him in an impossible position, and if it had not given him categorical orders to defend an indefensible post, it had at least created an environment that made it impossible to command successfully. He had done his best with a hopeless situation, and now politicians had cooked up a court-martial to torment and scapegoat the man whom they had placed in this predicament.

By contrast, Seth Warner was not a writing or even much of a talking man; we do not have his views of the campaign. He fought his fight, and went back to look after his people, the people of Vermont. He had fought again at Bennington, helping to consummate that victory of the militia of the Hampshire Grants against a foolhardy expedition by Burgoyne's Germans, who had attempted a stealthy march by horseless dragoons in cavalry boots led by a military band. He showed up in time for the final drama of Saratoga, and then, promoted to general of the Vermont militia, guarded that republic's borders until 1781, receiving a wound in a skirmish in 1780. Prematurely aged and ill from five years of ceaseless campaigning, he died a year after the war for American independence that he had helped win.

At Hubbardton, Warner had chosen to delay for reasons that made perfect sense to a militia leader: he was going to collect the local people, his sick, and his wounded and protect them from the ravages of Burgoyne's Indians. He did not make excuses for violating the letter of his orders, and did not need to. He fought a short, sharp battle that halted the British advance, inflicted losses the enemy could not afford, and then dispersed his own force, which he knew could, and would, reassemble to fight again.

St. Clair wore himself out, too, but in a different way. One of Schuyler's aides later recalled of St. Clair:

> I do not remember, tho' I lived in the same quarters with him the greater part of the time during the siege, that he ever undressed himself at night. All night, indeed, he would scarcely ever permit himself to sleep. If he did, it was not above an hour or two, tho' the gentlemen about him would frequently observe that he would certainly injure his health unless he indulged himself with more sleep.[61]

St. Clair worried himself sick; but what exactly did he accomplish? At his court-martial several sympathetic officers repeated that St. Clair had told them that "if he remained there, he would save his character and lose the army; if he went off, he would save the army and lose his character."[62] At the same time, however, he was telling his men "that he wished for nothing more than a serious attack, and did not doubt but we should repulse them if they did attack."[63]

St. Clair and Warner came from two very different strands in the American military tradition—the regular and the citizen soldier. Neither had much use for the other, until, in the late twentieth century, the professional soldiers finally triumphed. For many years after independence, however, they clashed, often bitterly. The United States evolved an unusual military system that placed a great deal of reliance on part-time soldiers and, no less, on part-time officers, often men, like Warner, of substantial standing in their own communities. Unlike most countries, in which reserve units are part of a centralized military, the United States to this day retains in the National Guard a system that retains features of the autonomous colonial militias. The officers of these units of citizen-soldiers consisted often of local notables, and, in today's National Guard, many battalions and regiments trace their lineage back to the earliest period of the Republic and even, in some cases, before.

More remarkably yet, the United States has clung throughout most of its history to the notion that civilians, often with relatively little formal military training, could succeed at command. The records of Revolutionary War commanders like Daniel Morgan and Civil War commanders like Bedford Forrest seemed to bear that out—although the list of politically connected incompetents was far longer. Plenty of West Point–produced generals had equally parlous records, of course. As late as World War II, it was not uncommon to find men receiving almost instantaneous promotions to the rank of colonel, particularly in the more specialized units such as civil affairs.

After World War II, however, the situation changed. President Lyndon Johnson refused, on political grounds, a large-scale mobilization of the National Guard in Vietnam, while George H. W. Bush mobilized only small elements in 1990 for the 1991 Gulf War. That only generated more friction, as professionals insisted that the Forty-eighth Georgia Army National Guard brigade spend more than two months in the broiling California desert before a deployment that never came. But in the Afghan and Iraq wars of the first decade of the twenty-first century citizen-soldiers again appeared, mobilized for overseas duty in the framework of a dominant professional military. The distinction between career soldier and citizen-soldier diminished after the first combat rotation or two, while at the upper ranks the lock on command held by professionals remained.

The tension between citizen-soldier and professional, however, will never quite go away. There is something deeply rooted in the American military tradition that looks with particular pride on the civilian, like Warner, who reluctantly goes to war to defend his country, fighting only for the duration—but for as long as that duration might be. There was no little irony in the adoption by Washington's former officers and their descendants of the term Society of the Cincinnati for their order (still flourishing today), created after the Revolution. The society was opposed precisely by some of those who most revered the notion of a Cincinnatus, a farmer who left his plow to command Rome's armies, and then returned to that plow as soon as the crisis had passed. Nor have the professionals walked away from the citizen-soldier. The United States Army's manual on leadership, has, as its longest example—five pages' worth—of superior performance the epic defense of Little Round Top at Gettysburg by Joshua Lawrence Chamberlain, professor turned warrior, and one of the ablest Union officers of his rank in the Civil War.

Washington and many of his commanders—the first professionals of the new United States—were wary of the militia, as St. Clair was. Indeed, his mistrust of them may have rendered him unsuited to command them. But the Saratoga campaign could not have succeeded without them. At Oriskany, Tryon County militia bought time for besieged Fort Stanwix at the expense of almost four hundred dead—one of the bloodiest battles of the Revolution. Their sacrifice enabled the Mohawk valley to resist St. Leger's column, and thus deprived Burgoyne of the supplementary stroke that would open the door to Albany. It was New England militia that annihilated Baum's column at Bennington, dooming Burgoyne's invasion, had he had the wit to acknowledge that fact. It was the militia of New England that swelled Gates's army to the point that no qualitative superiority of British or German soldier could overcome them. And throughout the war it was the militia—unstable, ill-disciplined, often demoralized, never entirely reliable, but still willing to fight—that suppressed local Tories and prevented the British from ever establishing real control in those areas that they reclaimed from rebel rule.[64]

In 1782, Benedict Arnold, now in British service, but as brilliant a strategist as ever, hit at this point, when he told King George III in a memorandum that the British could not hope to succeed unless they set up civil governments in America, rather than military rule. The average loyalist, he said, would serve under a civilian government that he accepted, but not under the British army.

> He has no objection to serve in the Militia *within* his own colony, under officers who are *of it*; and to assist in supporting its government and defending himself *in it*; and may perhaps pursue the Rebel out of it, or meet him on a Menaced Invasion near the borders.[65]

Arnold, a rebel who had often commanded militia successfully, knew whereof he spoke, and his words applied just as well, as he understood (and Burgoyne to his sorrow learned), if one replaced the word "rebel" with "king's soldier."

The outcome of St. Clair's court-martial was never much in doubt. The fall of Ticonderoga had seemed catastrophic at the time but the victorious conclusion to the Saratoga campaign, and its culmination in the French alliance, anesthetized the sting. Sitting on the bench were St. Clair's friends and colleagues, who themselves had reason to fear congressional scrutiny if they made a similar misstep. And really, he had been dealt a very difficult hand. The court voted unanimously, and, it appears, without much deliberation, to acquit St. Clair on all charges. He returned to serve as a senior aide to Washington throughout the Revolution, down to the Battle of Yorktown. And why not? St. Clair was the model of the conscientious, hard-working, selfless professional soldier, diligent, physically brave, and willing to suffer physical and financial hardship for his country.

————•◆•————

Would you be willing to have a son or daughter serve under him?

Some 220 years after the court-martial of Arthur St. Clair, forty American officers, most of the rank of colonel or the civilian equivalent in the Department of Defense, settled into their chairs, cradling mugs of coffee or tea. They had spent a full day inspecting the Fort Ticonderoga historical site on a staff ride—a kind of historical case study in which they think through problems of strategy and command by close investigation of a past battle. The heart of the technique is role play: each member of the group has taken on a character from the past—John Burgoyne, commander of the British forces, American loyalists, members of Congress. Throughout the day they explored the decision to abandon Fort Ticonderoga in July 1777, in the face of the second British invasion from Canada. They visited the ruins of Crown Point, where the British staged their forces; they climbed Mount Defiance, overlooking Ticonderoga, which the British had seized on July 5, 1777. They meandered through the outer ruins of Ticonderoga, the remnants of the old French field fortifications that the Americans had refurbished in 1776 and 1777, and wandered through the reconstructed fort itself.

Interestingly, in a narrowly professional sense, these American officers identified less with the beleaguered garrison of Fort Ticonderoga than with its opponents. The late-twentieth-century United States Army, after all, had much more in common with Burgoyne and the British army that had come marching out of Canada than it did with the ragtag assortment of Continentals, state troops, and militia who opposed them. The British were conscientious regulars, experienced in conventional war, well-read in its theory, and led by experienced and competent commanders. They moved cautiously, with due attention to the logistical needs of a force moving through a desolate wilderness. Like today's American forces, they operated at the end of a supply chain that stretched across the globe. These British soldiers had the edge in firepower (some eighty cannon, twelve howitzers, forty-six mortars), and although that made them cumbersome, it also made them formidable in the extreme.[66]

Burgoyne and his immediate subordinates found themselves, like American soldiers more than two centuries later, operating in a coalition. A large part of his army was German; but he also had to consider the attitudes and inclinations of Canadian and American loyalist auxiliaries, and the Indians. He was waging a mixture of conventional operations and counterinsurgency that sounded familiar to the colonels of the late 1990s, and would have sounded even more familiar to them a decade later. Like the American professionals, he had to wage a war of information, propaganda, and persuasion—all the while understanding that he could not control precisely the amount of violence his subordinates and local allies might deal out.

The culminating exercise of the staff ride was a reenactment of the court-martial of the commander of Fort Ticonderoga, Major General Arthur St. Clair. One of the officers, playing St. Clair, had to defend not only his decision to withdraw from Ticonderoga but the shambolic retreat that followed—the loss of stores at Ticonderoga and at Mount Independence, the destruction of what was left of the American fleet on Lake Champlain, the near disintegration of his army. The twentieth-century staff riders narrowed the charges down to one: "incompetency as a general," in the quaint wording of the eighteenth century.

The officers explored the case, some arguing that St. Clair, totally outnumbered, had been put in an impossible position. In fact, some contended, the very notion of a court-martial was unfair and wrong, a product of congressional ignorance of and meddling in military affairs. If the group reacted badly to one character on the staff ride, it had been to John Adams, head of the Congress's Board of War, passing harsh judgments about generalship while far from the scene of action.

Some of the soldiers in the room took a more skeptical view: St. Clair should have called earlier for militia reinforcements; he should have stationed forces on Mount Defiance; he had an obligation to at least put up a robust fight before withdrawing. But the weight of opinion rested with the conscientious but outnumbered and outmaneuvered general. The group voted, by a serious if not overwhelming margin, to acquit. Why they did so had much to do with the facts of the case. Perhaps it had something to do with sympathy for a professional soldier trying to cope with the unreasonable demands of politicians and military amateurs. Like St. Clair and most career soldiers of the period, the colonels had grave doubts about the utility of the militia—those farmers and artisans who showed up for a few months, barely trained and poorly disciplined, and then scattered in the face of the British army.

Having completed the exercise, the instructors made some final remarks, summing up arguments on both sides, suggesting parallels with the kinds of problems the colonels might find themselves dealing with in the future, saying a few words about the carefully reconstructed site of Fort Ticonderoga itself. And then a poll: "Could all of you who voted to acquit St. Clair please raise your hands once again?" About twenty-five of the forty raised their hands. "Now, would all of you who would be willing to have your son or daughter serve under him please keep your hands up." One by one, the hands went down.

After a pause to digest this ambivalent outcome, the instructors recounted St. Clair's further career. After the Revolution (during which he continued to serve, but never in command), he became, in 1787, president of the Continental Congress for one year, just as the new Constitution was being drafted. Thereafter he was appointed territorial governor of the Northwest Territory. A member of the Society of the Cincinnati, he helped found the city of that name. And in the summer of 1791 he went to war again.

St. Clair led the bulk of the United States Army, such as it was at the time, against the Northwest Indians, who in confederation had mounted a fierce opposition against the settlers pouring across the Appalachians. After months of painful marching and the construction of isolated forts, the Indians attacked St. Clair and his army along the Wabash River on November 4, 1791.[67] Neither the regulars nor the militia accompanying them could hold their ineptly fortified camp. The Indians pounced, killing over 600 soldiers and wounding another 250, inflicting the greatest defeat ever suffered by the United States Army at the hands of Native Americans, before or since. After careful deliberation, Washington replaced St. Clair with none other than the defeated general's predecessor, fifteen years before, at Ticonderoga—Anthony Wayne. In the meantime, Congress, once again, investigated St. Clair. Once again, upon due consideration of the quality of his troops, the difficulty of his logistical predicament, and the challenges of the terrain, he was acquitted. "Well, asked the instructor, whose fault was it? St. Clair's, or the people who kept him in command?"

There was a prolonged silence and then, pondering the last question, the reflective colonels filed off to a pleasant dinner in a comfortable dining room overlooking the dark waters of Lake George, and the green hills that loom over them.

CHAPTER EIGHT

Phantom Campaigns, 1778–83

America most probably will be lost to Great Britain forever

After the defeat and surrender of Burgoyne's army in October 1777, no more fleets prepared for battle on Lake Champlain; no more armies, equipped with trains of artillery, marched and countermarched. On both sides, thousands of soldiers melted away. The vast numbers of militia— well over ten thousand—who had assembled to surround and defeat him returned to their homes in Massachusetts, Vermont, and other states. Burgoyne's men shuffled off into a prolonged captivity: As the Convention Army they were hustled to Boston, and eventually, the South. A hard-pressed George Washington was desperate to return the Continental regiments he had sent north to New York to Valley Forge, his camp opposite Philadelphia, the lost capital, and he immediately summoned them back.

In the ensuing months and years of the war, the landscape changed, too. The Americans retained their positions at Fort Edward and Fort Anne, just south of Champlain and along the Hudson River, but held them weakly; the British, for their part, evacuated Fort George at the

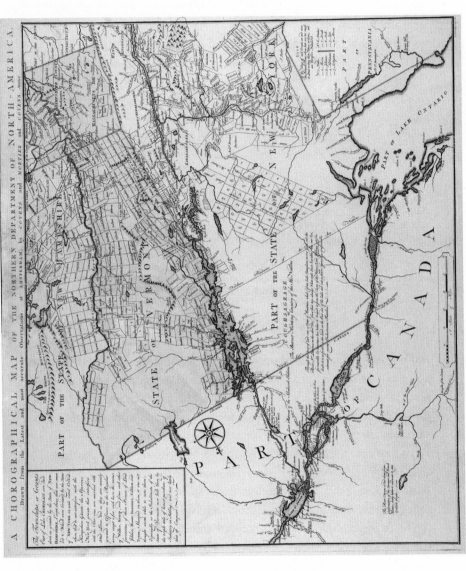

The border region, as mapped in 1780. *Courtesy, Osher Map Library, University of Southern Maine*

southern end of the lake, destroyed the rebels' works on Mount Independence and burned Fort Ticonderoga, although they continued to use the
site and its northern neighbor, Crown Point, as staging areas for raiders
venturing into the United States. The fleet that Carleton built in 1776
patrolled Lake Champlain, but its coasts, sparsely settled before the war,
were increasingly deserted. The loyalists fled north to Canada; the rebels
fled south, to Albany and its environs. War parties of regulars and irregulars, white men and red, rebels and king's men, burned farms and mills.
Each side took turns pillaging and burning Skenesborough, once the site
of a small, thriving manorial plantation, then of a humming shipyard.

There was, however, plenty of movement along the lake: raiding parties, some quite large, as many as a thousand men; scouting parties,
twenty or thirty strong, but oftener no more than half a dozen; lonely
spies, slinking through the woods to safe houses owned by fearful sympathizers, or to the blockhouses that served as listening posts in a shadow
war. There were no more big battles along the Great Warpath for the
duration of the conflict, but plenty of action—ambushes, the smashing
and burning of public and private property, a kidnapping here, a killing
there; a settling of scores. This was civil war, and also war in which alle-
giances were shifting and uncertain. As in most civil wars, allegiance
could be a slippery thing.

Take, for example, the case of sixty-year-old Joseph-Louis Gill, or as
he was sometimes known, "Magouaouidombaouit." The child of an
English couple captured and then adopted by Abenakis of New England,
he married the daughter of a chief of the St. Francis Indians, and became
one of five principal chiefs of that town, composed largely of Abenaki
refugees from the Americans. He lost his wife and one child in Robert
Rogers' murderous raid on St. Francis in October 1759. He became the
chief spokesman of the tribe in dealing with the British but seems to have
played both sides: In the summer of 1778 another group of Abenaki
scouts captured five Americans who had escaped prison in Quebec. In
their possession was a map, drawn by Gill, that was to have guided them
safely to New England. They reported their discovery to British authorities, and Gill fled across the border to Newbury, Vermont. In August
1780, following a clandestine overture from the superintendent of Indian
affairs in Montreal, he redefected. A year later he led a small band back to
Vermont, capturing there the notorious ranger Major Benjamin Whit-

comb, leader of St. Clair's scouts at Ticonderoga, and wanted by the British for the ungentlemanly act of picking off a British general from ambush. Whitcomb escaped on the way back—by arrangement, some of the suspicious Abenakis believed—but if so was not particularly grateful to Gill, since he then planned a retaliatory snatch operation that would have burned down St. Francis a second time.[1]

The leaders changed as well. The generals commanding armies in the field—Arnold and Burgoyne, Fraser and St. Clair—gave way to younger, more junior men, majors or lieutenant colonels, sometimes captains, commanding detachments on the front lines. They were harder, perhaps, more adventurous, and possibly more ruthless. And behind them, in cities remote from the front, the generals-in-chief played a far larger role. In Quebec, Frédéric Haldimand, a Swiss officer in British service, replaced Guy Carleton as governor of Canada and the commander in chief there.

Haldimand, a Swiss veteran of the Royal Americans in the last war, returned to Canada in June 1778 and after a month surveying the scene, reported back to London that "this extensive province by which alone, in the present circumstances, at least as far as we know, Great Britain can seize fast hold of America is in its present condition, quite open to the insults and ravages of the colonies in actual rebellion." His somber conclusion: "If this goes, America most probably will be lost to Great Britain for ever."[2]

Haldimand's great opponent was no longer Philip Schuyler (who had been relieved the previous summer) or even simply those who succeeded him in command of the Northern Department. Rather, it was a variety of political and military figures in the United States who had never given up on the idea of conquering Canada. Less than a month before Haldimand arrived in Quebec, on May 30, 1778, George Washington himself had written to a friend, Virginia politician Landon Carter:

> Your ideas of [Canada's] importance to our political union coincides exactly with mine—if that country is not with us, it will, from its proximity to the Eastern States—its intercourse, & connection with the numerous tribes of Western Indians—its communion with them by water, and other local advantages, be at least a troublesome, if not a dangerous neighbor to us; and ought, at all events, to be in the same interest & politics of the other States.[3]

The balance of initiative had shifted: It was now the Americans on the offensive, buoyed enormously by their alliance with France, and the British, weakened and dismayed, on the defensive.

Haldimand took a gloomy view of his task. The fortifications of Quebec (which he feared might soon experience a siege from a French fleet backed by American soldiers) were "entirely rotten" and the colony's forts and posts "in a very defenceless state." With the exception of the clergy and nobility, the Canadians were unreliable, and would be more so if French forces broke into the colony. The rebels had spies throughout the province, knew its geography, and drew supporters from the "many favourers of rebellion who are indefatigable in their endeavours to poison the minds of the Canadians." He had few troops, poor woodsmen in the case of the English, in the case of the Germans "only fit for garrison duty." Nonetheless Haldimand saw a political vulnerability on the opposing side that he could exploit:

> The seeds of jealousy and dissension between the colonies have long been sown; they are ripe for breaking out whenever they have peace at home, and from hence it will be easy whenever these internal commotions break out to make the most of them.[4]

Here lay his opportunity and he intended to take it.

For his part, although Washington certainly favored what he called "the emancipation" of Canada, he thought it a second priority: First he had to contain the main British forces in Philadelphia and New York, while preserving an army always on the point of dissolving through desertion and expiring enlistments. He had to cope, if not with conspiracies against him, then with the grumblings and envy of subordinate generals, and even more with the rising star of Horatio Gates, victor of Saratoga, who some saw as a potential replacement for the commander in chief. He had to advise Congress, and while deferring to its authority, restrain its ill-informed eagerness to direct military operations, overcome as it was with exuberance at the possibilities opened up by the appearance of a French fleet and a French army in America. He had, as well, to cope with an enervating war weariness and the petulant, sometimes vicious, internal disputes and jealousies of those who led the new country—a spirit of exhaustion, disillusionment, and resentment that spawned the greatest shock of the war, the desertion of his most brilliant general, Benedict Arnold, after some sixteen months of undetected treason.

These two strategic chess players, Haldimand and Washington, conducted much of their game along the Champlain corridor and some of its tributary rivers and valleys. The Great Warpath thus became a theater of phantom campaigns—operations cloaked in secrecy and subterfuge, covert action by spies and raiders, projected military and political maneuvers, pregnant with large possibilities, that had large indirect effects even if they never came to fruition. The issue was, in one way, that of 1775: Would the Americans take Canada? But it was also, as it turned out, even greater: What kind of United States would emerge from a war that seemed increasingly likely to end in American independence?

The child of folly

Upon learning of the surrender of Burgoyne's army at Saratoga a few days after it occurred on October 17, 1777, George Washington sent his trusted aide, Lieutenant Colonel Alexander Hamilton, north with a pressing task: to secure the return of eighteen regiments—perhaps five thousand men—to the main army opposite Philadelphia, whence they had come. If Gates intended to use some of that force to take Ticonderoga, he could send fewer, but the urgent need of the army was to prevent the British from breaking out of the occupied capital. Hamilton arrived on November 5, and ran into implacable opposition. To send such a force southward would expose Albany, which Gates described as "the finest arsenal in America."[5] It would uncover the New York highlands, where a belated minor offensive by General Henry Clinton had seized several forts and unnerved Gates on the eve of the surrender. Gates, now tasting glory for the first time in his career, rather enjoyed it, and seemed ready to use his prestige for advantage in getting his way. Hamilton "found insuperable inconveniences in acting diametrically opposite to the opinion of a Gentleman, whose successes have raised him into the highest importance."[6]

Although much of the credit for the success of the Saratoga campaign belonged to Schuyler, Arnold, and Daniel Morgan, Gates had become the hero of the New England states. In a rash act of tribute, at the end of November, Congress appointed him president of the Board of War, technically, at least, making him Washington's superior, although the latter clearly did not see it that way. Meanwhile, the contrast between Gates's smashing victory, even if he was hardly the sole author of it, and Washington's defeats at Brandywine and Germantown, and the loss of Philadelphia, made some wonder whether the country had the right general in chief. Certainly, there were murmurings, although it remains unclear whether there was a formally organized Conway Cabal—a plot to replace Washington with Gates, led by Thomas Conway, an Irish exile who had made a military career first in France, and then, when the Revolution broke out, in America. But whether Conway had formally plotted or not, he was, at the very least, indiscreet.

It was with a shock that General Conway received from Washington the following letter written on November 5:

> *Sir,*
> *A letter which I received last night, contained the following paragraph.*
> *In a letter from General Conway to General Gates he says—"Heaven has been determined to save your Country; or a weak General and bad Counselors would have ruined it."*
> *I am Sir Your Humble Servant*

The commander in chief's unstated, icy scorn had the desired effect. Conway's response that evening began with a grovel, "You are a brave man, an honest man, a patriot, and a man of great sense," as he weakly admitted that the offending words might have slipped from his pen.[7]

Whether or not a serious scheme to replace Washington with Gates actually existed, the fact was that for the moment, Gates had, if not the upper hand, a kind of influence that Washington and his loyal lieutenants could not ignore. Gates seems to have proposed "an irruption" into Canada that winter, and Congress enthusiastically ordered it in late January. The notion was to concentrate a force of twenty-five hundred to four thousand men who would rendezvous at the mouth of the Onion River, at the location of present Burlington, Vermont. This would be a winter campaign, conducted on snowshoes, and would have the object of winning the province, if possible, or at the very least of destroying the British fleet in its icebound river port of St. Johns. If the expedition could do that—if it could wipe out the sole advantage the British had left in the north, their maritime command of Lake Champlain—the way lay open for the unification of Canada with the United States. Congress had just finished drafting its Articles of Confederation on November 15, and Article 11 provided that Canada could join the United States without any further ado as the fourteenth state. Any other would-be states would have to win the approval of at least nine of the original thirteen.[8]

Gates would not command the "irruption." Instead, Congress turned to one of the French officers serving in the Continental Army, on the reasonable theory that a French general in command of an invading army would impress and win over the Canadians. The twenty-two-year-old major general Congress chose was Marie Joseph Paul Yves Roch Gilbert du Motier, Marquis de Lafayette. He had, despite his youth, six years of military service under highly competent French soldiers before sailing to the United States, where he arrived in June 1777. In a few short months he had fallen under Washington's spell, and remained, for the rest of his life, a passionate defender of the man who was, in many ways, a father to him in a foreign land. When he received, in late January 1778, the letter from Gates appointing him commander of the expedition to Canada, his emotions were decidedly mixed. On the one hand, he had already begun to sniff out the murmuring aimed at Washington amongst Gates, Conway, and some in Congress, including, possibly unfairly, John Adams. The politicians he described as "rigid republicans, but more capable of destroying than preserving the republic." Gates he considered "a good officer" who had, however, "neither the talent, the intelligence, nor the willpower necessary for supreme command."[9] Conway, despite his long service in the French army, he viewed as an intriguing adventurer. Washington, as he told his father-in-law, was something utterly different: "a man truly made for this revolution which could not succeed without him. I admire him more each day for the beauty of his character and spirit."[10] Lafayette wished to serve under Washington, and indeed, wrote to Henry Laurens, president of Congress—to whom he reserved the right of direct communication—that even in command of such an expedition, he wanted to be considered as commanding a detached element of Washington's army.

On the other hand, Lafayette's vaulting ambition, his insatiable desire for glory, and his twin patriotism, for the United States and

France, made the idea of liberating the French Canadians from British rule intoxicating, even if it meant leaving Washington behind. "It is, Sir, an highly pleasant idea for me, to think of a large parcel of my countrymen, driving their natural and tyrannical enemy out of the lands they had taken from them, and enjoying all the advantages of liberty by their strict union with thirteen other states." [11] He intended, however, to lead the expedition on his own terms.

In a move hardly likely to dispel Washington's suspicions of a plot to replace him as commander in chief with Gates, Congress had appointed Conway as the northern army's deputy commander. Disliking the thought of having someone disloyal to his beloved chief as his own deputy, Lafayette asked for Major General Alexander McDougall, a steady, if ailing veteran, to serve instead, arguing that an American army should not have two foreigners at its head. Congress found this reasoning convincing. But Lafayette wanted French officers already serving in the Continental Army, including the Baron de Kalb, assigned to him in lesser roles in order to ease the army's path in raising the Canadians against the British oppressor. As he confessed to his wife: "Canada is oppressed by the English and (between us) has had no reason to be satisfied with the Americans." He believed, however, that he and other French officers could overcome the diffidence of the Canadian peasantry. Meanwhile, he had already outmaneuvered Conway, and on his way north mischievously unnerved Washington's denigrators by insisting that they join him in a toast to the commander in chief.

As for Washington himself, although he described the expedition as "the child of folly," which "must be productive of capital ills," he declined to oppose it openly, prudently deferring to the newly empowered Board of War. [12] When, however, Gates condescended to ask Washington's opinion of the project, the commander in chief coldly replied that "as I neither know the extent of the Objects in view—nor the means to be employed to effect them, it is not in my power to pass any judgment upon the subject." [13]

Lafayette's pleasant dreams of the swift liberation of Canada crumbled when he arrived in Albany on February 17, 1778. He found Colonel Moses Hazen, last seen feuding with Benedict Arnold, making various excuses and promises—all equally unconvincing—about sleighs, clothes, and cattle. In fact there were not twenty-five hundred men awaiting

Lafayette (the minimum he had been led to expect), but rather twelve hundred. There was no money, no food, little clothing, no snowshoes, nothing, in short, with which to launch a hazardous winter assault two hundred miles northward over ice and snow. "You will be more surprised that General Gates seems not so well acquainted with the northern department as myself who am here since two days," Lafayette wrote the president of Congress. But he had more in mind than a mere dig at Gates, the overweening victor of Saratoga. "There is in [this] ridiculous and shocking affair a piece of folly or a piece of villainy beyond all expressions," he fulminated. [14]

Within two days of arriving in Albany, Lafayette concluded that his meager, ill-equipped, unfunded, demoralized, and dispersed command simply could not launch a winter assault. And, in a fit of mortified self-pity understandable in a twenty-two-year-old French aristocrat if unbecoming in a major general in the Continental Army, he imagined news of this failure spreading throughout Europe. "The whole world has their eyes fixed upon me," he somewhat improbably declared, and writhed at what that world would think when he would have to liquidate this operation in a "ridiculous way." "Men will have a right to laugh at me." [15] What could be worse? In March, Henry Laurens mustered his resources of good sense to get Congress to cancel the winter operation and to reassign Lafayette to Washington without too much fuss. Lafayette, somewhat mollified, took the high road, telling the Baron von Steuben, another European soldier just arrived in America, that such treatment in Europe would have been unthinkable, but aristocratic forebearance restored, he observed that "in a young country one must have patience and yield to circumstances." [16]

Washington wrote dismissively of Congress's decision, "I shall say no more of the Canada expedition than that it is at an end. I never was made acquainted with a single circumstance relating to it." [17] In mid-April, Congress sent Gates back to command the Northern Department, subsequently sending him to Boston, where, safe among the New Englanders who admired him, he was well out of the way of possible intrigues against Washington. For six months after the cancellation of the "irruption," events distracted Congress and the American high command from contemplating more such adventures. In February 1778, the United States and France signed treaties of alliance and commerce, which Congress ratified in early May. France's overt participation in the war of American independence transformed the conflict from a colonial insurrection to a global war, to be fought out in the Caribbean (where both England and France had valuable sugar islands), the Mediterranean, and even India. In North America it meant the appearance of a French fleet in early July 1778, and with it the possibility of combined operations.

In a frantic reaction to the debacle of Saratoga, the British government put together in February a new peace commission led by the Earl of Carlisle offering terms that yielded to virtually all American demands (particularly on taxation), save a nominal independence. They were at least two years too late, and Congress rebuffed the overtures. On the continent of North America, the new commander in chief, competent, pessimistic, and harried Sir Henry Clinton, realized that he must now compete for resources with other theaters, including the financially lucrative West Indies. For his part, Washington anticipated, correctly, that the British would evacuate Philadelphia, which they did in mid-June, adroitly fending off American attacks in a withdrawal to New York. The Americans, in their first substantial combined operation with the French, then attacked an isolated British garrison at Newport, Rhode Island, in August. In the incapable hands of John Sullivan (last seen delaying the withdrawal from Canada until catastrophe was nigh), who spent almost as much time quarreling with his counterpart, a French admiral, as fighting his enemies, the expedition failed, and the French fleet withdrew to Boston.

Still, in midsummer 1778, American prospects looked remarkably good. They had a powerful ally, whose fleet seemed capable of disputing command of the sea with Great Britain. The army had come through the winter of Valley Forge better organized and disciplined than ever before, thanks partly to the good work of Baron von Steuben, one of Frederick the Great's junior officers who found his real vocation in training American soldiers. The British government had made overtures that made it look weak, if not desperate. The British army had withdrawn from Philadelphia, the American capital—now triumphantly reoccupied—and seemed unlikely to resume offensive operations anywhere. Indeed, as Washington wrote the Board of War in early August 1778, "We have a prospect that the British army will ere long be necessitated either to abandon the possessions they now hold and quit these states, or perhaps to do something still more disgraceful," that is, surrender.[18] Under what appeared to be such favorable circumstances, the possibility of invading Canada arose once again, giving birth to a new, more comprehensive and more realistic plan that would bring America's French allies to center stage.

———————•◦•———————

No Nation is to be trusted farther
than it is bound by its interest

The immediate occasion for the new scheme was the dispatch of Benjamin Franklin to Paris in the autumn of 1778 as minister plenipotentiary. Congress instructed him to dangle under French noses the prospect of destroying the British fishing industry, and with it one of the bases of British naval power, by the occupation of Halifax and Quebec. To that end, Congress provided a plan for operations to commence by late spring 1779, drafted in large part by a board of officers composed of Gates, Hazen, and Brigadier General Jacob Bayley, a Vermonter who held a New York commission. They had produced an extraordinarily ambitious concept, calling for thrusts from multiple points at Detroit, Niagara, and Oswego, the formerly French forts along the northwestern frontier. The central effort would be a winter attack up the Connecticut River valley (along what is now the Vermont–New Hampshire border), parallel to Lake Champlain and aimed, like the abortive winter campaign of 1778, at destroying the British naval base at St. Johns, seizing Montreal, and opening up Lake Champlain to a maritime line of supply. On their own the Americans might just do this in one year's campaign; they could not, however, also hope to take Quebec city in one season and complete the conquest—or rather, the "emancipation"—of Canada in 1779. Therefore, Congress contended, Franklin should attempt to persuade the French to launch a major naval expedition in the spring of 1779 that would sail up the St. Lawrence and besiege Quebec much as Wolfe had in 1759. Some four or five thousand French troops, when combined with much larger American forces moving north along the Great Warpath, should together complete the conquest.[19] By the winter of 1779, or the spring of 1780 at the latest, the allies would have seized Canada.

Rather belatedly, it occurred to Congress that it might be wise to consult the commander in chief about this plan before asking Franklin to put it before the French. Washington, fully aware that Congress desired to take Canada, and sympathizing with the idea himself, had already begun preparations. He had ordered General Bayley, stationed in Newbury, Vermont, and at the southern edge of the no-man's-land between Canada and the states, to begin collecting intelligence—on the size of the British garrison, its locations, the mood of the Canadians, the disposition of the Indians, the status of the crops, and much else. He had also corresponded with his friend and long-suffering colleague in the north, Philip Schuyler, who strongly doubted the possibility of any successful operation against Canada that did not follow the Lake Champlain route. Brigadier General John Stark of New Hampshire also chimed in: It would be impossible to mass the kind of provisions needed for several thousand men for an attack delivered by land roughly along the Connecticut River valley route.

But the news was not entirely bad. Schuyler thought it possible to take St. Johns by a *coup de main* launched on the frozen lake in February or March 1779, and then rush reinforcements and supplies north along Lake Champlain once the ice melted; Bayley's agents—a mixture of Indians, disaffected French Canadians, and Americans masquerading as Tories—accurately reported that there were barely fifty-five hundred troops in all of Canada, many of them dispirited Germans, that the French Canadians had been affected by France's entry into the war, and that some of the Indians of St. Francis, long the terror of the New England frontier, were willing to come to terms with the Americans. The mood of defeatism in Canada, it seemed, was contagious.

Congress had asked Washington for his observations on the draft plan, requesting that he send a copy to Lafayette, who was shortly to return to France for some months of leave. Washington wrote three letters, the first on November 11, 1778, to Henry Laurens, president of Congress, which might be shared with other members of Congress; the second, a private note on the fourteenth; the third, a letter to the new president of Congress, John Jay, on December 13.[20]

Washington's first, semipublic letter began by politely saying that he would not send a copy to Lafayette as requested, because of necessity he must discuss "our wants and our weaknesses," which "ought only to be known to ourselves." He favored an attack on Canada, he said, but opposed launching it now. The United States, in its first alliance as an

independent country, should not make an agreement on a coalition operation "without a moral certainty of being able to fulfill our part, particularly if the first proposal came from us." The Americans would need a
large force to execute the plan—12,600 on the front lines, he estimated,
but, he reminded the politicians, at least as many would be needed to
build roads, guard supplies, and move them forward. The shortage of
hard money in the United States would make it difficult to buy the
needed supplies, which they would not likely find in Canada. The Americans would have to wage "war at an immense distance, in a country wild
and uncultivated—incapable of affording any aid—and a great part of it
hostile." Moreover, he thought, the Americans ran the risk of underesti-
mating British recuperative power, particularly when confronted by a
mortal threat. To lose Canada would be to lose Britain's entire North
American position, "a deadly blow to her trade and empire," and if Halifax
fell as well it would mean the loss of the "finest port and best naval arsenal
in America." Britain would throw naval and military resources into the
fight, and would contest fiercely such a stroke.

Washington also criticized the complexity of the plan. It called for
multiple, coordinated attacks, by forces composed largely of militia, many
of whom would be reluctant to fight outside their states, or endure the
grueling conditions of siege warfare. He concluded, however, on an emol-
lient note. If the British evacuated Rhode Island and New York, dispersing their army as they did so, the possibility of taking at least some of
Canada would open up. But for the moment, the commander in chief
thought the plan a bad one, the risks excessive, and the chance of failure
high. Nonetheless, he continued, as ordered by Congress, he would begin
amassing resources in Albany, and continue gathering the intelligence
that would be necessary for an attack if ordered.

These were all sound arguments, if put with unusual firmness, but
Washington's second private letter of November 14 revealed his real
thinking. "My solicitude for the public welfare," and his confidence in
Laurens's discretion, allowed him to unburden himself of his deepest,
indeed, "insurmountable" objection to the plan for a combined conquest
of Canada by French and American troops. At heart, Washington did not
trust French intentions, and even if their intentions were pure, he had no
confidence in their ultimate behavior. For that matter, he did not entirely
trust Lafayette, either.

It would violate the "true and permanent interests" of the United States to place thousands of French troops in Canada, a province connected to its motherland by the ties of blood, religion, and history. The population of Canada would rally around their French liberators, and help her hold it against all comers, including Americans. Even if the French entered the enterprise with the intention of allowing Canada to join the United States, once there, retaining it as a colonial possession would prove an irresistible temptation. Canada offered raw materials (particularly naval stores), a renewal of her previous trade with the Indians, bases for her navy, control of the Newfoundland fisheries, and the power, "finally, of awing and controlling these States, the natural and most formidable rival of every Maritime power in Europe."

"No Nation is to be trusted farther than it is bound by its interest," Washington believed, and so the Americans could trust no solemn pledge from their allies. France might claim Canada as security for American debts to France. And if it came to a confrontation, the United States could do little against a French fleet occupying the St. Lawrence, some four or five thousand French troops holding the conquered citadel of Quebec, and a population overjoyed at returning to rule by Frenchmen.

And it could get even worse. If France and Spain, aided by the United States, defeated Great Britain, the United States would find itself flanked in the south by a Spain allied with France, in the north by France herself, and to the west, by the Indians, whom the French had always known how to manage. France would, in this case, "have it in her power to give law to these States." Under such conditions, "resentment, reproaches, and submission seem to be all that would be left us." He warned Laurens that "men are very apt to run into extremes, hatred to England may carry some into an excess of confidence in France," and even Lafayette did not escape his suspicion. The marquis had offered the idea of a combined attack on Canada as though it were his own, but Washington suggested that the idea had been conceived in Paris, and planted on Lafayette as a witting or unwitting tool of French policy.

Here was a very different Washington than Lafayette may have supposed he knew—cautious and coldly suspicious. On December 5, a committee of Congress, responding to Washington's first letter, conceded the force of his logistical arguments, and agreed to postpone an invasion of Canada unless the British abandoned their positions along the American coast. Nonetheless, they asked Washington to prepare attacks on the string of British forts to the northwest, including Niagara, and continue contingency planning with the French, including Lafayette. On December 13, Washington wrote a third letter, to John Jay, the new president of Congress, quite remarkable in its combination of formal deference to civilian authority and implacable opposition to its desires. A servant of Congress, he insisted, he found himself in the "greatest uneasiness when I find myself in circumstances of hesitation or doubt with respect to their directions." But, he insisted, it would be impossible to plan an attack in collaboration with the French. He would continue preparations for an attack on Niagara (which, parenthetically, would require no French cooperation), and he offered to brief Congress in person about the logistical difficulties attendant on a Canadian campaign. But he refrained from writing to Lafayette as directed, until he had had the chance to speak privately with his political masters.

Washington spent all of January 1779 in liberated Philadelphia. But he clearly had carried his point earlier, because when he wrote on December 29 to Lafayette, who was heading back to France, it was with bland assurances of friendship—and an enclosed report from Congress regretfully postponing the operation in Canada indefinitely. Lafayette sailed from Boston on January 11, probably just after receiving Washington's letter. But before leaving, in the cheerful and mistaken belief that the enterprise would eventually take place, he had drafted an address to the Indians of Canada that would have unnerved Washington further. "You remember that your fathers told you on leaving Canada that you would see them appear again one day or other. . . . Well, my children, they are going to keep their word to you."[21] His mentor and friend had, however, made certain that they could not.

Lafayette still longed for the expedition. In the summer of 1779 Lafayette wrote about what he called "my favourite scheme" to the French foreign minister, Count Vergennes. He outlined two French views of Canada after the conclusion of the war, the first that it would be good to have that country remain under British control, threatening the United States and thereby reinforcing American need for an alliance with France; the second that a liberated Canada subsequently joining the United States would give France all the advantages of trade, raw materials, relations with the Indians while adding to the balance of the new world a fourteenth state, which will always be attached to us and which by its situation would offer a great preponderance in the troubles that will one day divide America.[22]

This last suggests that Lafayette could take a dark, or at least a complex view of Americans. He clearly favored the second approach: Canada should become the fourteenth state, but closely linked with France. The French government, however, adhered to the first view: Much better to have a United States confined by, and at odds with, an antagonistic British presence to its north, and hence perpetually dependent on France. Ironically, in view of Washington's dark suspicions, no French statesman seems to have wished to recover Canada—a colony ever costly to maintain, difficult and in the end impossible for France to defend.[23]

When Lafayette returned to the United States in the spring of 1780, however, Washington was quite happy to exploit him and his zeal for the reconquest of Canada to support one of the deception schemes the commander in chief enjoyed. In this case, Washington wanted to persuade the British to draw off troops to defend Canada, weakening their army in New York and the South. He therefore encouraged Lafayette to spread declarations in Canada suggesting that a French fleet and army would appear in the St. Lawrence, and hinting that he would command the American corps working with the French. "The more mystery in this business the better. It will get out and it ought to seem to be against our intention."[24] Washington did that better than he realized, because he passed a draft proclamation of this kind for surreptitious printing in Philadelphia to the military governor of that city—and Benedict Arnold, at this point deep into his treason, promptly passed it to his British contacts, where it had the desired effects. Lafayette does not seem to have understood the extent to which this was all a ploy, writing as he did to the French foreign minister, and the French ambassador to the United States, that if French troops were not sent to the West Indies they should be directed to the conquest of Canada. To the end of the war and even beyond Lafayette pined for the opportunity to liberate his countrymen in Canada from the British yoke while uniting them with his adopted second homeland. When he finally left the United States at the end of the war he told Congress that he had no personal regrets, "but independent of personal gratifications, it is known that I ever was bent upon the addition of Canada to the United States."[25]

----•-•----

There remain no more of these traitors on either side of Lake Champlain

In Quebec, Frédéric Haldimand took the schemes of his enemies and the weaknesses of his own position with the utmost seriousness. Even before arriving in Canada he warned that it "will be the principal object of the designs of the French as well as of the rebels"—a conviction that only strengthened over time—and asked for reinforcements and authorities commensurate with his task.[26] In the meantime, British intelligence in New York had picked up the first set of American plans for a winter raid on St. Johns under Lafayette and Conway in the early winter of 1778. The British government knew in advance of Lafayette's impending return to France at the end of that year, and suspected that he did so "to solicit and promote some conjunct operation against Canada."[27] Haldimand had good sources: British spies were no less active in New York and New England than the Americans were in Canada. Indians, loyalists, and ambiguous characters of various kinds slipped back and forth with gossip, news, and information.

Haldimand understood all the reasons a renewed invasion of Canada might appeal to both the Americans and the French, and even if their interests might ultimately oppose one another, that would make little difference to a Great Britain that had lost her North American possessions. He had doubts about the abilities of his loyalist troops ("a useful corps with the axe, not altogether to be depended on with the firelock") and even more about the Germans ("the refuse of those who accompanied General Burgoyne"), whom he thought prone to desertion. The Indians were wavering—as the case of Joseph-Louis Gill suggested. The British fleet on Lake Champlain could stop a naval attack by that route, but a winter raid on the ice might get through. The Americans could assault along the Niagara frontier, or infiltrate units across the Vermont and New Hampshire borders and raise the Canadians against British rule.

Haldimand pondered as well the gravest threat of all: a French amphibious assault on Quebec. Any British setback "would raise the whole country in arms against us," he informed London, insisting that his opinion rested "upon a precise knowledge of the general disposition of the inhabitants."[28] He could no longer count on the priests to keep their flock in line: "The clergy, who in general behaved so well in 1775 and 1776, since the French alliance with the rebel colonies are cooled very much to the British interests." Mistrusting even the Canadian gentry, Haldimand declined La Corne St. Luc's request for promotion in the militia to the rank of colonel, leaving the dissatisfied old man to console himself with rebuttals of Burgoyne's accusations, his considerable wealth, and the company of his third, and much younger wife, who survived him (he died in 1784) by a good thirty-five years. Haldimand feared the appeal of French soldiers to *habitants* and aristocrats alike. He knew, among other things, that the French had sent an able naval commander, Louis Antoine de Bougainville, to Boston with a squadron of warships. This was the same Bougainville who had served as an aide to Montcalm at Fort Carillon in 1758, and Haldimand was convinced (incorrectly, as it happened) that this was part of a carefully concerted French plan to reconquer the old colony using a distinguished veteran of the previous war.

To counter these threats, real and imagined, Haldimand took various measures.[29] Much of his activity was of necessity purely defensive—he set Captain William Twiss, the indispensable engineer who had cut the path for Burgoyne's artillery to the top of Mount Defiance, to reconstruct the defenses of Quebec as well as St. Johns. He reinforced other outposts, including Detroit and Niagara, strengthening their fortifications and replenishing their garrisons with the aid of modest reinforcements sent from New York (with much grumbling from General Clinton) as well as Europe. He expanded his intelligence networks in New York and New England and built a chain of small outposts to help intercept American agents moving north. Like Carleton before him, he worked closely with French clergy (to the extent he trusted them) and *seigneurs* to tamp down any Canadian sympathy with the Americans. But he took the offensive as well. In doing this he followed the strategy dictated in Britain. Germain

had instructed the new commander in chief, Sir Henry Clinton, to reinforce Canada, both "to secure the province and to annoy the rebellious
colonies on that side and oblige them to keep a considerable body of their
troops on foot for the defence of their frontiers."[30] The way to defeat
American ambitions was first, to strip the country bare of provisions to
prevent an invasion; second, to distract them with attacks on their own
frontiers; and third, to terrify the border populations into, if not submission, then at least quiescence.

On October 24, 1778, Major Christopher Carleton, twenty-nine-
year-old nephew of the previous governor, General Sir Guy Carleton, led
a flotilla south from Isle aux Noix. Orphaned at age four, Carleton had
begun a precocious military career at age twelve that early on took him to
America, where he spent most of his time living among the Mohawk
Indians. According to some sources, he went through the harrowing
ordeals of the Mohawks, had himself tattooed, painted his face, and even,
for a time, had a ring in his nose.[31] He did, however, marry in the English
fashion, and to none other than his uncle's wife's older sister, a somewhat
improbable, but apparently happy connection.

Carleton's force included regulars from three British regiments, loyalists, and the Royal Artillery—some 350 in all, plus a few Germans and one
hundred Indians whom he had a superb gift for managing. Haldimand
ordered him (in French, the language in which Haldimand was still the
most comfortable) to destroy American foodstuffs, mills, and forage along
the shore of Lake Champlain, seizing rebels, destroying boats and farms.[32]
Haldimand wanted to make it impossible for the Americans to mass the
provisions along the Great Warpath that they would need for the winter
attack he believed they were planning. During the next two and a half
weeks, Carleton and his men did a brilliant job of destruction. Provisions
enough for twelve thousand men ruined, hundreds of horses, hogs, and
cattle slaughtered or seized, forty-seven homes, twenty-one barns full of
wheat, a sawmill and a grist mill burned, forty prisoners taken (men
only—the women were released). A grimly pleased Haldimand informed
London, "At present there remain no more of these traitors on either side
of Lake Champlain from near Ticonderoga to Canada."[33]

For the next three years, Haldimand expanded this policy of raiding,
making use of Carleton and other commanders, including Guy and John

Johnson, cousin and son of William Johnson respectively. In 1780 Christopher Carleton conducted an even larger operation: With nine hundred men—again, a combination of regulars, loyalists, and Indians—he struck more deeply. Launching from the ruined site of Fort Ticonderoga, he burned down Fort Anne, one of the Americans' forward outposts in New York, and Fort George at the site of Fort William Henry. He burned two hundred dwellings and destroyed 150,000 bushels of wheat, and again, took male prisoners, sending the women and children back to American lines.[34]

This differed in some respects from border warfare as the French had waged it. Carleton moved with large, more conventional parties; he treated his prisoners well, and seems to have been able to control, or at least limit, Indian atrocities. Because of American participation on both sides it partook more of civil war, however, than a clash between nations. In the Mohawk valley and along the New York and Pennsylvania frontiers it did become savage, as neighbor fought neighbor, and as the Indians—who in many ways had hoped to stay out of this fight—were drawn in.

For the Iroquois, in particular, the war was a near-fatal calamity. It had already brought internecine fighting between those who supported the British and those allied with the Americans. It now brought further suffering in the Iroquois heartland. In 1779, Washington had ordered John Sullivan—usually unlucky in war, as in Canada in 1776 and Rhode Island in 1778, but always ready to engage in it nonetheless—on a major offensive in Iroquois country in the Finger Lakes region of New York. Sullivan encountered the Indians (whom Haldimand had failed to reinforce in time) in only one battle, a relatively minor clash. But in a campaign more significant than the casualty bill might suggest, he destroyed the villages and farms of the Indians, who had wisely evacuated in his path. The impoverished families fled to Canada, adding to Haldimand's burdens. The braves, however, returned, quite literally with a vengeance, to the warpath, led by Joseph Brant, brother of William Johnson's Indian wife, Molly. The border regions smoldered and burned.[35]

It was at this point that Haldimand, acting on instruction from London, played his most daring card. He attempted to pry the United States apart, with independence as his unlikely lever, and Vermont as his fulcrum.

He professes so much honesty accompanied with so many
sincere gestures that he rather seems to overact

Thirty-three-year-old Captain Justus Sherwood of the Queen's Loyal
Rangers picked his way to the American camp commanded by Colonel
Herrick carefully, but not clandestinely. It was the end of October 1780,
and the fife and drum and flag that accompanied him and his half dozen
companions signaled that he came to parley. He had sailed to ruined
Skenesborough and walked the rough road to Herrick's outpost, whence
he asked the Vermont citizen-soldiers on duty to convey him to Castleton, the nearby headquarters of General Ethan Allen, commander of Vermont's militia, to discuss a prisoner exchange. That was the nominal
purpose of the mission: The real purpose, following upon an initiative
from Governor Chittenden of Vermont in July 1779, was a broader set of
political talks about Vermont leaving the war.

Sherwood took care: Some of these men considered him an even
more grievous traitor because he had once been one of them. A Connecticut native (like many Vermonters) who had helped settle the eastern
shores of Lake Champlain on Otter Creek, he had helped found the
Green Mountain Boys. A friend and companion of Seth Warner and
Ethan and Ira Allen, he had defended the New Englanders who had settled Vermont against the claims of the hated New Yorkers. But in the
summer of 1776 he had argued with his neighbors against taking up arms
against Great Britain. A few weeks later a mob plundered and ransacked
his home, terrified his pregnant wife and his child, scattered and trampled
his personal papers. That was the beginning. They came back again,
whipped him with beech rods, and sentenced him to life, and probably a
short life at that, in the Revolution's gulag—the Simsbury Mines in Connecticut, an abandoned copper mine eighty feet below the surface of the
earth.

Luckily Sherwood had escaped before getting to that deathly prison.
He gathered forty other Tories and hid in the mountains he knew well,
eventually making his way to Crown Point, where he joined the British
army, serving as a scout. He served in that band of loyalists who had

swept through Hubbardton the day before the battle, alarming his old friend Seth Warner. He scouted for the hapless German lieutenant colonel Baum at Bennington. He rejoined Burgoyne but knowing what awaited a recaptured loyalist, slipped away just before the surrender, and, reunited with his no less courageous wife, who had made her way to Crown Point, went to St. Johns, where he became one of the leading figures in Haldimand's secret service based there.[36]

Vermont had declared its independence in January 1777 and adopted a constitution in July, but Congress had not recognized it, and New York, led by Governor George Clinton (no relation to Sir Henry, the British commander in New York City), opposed it violently. Sherwood and Haldimand believed that the new republic had had enough of war. It had a small, understrength regiment under Seth Warner serving in the Continental Army, stationed in New York; the rest of its militia occupied a string of blockhouses running east from Castleton (slightly northeast of Skenesborough), across the mountains, and then on a sharper angle northeast to Newbury on the New Hampshire frontier. Vermont controlled less than half of its territory, in other words: The large area to the north of this line lay either uninhabited or, like the settlements at the mouth of the Onion River and Otter Creek, devastated by Haldimand's raids. Sherwood and Haldimand saw an opening here, as did Lord George Germain in London. He wrote Haldimand in March of 1780:

> The drawing over the inhabitants of the country they call Vermont to the British cause appears a matter of such vast importance for the safety of Canada, and as affording the means of annoying the northern revolted provinces, that I think it right to repeat to you the King's wishes that you may be able to effect it, though it should be attended with a considerable expense.[37]

Benedict Arnold, now in 1780 turning his formidable talents to the king's service, agreed. Some of his suggestions had gone beyond a conservative English statesman's zone of comfort—why not, he asked, simply offer to pay the salary of the Continental Army, now two or more years in arrears, and offer titles of nobility to its officers? Less controversially, he, too, saw in Vermont an opportunity. "An offer to establish the people of Vermont in their assumed government might bring them over to the interest of Great Britain; their defection from the rebels would have a happy effect."[38] British agents reported what many in the colonies knew: that the Allen brothers and other leading figures, including Governor Thomas Chittenden, and Jonas Fay, son of the owner of the Catamount Tavern, headquarters of the Green Mountain Boys, were desperate about their state, ravaged by its enemies, yet deemed illegitimate by its neighbors. Ethan Allen, in particular, was viewed as a prospect for talks. The British may have tried to recruit him when he was a prisoner in 1776–77. After he was exchanged back to the Americans, in July 1780, he had received a letter from a loyalist colonel, Beverly Robinson, who engaged in secret service work for General Sir Henry Clinton in New York. The Tory wrote to Allen offering Vermont "a separate government under the king and constitution of England." Allen was too shrewd to reply in writing, but neither did he disclose to the public that he had received this communication. Now, in October 1780, he finally had the chance to pursue a discussion in person, rather than in writing.

Ethan Allen asked Sherwood for a brief private discussion before the larger talks began. Hesitating, the loyalist, surrounded by personal as well as political enemies, asked him to "take no advantage of me nor ever mention it while I remained in the country" and then proceeded to say that he had a proposition that went beyond a prisoner exchange. "If it was no damned Arnold plan to sell his country," Allen said, he would. Arnold's treason had just broke the month before, which no doubt made Allen sensitive. So, too, had a destructive British-led Indian raid on Royalton, Vermont, just a few days before, which had killed four locals and taken several dozen captive. Even so, he was prepared to listen, so Sherwood made his pitch to Allen. Governor Haldimand knew, Sherwood said, about New York's determination to persecute Vermont, and that Congress had refused, and would refuse, to recognize the fledgling state. He, Sherwood, their former friend and neighbor, wanted nothing but the best for the suffering people of Vermont. Allen stopped him abruptly, said that they had lingered away from the larger group for too long. They would continue the discussion later.

They did continue the discussion in private, staying up until two in the morning. Allen declared that he was surrounded by enemies on every side, weary of war, and eager to return to his philosophical pursuits. He supported the cause of American liberties, but stood first for the people of Vermont, now exposed to tyrannies from Congress no different in kind from those of the king. If Congress would accept Vermont as an equal state, well, the matter would end there. But if the British could aid Vermont against an invasion from its neighbors, if Britain would guarantee Vermont's independence, above all, if it gave it all the privileges of self-governance, including the right to select its own officials—why, there was something to be talked about. They would have to tread carefully, for New York had its spies all about. And, he admitted, his own people would "cut off his head" if he proposed peace with Great Britain without careful preparation. But let the negotiations continue, under the guise of prisoner exchanges, while Britain and Vermont maintained a truce with each other.

The conversation greatly encouraged Sherwood, although getting the word back to Haldimand proved difficult. Allen bade him a cheery good-bye, but the loyalist's escorts reported that an Indian raid had occurred in violation of the truce and told him that if Major Carleton had violated the good faith of the parley, Sherwood's life should answer for it. The militia had turned out in alarm, and the parties they encountered on the road were hostile and belligerent. Luckily, this Indian raid turned out to be a fiction, the Vermont authorities intervened to protect Sherwood, and he had only to contend with the elements on his way back to Canada, rather than men with gun, knife, or noose. Snowstorms, ice on the lake, short rations, and headwinds made the trip back to his own lines last nearly three weeks. But by the end of November he arrived in Quebec, and reported directly to Haldimand.

A delicate set of negotiations now ensued. The leaders of Vermont found themselves in a bind. They had pestered the leaders of Congress for recognition, with appeals to principle backed by offers of inexpensive land in Vermont—a set of payoffs that helped, but did not overcome the opposition of New York.[39] Vermont's apparent desire to expand did not make matters better: Vermonters cast greedy eyes on the slice of land between their border and the Hudson (the so-called Western Union), largely inhabited by New Englanders who had no particular affinity with New York. On even more tenuous legal grounds, they had received applications for admission to Vermont from sixteen townships east of the Connecticut River in New Hampshire (the Eastern Union). For a state with barely forty thousand inhabitants, it made for an ambitious agenda, and in the summer of 1779 Congress addressed the "pretended state of Vermont," telling it to withdraw its claims on both points of the compass, which the Vermonters prudently did. But Congress continued to refer to the state as "the New Hampshire grants," and refused to recognize what had, after all, been a functioning, self-declared government since 1777.

At the end of July 1780 Governor Chittenden and his council sent a letter to Congress, read in September. After noting that Vermont was not one of the thirteen states of the Union, they declared that under the pressure of necessity they conceived themselves

> *at liberty to offer, or accept, terms of cessation of hostilities with Great Britain,* without the approbation of any other man or body of men.[40]

Vermont had been at war for five years, and if Congress chose to usurp her rights the state had the right to reconsider the very purposes for which she had fought. This letter to Congress confirmed that something was up. Schuyler in Albany guessed correctly that Sherwood's mission—which he knew about within days—was "only a cover to some design of the enemy," and Washington instructed him to lay Sherwood by the heels if possible.[41] Washington, still reeling from the Arnold treason, suspecting that the Carleton raid was but the opening of a British campaign along the lines of Burgoyne's 1777 invasion, and coping with an increasingly discontented and possibly mutinous army, feared a grand scheme by the British. Governor George Clinton of New York was more paranoid yet, particularly when his spies in Vermont reported back Allen's remark that "he will fight, nay even run on the mountains and live on moose meat, before he will subject himself to New York, or Congress."[42] Allen had in fact much earlier come to the conclusion that Congress would not accept Vermont as a state, and might, indeed, threaten its independence. "There is a North pole as well as a South pole," the oracle of the mountains declared, "and if thunder should threaten from the South, we will shut the door opposite that point and open the door facing North."[43]

Allen had agreed to a truce, albeit one which he suggested—for cover—should include part of New York as well. He meekly accepted a request to resign as brigadier general of the Vermont militia, although he may have orchestrated that move in order better to manage the British relationship without attention. He had taken enough heat already: When it became clear that the Robinson letters would leak he promptly informed Congress of the correspondence, asserting, correctly, that he had never written back to Robinson. He chose not to burden Congress, however, with knowledge of his purely verbal discussions with British agents. But having written to the president of Congress in March 1781 that "rather than fail, [I] will retire with hardy Green Mountain Boys into the desolate caverns of the mountains, and wage war with human nature at large," there was plenty of grounds for alarm in the patriot camp. Schuyler, Washington, George Clinton, and others did indeed suspect, but did not know the truth: that Vermont's leaders had begun negotiations with the aim of bringing Vermont into the harbor of a neutral peace, ultimately as a province or protectorate of Great Britain.

The negotiations did not run smoothly. In April 1781 Chittenden sent Ira Allen, Ethan's even wilier younger brother and another emissary to Isle aux Noix, ostensibly to negotiate further prisoner exchanges and an extension of the truce. In July, Joseph Fay came to Crown Point for a prisoner exchange but, again, with a larger purpose. "He professes so much honesty accompanied with so many sincere gestures that he rather seems to overact," an exasperated Sherwood—a decent man in an indecent business—reported back.[44] Indeed, the loyalist's opinion of his erstwhile friends had gone down considerably over time. He now viewed them as a rough but negligible set who had "made themselves popular in the present rebellion by actions at which a man of honor and integrity would revolt."[45] And as for their people, Sherwood thought perhaps two-fifths ready for reunion out of loyalty or self-interest, while the rest were "mad rebels."

Haldimand, exasperated by the hesitations and maneuvering of the Vermonters, prepared a final offer in the form of a public proclamation. Vermont would be treated as a "separate province, independent of and unconnected with every government in America," it would receive every privilege offered to the United States by the Carlisle Commission, and indeed would have all of the liberal provisions of the charter of Connecticut (one of the more lenient in the country before the Revolution). Only the right of appointing a governor would remain with the Crown. He promised to Vermont, moreover, the territory of the Western Union, that is, the land from the Hudson east, a border that would place Great Britain within easy range of Albany, and on the water route to New York City.

260 CONQUERED INTO LIBERTY

Vermont would have completely free trade with Canada, and most important, a British army would stand ready to protect it from the southern states.[46]

To make the offer more pointed—to overawe the Vermonters while, at the same time, suggesting the tangible benefits of an association with Great Britain—Haldimand dispatched Colonel Barry St. Leger, the commander of the Mohawk valley expedition in 1777, with two thousand troops to Crown Point. St. Leger, not the most politically adroit of British officers, thought he could best convey Haldimand's final offer to Chittenden and the others by capturing a Vermonter and using him as a courier. His scouts caught several, but only after shooting a sergeant, whose body the British apologetically returned to the Vermonters. The meek good manners of the British in extending this courtesy reinforced the suspicion not only of Vermonters innocent about the negotiations, but also of the numerous New York spies in that state. To make matters worse, Simon Hathaway, the prisoner picked to deliver Haldimand's proclamation, read it and shared it with most of those he encountered en route to Governor Chittenden.

Ira Allen did his best to calm the furor. He described Haldimand's offer as a surprise, a ploy, anything but what it was—the consummation of a prolonged discussion between the leaders of Vermont and the British governor of Canada that would make Vermont a province of the British Crown. Where the negotiations might have gone from there one cannot tell, because shortly thereafter, news of Cornwallis's surrender (which had taken place on October 19, 1781) trickled north, and with it the realization that the tide of the war had turned decisively against the British. The leaders of Vermont backed off, and Haldimand, who had finally come around to the view that they were indeed of a mind to leave the United States, stayed in touch, but suspended the active negotiations.

Tension did not immediately abate, however. That winter several hundred New York and Vermont militia squared off against each other in the Western Union; it did not come to blood, but it could have. The New Hampshire border was also unquiet, while George Clinton of New York raved about the "traitorous correspondence between the leaders of the New Hampshire Grants and the enemy."

George Washington had followed these events with growing alarm,

paying particular heed to reports by that hard-bitten old veteran John
Stark, once of Rogers' rangers, and more latterly, the hero of Bennington.
In January 1782, Washington wrote directly to Governor Chittenden,
writing—as a purely private opinion, of course—that Vermont's disputes
with New York and New Hampshire constituted a serious threat to the
public peace. And although he said that he accepted at face value Chittenden's assurance that there had been no negotiation with the British,
still, he thought he should point out that:

> There is no calamity within the compass of my foresight, which is more
> to be dreaded, than a necessity of coercion on the part of Congress; and
> consequently every endeavor should be used to prevent the execution of
> so disagreeable a measure. It must involve the ruin of that state against
> which the resentment of the others is pointed.[47]

If Thomas Conway had felt Washington's ice, if Lafayette had unwittingly
encountered his disingenuousness, Thomas Chittenden could see the
glitter of his steel. At the same time, a way out opened up. Congress, in a
fit of alarm in August 1781, had de facto acknowledged the boundaries of
Vermont minus the Western and Eastern Unions, offering to incorporate
Vermont into the Union if that state abandoned those territories. If she
did not, "Their neglect should be considered hostile to the United States,
and thereupon the confederate military power should be used against
them."

Chittenden penitently replied to Washington, "The glory of America
is our glory, and with our country we mean to live or die, as her fate shall
be." But still the standoff persisted. Congress, which would have accepted
Canada without a vote, could not muster nine states to take in Vermont—New York opposed it, of course, but so too did Virginia, North
Carolina, South Carolina, and Georgia, partly for sectional reasons (Vermont's constitution had banned slavery), partly because they feared Vermont would oppose their extensive western land claims, and partly for
fear of a precedent for the dismemberment of states through secession.

Haldimand watched, and continued to correspond with the Vermont
leadership, but without much hope. He continued Carleton's raids against
New York but shielded Vermont from further pressure; meanwhile Ethan

Allen, now writing to Haldimand under cover, bitterly told the British governor, "It is liberty which they say they are after, but will not extend it to Vermont. Therefore Vermont does not belong either to the confederacy or the controversy, but are a neutral republic."[48]

In Philadelphia, an anxious James Madison reported to his fellow Virginian John Randolph about rumors of Vermont receiving a royal charter. In September 1782, New Yorkers who had settled in Windham, Vermont, rose against the government of the state; once again, bloodshed was barely averted, partly because of the shrewd histrionics in which Ethan Allen excelled. Promising that he would "give no quarter to Man, Woman, or child who should oppose him, and that he would lay it as desolate as Sodom and Gomorrah," he overawed the Yorkers—and his combination of intimidation and selective banishment worked. Congress denounced him again, of course, but that was the end of New Yorker covert operations in Vermont.[49] Once again, Washington intervened, but this time to tamp down indignant congressmen looking to suppress Vermont by force of arms. "The country is very mountainous, full of defiles and extremely strong. The inhabitants, for the most part, are a hardy race, composed of that kind of people who are best calculated for soldiers." And, what is more, they would fight desperately, "well knowing that they were fighting with halters about their necks." After all, that was the position he and many others had been in in 1775. And Washington gave it as his opinion—as well as that of leading officers—that the consequences of war with Vermont, which would have numerous sympathizers in New England, might be like "the quarrel with Great Britain, who thought she was only to hold up the rod and all would be hushed."[50]

Peace with Britain, signed in November 1782, although not reflected in a complete cessation of hostilities until April 1783, put an end to the immediate prospect of detaching Vermont from Canada. Haldimand, through either Sherwood or his military secretary, Robert Mathews, wrote to Ira Allen, accepting that Vermont would probably not rejoin the British empire. It left open the possibility, of course, that "should anything favourable present, you may still depend on his Excellency's utmost endeavours, for your salvation."[51] Amicable correspondence continued, and indeed, by the end of May, Ira Allen and Jonas Fay had a different proposal for Governor Haldimand:

Since the powers at War have concluded on a general peace, which opens the way for a general commerce; we take the freedom to propose to your excellency to contract for supplying the troops in Canada under your command with fresh and other provisions which shall be done at as cheap a rate as possible.[52]

I shall do everything in my power to render this state
a British province

In the late 1780s Vermont found itself, curiously, in a comfortable position. The rest of the states had followed Washington's advice and forsworn armed coercion, and in any case, a majority of them favored Vermont's admission to the Union. Leading officials, with substantial holdings in Vermont in their portfolios, had no desire to throw the legitimacy of their claims away. Internally, the advocates of New York's claims had been cowed by the Green Mountain Boys. And the state, finally, having funded its war with land sales, found itself in the enviable and unusual position of having no debts, unlike many of its counterparts. The thrifty Yankees were not overeager to assume such debts as members of the new Union. Meanwhile, a comfortable trade had opened to the north with Canada, and the settlement of the northern half of the state had begun. Vermont joined the Union in 1791 with Kentucky just behind in 1792, but in no great rush.

The Allens, Chittenden, and patriotic historians in the century that followed the Revolution made the case that the wily Vermonters had never intended to link themselves with Great Britain. Rather, they claimed, they had outwitted Haldimand, gained a breathing space for the hard-pressed farmers of Vermont, and secured the exchange of their prisoners held in Canada. This is likely untrue. The leaders of Vermont seem to have been deadly serious about the negotiations, if prudent in how they went about them. Ethan Allen wrote to Haldimand in mid-June 1782, "I shall do everything in my power to render this state a British province," and if there was characteristic bombast in this, there was truth in it as well. Rather than yield Vermont's independence, he would try to reunite it with the Crown. Indeed, one has to wonder whether, if the British had offered the Vermonters the right of electing their own governor—in effect, making the republic a dependent client state of the empire rather than a colony—they might not have gone further yet.

Campaigns that might have occurred but do not, do not loom very large in history, for they belong in the realm of counterfactuals. It is hard enough to figure out what *did* happen. But from the point of view of participants, possible campaigns mean a great deal, and color all kinds of real actions and behavior. Statesmen and generals live forward in time; historians look backward. The latter know far more than the former ever can. But a retrospective look fails to understand what the making of decisions really is like, because we know how it all turned out. In the war of American independence, as in all wars, leaders understood matters very differently than those who came after them.

Beyond this general lesson, the phantom campaigns of 1778–82 teach three things, broadly: the enduring role of Canada in the revolutionaries' conception of the war, the strategic capacity of British leadership, and the contingency of the final outcome.

The abortive campaigns of 1778 and 1779 testify to the allure of Canada to a revolutionary leadership that deeply desired the incorporation of Canada into the American Union. As late as 1782, Benjamin Franklin strove mightily to achieve by diplomacy what his countrymen had failed to win on the battlefield. He argued fruitlessly to his British interlocutors negotiating the final peace treaty that handing Canada over to the United States would eliminate a future source of friction. The Americans wanted Canada for multiple reasons. To take Quebec would probably be, eventually, to take Nova Scotia and with it the finest port in North America, Halifax, and to do all that would be to cripple British power in the hemisphere permanently. It would help America gain control of the fisheries of the Grand Banks—a source of food, income, and a nursery of sailors for many countries. It would help establish the United States as Washington and others wished it to become: a great power—an "empire" was the word he used—that could stand on its own against all Europe. Franklin did not achieve by guile what the Americans could not achieve by force—but that was hardly inevitable, given the weakness of British forces in Canada and the disaffection of the Canadian population.

Which is why Haldimand deserves more credit than he often receives for strategic acumen. He made sure that schemes like those of Congress in 1778 for a 1779 campaign could not succeed. He conducted campaigns of destruction that differed from those of his French predecessors: The torch rather than the scalping knife was the key weapon. This does not diminish the ruthlessness of war along the frontier. Indeed, along the margins of the Champlain corridor, particularly the Mohawk river valley, the war was brutal, albeit in part because it was a civil, as well as a national and ethnic conflict. But his cruelty was not gratuitous. He conducted his negotiations with Vermont as shrewdly as he could within the confines of his instructions. Had the French fleet been defeated outside Yorktown, had Sir Henry Clinton rescued Cornwallis, had the active war, in other words, continued to drag on beyond late 1781, one has to wonder whether Vermont, besieged on all sides, might not have risked a plunge into Britain's embrace.

And that is in some ways the greatest lesson of the phantom campaigns. It could have been different. Had Washington—who very much approved of the effort to take Canada, indeed, had pushed the original efforts to do it in 1775—thrown his weight behind it, it would have been natural to have given Lafayette his opportunity. Vergennes might have opposed it, but would have found it difficult to resist the blandishments of Lafayette, the concerted pressure of his ally, and eventually his own side's desire for a particularly sweet revenge on the British. Even without a French fleet in the St. Lawrence, the Americans might have tried again—and whether they succeeded or failed, the consequences would have been large. Washington, often derided as a strategist, showed himself a shrewd politico-military operator in this case—and no less so in dealing with Vermont.

The Haldimand negotiations look, in retrospect, like comic opera. They were not. Although both the British and the Vermont leadership tried to keep the talks secret, the negotiations were well enough known that they might have triggered a crisis leading either to an invasion by the other colonies, or a Vermont accession to the Crown, or both. Again, Washington's shrewd combination of threat, restraint, and quiet pressure on Congress to come to terms with what John Stark called "these turbulent sons of freedom" prevented a strategic calamity or a bloody civil war.

Leadership is the most contingent of all historical forces. Americans of today often understand the outcome of conflict as a product of masses of forces, strategic concepts, and technology. But in truth, it is personalities that often dictate outcomes. It had mattered enormously that the British had had a Thomas Gage and a John Burgoyne at center stage in 1775 and 1777. Both inadvertently contributed to American success by making the spectacularly bad decisions that led to Lexington, Concord, Bunker Hill, and the evacuation of Boston, as well as the culminating disaster of Saratoga. The British could consider themselves fortunate that they had a Guy Carleton and a Frédéric Haldimand as well, to contain the damage and preserve Canada as a British colony and ultimately an independent country.

Contingent personalities favored the Americans, too: on the field of battle, as we have seen, no one did more in the northern campaigns than Benedict Arnold. Had he died of his wounds at Quebec in January 1776, for example, one may wonder if the Americans would have built the fleet and fought the battle that bought an invaluable year along the Great Warpath. But perhaps the greatest and most beneficial contingent feature of the war of American independence as fought along the Great Warpath lay in the icily unsentimental good judgment and restrained but real ruthlessness of someone who had never defended its forts, and who only sailed its waterways and walked its trails after hostilities had ceased— George Washington, commander in chief.

Far more remote, in some ways, than Abraham Lincoln, the only figure in American history with whom he is to be reasonably compared, he is often portrayed as a figure of unshakable rectitude, patriotism, and integrity, if occasionally uncertain military judgment. True, by and large. But along the Great Warpath he also demonstrated deep suspicion of his allies, manipulativeness toward an adoring protégé, and ruthlessness toward his own side that kept the French out of Canada, and Vermont in the United States. It says something about the nature of war along the Great Warpath from 1778 through 1781 that, in that context at least, those were indispensable virtues.

CHAPTER NINE

Plattsburgh, 1814

The lightest of a succession of calamities

On September 10, 1814, John Quincy Adams, son of the second president of the United States and destined to become its fifth, the most accomplished American diplomat of his generation (and perhaps the most able in American history), conversant in half a dozen languages, was, as usual, dissatisfied with his colleagues, his compatriots, his predicaments, and most of all, himself. He had just turned forty-seven, noting in his diary that "two-thirds of the period allotted to the life of man are gone by for me." As he contemplated the days of his life, his remorseless New England conscience informed him, "I have not improved them as I ought to have done."[1] Nonetheless, on this autumn day he continued conscientiously to discharge one of the many duties that gave structure and meaning to his life. It was a duty that he performed after rising—as he usually did—between five and six in the morning, lighting a candle and kindling a fire, reading in the Bible (with commentaries) for an hour, followed by an austere breakfast consumed alone.

He was writing a long, gloomy letter to his mother, Abigail Adams.

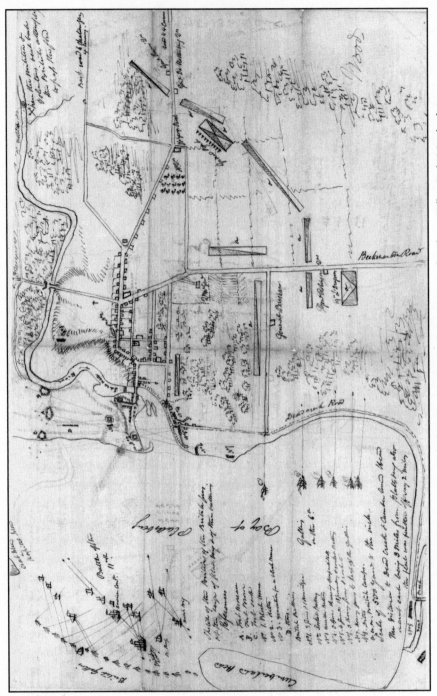

General Alexander Macomb's sketch of the battle. *Courtesy, National Archives, College Park, Maryland*

Adams wrote from Ghent, in what is now Belgium, where he led (after a fashion) a delegation of five peace commissioners negotiating with their British counterparts for an end to the War of 1812. He had told Abigail at the outset, in January of that year, that he thought war a bad idea. Writing from St. Petersburg, where he then served as minister representing the United States to Russia, he had said, "We could gain nothing and could not fail to lose something of what is worth more than all other possessions to a nation, our independence" from such a war.[2] He had no doubt about the justice of America's stand, of course. Both Britain and France had treated the United States badly, in his view, the former attempting to reap commercial advantage from her naval dominance of the globe, in the process abusing American rights by impressing her seamen and blocking her trade. Napoleon's France, as he knew from close observation in Europe, had embarked on a course of limitless expansion.

Adams considered these injustices and their remedies with characteristically cold clarity. He thought both England and France were doomed to fail in their overreaching ambitions, their insane "spirit of ambition, glory, and conquest." At some point, he acknowledged, the United States might have to defend itself—"to forego the right of navigating the ocean would be a pusillanimity which of itself would degrade us from the rank and rights of an independent nation," he wrote Abigail in May, as his views hardened.[3] But though he favored military and naval preparedness, he understood the odds. Even if the United States Navy were four or five times its current size, a fleet of thirty frigates (rather than the actual seven), and a squadron of ships of the line (rather than none) it could only irritate the mighty Royal Navy with its 180 frigates and 150 ships of the line.[4] An army of five or six thousand, backed by an undisciplined and ill-trained, if numerous militia, could barely hope to defend American ports.

England "has vulnerable parts," he thought, and the United States might strike at them. But he expected little in the way of sustainable military success, and events proved him correct. An initial run of spectacular but strategically meaningless victories in individual sea fights had given way to a clamping, crushing British naval blockade of the Atlantic coast. American attempts to penetrate Canada had collapsed in campaigns as nugatory in their results as they were discreditable to the undisciplined troops who fought them and the superannuated veterans of the war of

American independence who led them. After recovering from the surprise of the war, the British prepared to launch devastating raids on the
coast, and even to seize parts of Maine. New England seethed with dis-
content at the administration of President James Madison, and, in displays of disloyalty that added to Adams's anguish, not only did a ripping
business in illegal trade with the enemy, but even, albeit in very limited
quarters, contemplated secession and a separate peace. And now, at Ghent
in the autumn of 1814, Adams and his colleagues faced a British negotiating team determined to exact a high price for what they understood as
American insolence, aggression, and betrayal of the cause of freedom.

After a failed attempt by the tsar of Russia to mediate a peace, the
Americans and British had agreed to direct negotiations at Ghent, which
began in August 1814. The Americans had a formidable team: Adams as
the nominal head, with Swiss-born Albert Gallatin, former secretary of
the treasury; Henry Clay, the Speaker of the House of Representatives
who had helped launch the war; James Bayard, the moderate Federalist
from Delaware whose political maneuvers had given the presidency to
Thomas Jefferson rather than the appalling Aaron Burr; and John Russell, a brilliant if insecure and not entirely honest diplomat who had represented the United States in London. Their British counterparts were
somewhat less impressive: at the top the bitterly hostile Henry Goulburn,
undersecretary of state for war and colonies, whose intellect had not been
impaired, although his looks had, by the experience of his nurse having
sat on his head when he was a baby; the aged evangelical admiral, James
Gambier; and William Adams, a colorless lawyer who has left no discern-
ible mark on the records of the negotiation.

The less talented men, however, had in the summer of 1814 the stronger cards to play. The allies had defeated Napoleon, and Great Britain
could now send its tough regulars to North America. The Americans had
hoped to negotiate a deal acknowledging their maritime rights. The British came in with an altogether different agenda: changes in the borders in
favor of Canada; American (but not British) disarmament on the Great
Lakes, both by water and by land; and perhaps most troubling of all, the
creation of an Indian territory in the West. The United States, the British
negotiators insisted, must extend peace to the Indian allies of Great Britain, demarcating their territory "as a permanent barrier between the

dominions of Great Britain and the United States." This provision they considered "a *sine qua non* of a treaty of peace."[5] The American negotiating team wriggled and fenced, writing lengthy memoranda and making their case over correct, if not entirely convivial dinners with their British counterparts, but the outlook remained bleak.

And bad news lurked over the horizon. In mid-July 1814, the British naval commander for the American war, Admiral Alexander Cochrane, had issued his orders to commanding officers off North America:

> You are hereby required and directed to destroy & lay waste such towns and districts upon the coast as you may find assailable; you will hold strictly in view the conduct of the American Army towards His Majesty's unoffending Canadian subjects.
>
> For only by carrying this retributary justice into the country of our enemy can we hope to make him sensible of the impolicy as well a inhumanity of the system he has adopted.[6]

Cochrane meant it, and his subordinate, Admiral George Cockburn, ably seconded by a small British expeditionary force, followed these orders with zeal. Adams could not know, as he wrote Abigail in September, that the Royal Navy had appeared in the Chesapeake on August 16 and that a combined force of soldiers and sailors had taken Washington and burned the White House, the navy yard, and other public buildings there on the twenty-fourth and twenty-fifth of that month. (When he did learn this grim news, Adams described it to his wife as merely "the lightest of a succession of calamities through which our country must pass.") Even before hearing the details of Cockburn's raid, however, Adams expected the negotiations to collapse. He foresaw a destructive British campaign, advertised as vengeance for the burning of some Canadian towns including York (today, Toronto), capital of Upper Canada, but really, he believed, a sustained effort to break and humble the United States. He told Abigail that he believed that the British were only waiting for some spectacular victory to break off the talks.

The day after Adams wrote his letter, however, on September 11, 1814, a battle occurred at Plattsburgh on the northern end of Lake Champlain. That battle confounded Adams's gloomy prognostications, upset British calculations, kept the negotiations alive, and shaped the curiously indecisive yet—as it turned out—altogether satisfactory Christmas Peace of 1814.

A mere matter of marching

The War of 1812 occurred after more than a decade of tension between the United States and Great Britain. Indeed, one might argue, it resulted from the unfinished business of the American Revolution, despite the Jay Treaty of 1794 that for a time completed the adjustment of claims and boundaries, and that secured the removal of British forces from their remaining posts in the Old Northwest. The American government in 1812, at the time, made the issue of maritime rights, including freedom from impressment of American sailors and neutral rights at sea, the primary cause. British politicians suspected a greedy desire to secure Canada while Britain was preoccupied with its life-and-death struggle with France. Both, to some extent, were right. The British government, insisting that once a British subject, always a British subject, gave its captains the right to take any British-born sailor off an American ship, and they duly took thousands, including some who were not, in fact, British subjects. Three sets of government directives in 1807 and 1809 (the so-called Orders in Council) also gave the Royal Navy authority to seize ships bound for any ports that British ships could not enter and imposed other restrictions on trade with French-dominated Europe.

These policies proved onerous to Yankee merchants and, particularly when accompanied by rough enforcement, outrageous to American dignity. The attack by HMS *Leopard* on the USS *Chesapeake* in 1807—an ambush of a newly fitted-out and hence unready American frigate by a British man of war searching for British deserters—was the most egregious such incident, but there were others. The United States retaliated with embargoes that failed, in part because of the unwillingness of northeastern merchants to comply with them. The British government actually withdrew the Orders in Council on June 16, 1812, but too late: An exasperated United States government, which would not know about the British move for weeks, declared war the next day. Had a trans-Atlantic cable existed to convey the news instantaneously, the war probably would not have occurred.[7] But even if this hypothetical is correct, one should not neglect the underlying spirit of nationalist resentment of England, and desire to expand the United States, that contributed to conflict.

President James Madison was, for so lucid a writer, remarkably unclear about his objectives and strategy in going to war. But there can be little doubt that Canada was on his mind, and on the minds of his chief subordinates. In June 1813, when Secretary of State James Monroe issued instructions to Gallatin, Adams, and Bayard as commissioners to negotiate peace with Great Britain, he noted that the British would probably wish to retain Canada. But he urged his representatives to argue "the advantages to both Countries which is promised, by a transfer of the upper parts and even the whole of Canada to the United States."[8] When the war began, former president Thomas Jefferson, with his customarily poor military judgment, declared that the conquest of Canada would be "a mere matter of marching," and he was hardly alone in this belief.[9] And certainly, it was no small or unimportant irony that the section of the country most directly affected by British restrictions on trade—the seafaring towns of New England—were the most opposed to the war.

Madison, having decided on war, and having secured narrow passage of its declaration (a vote of 79 to 49 in the House, and 19 to 13 in the Senate), decided to begin with an invasion of Canada.[10] The odds looked good, initially. America's population numbered over seven million, and was growing rapidly. Admittedly, it had barely six thousand regulars of uneven quality under still more uneven commanders, but behind them lay a vast, if ill-organized, mass of militia. Canada's population numbered something on the order of four hundred thousand, with well under one hundred thousand in Upper Canada (now primarily the province of Ontario), an area in which numerous Americans of doubtful loyalty to the Crown had settled, as British authorities knew very well.[11] But Madison and his advisers miscalculated in numerous ways. The population of Canada now included the exiled loyalists of the American Revolution and their descendants, as well as others (Scottish emigrants) who had no particular desire to join the Union. The French-speaking population was not as disaffected as it had been in 1775, when it had maintained a cool neutrality between the English and the Americans. There was no question, as during the Revolution, of the Royal Navy losing command of the sea to a French fleet, and in any event, the United States had not entered this war in alliance with any country, including France, with which relations had been almost as fraught as those with the mother country. The governor general of Canada, Sir George Prevost, son of one of the founders of the Sixtieth of Foot, the Royal Americans, spoke French fluently, and like Carleton and Haldimand before him, went to great lengths to secure French Canadian support. The Indians of the old Northwest, aroused by the threat of American immigration, and finally blessed with able leaders, fought, with some notable exceptions, on the British side. And although British generals fretted at the state of the Canadian militia, it was probably better organized and trained than its American counterparts. They had in Canada almost as many regulars as the Americans, and of better quality, including British troops and fencibles, Canadians recruited for service at home.

The invasions of Canada that characterized the first two years of the war took place chiefly along the Niagara frontier, on the narrow sector between Lakes Erie and Ontario, with occasional fighting to the north and west of Lake Erie, particularly along the Thames River Valley, and at the eastern end of Lake Ontario. The Lake Champlain sector remained much quieter. When the war began the American administration rushed troops to the Niagara frontier, pursuing operations along the eastern Lake Ontario littoral, thinking that by winning naval superiority on that lake and seizing the chief British base at Kingston, it could then follow the route of Amherst's triumphant march to Montreal in 1760.

The Americans concentrated their efforts by land on the Niagara frontier and to the west rather than on the more direct Great Warpath route for several reasons. The availability of America's minuscule army in the region, much of it engaged in chronic warfare with Indians in the Old Northwest (roughly, Ohio, Illinois, and Indiana), plus the undoubted eagerness of westerners to fight the British and Indians, played some role. Misled by the undoubted disaffection of Americans who had settled in Canada, they anticipated a warmer reception in that part of Canada than they got. Moreover, operations along the Lake Ontario littoral offered the opportunity to cut western Canada off from "Lower Canada"—what we now think of as the province of Quebec.

There were a few American strategists who desired an invasion along the direct and traditional Lake Champlain route. Most notable of these was Secretary of War John Armstrong, himself a veteran of the Saratoga campaign. Unfortunately, Armstrong did not combine insight with skill in making his case, or the power of decision.[12] His generals, James Wilkinson (fellow aide to Horatio Gates during the war of independence), and his predecessor, Henry Dearborn (an elderly veteran of Arnold's march to Quebec), made halfhearted thrusts north from their base at Plattsburgh at the northern end of Lake Champlain, but the Lake Ontario sector drew off most of the American effort. And in truth, a thrust north along the Great Warpath posed numerous challenges. The Richelieu River offered an avenue for such an attack, but the British garrison at Isle aux Noix, which had surpassed the river port of St. Johns in importance, could block it. The island's fort was crumbling, but the Americans hardly had much to throw at it, and Prevost moved swiftly to garrison it with regulars and mobilized militia, posting gunboats, planting obstacles in the river, and clearing the banks so that artillery could sweep them. The core of Canada—the citadel of Quebec and Montreal, the most important commercial city—had the largest garrisons of British troops, and the Royal Navy remained supreme on the St. Lawrence. Unlike the case in 1775–76, no American force could hope to cross north of the river without becoming cut off from the southern bank. The British could move forces easily along the waterway to any threatened point.

Politics, too, made the Champlain corridor less promising than before. Governor Daniel Tompkins of New York was a stout Republican, but his counterpart across the lake, Martin Chittenden of Vermont (son of the Thomas Chittenden who had nearly negotiated Vermont's return to the British empire), was a no less vehement Federalist. Both states had populations ambivalent about the war, and until 1814, Tompkins had to confront a hostile legislature. He was, even so, a superbly active governor, mobilizing the militia and directing military resources to the frontier. Chittenden, however, refused to allow Vermont militia to serve outside the state. But on both sides of the lake there were many who were just as happy selling to the British as shooting them. Happier, in fact. General George Izard, the American commander on the frontier, declared in disgust that the cattle moving across the border resembled herds of buffalo, that "press through the forest, making paths for themselves. Were it not for these supplies, the British forces in Canada would be suffering from famine."[13] He was right. The British army in Canada fed itself on American beef, fairly bought. A more sinister, and even less scrupulous trade occurred as well, as when, in June 1814, an American naval patrol, alerted by timely intelligence, pounced on smugglers towing two spars, one eighty feet and the other eighty-five feet long, to the British naval base at Isle aux Noix. They would have served as the fore and mizzen masts of a ship of war in the British fleet, the American commander realized.[14]

The valley itself had changed during the years since the Revolution. Wilderness had given way to a number of small towns: On the New York side, Plattsburgh, founded in 1785, numbering some three thousand residents, and including stores, mills, a forge, and a tannery, had become the seat of newly established Clinton County. On the Vermont side, across the lake and some nineteen miles to the southeast, lay Burlington. Smaller (some one thousand inhabitants), it too was the seat of a new county with nearly twenty thousand residents. Plattsburgh and Burlington offered harbors. The former served as a base for troops and materiel moving in the direction of Lake Ontario and that sector of the St. Lawrence River that flows from it; Burlington was a strong and (by 1814) a well-defended base for troops whose job was both to defend the frontier and to intercept smugglers. Vergennes, twenty-eight miles south of Burlington, situated along Otter Creek several miles from the lake, had roughly the same size population, but because of the waterfalls boasted industrial assets that would prove invaluable in the building of a fleet: blast and air furnaces, mills and forges, a wire factory and a shot tower.[15] Whitehall (formerly Skenesborough), the remotest place on the lake and the construction site for Arnold's fleet, served as a refuge where ships could be laid up during the winter, far from British raiders.

The War of 1812 began with the initiative and advantages squarely on the American side. Through 1813, however, the British, assisted by Canadian regulars and militia, fended off most of the American attacks along the border. On the Great Lakes, the two sides began furious shipbuilding campaigns. On Lake Erie, this culminated in a battle on September 10, 1813, that effectively deprived the British of control of that body of water; on Lake Ontario command seesawed back and forth, depending on the state of building programs at Kingston (on the British side) and Sacket's Harbor (on the American side), at the eastern end of the lake. But during

1813, the overall advantage shifted to the British, as naval reinforcements allowed the British to blockade America's Atlantic ports, and to begin a campaign of destructive raids designed to punish, cow, and pin down American forces along a battered seaboard.

Secretary of War John Armstrong tried a dual thrust at Montreal. The first, from the Lake Ontario side, he entrusted to the egregious Major General James Wilkinson, no stranger to the Great Warpath as Horatio Gates's aide and confidant—a conspirator, friend of Aaron Burr, traitor (in Spanish pay), and military incompetent, but also, unfortunately, the commanding general of the United States Army. The second, northward from Plattsburgh, he consigned to Major General Wade Hampton, yet another veteran of the American Revolution. Hampton, a fifty-nine-year-old South Carolina slave-owning planter and politician in uncertain health, had crushed a Louisiana slave revolt in 1811 in a campaign that included mutilation, summary execution, and the display of heads on pikes. He despised Wilkinson. At the Battle of Chateaugay on October 26, 1813, sixteen hundred Canadian regulars, militia, and Indians, led by a French Canadian colonel, rebuffed a numerically superior force of about twenty-six hundred Americans under Hampton, who subsequently retired in disgrace. Casualties were light on both sides, but Canada acquired a unifying legend of heroic resistance, while the Americans, marching back to their base in the mud, added one more bungled campaign to the ledger.

When the United States had declared war in June 1812, Napoleon stood on the verge of his invasion of Russia. A year later, however, Napoleon, defeated in Russia (as John Quincy Adams had anticipated), and again at the monumental Battle of the Nations at Leipzig in October, had recoiled back into the core of his empire. In March 1814, the allies entered Paris, and on April 6 the tyrant abdicated. The British government, now relieved of many of its military burdens and free to indulge its anger at the Americans, had already extended that war, blockading New England ports as of that month. The British government immediately began sending reinforcements from the Duke of Wellington's army, which had repeatedly beaten Napoleon's forces in Spain and southern France, to Canada. Four brigades under able generals who had learned their trade under the greatest British commander of the war, a thousand artillerymen, plus engineers, over sixteen thousand soldiers in all, began sailing from French ports in May and June, the first units arriving in Canada in time for campaigning during August and September.[16] The British negotiators at Ghent had anticipated this pulse of military activity across the Atlantic. The stunning scale of their demands to the Americans as the talks began reflected their confidence in the increasing military and naval leverage behind their diplomacy.

The British intended to take territory that would permanently secure Canada. Thus, when, in early June 1814, the Earl of Bathurst, secretary for war and the colonies, gave his guidance for the upcoming campaign to General Prevost (who, like Carleton before him, was both governor of Canada and the field commander of the army there), he notified him that most of the reinforcements from Wellington's army would go to him. He should launch offensive operations with two objectives: to protect Canada and "to obtain if possible ultimate security to His Majesty's Possessions in America." Bathurst spelled out what that meant: the destruction of the American naval base at Sacket's Harbor and with it the American fleet on Lake Ontario; the elimination of the American naval establishments on Lakes Erie and Lake Champlain; the occupation of Detroit and the Michigan territory; and finally, an advance south along Lake Champlain to a line of Prevost's choosing, "always however taking care not to expose His Majesty's Forces to being cut off by too extended a line of advance."[17] In other words, as the commissioners in Ghent made clear to their appalled American interlocutors in one of their first sessions, the British aimed at the complete and permanent elimination of American forts and naval forces on *all* of the lakes. Henry Goulburn twisted the knife a bit further, insisting that this demand offered "proofs of moderation of Great Britain, since she might have demanded a cession of all the borders of the Lakes to herself."[18]

This, then, was the context of operations along Lake Champlain in the late summer and fall of 1814. The British had in view an assault—of necessity both on land and by water—to eliminate all American naval forces and occupy land that would, at least, serve as a bargaining chip for the delegation in Ghent, and at best, permanently thicken the belt of British territory protecting the core of Canada. For a year and a half the two sides had merely shadow-boxed along the Great Warpath. Now the real match would occur.

This war of Broad Axes

In a war so often characterized by the haphazard selection of incompetent commanders, logistical mismanagement, and a haze of general confusion, the secretary of the navy had made an excellent decision in the early months of the war. He decided to replace Lieutenant Sidney Smith, in command of American naval forces on Lake Champlain, with Lieutenant Thomas Macdonough. Smith had not shone, but he did not have much of an opportunity to do so. His command, he plaintively noted, had consisted of two gunboats, one sunken, the other with seams opening up to the width of one hand, and, as he wrote the secretary, his instructions had been taking three months to arrive at Basin Harbor, Vermont.[19] But the vigilant Governor Tompkins of New York had begun peppering the Navy Department with urgent demands for preparedness, so, on September 28, 1812, the navy sent the twenty-nine-year-old naval officer north.

Macdonough represented a new breed of American officer. He had served at sea since age seventeen, taking part in the Barbary war with Tripoli in 1804, where he had caught the eye of one of the most able and dashing of American naval officers, Stephen Decatur. He had joined that audacious officer in the nighttime boarding and destruction of the frigate *Philadelphia* that had run aground and been captured in Tripoli harbor. After a variety of duties, he had taken a furlough to command a merchant ship trading in the East Indies, returning just in time for another assignment on board USS *Constellation*, and then a gunboat command in Maine. There was nothing particularly colorful about Macdonough: He was merely devout, intelligent, even-tempered, and competent.

Upon arriving at his station in upstate New York, Macdonough began writing to his superiors. His complaints to the secretary of the navy had, at first, a superficial similarity to those of Benedict Arnold nearly forty years before—few seamen, command squabbles (the army refused to give up its four sloops), and shortages of equipment. But in truth he had considerable advantages over his predecessor. Guns, ammunition, and fittings for ships soon streamed north, and although the shortage of seamen remained a problem, he had able carpenters and shipbuilders at Burlington and Vergennes, the two key naval bases on the lake. Macdonough himself supervised the building and training of the fleet, and remained cool even when the hapless Lieutenant Smith, perhaps seeking to redeem himself in the Navy Department's eyes, forayed north to Isle aux Noix on June 3, 1813, and managed to lose sloops *Growler* and *Eagle* to British shore batteries. The British, having briefly achieved superiority on the lake, sortied from July 29 through August 3, burning blockhouses, barracks, and storehouses at the northern end of the lake, including Plattsburgh. They poked at Burlington, found its batteries too forbidding, and withdrew, and Macdonough went back to his shipbuilding.

In the winter of 1813–14, however, matters took a far more serious turn. The Navy Department, like the rest of the government, realized that Napoleon's impending doom would free British resources for the lakes. Reports from Isle aux Noix indicated an active program of shipbuilding, and although Macdonough believed that with the forces then in hand he could hold the lake for the moment, the same could not be said for the upcoming season.

In February 1814 Secretary of the Navy William Jones gave Macdonough (promoted now to the rank of master commandant) a piece of welcome news. He had sent master shipbuilder Noah Brown to Vergennes (the winter quarters of the American fleet) to build a serious man of war. Noah and his brother Adam built good ships, and quickly; they had built, among other vessels, the seagoing sloop of war *Peacock*, of twenty guns, that would distinguish herself in one of the last ship-to-ship combats of the war. And they were patriots, willing to advance funds out of their pockets to get the job done. The navy asked them to build a new ship with unheard-of speed, sixty days from keel laying to launch. They delivered. As Macdonough informed Secretary Jones on April 11, the shipwrights had worked wonders. The small shipyard at Vergennes launched the ship—tentatively named after Secretary Jones, but later christened *Saratoga*—"this day, being the thirty fifth day after her Keel was laid, and all her Timber taken from the stump."[20] The armament had not arrived, the early spring roads near Vergennes being in a dreadful state, but when they did they were formidable: six twenty-four-pounder long guns, and twenty thirty-two-pounder carronades, the former being heavy, long-range weapons, the latter smaller, less accurate but easier to manage weapons for close-in work.

Launching a ship was one thing—fitting it out with all the necessary equipment, beginning with guns, but including rigging and maritime hardware, was another. Manning was an even more formidable problem: Macdonough reported his fleet 250 short, or at best two-thirds of what he needed. And even with full crews he would need time to train his men, particularly those who were landlubbers or loaned by the army, let alone weld the flotilla into a coherent unit. Still, this achievement, and others, bears reflection.

Lake warfare in the War of 1812 was a peculiar affair.[21] The battle on Lake Erie aside, it consisted chiefly of feverish campaigns of construction in protected harbors, with each side alternating brief periods of ascendancy, which, however, neither could fully exploit. On Lake Ontario this went to lengths that seemed to some observers ludicrous, and by the end of the war both sides had warships as large as the ships of the line at Trafalgar under construction. But experienced sailors—and that is who both sides put in command on the lakes—saw these as contests in which having just one ship substantially more powerful than that of an opponent could tip the scales completely. As a result, the competition became one of a protoindustrial competition, a foreshadowing of the far larger mobilizational campaigns of the Civil War and the world wars. As in later conflicts, builders resorted to hasty expedients—in this case green timber of different varieties thrown together, which meant that the ships would not last very long, but could get the job done.

Thrifty administrators disliked this reckless spending of money on ever more grandiose projects to build ships that could not last more than a few years. Secretary Jones wrote Macdonough in July, "I had hoped that the irksome contest of Ship building would have been superseded, by the possession and fortification of the point which the Secretary of War had designated, for the purpose of repelling any attempt of the enemy, to pass into the Lake." He referred to the hope that General Wilkinson, from his base at Plattsburgh, could fortify Rouse's Point at the northern end of the lake and seal it off, although even that egregiously mendacious general promised no such thing. Meanwhile, the anxious secretary feared, "The enemy's means and facility of increasing his naval Armament, greatly exceed those which we possess, either in equipment, transportation or manning." "I see no end to this war of Broad Axes," he concluded unhappily.[22]

This was a competition in which the Americans had performed remarkably well—and far better than they had during the Revolution. In the years since that conflict, American trade, and with it the shipbuilding and maritime industries more generally, had taken off. In the twenty years between 1790 and 1810 alone, the gross tonnage of American merchant ships had more than trebled, in both foreign and internal traffic.[23] With the shipyards and carpenters to build them, and the sailors to man them, had come as well the industry to equip them. Whereas the rebellious colonies had struggled to acquire the guns to equip Arnold's fleet with an odd assortment of naval artillery, Macdonough and his men received American-made equipment comparable in quality to anything the Royal Navy could bring to bear.

One can nevertheless understand Jones's anxiety about the naval building races. He had to sustain three fleets on the lakes (Erie, Ontario, and Champlain), as well as shipbuilding programs along the blockaded coast. And he knew that the Royal Navy had, after twenty years of unremitting naval conflict with France and its allies, created the most formidable maritime industry and shipyard infrastructure of its time. He knew, moreover, that the United States government teetered on the edge of bankruptcy throughout the war. Nonetheless, he poured resources into the naval building race on Lake Champlain, as elsewhere, and when he hesitated, President Madison, in a rare act of operational foresight, ordered the construction of one more vessel, which became the brig *Eagle* (not to be confused with the sloop of that name that Smith had lost by his ill-conceived sortie earlier that year).

Indeed, and again in a foreshadowing of things to come, the Americans contemplated seizing a technological march on their opponents. Governor Tompkins, ever alert, had informed Jones that the Lake Champlain Steam-boat Company, which had had an exclusive contract before the war for navigating the lake with steamships, had begun building a four-hundred-ton ship at Vergennes. He urged the Navy Department to build what would have been the first steam warship of its kind, arguing that it would economize on manpower, be able to tow other ships, always be ready to fire red-hot shot heated in her furnaces and—at war's end—revert to the useful commercial purpose of ferrying passengers around the lake.[24] Macdonough thought seriously about this, but upon inquiry discovered that much of the machinery for the engine had not yet arrived at Vergennes and that the equipment itself was unreliable, and concluded that the delays would not be worth it. He ordered the ship converted to sail and fitted out as a schooner, and under the name *Ticonderoga* it sailed onto the lake in mid-May. To complete the fleet he needed only *Eagle*, which could not appear on the lake until the end of August at the very earliest.

Macdonough ruthlessly trimmed his fleet, disarming two sloops, in order to give himself a compact but effective force. He knew that the British would, following the pattern of lake warfare, attempt to destroy it before his force could put out from the shipyard. As he anticipated, on May 14, 1814, they tried—a British flotilla with a small military force appeared opposite Otter Creek, but after ninety minutes of gunfire from a battery carefully placed to protect against such an eventuality, withdrew. Twelve days later, in his flagship *Saratoga*, the young fleet commander sailed north to Plattsburgh. Aside from *Saratoga* he had the converted steamship *Ticonderoga* of seventeen guns, two sloops (*Preble* and *Montgomery*, seven and six guns respectively, the latter subsequently dropped from his battle line), plus six galleys with two guns each and four gunboats with one gun each. Against this he expected a British force led by a large ship of war being built at Isle aux Noix, the brig *Linnet* with eighteen guns, two sloops stronger than his own, and seventeen galleys variously mounting one or two guns, plus a boat for launching the Congreve rockets later so memorably, if ineffectively, used at the siege of Baltimore. Until the American brig *Eagle* arrived, he would be badly outgunned; when it did he would have rough parity in weight of metal, although a disadvantage in terms of the range of his weapons.

The British had their own robust building program at Isle aux Noix, but had not managed to build quite so quickly or effectively as the Americans. Macdonough's intelligence, obtained from prisoners and deserters, was sound, but slightly overestimated the number of gunboats (the British had only twelve rather than the estimated seventeen), and underestimated the power of the big ship, HMS *Confiance*, which mounted thirty-six guns, including ten twenty-four-pounder and thirty-two-pounder carronades and twenty-six long twenty-four-pounders, with a crew of 270 men. Fortunately for Macdonough, *Confiance*'s completion lagged until the end of August.

Thus, as that month came to an end, the two sides girded themselves for a major clash at the northern end of the lake. General Prevost mustered an army of ten thousand men, more than Burgoyne had brought to bear a generation before, including some of Wellington's superb, unbeaten veterans of the Peninsular War. These forces arrived just in time for a late summer–early autumn offensive: As of the beginning of August Prevost knew that the last two brigades sent from Europe were approaching Quebec by sea, but would not complete disembarkation and a march to the front until the end of the month.[25] Given his orders, Prevost decided that he would strike at Plattsburgh rather than on the eastern shore of the lake: "The State of Vermont having shewn a decided opposition to the war, and very large supplies of specie daily coming in from thence, as well as the whole of the cattle required for the use of the troops, I mean for the present to confine myself in any offensive operations which may take place to the Western side of Lake Champlain."[26]

Prevost aimed to defeat the American garrison of Plattsburgh and occupy and destroy the town, while facilitating the destruction of the American fleet on Lake Champlain. He would then throw his force at Sacket's Harbor on Lake Ontario, assuming a naval offensive there as well. All prospects of success hinged on intimate cooperation with the navy.

Macdonough's fleet, basing itself at Plattsburgh, patrolled the northern end of the lake, waiting anxiously for word that *Confiance* had joined the British fleet, which would then sortie from Isle aux Noix, its new flagship in the lead. A relatively strong American military contingent of over five thousand regulars held the lines at Plattsburgh. Wilkinson, dismissed in disgrace, had given way to Major General George Izard, one of the best of the younger generation of American commanders, educated in European military academies, scholarly but decisive, who had spent the spring training and organizing them. The stage was set for battle.

The Almighty has been pleased to grant us a signal victory

The campaign opened, characteristically, with an American military blunder. Secretary of War John Armstrong, seeing an opportunity where none existed, ordered Izard to march with four thousand men to Ogdensburg, whence he could threaten the British naval base at Kingston from the rear. Armstrong, who unaccountably managed to convince himself that the British had not sent substantial reinforcements to Canada, thus stripped the Plattsburgh area of its best troops and most capable commander. Izard protested but, receiving orders to proceed as instructed, on August 29 dutifully began a march of several hundred miles to the west and the extinction of a promising military career. Izard's departure opened the way for a true debacle, as the British began their invasion three days later. Izard's deputy, Major General Alexander Macomb, commanded a small force of regulars that Izard had left behind, including recent recruits and convalescents, some fifteen hundred effectives in all. Luckily, their thirty-two-year-old commander, one of the very first students to attend the military academy at West Point, and former adjutant general of the army, was a highly competent professional soldier.

Prevost, despite his overwhelming superiority in number and quality of troops, had his troubles. He needed naval support, for one thing: Supply along the muddy roads of New York would fail him, and, as he soon learned, an active American naval force could make life miserable along a coastal march. Moreover, as long as the Americans controlled the lake, they could move reinforcements and supplies from Vermont and New York to Plattsburgh with ease. He doubted whether even after the launch of *Confiance* the Royal Navy would match Macdonough's fleet, which had, throughout the summer, kept the British bottled up at the northern end of the lake. His army, composed of two brigades of Wellington's veterans and one of regulars who had served in Canada, did not particularly care for their commander in chief, who, despite a creditable combat record early in his career in the West Indies, had spent a decade in military government in North America. It did not help that after years of rough-and-ready living under Wellington, who cared chiefly that his men marched and fought as he wished them to, their new commander welcomed them by issuing a severe rebuke about their slovenly uniforms, which reflected "a fanciful vanity inconsistent with the rules of the Service," and enjoined all commanding officers to make sure that "the Established Uniform of their Corps is strictly observed by the Officers under their Command."[27]

The Royal Navy also had its own self-inflicted wounds. Commander Daniel Pring, an able and active twenty-six-year-old naval officer, had organized and directed the dockyard and naval establishment at Isle aux Noix and commanded the British fleet on Lake Champlain since the summer of 1813. Energetic and able though Pring was, his superior, Captain Sir James Lucas Yeo, the brilliant thirty-two-year-old commander of naval forces in Canada, thought him too junior to command the British flotilla once *Confiance* was launched. Instead Yeo dispatched Captain George Downie, his own second in command, to take charge. Downie, an experienced, long-serving sailor aged fifty-four, arrived on September 1, just as Prevost crossed the border. The flotilla commander, new to his fleet and the lake, would find himself subject to extraordinary pressures in the ten days remaining to the campaign, and his life.

On the other side of the border, the thirty-two-year-old American commander, Alexander Macomb, scrambled to prepare for the British attack. Now he found himself commanding barely fifteen hundred regulars plus, as of the beginning of September, some seven hundred militia—little more than a third the size of the force that had occupied Plattsburgh only two weeks before. He made three swift decisions. He asked the commander of the district's militia, Major General Benjamin Mooers, to summon them—which Mooers, a veteran of the Canadian campaign of 1776, did promptly and effectively, bringing in some three thousand men. Macomb repeated the appeal to Vermont's Governor Chittenden, who, despite his personal opposition to the war, could not withhold support on the eve of actual invasion. He released volunteers from the Vermont militia to join Macomb. These soon swarmed across the lake and performed well in the subsequent battle, despite their state's ambivalence about the war. Macomb put most of his men to work strengthening his army's position in southern Plattsburgh, the part of the town bounded on the north by the Saranac River, on the east and south by the lake, but open by land to the southwest. Three forts, amply equipped with artillery, blocked any attack there, and blockhouses and batteries augmented Macomb's defenses. Another of the first graduates of West Point, Major Joseph Totten, had designed the earthworks, and it would require more than a mere sudden onrush to take them.[28] And finally, the general sent out some of his regular riflemen and militia under the command of Major John Wool, a thirty-year-old lawyer turned regular soldier, to delay the British advance by skirmishing, breaking bridges, and felling trees.

The British columns, numbering just under ten thousand men (the rest either protecting the lines of communication or ill), crossed the Chazy River on September 3, but were slowed by the obstructed roads and, increasingly, afflicted by wretched weather. When the British pushed farther on the sixth from a position eight miles from Plattburgh, the militia broke at the mere sight of the ordered British columns, which did not even form into line, trusting their own skirmishers to disperse the anxious citizen-soldiers. These latter panicked further at the sight of their own red-coated New York dragoons, who they thought were the enemy having taken position behind them. Macomb's regulars—small units of riflemen under Major Wool—did little more than harass the British column and withdraw.[29] The militia rallied when it got back to friendly lines, and by the seventh something approaching a siege had begun. The enemy occupied the northern bank of the Saranac and began hauling up artillery, but Prevost hesitated to launch a frontal assault across the fords and up the ridge on the dug-in Americans (who were strengthening their position with a speed that would have done their revolutionary ancestors credit) without naval support.

The British commander had experienced harassing fire from Macdonough's fleet as he and his men had crossed Dead Creek on the approach march to Plattsburgh, and did not like it. Prevost urged Captain Downie to attack the American fleet, now moored in Plattsburgh harbor, pledging a simultaneous attack on two bridges and a ford across the Saranac. On September 9, the soldier and the sailor exchanged messages. Prevost informed Downie that he had postponed an attack on the south bank of the Saranac "until your squadron is in a state of preparation to cooperate with this Division of the army," and he continued, "I need not dwell with you on the evils resulting to both services from delay," adding, for reassurance, that deserters had told him that the Americans were "inefficiently manned," and had taken to filling their ranks with prisoners. Downie responded that he intended to sail at midnight that night and conduct an attack: "I rely on any assistance you can afford the squadron," he told Prevost.[30] Each commander believed he needed the other— Prevost needed Downie in order to cross the Saranac and open an attack on the final American position in Plattsburgh, Downie needed Prevost to prevent American shore batteries from hampering his own attack on the fleet. And, of course, Downie may have hoped that British shore-based artillery (including guns captured from the Americans during a successful land attack) would catch Macdonough between two fires.

Macdonough, reinforced at nearly the last minute by *Eagle* (which had only been launched August 11 and sailed on the twenty-sixth), had taken up his position in Plattsburgh Bay on September 1, sheltering at the northern end of the bay, just behind the mass of Cumberland Head. On the fifth he summoned his officers and laid out his plan of battle, which, as it transpired, they had six days to rehearse.[31] Like Arnold before him, he chose his position shrewdly, intending to make the British attack him to their disadvantage. In the bay, measuring two miles by two miles, he anchored his ships as far north as he could, in a line consisting, from the north, of *Eagle, Saratoga, Ticonderoga,* and *Preble;* inshore and to their west he stationed his gunboats in groups of two and three, where they would be sheltered from the main action but able to engage in the gaps between his ships as circumstances allowed. By taking a position at the northern end of the bay, he would make it difficult for the British to get at him as they rounded Cumberland Head; the geometry of the position also made it more likely that the British would come within range of the short-range carronades with which he was plentifully equipped. His ships, moored bow and stern in the sheltered bay, would have steady platforms from which to fire, while the British would have to sail in exposed to raking broadsides as they maneuvered into position. Furthermore, Macdonough had his men rig springs, hawsers running along the ship attached to the stern and to the ship's bow anchor. If the starboard side of the ship—the side facing the enemy—were badly mauled, by winding these cables in the sailors could winch the ship around, presenting the larboard broadside, which originally faced the shore, to the enemy. The enemy's flagship, *Confiance,* which had most of the British firepower, was the key: Sink, disable, or take her, and the battle was won.

An adverse wind delayed Downie one day, but early on September 11, he reconnoitered in a rowboat just beyond Cumberland Head, took in the American line of battle, and planned his attack. It was vintage Royal Navy, a microcosm, on a petty scale on a lake in the American wilderness, of the tactics that had given the British crushing victories in the great fleet engagements of the wars of the French Revolution and Empire. The British intended to break the enemy line, overwhelming one segment of it while the remainder of their fleet held the rest of the enemy line at bay; having crippled, sunk, or captured the enemy's van, the fleet would unite to finish off the rest of the enemy fleet. The concept worked at, among other great sea fights, the Battle of the Nile in 1798, when Admiral Horatio Nelson had led his squadron in against a moored French fleet of equal if not slightly superior strength, destroying or capturing eleven of the thirteen enemy ships of the line.

The *Confiance*, more powerful than any of her American counterparts, would sail past the first American ship, the brig *Eagle*, giving her a broadside, and then cross the American line, sailing across the bow of Macdonough's flagship, *Saratoga*, which she would then engage with a raking fire, the most destructive possible, since every shot that went home would travel the length of the enemy ship. Brig *Linnet* and sloop *Chub*, following on, would overwhelm *Eagle*, already weakened by *Confiance's* broadside. Sloop *Finch* and the gunboats would take on the American schooner *Ticonderoga* and sloop *Preble*. *Finch* was to start with the more dangerous opponent, *Ticonderoga*, assisting the gunboats in taking her, and only then going after the sloop. (See the table on p. 290). At best, this part of the British line would take the American schooner and sloop, but in any event they would pin them down while *Linnet* and *Chub* took *Eagle*, and *Confiance*, with its superior firepower and positioning, destroyed the *Saratoga*. With *Eagle* and *Saratoga* taken or destroyed, all that would remain would be mopping up and assisting the British land assault into Plattsburgh. This was not a desperate scheme, but rather a quintessentially audacious plan by a fighting captain of the Royal Navy, which received no criticism from naval colleagues after the battle.

Downie's concern about American shore batteries was misplaced—they seem not to have engaged at all. But he faced far more serious problems. Some of these he understood: The British would have to approach the American position under constant fire from gunboats as well as the moored ships. British tactics in this as in other great sea battles of the past two decades depended for success not on numbers, superior ship design, or better cannon, but on adroit seamanship and ship handling, and on rapid, close-range fire followed by boarding. The key to British supremacy lay in well-trained crews, highly competent officers, and superior command and control.[32] But although Downie had the advantage of

Forces Engaged at Plattsburgh (British Plan)

U.S. (as moored, north to south)	Armament	Royal Navy	Armament	British plan	The reality
Eagle (brig)	12 x 32 pdr carronades 8 x 18 pdr long guns	Linnet (brig) Chub (sloop)	16 x 12 pdr long gun 3 x 6 pdr carronades 8 x 18 pdr carronades	Linnet and Chub to attack Eagle after Confiance fires into her	Confiance does not engage Eagle; Chub, damaged, drifts south
Saratoga (ship)	8 x 24 pdr long guns 6 x 42 pdr carronades 12 x 32 pdr carronades	Confiance (ship)	27 x 24 pdr long guns 6 x 24 pdr carronades 4 x 32 pdr carronades 2 x 18 pdr long guns	Confiance to cross Saratoga's bows and rake her after firing a broadside at Eagle	Engages alongside Saratoga approximately one hour
Ticonderoga (schooner)	8 x 12 pdr long guns 4 x 18 pdr long guns 5 x 32 pdr carronades	Finch (sloop)	6 x 18 pdr carronades 4 x 6 pdr columbiads 1 x 18 pdr columbiad	Finch and gunboats to attack Ticonderoga, then Preble	Finch attacks Preble first, later disabled by Ticonderoga
Preble (sloop)	7 x 12 pdr long guns	2 gunboats	1 x 18 pdr long gun 1 x 18 pdr carronade	British gunboats to support Finch against Ticonderoga and swarm Preble, taking her	Gunboats attack Preble and Ticonderoga, but most withdraw prematurely
Gunboats (moored inshore of the fleet)	Six with 1 x 18 pdr columbiad and 1 x 24 pdr long gun; Four with 1 x 12 pdr long gun	3 gunboats 3 gunboats 4 gunboats	1 x 24 pdr long gun 1 x 32 pdr carronade 1 x 18 pdr long gun 1 x 32 pdr carronade		

Note: "pdr" = "pounder." Armaments as actual, not as believed by combatants; Chub and Finch were the captured American sloops Growler and Eagle, respectively. Columbiads were hybrid weapons midway between carronades and long guns, and capable (in theory at any rate) of firing shell as well as shot.

Ship data: David Curtis Skaggs, Thomas MacDonough: Master of Command in the Early U.S. Navy (Annapolis: Naval Institute Press, 2003), pp. 119–20.

more experienced sailors than the Americans, he lacked experienced crews. His claim to parity in firepower with the Americans rested on the strength of the *Confiance*. But *Confiance* had entered the river less than two weeks before. According to its sailing master, most of the crew had come aboard only six days before the battle, and some only two days before. Its armament had lacked modern gunlocks for their cannon and carronades; its crew consisted of detached sailors from Royal Navy ships in Canada plus some soldiers who knew neither one another nor their officers; the roughness of the new deck made the guns difficult to work, and as it was, the British had only exercised the guns a few times before the battle.[33] Furthermore, although the British had considerably more long-range firepower than the Americans, they bore a disadvantage in the short-range "smashers"—the carronades that threw heavier shot at slower velocities for short distances, but that expended all their energy on their target. And this would be a close-in fight by virtue of Macdonough's careful positioning of the fleet as well as Royal Navy preference.

Macdonough had his problems, too. His crews remained understrength, and it is quite true that he accepted a draft of forty men under sentence for various disciplinary infractions who gladly (if possibly unwisely) exchanged ball and chain for ship duty.[34] Moreover, Robert Henley, the skipper of the newly arrived *Eagle*, was jealous of his superior's command, having served alongside him earlier in his career, and initially did not even consider himself subordinate to him. Still, Macdonough had built this fleet, knew these waters, and most important, had had months to train his crews and nearly a week to prepare his tactics for this particular fight in Plattsburgh Bay. Downie, under severe pressure from Prevost, whom he had been instructed to support, had none of these advantages.

The British made sail at 7:40 A.M. on September 11—and just as they entered the bay the wind shifted from north-northeast (the prevailing direction) to west-northwest.[35] As a result, Downie's ships now had to sail into the wind, which, to make matters worse, began fading away. His plan fell apart as it did so. *Linnet*, under the superseded Commander Pring, did indeed lay itself alongside *Eagle*. *Confiance*, however, could not get in position for a broadside at *Eagle*, or maneuver to break the American line. Instead, it moored some three hundred yards away from *Saratoga*. American fire during the British approach also disrupted the British plan. The

British sloop *Chub*, which had been intended to join *Linnet* in the attack on *Eagle*, lost its cables, bowsprit, and main boom to American fire and its commander lost control of the vessel after firing one broadside.[36] The disabled sloop drifted off to the south, and, to make matters worse, ended up slipping between *Confiance* and *Saratoga*. Macdonough took the opportunity to pour two broadsides into the hapless sloop, crippling and leaving it prey for the American gunboats. *Finch* engaged *Preble* and only then attempted to close with *Ticonderoga* (the plan had been the other way around), but, badly damaged, drifted off to the south, where it ran aground off Crab Island, a small island that included a hospital and a small American battery.

Beginning at 9:30 A.M., the real battle between *Confiance* and *Saratoga* began, with a well-aimed British broadside, the long guns being loaded with two shot each, plus a charge of canister (small shot and metal scraps)—a devastating, hammering blow that knocked more than half of the American crew, including Macdonough, off their feet, killing his first lieutenant and killing or wounding forty more. The return fire of the American flagship inflicted a no less grievous loss on the British, knocking a gun off its carriage on *Confiance*, where it smashed into Downie's groin, killing him instantly and flattening his watch (recovered after the battle), which showed the exact moment of its owner's demise. A brutal slugging match ensued at close range that, as Macdonough had anticipated, benefited *Saratoga*, with its armament composed chiefly of carronades, unlike the *Confiance's* much larger armament of long guns. Macdonough was knocked off his feet twice more, once by a falling spar, once by the decapitated head of one of his gun captains hit by an enemy cannonball.

At the southern end of the line the American sloop *Preble*, pummeled by *Finch* and the gunboats, cut her cable and drifted to shore, either surrendering (according to the British) or merely avoiding capture (according to its commander). But the *Ticonderoga* battered *Finch* and the gunboats, driving off the latter without too much difficulty, its thirty-two-pounder carronades loaded with grapeshot dissuading the British from trying to board.

The one part of the battle going well for the British at this point was Pring's combat in *Linnet* with *Eagle*. *Linnet* had a weaker armament (sixteen twelve-pounder long guns, versus twelve thirty-two-pounder carronades and eight eighteen-pounder long guns for *Eagle*) but a better-trained crew and an altogether superior commander. After an hour-and-a-half duel, during which both ships were badly mauled, *Eagle's* commander attempted to turn his vessel using springs, could not, cut his cable, and slipped out of the line of battle. At the vexed Macdonough's urgently shouted order, however, Henley managed to reposition himself in the gap between *Saratoga* and the next American ship, *Ticonderoga*, where he opened up on *Confiance*. Macdonough's report to Secretary of the Navy Jones made it clear what he thought of Henley's "unfortunately leaving me exposed to the galling fire from the Enemy's Brig"[37] in addition to the battering of *Confiance's* diminished, but still powerful batteries.

The critical point in the battle had now arrived. British fire had battered in *Saratoga's* starboard side. Nearly all of the American flagship's guns were dismounted or obstructed by wreckage and thus unable to fire. Macdonough ordered his men to cut the cable of the stern anchor and wind in the hawser, slowly turning the ship in an arc to bring the port side to face the enemy. It was a fearful moment, because it meant exposing the vulnerable stern of the *Saratoga* to raking fire from *Confiance*, and, what was immediately worse, *Linnet*. After a heart-stopping hitch, and a well-aimed broadside from *Linnet*, however, Macdonough's men succeeded in pivoting *Saratoga* around. *Confiance*, which itself had only four working guns opposite the Americans, attempted but could not accomplish the same maneuver. With a fresh broadside toward the enemy, *Saratoga* soon put *Confiance* out of commission, the British flagship striking around ten-thirty in the morning. *Saratoga* then turned on *Linnet* and compelled her to strike as well, fifteen minutes later. The engagement had lasted little more than two and a half hours in total, with the principal part of the fighting between the two flagships having gone on for only one hour.

Because of the close range, the still waters, and the heavy guns on both sides, however, that one hour of battle had been, for its size, as brutal an encounter as any fought in the age of sail. According to Macdonough's initial report, *Saratoga* had taken 55 shots to its hull; *Confiance*, much of whose fire had gone high (partly because the crews were unfamiliar with the long guns that had formed the major part of their armament), had taken no fewer than 105. (On closer inspection, Macdonough learned *Confiance* had suffered almost twice as many hits). American fire had killed and wounded roughly half of *Confiance's* crew of 270, while *Sara-*

toga had suffered more than a quarter of its own men killed and wounded. It was not until sunset that the Americans could get their prisoners ashore, their own vessels being been crippled by lost spars and cut rigging as well as damage to their hulls. But Thomas Macdonough, pious, clear, concise, and accurate, put it simply in his victory dispatch, which read, in its entirety, "The Almighty has been pleased to grant us a signal victory on Lake Champlain in the capture of one frigate, one brig, and two sloops of war of the enemy."[38] He and his men had wiped out the British fleet, save for a few gunboats.

General Prevost quickly drew his conclusion: The campaign had ended almost as it had begun. He had ordered attacks across the bridges and ford along the Saranac as the Royal Navy attacked, but called them off as soon as he saw the British defeat in the bay, as a result of "unfortunate events to which Naval Warfare is peculiarly exposed"—a phrase that outraged his naval colleagues later on.[39] He subsequently ordered his forces to withdraw to Canada, leaving behind, in a hasty if unforced evacuation, large quantities of supplies, including ammunition, tents, and (according to General Macomb) some three hundred deserters. In a private letter to the secretary at war and of the colonies, the Earl of Bathurst, Prevost made his case for what seemed to many in the army, in Canada, and subsequently, in London, an ignominious retreat. He could not destroy the American naval establishment without a naval force; the roads were appallingly bad and deteriorating in the rain. Furthermore, he declared, "The enemy's militia were raising *en masse* around me, desertion increasing, and the supply of provisions scanty." Understanding that he would be condemned for doing so, he decided to withdraw rather than launch an assault on the American fortifications that might very well fail, given that the Americans had been "cheered by the sight of a naval victory."[40]

Prevost did indeed attract furious denunciation. Alicia Cockburn, wife of a British major attached to a unit of Canadian regulars, wrote to her cousin in late October, "Had any man with common abilities been at the head of this Government, unbiased by the invidious counsels of fools and sycophants, we must long ago have taught the Yankees submission and been at peace. Such is the *decided opinion of every military man in the Province.*"[41]

Commodore James Yeo, grieving for the loss of his former second in command, and furious at Prevost for pressuring Downie to launch a premature attack on Macdonough, immediately began a campaign to pin the blame for the failure of the attack on the general. Less than two weeks after the battle, he wrote to John Croker, the powerful secretary of the Admiralty, that "Captain Downie was urged, and his ship hurried into action before she was in a fit state to meet the enemy." [42] Moreover, he insisted, and British naval opinion agreed, that had Prevost played his part by seizing the American batteries on the shore or emplacing his own, they would have defeated the American squadron. These two contentions, of course, were not entirely compatible: If Downie and his fleet were not "in a fit state to meet the enemy," how could the attempt have succeeded no matter what Prevost did?

That, however, was hardly the point. British naval *amour propre* suffered multiple wounds during the War of 1812. Of course it could blockade the American coast and wipe out American commerce—the navy, and the British public, expected that as a matter of course. But in a series of operationally insignificant but politically important ship-on-ship battles, the Royal Navy had been worsted, and even some countervailing successes (the capture of the frigate *Chesapeake* by *Shannon*, for example) did not take the sting away from a service and a country used to unvarying triumph on water. The Royal Navy never suppressed American privateers, which did not cripple British commerce, but did hurt it. As the Battle of Baltimore proved, it could not force a defended American harbor. And most important of all, it had failed on the lakes in the heart of the continent. On Lake Ontario it had fought and built its way to a mere draw with the Americans; on Lakes Erie and Champlain the fleets it had sent out under capable commanders had experienced not merely defeat, but annihilation.

The court-martial that, in accordance with naval practice, took place a year later, cleared Downie and his principal subordinates of all responsibility for the defeat, which the naval officers present insisted was "principally caused by the British squadron having been urged into Battle previous to its being in a proper state to meet its Enemy by a promised Co-operation of the Land Forces which was not carried into effect." [43] The court was implicitly critical of the commander of *Chub* and explicitly so of most of the gunboat commanders and crew (many of them Canadian militia), "who failed in their duty" by not taking *Ticonderoga*. The Royal Navy was not going to take responsibility for this debacle.

Neither, if he had his way, was George Prevost. His opportunity, however, never came. On March 1, 1815, he learned that the United States government had ratified the peace treaty signed in Ghent at the very end of December 1814, officially bringing the war to an end. The next day, he learned that the British government had recalled him: Ill, depressed, and deeply wounded by criticism from the press, the navy, and British Canadians (many of whom resented his good treatment of the French speakers), he looked forward to his own court-martial to clear his name. He would have received it, had he not died at the very beginning of 1816, his health crushed in part by the burdens of office during a long and difficult war.

There was, in fact, much to respect in Prevost as governor and commander.[44] Like Guy Carleton before him, he had little natural charm, but considerable administrative skill; like Carleton, too, he understood the importance of maintaining the allegiance of French Canadians, even at the expense of exciting the animosity of English settlers who disdained their papist neighbors. The forces under his overall command had parried repeated American assaults on Canada, and none had suffered the debacles that afflicted the Royal Navy on Lakes Erie and Champlain. In 1814 he proceeded cautiously, but not without reason. He may have realized better than those in London that the Americans had winnowed out the incompetent and decrepit generals of the war's early days. Macomb made an altogether more formidable foe than Dearborn or Wilkinson. American regulars had shown themselves as competent and determined as their British counterparts in the skirmishing before Plattsburgh, and in more substantial fighting along the Niagara frontier. And although the militia scattered before British columns in the field, when positioned behind fortifications, amply supplied with weapons and ammunition, excited by the naval victory, and supported by the fleet that had won it, they might very well have repulsed a British attack, or inflicted such a heavy price that success would hardly have been worth it. Had Edward Pakenham, Wellington's brother-in-law, made a similar calculation when encountering Andrew Jackson's southern militia at New Orleans four months later, he (and two thousand of his men) might have survived the war unscathed.

As for the relationship between the two services, Prevost undoubt-edly pressured Downie, but it is not clear that Downie resisted all that much. After the war, Prevost's liaison with Downie reported that in his meeting with the British fleet commander the latter had thought that the enemy was superior in weight of guns, but "expressed himself full of con-fidence in a successful issue to the Battle." [45] No doubt, Downie would have preferred to have British shore batteries playing on the American fleet (though they would have had to do so at extreme range), but there is no record that suggests that he viewed that as a prerequisite for success. Rather, the defeat of the British fleet stemmed from overconfidence despite the unreadiness of the force to execute a standard Royal Navy tac-tical plan, the vagaries of wind, and most of all, a highly competent and creditable defense by an American commander and his fleet. There was a profound lesson here. Only one British strategist understood it, but, as will be seen, he was the only one who mattered.

The victory remains with the Americans

In Ghent throughout the autumn of 1814 the wearisome negotiations continued. The Americans had reluctantly accepted a compromise on the Indian issue, much to the chagrin of John Quincy Adams, who disliked even the anodyne agreement that the Americans would conclude peace with the Indians with whom it had fought during the war and restore their possessions. Adams's lectures to the British wearied them and his own colleagues, although they agreed with the underlying argument. Adams saw a future of American expansion, and the displacement and compensation of American Indians as a relatively benign alternative to the other fate that would await them—extermination.

> To condemn vast regions of territory to perpetual barrenness and soli-tude that a few hundred savages might find wild beasts to hunt upon it, was a species of game law that a nation descended from Britons would never endure. It was as incompatible with the moral as with the physical nature of things. [46]

The British government, and for that matter, the American government, could not prevent the movement westward without massive violence, and a fixed boundary to Indian country would not do much good either. "It was opposing a feather to a torrent," Adams declared.

The British negotiators ground their teeth at Adams's rhetoric, but they conceded this point. Still, having beaten down American insistence on making maritime rights a part of the peace treaty, they persisted in the belief that they could, and would, gain more. The prime minister, the Earl of Liverpool, told Castlereagh, his foreign secretary, that "if our commander does his duty, I am persuaded we shall have acquired by our arms every point on the Canadian frontier which we ought to insist on keeping." [47] And throughout September the British government, to which the negotiators at Ghent referred constantly, aspired to retain territory seized during the war. By the end of the month matters looked particularly promising. The British government had learned of the operations in the Chesapeake and the capture of Washington; the prime minister informed the Duke of Wellington in Paris and Lord Castlereagh that the British would soon occupy Rhode Island, destroy Baltimore, and seize other coastal positions, while Prevost took Plattsburgh and Sacket's Harbor.

Thus, just before news of Plattsburgh arrived in London, the British government offered the Americans peace on the basis of *uti possidetis*, namely, both sides' keeping the territory held at the end of the war. Given that the British had various bits of American territory, and had expected more after this campaign (including Plattsburgh and even Sacket's Harbor on Lake Ontario and possibly New Orleans, as well as key forts in the Northwest), it would have been a major advantage. Given this, the British were willing to let slide their earlier demand that the United States recognize an Indian frontier. They were stunned, however, at the American insistence on the "extravagant doctrine of some of the revolutionary governments of France, viz., that they will never cede any part of their dominions, even though they shall have been conquered by their enemies." [48] The Americans simply refused to play by the normal rules of European politics.

Into an otherwise pleasing prospect of humbling American pride, punishing its dastardly attack on Canada, and securing that colony's security through strategically acquired points of territory, came crashing, first, word of the failed attack on Baltimore, and then the news of Plattsburgh.

Henry Goulburn, the chief British negotiator, could not interpret the latter as anything other than a major defeat, and, his dislike of Americans deepening the more he dealt with them, he told his government that "even our brilliant success at Baltimore, as it did not terminate in the capture of the town, will be considered by the Americans as a victory, and not as an escape." [49] Plattsburgh, however, admitted of no such interpretation.

The *Times* of London, equally sour, had to acknowledge that "the victory remains with the Americans. The invasion and threatened occupation of their territory has been frustrated, and we know enough of their propensity to magnify their successes, not to doubt that the exploits of Commodore Macdonough and General Macomb will be placed on a par with the greatest feats in history, ancient or modern." [50] To be sure, the paper called for renewed efforts to continue the war. Contemplating the American situation, it foresaw "a fund of the bitterest animosity laid up against us in future, with our flag disgraced on the ocean and on the lakes, and with the laurels withered at Plattburgh which were so hardly but so gloriously earned in Portugal, and Spain, and France." It called for sending the Duke of Wellington to North America. John Quincy Adams, flinty son of New England, dismissed all this as blubbering. [51]

The British government thought hard about doing what the *Times* recommended, Liverpool writing to Wellington on November 4 proposing sending him to America to "make peace, or to continue the war, if peace should be found impracticable, with renewed vigor." Wellington, while ready to do whatever the government asked him, advised against it. The situation in Paris had deteriorated: The occupied French were turbulent, and peace negotiations required his presence. Under even moderately competent generals his veterans could defend Canada, he felt quite sure. But without naval superiority on the lakes the British government could accomplish nothing, and he saw no prospect of changing that. And as for the present negotiations, "I confess that I think you have no right from the state of the war to demand any concession of territory from America." [52] Moreover, he pointed out, with justifiable self-regard, to send him over would be a kind of "triumph for the Americans," making them out to be a more formidable enemy than they were. A lion should not pay a pole cat that kind of compliment.

The British government, weary of war, anxious about domestic unrest, reluctantly went along with the Iron Duke's advice—although it did retain a hope that if the Americans refused to ratify the treaty the British might be able to retain New Orleans, or even offer a separate peace to the New England states, believed to be on the verge of secession.[53]

Goulburn hated it. He never wanted to accommodate any American wishes, found the outcome of Plattsburgh "unaccountable," and despised "the fixed determination which prevails in the breast of every American to extirpate the Indians and appropriate their territory." Still, he dutifully implemented instructions.[54] His no less acidic American counterpart recorded in his diary his irritation with Goulburn, with his colleagues ("Mr. Clay is losing his temper and growing peevish and fractious"), and, of course, with himself. Adams had completed (re)reading the Old Testament, but found fault with his own increasingly frivolous habits. "I have this month frequented too much the theatre and other public amusements; indulged too much conviviality, and taken too little exercise." He was becoming fat and lazy, and teetered, he feared, on the edge of indolence and dissipation as a way of life.[55]

Six weeks of haggling produced the so-called Christmas Peace, the Treaty of Ghent. It is a remarkably boring and disappointing document, because it merely established peace on the basis of *status quo ante*—going back to where both sides were in May 1812. Most of its articles talk about the mechanics of establishing peace, restoring prisoners and property, and demarcating a boundary with the aid of a neutral commission. Both Americans and British promised, in the ninth article, to restore to their Indian enemies "all the possessions, rights, and privileges which they may have enjoyed or been entitled to in one thousand eight hundred and eleven previous to such hostilities," providing the Indians ceased hostilities. But since in 1811 the Indians were already being swamped and dispossessed by a tidal wave of American migrants, that could provide no comfort to Britain's Indian allies, who had, parenthetically, played a vital role in the defense of Canada. Of other issues—maritime rights and impressment, the supposed *casus belli*, above all—not a word.

Ultimately, Canada and Canadians won the War of 1812. If the conquest of that country had not been an American objective when the war began, it surely had become such shortly after it opened. Not only did the colony remain intact: It had acquired heroes, British and French, and a narrative of plucky defense against foreign invasion, that helped carry it to nationhood. As for the British government, it might have desired a more punitive peace, and the several naval defeats still stung, but on the whole the British government had done well: It had defended its colony against considerable odds, yielded nothing in terms of what it understood to be its rights as the dominant naval power, and had given Jonathan (as the British press called the Americans) several good drubbings. The Americans, some (and not only British) historians contend, lost.[56] The nominal causes for which they had fought the war had advanced not an iota; they had failed in their objective of conquering Canada; they had suffered humiliating defeats at the hands of numerically inferior enemies; the Royal Navy had driven American commerce from the seas; and American national finance had suffered severely.

Americans at the time, and, by and large, since, did not see matters that way.[57] Some of this has to do with myth, understood as powerful stories that frame a deeper conception of one's own history. They clung to the victorious naval duels of the USS *Constitution*, the "bombs bursting in air" over Fort McHenry, the fleet action on Lake Erie, the battle of New Orleans (which did *not* take place after the war had ended, as some believe, because the peace had yet to be ratified by Congress)—and, very much, Plattsburgh. Nor did Americans alone see the War of 1812 as something of a success. After the war Adams, an observant diplomat, remarked to a friend that "the effect of the war had been to raise our national character in the opinion of Europe."[58]

The American sense of self-confidence coming out of the war, merited or not, helps explain why it is that just three weeks after ratifying the Peace of Ghent, President James Madison requested, and Congress heartily approved, sending virtually the entire United States Navy to the Mediterranean to impose a victor's settlement on the states of North Africa, which had continued to attack American commerce. The United States, delusionally or not, took from the War of 1812 a tremendous boost to its self-confidence. It was the kind of outcome that infuriated many scorekeepers then and since tallying up the numbers of defeats, casualties, and destruction, but it was a psychological, and hence a political reality nonetheless.

Before Plattsburgh, the British had already abandoned the idea of an Indian buffer state (presumably under British protection), which would have been a serious threat to the future expansion of the United States and, from the American point of view, the most dangerous outcome of the war.[59] But even so, Plattsburgh was a decisive battle, one of the few that deserve that description. Even without the projected buffer state, the British had hoped forever to neutralize American threats to Canada by seizing key territory and demilitarizing the American side of the border. The British could, and did, interpret the rebuff before Baltimore as of less significance, particularly given the context in which it occurred, namely, the occupation of Washington and punitive destruction of public buildings there. After Plattsburgh they gave up on the idea of seizing American territory to physically limit the United States, including by holding New Orleans (although the expedition there had already been launched).

Plattsburgh was also a profoundly revealing battle. As Wellington's correspondence indicates, Plattsburgh provided conclusive proof that Britain had failed on America's inland seas. It not only shook the confidence of British statesmen: It revealed a deeper truth, that henceforth no European power could project into North America military power capable of seriously threatening the United States. When a rising young politician, an acolyte of Henry Clay, considered his country's future a quarter of a century after these events, he asked, "Shall we expect some transatlantic military giant to step the Ocean, and crush us at a blow? Never! All the armies of Europe, Asia, and Africa combined, with all the treasure of the earth (our own excepted) in their military chest; with a Buonaparte for a commander, could not by force, take a drink from the Ohio, or make a track on the Blue Ridge, in a trial of a thousand years."[60] Abraham Lincoln's certainty owed something to what Plattsburgh had demonstrated.

Americans in later years have taken for granted the idea that foreign enemies might raid the United States, as at Pearl Harbor in 1941 or New York and Washington in 2001, but could never project conventional armed forces into the heartland. This was far from being the case until Plattsburgh. Moreover, the Lake Champlain campaign of 1814 demonstrated America's enormous potential military strengths—the extraordinary speed with which the Brown brothers built effective warships bespoke the new country's military-industrial capacity, while the ability of a small cadre of professional officers like Macdonough and Macomb to train and lead a large body of citizen-soldiers suggested the country's capacity for rapid and effective mobilization should the need arise.

By the end of the negotiations, John Quincy Adams had achieved a modicum of fellow feeling for his colleagues. He had even come to see in

Henry Clay "the same dogmatical, overbearing manner, the same harsh-ness of look and expression, and the same forgetfulness of the courtesies of society" that he sadly recognized in himself. Upon signing the treaty on Christmas Eve, 1814, he again sat down to write to his mother, more cheerfully than he had three months before, but still cautiously. "We have abandoned no essential right, and if we have left everything open for future controversy, we have at least secured to our country the power at her own option to extinguish the war." [61] He could not know that the flames would never again leap up so high as they had at Plattsburgh, but, as Adams knew very well, embers remained.

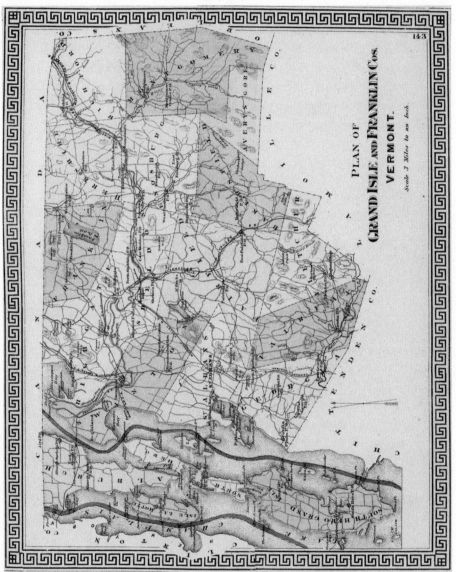

The area around St. Albans and the border, shortly after the Civil War.
Courtesy, David Rumsey Map Collection, www.davidrumsey.com

CHAPTER TEN

Rumors of War, 1815–71

The approach for invasion most to be dreaded

In February 1862, at age eighty, Britain's inspector-general of fortifications still served the queen as he had since she had ascended the throne twenty-five years before, and as he had served her uncles and grandfather before that. John Fox Burgoyne was a pillar of Victorian virtues, "brave, able, intelligent, upright, a humble Christian, a modest citizen," as Reverend G. R. Gleig would describe him when he finally passed away in 1871. He was also none other than the eldest son—illegitimate, the product of an affair with an opera singer—of the General John Burgoyne who had traveled the Great Warpath south, headed to the disaster of Saratoga, eighty-five years before.

This Burgoyne had served as chief engineer of British forces in Spain during the Napoleonic Wars, received wounds to neck and jaw, and had sailed to America in 1814 with Major General Edward Pakenham's expedition to New Orleans. He had captured an American fort at the entrance to Mobile Bay, but his success could not redeem that disastrous campaign. He served in the Crimea with distinction. He wrote widely and well, about the pacification of Ireland, the need for coastal defenses, the design of saddles, and the interesting subject of "officers throwing responsibility upon others." Now, however, he had more urgent matters to analyze: the defense of Canada in the event of an American invasion.

At this point Great Britain had already sent almost thirteen thousand troops to Canada (meaning present-day Ontario and Quebec), and had deployed five thousand more to man the defenses of Halifax, New Brunswick, and Newfoundland. British armories had disgorged tens of thousands of rifles to arm the Canadian militia as well. The old general believed that the American Civil War, raging since the previous spring, had in some measure ameliorated an intractable strategic problem. The United States, with a large population, vast wealth, and attractive institutions, might have overrun Canada, seducing vast numbers of British subjects from their allegiance as it did so. "In an all-powerful condition," he wrote, the United States "could have rapidly brought to bear upon this, our weak point, such a force as we could hardly expect to withstand."[1]

Now, however, matters looked a bit better. The United States were (he used the plural) disunited, and likely to remain so; financially drained by their war; and less likely than before to appeal to disaffected Canadians. On the other hand, frustration at losing the conflict with the seceding southern states might goad the northern states into an attack on Canada. In that case, British naval superiority could not save the day: "That any of our colonies can obtain absolute protection from our navy is a fallacy." Canada's thousand-mile land border was acutely vulnerable, and there were severe limits to how Britain could defend it. The difficult strategic question was not whether, as some thought, "the colony shall defend itself, which in fact it cannot do, but whether it shall be abandoned to the enemy on the first war that may occur."

Of all the vulnerable points on the frontier, he singled out one for concern. "The approach for invasion most to be dreaded, would seem to be decidedly from Lake Champlain towards Montreal."[2] This offered the most direct route to "the heart of our resources," and here the greatest efforts must be made to renew fortifications, train militia, and deploy the few regulars Britain had available. Conceivably, the British high command in Canada might contemplate preemptive attacks on American forces, but opportunities for such daring operations seemed unlikely. During the next year, 1863, the old general sent a much brisker young subordinate, Lieutenant Colonel William Jervois, to reconnoiter Canada and even the American side. The ingenious Jervois performed this latter task by pretending to be an artist in a rowboat whose carefully drawn sketches somehow always featured harbor fortifications. Jervois's analyses only reinforced the fundamental pessimism of the old general of engineers. Britain would be lucky to hold Montreal and Quebec against a determined attack for even a brief period of time.

Burgoyne, it is said, had an excellent sense of humor. In that case, it must have been at least a source of ironic reflection that he was considering the desperate defense of a colony that his father had used as a base from which to crush the bumptious rebels who had now built this great power, in turn rent by civil conflict. The same Great Warpath his father had viewed as a highway into rebel territory, he now viewed with trepidation as an avenue for invasion of Canada by the American enemy, in the not unlikely event that war should break out yet again.

———— •◆• ————

It is impossible for Her Majesty's Government to withdraw from these Dominions without disgrace

The possibility of a third Anglo-American war had existed ever since the end of the second, the War of 1812. "The myth of the unguarded frontier," as some have called it, was just that.[3] Particularly during two decades of the nineteenth century, from the mid-1830s through the mid-1840s, and again during the 1860s, war between the United States and Canada loomed as a serious possibility for both sides. That it did not occur had more to do with statecraft and luck than with the innately pacific qualities of the two countries. If, as we have seen, phantom campaigns can have real consequences, one might say that phantom wars deserve at least a small fraction of the attention their real counterparts attract.

The Peace of Ghent, based on the *status quo ante*, resolved no fundamental issue between Great Britain and the United States. The War of 1812 had, however, two large strategic effects: It disinclined the British to attempt to project military power into the American heartland (although some commanders in Canada would later toy with the idea), and it helped convince most in the United States that the project of conquering Canada would prove expensive and difficult (which did not discourage those who hoped that the provinces would, of their own free will or under moderate pressure, join the Great Republic as states). Three sources of potential friction remained between Great Britain and America over Canadian issues: border disputes left over from the resolution of the two previous wars; internal convulsions on either side of the border that might spill over; and an explosion along the Canadian-American frontier detonated by fuses lit elsewhere, most notably on the high seas.

The geographical focal point for a future war still lay on the Great Warpath, as John Fox Burgoyne shrewdly discerned. Had the War of 1812 continued another year, the war plan for 1815, drafted by Secretary of War James Monroe (John Armstrong having resigned after the burning of Washington by the British in August 1814), envisioned a direct thrust north along the Champlain corridor toward Montreal.[4] If one lesson of that war seemed to be that Great Britain would find it difficult, if not impossible, to maintain control of the Great Lakes, a second had been that the Americans would be better advised to take the difficult but shorter route to Canada's heart rather than, as in 1812–13, the long way around via the Niagara frontier and Lake Ontario.

Thus it was that the advent of peace in 1815 brought no surcease to military planning for war along the Great Warpath. The severe limitation of armaments on the lakes agreed to by American and British diplomats (the Rush-Bagot Agreement, ratified in 1818) limited the two sides to one small armed vessel each on the Great Lakes and Lake Champlain. In truth, however, this deal merely recognized two facts: the need for post-war economy in both countries, and the futility of keeping wooden navies permanently afloat in the harsh northern climate. Fortifications, however, were a very different matter. Lieutenant Colonel Joseph G. Totten, architect of Alexander Macomb's field fortifications at Plattsburgh, now began supervising construction of a major fortification in March 1817 at Rouse's Point. He ordered half a million bricks and twenty thousand bushels of lime for the massive new site, which he showed off to the newly elected president James Monroe that summer. The next year, in June 1818, he deployed several companies of infantry from the nearby Plattsburgh barracks, to protect the site against sabotage from across the border—a border barely a mile away.[5]

The American government had decided to plant a fort here, at the very northern end of Lake Champlain. The structure was planned as a massive building, with three tiers of artillery (two in casemates, one in the open, or as the engineers put it, *en barbette*, on the upper platform), and could bar any British vessel sailing south from the Royal Navy's base at Isle aux Noix. Thus bottling up any future British flotilla, the Rouse's Point fort would not only protect Lake Champlain; it would, as Totten recognized then and thereafter, provide a base from which to invade Canada.[6] Unfortunately, the sand island chosen as the building site made for a weak foundation for the fortress. What ruined it, however, was not so much the crumbly soil beneath it as the scientific observations of a British astronomer and the first head of the American Coast and Geodetic Survey. In a survey of the boundary commissioned by both governments, the two experts came to the unfortunate conclusion that the unnamed fort lay on the wrong side of the border, in Canada. The chagrined Americans abandoned the project in December 1818, and "Fort Blunder," as the locals called it, entered regional folklore.

On the other side of the Atlantic, the Duke of Wellington had not forgotten his apprehensions about the United States. In 1819 he had become master-general of the ordnance, and by virtue of this position and his unparalleled reputation the government's senior military adviser. One of his first tasks that year was a review of North American defense plans. In 1825 he sent one of his chief engineers, Sir James Carmichael Smyth, to conduct a survey of Canada's defenses and develop a plan for strengthening them. The resulting blueprint envisaged a massively expensive (£1.6 million) program, including the construction of the Rideau waterway, some 125 miles of rivers and canal that would bypass the St. Lawrence and allow a connection between the critical naval base at Kingston on Lake Ontario and Ottawa. The Rideau canal was only part of a vast construction program, which included the strengthening of Kingston (where one of six planned forts survives as Fort Henry), the building of a defended supply depot at Montreal, and the massive fortification of Quebec in a style much admired by twenty-first-century tourists.[7] Wellington and Smyth also advised a substantial fortification at Isle aux Noix, which became Fort Lennox, to block an attack along the Lake Champlain corridor.[8]

Although the British government never brought itself to expend anything like the full amounts envisaged by Wellington and his planners, it nonetheless began the fortification and strategic canal scheme. Still, although there was plenty of reason for friction in the 1820s, including British suspicion of American intentions to annex Cuba, the two countries achieved a *modus vivendi* that allowed both sides to relax their military preparations. Nonetheless, the apprehensive British government did make a point of keeping a larger garrison in Canada than it had before the War of 1812.

During the 1830s, however, matters took a decided turn for the worse. American expansion in the direction of Mexico, beginning with Texas achieving independence in 1836—surely, only a prelude to annexation by the United States—prompted another bout of British suspicion, on the grounds that northerners would seek to balance the entry of a new slave state into the Union by adding a Canadian province or two as free states. And America's boisterous expansionism to the West augured ill for her neighbor to the north. But the real source of conflict was, oddly, in Canada itself. The country seemed ripe for insurrection, and the Americans prepared to take advantage of it.

In 1837, democratic unrest disturbed Upper Canada (now Ontario) and Lower Canada (Quebec). Since American independence, Lower Canada had remained under the rule of a powerful governor general assisted by an appointed executive council and a weak representative assembly based on limited suffrage. The government of Upper Canada seemed to serve the interest of the well-connected few—the so-called Family Compact. Members of the small French Canadian middle class resented the powerful grip of the church and the *seigneurs*, who had long provided the empire with reliable local allies; English Canadians sought more representation. Many, in both Canadas, observed and approved the roistering democracy to the south, and had supporters there.

The frontier region in the north was, in the 1830s as before, a distinctive trading and social area made more turbulent by economic recession; cross-border contacts were extensive, and Americans followed what was going on to their north. *Patriotes* (as the French revolutionaries were called) and English rebels received a great deal of sympathy from their neighbors. Men and weaponry flowed north, and dissidents fled south, all to the mounting anger of British authorities. It was not long before actual violence broke out, leading the British to increase the size of the permanent garrison of Canada to ten thousand regulars from scarcely a fifth as many, and to augment that force with militia and new, more reliable volunteer units. The British also strengthened the Royal Navy in American waters.

Along the Niagara frontier the trigger to conflict proved to be the use of a steamship to ferry arms and men to a rebel base in the middle of the river, Navy Island, barely three miles upriver from Niagara Falls. William Lyon Mackenzie, a Scottish emigrant, journalist, and agitator for democracy who had been recruiting supporters in Buffalo, seized the island and fortified it. He and his supporters hired the forty-six-ton steamer *Caroline* to supply them from the American side. On December 29, 1837, some fifty Canadian volunteers in seven rowboats under a British naval officer crossed the river to the New York side, stormed the *Caroline*, captured the boat, and set it afire, cutting it loose from its moorings and allowing it to drift to what would have been a spectacular end, plunging in flames over Niagara Falls, had it not unromantically sunk before going over the cataract. In the melee, and in murky circumstances, one American lay shot to death on the New York shore.

The pacifically inclined administration of President Martin Van Buren attempted to tamp down the resulting furor. He succeeded, in part through the diplomatic efforts of Winfield Scott, one of the heroes of the War of 1812 and the greatest figure in American military history for the first half of the nineteenth century, whom he dispatched to quiet the New York frontier. Colonel John Wool, who had led the riflemen harassing Prevost's columns at Plattsburgh, now inspector general of the army, embarked on a similar mission in Vermont. Supervising both was the former Plattsburgh commander himself, Alexander Macomb, now the army's general in chief. Neither Scott nor Wool had more than reputation and dignity to enforce the administration's aim of quieting the frontier, but luckily both had these qualities aplenty. Wool, like Scott, soon realized that the local population was restive, armed, and inclined to support the rebels, and that on the other side of the line, irate and jumpy British officers commanding regulars and militia were inclined toward hot pursuit into American territory.[9] Wool mobilized small units of New York and Vermont volunteers, and with a combination of diplomacy and threats of force broke up units of armed rebels and their American sympathizers attempting to cross the border heading north.[10]

The Americans and British composed their difference, in part through the successful diplomacy of Daniel Webster, secretary of state, but the northern border remained turbulent, with secret societies (the so-called Hunters' Lodges) along the border and bands of armed men periodically crossing into Canada and back. Eventually, an additional infantry regiment helped the United States government regain control of the border.

Given that the entire American regular army numbered no more than the British garrison of Canada, and was, in any case, mostly tied down fighting the Seminole Indians in the South, the balance along the border did not favor the United States. President Van Buren did not desire, and was not really in a position to launch, a war with Great Britain, but popular antipathy continued to bubble up, spiking again in 1840–41 when New York authorities arrested and charged with murder Alexander McLeod, a British veteran and deputy sheriff of the Niagara district, who had supposedly boasted of his role in the *Caroline* affair. Britain's Foreign Secretary Palmerston, pursuing a "diplomacy of menace," threatened war if the Americans executed McLeod, and for a time the crisis brought the countries even closer to war than in 1838. In violation of the Rush-Bagot Agreement demilitarizing the Great Lakes, the British began a naval buildup there under a Royal Navy officer who declared that "war with the Yankees" was inevitable." The crisis was finally resolved when—much to the relief and surprise of all concerned—the court acquitted McLeod. Governor William Seward of New York quietly assured Secretary of State Webster that McLeod would be pardoned if convicted. Webster, for his part, had quietly made sure that McLeod had an outstanding lawyer to make his case.

The Webster-Ashburton Treaty of 1842 (named after the new secretary of state and his new, more pacifically inclined British counterpart, Alexander Baring, Baron Ashburton), abated Anglo-American tension for a time. It settled most of the outstanding border issues, including American agreement to a line that favored New Brunswick at the expense of Maine in return for recovering Rouse's Point, where a new fort began to rise in place of the ruined Fort Blunder. But in the far West the border of the Oregon Territory inflamed tensions once again, leading to a further crisis in 1845.

Again, war clouds gathered. The governor general of Canada, Sir Charles Metcalfe, wrote to Lord Edward Stanley, secretary of state for war and the colonies, on July 4, 1845, that to defend Upper and Lower

Canada together would require some fifty thousand regulars—but that if such a number were in fact available, it would be better to go on an immediate offensive in the Northeast, taking Maine, New Hampshire, and Vermont.

> I presume that war may be carried on in North America, on the same principles, and with the same results, as in Continental Europe. I may best perhaps explain my meaning by suggesting the supposition that Napoleon Buonaparte had possession of Canada with the resources of Great Britain, and the command of the ocean. He would, it may be imagined, make short work of a war with the United States, if his object were as moderate as ours would be, namely an honourable peace. Why might not England do likewise?[12]

The aged Duke of Wellington, still advising on Canadian affairs, pressed during the crisis for an acceleration of the canal and fortification construction programs he had long urged, and for the mobilization and training of the Canadian militia. Wellington again pointed to the Lake Champlain route as the most obvious and dangerous pathway into Canada. Economic development on both sides of the border had favored the Americans in this connection. More roads (and now the Champlain canal) led to the northern border, while the expansion of roads along the Richelieu valley meant that Fort Lennox could no longer block an invasion. With rather more experience of war than Metcalfe, he focused on the defense of Canada rather than a preemptive attack on the United States. "It is impossible for Her Majesty's Government to withdraw from these Dominions without disgrace," Wellington insisted.[13]

The Americans eventually climbed down over the question of the Oregon border, for a number of reasons, including the hovering fact of British naval supremacy. In 1845–46 the Royal Navy vastly outstripped that of the United States by a factor of four or five in ships, men, and guns; even with France added into the balance, the Royal Navy still seemed supreme, if on shakier ground.[14] But in truth, neither party wanted war: For neither a Britain painfully reforming itself and coping with the consequences of the potato blight and famine in Ireland, nor a United States sensing the opportunity to gobble up large slices of Mexico, did war seem a sensible choice.

Over the next fifteen years relative peace obtained, bolstered by a variety of commercial agreements that increased the already burgeoning trade between the United States, Canada, and Great Britain. But underlying hostility remained, and throughout the mid-1840s Canadians on the Champlain border would have heard the slow but relentless slamming of steam engines driving in over four thousand piles to support the construction of Fort Montgomery at Rouse's Point. In ensuing years they would have noted the slow rise of the new fort's walls, casemates, and embrasures supervised by a young captain of engineers, Montgomery Meigs, who would later make his mark as the quartermaster of the United States Army. And the more historically minded of the fort's northern neighbors would have noted uneasily that the Americans had named it after the renegade British officer turned American general who had led the first invasion of Canada seventy-five years before.

———— ◆ ————

The resources of the Union are as exhaustless as its spirit

Fort Montgomery, whose building slackened as the 1850s wore on, assumed a new importance when the American Civil War broke out in 1861, for it was the northernmost point on what might very well become a second front in that war. Since the beginning of the Civil War, Great Britain had maintained a position of neutrality, recognizing Confederate belligerency but refraining from formally acknowledging southern independence. This in itself angered the American government, infuriated by Confederate arms purchases in Britain, and above all by the construction of Confederate cruisers in British shipyards. Although the British government refused to permit the arming of Confederate ships in its ports, thus maintaining that it had not breached its neutrality, this did not appease the Americans. Overt British sympathy with the Confederacy—most prevalent among the upper class, though not shared by those ideologically opposed to slavery—was common. Upon the outbreak of war the British immediately, and conspicuously sent two battalions of infantry in the *Great Eastern*, the world's largest steamship, to reinforce the garrison in Canada. More troops, arms for the Canadian militia, and a substantial naval reinforcement to Halifax and the West Indies soon crossed the Atlantic.[15]

Even liberals such as Walter Bagehot, founding editor of the *Economist*, confessed to a profound mistrust of the United States. It had been unfortunate, this brilliant student of politics and finance wrote, that the United States had so swiftly and without apparent setback become prosperous, populous, and powerful.

> They were so rough, so encroaching, and so overbearing, that all other governments felt as if some new associate, untrained to the amenities of civilized life, and insensible alike to the demands of justice and of courtesy, had forced its way into the areopagus of nations;—yet at the same time they were so reckless and so indisputably powerful, that nearly every one was disposed to bear with them and defer to them, rather than oppose a democracy so ready to quarrel and so capable of combat.

For that reason, Bagehot declared, "We do not see why we should hesitate to declare our belief that the dissolution of the Union will prove a good to the world, to Great Britain, and probably in the end to America herself."[16] This attitude seemed to President Lincoln and his subordinates a peculiar and unwelcome form of benevolence.

One more time—the last, as it turned out—in the fraught relationship between mother country and former colony, the United States backed down in the face of a confrontation at sea. At the end of 1861 an overzealous navy captain intercepted the British ship *Trent* and carried off the Confederate commissioners to France and Great Britain who had been on board. Ironically, it was now the British government that harped on the rights of neutrals, and the Americans who insisted on a free hand in snatching persons from the ships of countries with whom they were at peace. The British government threatened war, but thanks to the last-minute intervention of a dying Prince Albert, did so in a note just gently phrased enough to allow the Americans to back down without too much indignity. The crisis, and the threat of a British alliance with the Confederacy, abated. But that sturdy veteran of Plattsburgh, General Totten, still chief engineer of the United States Army, hastened to pay another visit to Fort Montgomery and accelerate plans for its completion.

Friction between Britain and the United States persisted. "We find we are drifting, not withstanding your most earnest and vigorous resistance," towards a war with Great Britain," wrote William Seward, formerly governor of New York during the *Caroline* affair, now secretary of state and Lincoln's chief adviser, in June 1863, to America's minister to the Court of St. James, Charles Francis Adams, son of John Quincy.[17] Seward's anger at, and disdain for, Britain reflected a judgment that Europe, including Britain, had undergone a moral decline since the days of Alexander the Great. "American society, on the contrary, is full of the vigor of youth."[18] This was the tone of much of the trans-Atlantic dialogue. In 1863 General Burgoyne meanwhile carried on a polite professional correspondence with General Totten, inquiring about the various practices of American armies, after respectfully noting their extraordinary size. Totten acknowledged the failures of some Union commanders, but pointedly reminded his colleague—and potential enemy—that "the resources of the Union are as exhaustless as its spirit."[19] Burgoyne (who privately complained of the Americans' "arrogant bullying system," and whose belligerence he declared worthy of "a spoiled child") acknowledged the truth that Totten had indicated. By 1863 the United States had, at last, shown the kind of war power that it could mobilize if it set its mind to it. Armies of hundreds of thousands amply clothed, fed, and equipped; suddenly sprouting rail and telegraph lines supporting and directing their advance; ironclad navies conjured out of nothing and equipped with the most modern armaments; and ingenious devices from mines to repeating rifles made manifest the latent power that British authorities had long tacitly understood to exist.

The tensions between the two countries were reflected in Canada as well as in chanceries and on the high seas. Canadians, like many Englishmen, shared mixed feelings about the United States, fearing its power, disliking slavery, but above all, hoping not to stir American desires to seize their country by force. As the war continued Canada became home—not for the last time—to a variety of American dissidents. Confederate soldiers who had escaped from northern prisoner of war camps, civilians who sought refuge from the fighting increasingly penetrating their homeland, northern draft dodgers, "crimps" seeking to recruit British subjects (including poorly paid British soldiers) for the Union army, all swarmed north of the border.[20]

War, narrowly averted over the *Trent* affair, could always spill into

Canada. But British naval supremacy, the ultimate guarantor of Canadian independence, no longer seemed as secure as it had only fifteen years before, during the last war scare. On March 8, 1862, the Confederate iron-clad *Virginia* (formerly USS *Merrimac*) had made short work of two Union wooden ships, the *Cumberland* and *Congress*. A revolution in naval architecture had occurred, making obsolete the wooden ships that were the staple of most fleets, including the Royal Navy. The United States Navy, with its peculiar-looking but lethal USS *Monitor* class of shallow-draft coastal ships, each mounting a powerful turreted battery, was build-ing ironclads at a furious pace, which meant that the Royal Navy might easily find itself outgunned on this side of the Atlantic.

As for Canada itself, Burgoyne's emissary, Lieutenant Colonel Jervois, had visited North America a second time, in 1864. By that time the Brit-ish knew that the Union could raise and deploy armies of hundreds of thousands, equipped with the latest weapons, and led by able generals— an opponent that they could not hope to match. Jervois concluded that the regular garrison of Canada simply could not defend it:

> Even when aided by the whole of the local militia that could at pres-ent be made available it would, in the event of war, be obliged to retreat before the superior numbers by which it would be attacked; and it would be fortunate if it succeeded in embarking at Quebec and putting to sea without serious defeat.[21]

Jervois merely told the governments in Canada and Britain what, in their hearts, they already knew: As matters now stood, if the United States wanted to take Canada by force, it could.

———— ·•·• ————

The war must continue until neutral nations interfere

In April 1864 the Confederate States of America had been cut in two by Union forces operating along the Mississippi River. The all-important rail junction of Chattanooga had fallen; soon, William Tecumseh Sherman would begin his march on Atlanta. Robert E. Lee's Army of Northern

Virginia had suffered its first large-scale defeat at Gettysburg the previous July and had not attempted large-scale offensive operations since. Opposite it, the Army of the Potomac had a newly appointed commander, Ulysses S. Grant—not only more capable than his predecessors, but utterly implacable in his determination to crush the rebellion even if that meant leaving Union prisoners to languish in deadly camps rather than exchanging them for Confederates held in the North. The blockade the United States Navy had wrapped around the Confederacy was squeezing the life out of its commerce, as one port after another succumbed to federal amphibious forces and an ever-expanding fleet.

At this juncture, on April 7, 1864, President Jefferson Davis inquired of Jacob Thompson, former secretary of the interior under President James Buchanan, if he would undertake a special mission abroad for the embattled Confederacy. Thompson agreed, and in short order he and former Alabama senator Clement Claiborne Clay slipped out of Wilmington, North Carolina, through the Yankee blockade, to Halifax, where they linked up with a third colleague, law professor James Holcombe of the University of Virginia. Their titles were commissioners *in* Canada, not commissioners *to* Canada, because their task was not representation but subversion, covert action, and political warfare.[22] And one of the most dramatic of their deeds, conducted along the Great Warpath route, nearly brought the United States and Great Britain to war once again.

The Confederate mission in Canada remains swathed in an obscurity, composed of verbal instructions not committed to paper, destroyed records, and a certain amount of innate incoherence. But its enterprises soon became apparent: to disrupt the northern war effort by lighting a variety of fires—some quite literal—in its rear. Drawing on the young veterans of some of the South's most capable light cavalry units (the Civil War counterparts of contemporary special operations forces) who had either escaped from captivity or deliberately infiltrated through Union territory to the north, they set out to wage covert war to an altogether astonishing degree.[23]

One part of the Confederate mission consisted of outreach to Confederate sympathizers or, at least, anti-Lincoln forces in a variety of secret organizations. So-called Copperheads (after a particularly vicious rattlesnake), the Confederates believed, abounded, particularly in the Northwest, and the commissioners conjured with the idea of a Northwestern

Confederacy that would combine with the South to crush New England. The commissioners played with Horace Greeley, the self-important and volatile editor of the *New York Tribune*, luring him to Niagara Falls for a backdoor negotiation to which Lincoln gave his reluctant and heavily qualified assent. The talks crumbled when it became clear that Greeley had failed to communicate President Lincoln's two preconditions: unconditional restoration of the Union and the end of slavery. And they seem to have thought about the possibility of provoking a war between Britain and the United States. "The war must continue until neutral nations interfere and command the peace," wrote Clay from Canada in August 1864 to the man who coordinated Confederate secret service activities, Secretary of State Judah P. Benjamin.[24] To the Confederate secret service headquarters in Saint Lawrence Hall in Montreal (supposedly, the only hotel in Canada to serve mint juleps) came a host of shady characters to muse, talk politics, dream of southern independence, and conspire.[25] Most remain in the shadows to this day; one, at least, achieved infamy— John Wilkes Booth.

Throughout the spring and summer of 1864, Thompson and Clay (Holcombe had returned to the Confederacy after helping to establish "rat lines"—escape routes for southern prisoners of war) spent their ample war chest engaging in political warfare, seeking to disrupt the impending election and foster anti-Lincoln sentiment. By September, however, Clay at least had come to a sober judgment: "The peace feeling of the North fluctuates with the vicissitudes of the war, increasing with their reverses and diminishing with ours."[26] And as the tide turned against the South, so, too, it seemed to them, did northern optimism and determination rise. The Confederate commissioners noted unhappily that the Democrats' candidate for president, General George McClellan, had now taken a position on reunion difficult to distinguish from that of Lincoln. The negotiations with Greeley had gone nowhere, and efficient Union police and counterintelligence had frustrated the Confederates' efforts to spark uprisings and political dissension in the Northwest.

In part as a result, the Confederate commissioners turned to more active measures, drawing on their share of the five-million-dollar secret service fund voted by the Confederate Congress in February 1864. They concocted plots—several of them actually attempted—to liberate thousands of Confederate prisoners by means of raids across the Great Lakes,

beginning with the seizure of the gunboat *Michigan*, the only federal warship in service there. They contrived plans to set on fire entire northern
cities, including New York, by simultaneously igniting incendiaries in
hotels that would overwhelm the ability of the citizens to extinguish
them. His aim, Thompson subsequently wrote, was "to burn whenever it
is practicable, and thus make the men of property feel their insecurity and
tire them out with the war."[27] They even connived at a scheme to spread
yellow fever in the North by distributing the clothes of patients who had
had the dreaded disease, not realizing that mosquitoes, rather than con-
taminated outerwear, spread it.

In the summer of 1863 General John Morgan, one of the most daring
Confederate cavalry leaders, had raided deep into the Union, penetrating
Indiana and Ohio almost to the Pennsylvania border near Pittsburgh. In
the van rode Bennett Young, one of his best and bravest scouts. Morgan
and his men were eventually cornered and captured, but Young subsequently escaped from his prison camp near Chicago and wended his way
to Canada, where he became a student at the University of Toronto.
Seeking to work his way home via Halifax and Bermuda (the home port
for many blockade runners), he met with the newly arrived Confederate
commissioners, who commended him to Secretary of State Benjamin.
Slipping into Richmond, Young had an audience with the secretary of
war, James A. Seddon, in which he seems to have convinced the Confederate official to use him to conduct raids across the border. Taking yet
another blockade runner back to Bermuda, and thence to Canada, Lieutenant Young now began his work in earnest in the Confederate secret
service.

Following his participation in an abortive scheme to release eight
thousand Confederate prisoners during the Democratic convention in
Chicago at the very end of August 1864, Young returned to his discontented superiors. A second mission took him across the border again, to
Buffalo, where he passed money to another Confederate operative to
fund a raid on the prisoner of war camp at Johnson's Island, Ohio. When
Young returned to Canada he found waiting for him a cipher message
from Secretary of War Seddon, now seething over Philip Sheridan's
destructive Shenandoah Valley campaign. Sheridan had been ordered to
make it impossible for the Confederate army to use the Shenandoah yet
again (as it had during the summer of 1864) for a raid on Washington. "If

the war is to last another year, we want the Shenandoah Valley to remain a barren waste," Grant had instructed Sheridan, who went to work making it so, lighting the valley with burning barns and homesteads.[28]

For revenge, therefore, as well as for motives of higher strategy, Seddon ordered Young to conduct raids into New England. "The people of New England and Vermont especially, some of whose officers and troops have been foremost in these excesses and whose people have approved their course, should have brought to them some of the horrors of warfare."[29] Seddon said nothing about provoking war between the Union and Great Britain, but such an outrageous violation of Canadian neutrality clearly troubled him not a whit. And Young accepted the mission with relish.

Yet again he slipped over the border, reconnoitering potential targets, and on returning, laid his plans. He would attack St. Albans, Vermont, a town of five thousand not two miles east of Lake Champlain, and some sixteen miles south of the border. It lay near an important railroad depot and contained the residence of the governor of Vermont, Gregory Smith, which Young intended to destroy in retribution for the deeds of the First Vermont Cavalry in the Shenandoah. On October 6, 1864, Clay approved the plan to burn the town and rob the banks there, and gave him a check for fourteen hundred dollars for expenses. He also assured Young that once he was back over the border into Canada, the Confederate commissioner could secure his release should the local authorities take it upon themselves to incarcerate him.

Young plotted the attack with the care one would expect of an experienced special operations soldier. He secured special munitions—bottles of so-called Greek Fire, an inflammable petroleum-based incendiary mixture. He arrived in St. Albans with two of his men on October 10, more than a week before the attack, and in succeeding days infiltrated seventeen more men in by twos and threes, having them stay at separate hotels; they spent several days continuing to inspect the town, including the stables whose horses they intended to seize. Their cover stories—young men on a fall hunting trip, invalids in search of rest, horse traders—excited little attention in a bustling town caught up in the lively northern trade and enjoying the spectacular foliage of a New England fall despite the gloom of recurrent rain.

On October 19, Young and his men struck.[30] At three o'clock in the afternoon, dressed in a carefully packed Confederate uniform, he announced to the stunned citizens that the town was being occupied by Confederate forces. The score of Confederates divided, as planned, into prearranged parties—to rob the three banks, steal horses, control civilians held on the town green, and lob the bottles of Greek Fire. They did indeed rob the banks, stealing over two hundred thousand dollars for use of the Confederate secret service. But the raid fell short of its destructive ambitions. Angry townspeople, led by a nineteen-year-old cavalry captain on furlough, William Conger, began reaching for their firearms, and workers from the local railroad yard joined them. In a flurry of shots one local citizen fell mortally wounded, while two others received slight wounds. The Greek Fire went up in sheets of flame but failed to ignite the buildings still wet from autumnal rains. And as the raiders fled the town—a trail of fluttering dollar bills scattering behind them—a posse led by Conger pursued them, to the border and over the border. The young Vermont cavalry captain returned after the first day, but receiving word that hot pursuit had been authorized, crossed back into Canada the next day, and with his posse, captured Young. The Confederate managed to break away from the wagon carrying him back to St. Albans and was recaptured by the angry Vermonters, who proceeded to beat him with their rifle butts. Luckily for the Confederate, a British officer at this point intercepted the party and, promising to place the Confederate under arrest, persuaded the Americans to go back over the line.

In all, Canadian authorities apprehended thirteen raiders including Young, and held them pending a hearing by Judge Charles-Joseph Coursol, an ambitious lawyer, politician, and reformer. First at the British military post in St. Johns, and later in the Montreal jail, the Confederates were treated more as celebrities—wined and dined by their hosts, posing for photographs—than as criminals. It seemed to these young men to have been at least a glorious escapade, if not an entirely successful enterprise. More than a few British officers and Canadian sympathizers, including their nominal jailers, admired their spunk.

From the headquarters of Union forces in New York, and from Washington, the view was very different. The St. Albans raid was but the most egregious of a set of cross-border operations, including an abortive raid on Calais, Maine, and the efforts to liberate Confederate prisoners in Illinois and Ohio. Major General John Wool had only the year before finally retired from the army, where his last command had been of the Eastern Department, which included Vermont and New York. His successor, another, if somewhat younger War of 1812 veteran, Major General John Dix, rushed reinforcements to the border and ordered the provost marshal in Burlington to "put a discreet officer in command, and in case they are found on our side of the line pursue them into Canada if necessary and destroy them."[31] The arrest of the raiders temporarily mollified Dix, but his fears for the frontier did not abate. In early November, he ordered a detachment of the First Vermont Cavalry—the unit whose depredations in the Shenandoah had infuriated Seddon—stationed in St. Albans while on furlough through the election.

All this was bad enough, when a capricious decision made on murky grounds plunged the United States and Great Britain into crisis. On December 13, 1864, Judge Coursol decided to discharge the St. Albans raiders on the dubious (and to Americans, outrageous) grounds that his court did not have jurisdiction over them, they being soldiers engaged in acts of war rather than common criminals. John A. MacDonald, the anti-American attorney general of Upper Canada and leading politician in the nascent movement to Canadian union, nonetheless described Coursol as "this wretched prig of a police magistrate," and ordered sheriffs to rearrest the raiders. But the damage was done. Dix, outraged, and receiving reports of further raids being prepared in Canada, issued General Orders number 97 on December 14. Units along the frontier would attempt to intercept raiders, of course, but Dix also ordered them "to pursue them wherever they may take refuge." Unlike the Vermont posse, moreover, Union troops should not hand their captives over to Canadian authorities or British soldiers—a policy likely to lead to confrontation, and probably an armed clash, across the border.[32] Dix had given a warrant for cross-border operations to destroy terrorist sanctuaries on the other side of a supposedly neutral frontier, in a country suspected of sheltering anti-American miscreants—a concept familiar to Americans a century and a half later, albeit in rather different contexts.

The crisis following the St. Albans raid had even greater potential to bring the United States and Great Britain to blows than the *Trent* affair—and not least because the Americans were in a good position, following Lincoln's reelection and the imminent collapse of the Confederacy, to avenge the attack from the north.[33] Fortunately for both sides, cooler heads prevailed. The embarrassed Canadians issued orders for the rearrest of the raiders, and President Lincoln directed Secretary of War Edwin Stanton to revoke Dix's order. Stanton did so, saying:

> The act of invading neutral territory by military commanders is, in the opinion of the President, too grave and serious to be left to the discretion or will of subordinate commanders, where the facility of communication with superior authority is so speedy, as it always may be with the chief authority in your department, and even with the President at Washington. . . . Subordinate military authorities, when left to their own will or discretion, are too prone to act upon views of military necessity where none really exists, to be intrusted with the power of crossing neutral territory without specific authority.[34]

But serious damage had been done. For the first time in the history of the border, the secretary of state temporarily imposed the use of passports on what had long been an open frontier—a move not repeated until after the attacks on the United States on September 11, 2001. And the United States further informed the British government that it intended to abrogate the Rush-Bagot Agreement and build up its gunboat fleet on the Great Lakes in order to intercept Confederate raiders there.

The immediate crisis passed, however, in part because American politicians restrained their military commanders, while Canadian and British politicians prodded their reluctant sheriffs and courts to make at least a pretense of controlling Confederate operations. But the St. Albans raid, the northernmost fight of the Civil War, profoundly unsettled an already difficult three-sided relationship. The United States government had an excellent idea of what transpired across the border, because Secretary of State Seward had appointed consuls the length and breadth of Canada to keep an eye on Confederate activities. He supplemented these official representatives of the United States with private detectives who slipped back and forth across the border—and they in turn were joined not only by their fellows appointed by border governors and military commanders, but by detectives working for the Canadians and the British. For their parts, the British governor general, Sir Charles Stanley Monck, and the British commander in Canada, Sir William Fenwick Williams (a native Canadian), saw eye to eye on the need to mollify the North and suppress

Confederate activities. As a result, the Confederate commissioners increasingly felt like men draped in sodden wool blankets, acutely uncomfortable and unable to move with anything like freedom. The government in Richmond agreed, and recalled them in late 1864, replacing them with a brigadier general charged with wrapping up the mission.[35]

But the St. Albans raid proved itself something more than a mere curiosity, an adventure tale fondly to be recollected by aging southern gentlemen as the nineteenth century ended and the twentieth century began. That there might be another act, even after the Civil War ended, was clear to at least one experienced statesman, Secretary of State William Seward. Five days after the St. Albans raid, he wrote to Charles Francis Adams in London—surely with the aim of having the American minister to the British government convey his thoughts in a tone of silky menace to his hosts—that

> political agitation is as frequent in the British American provinces as it is here. It is not easy to foresee how soon revolutionary movements may appear there. Every provocation now given to Americans will likely be claimed as a precedent in that case for intrusion from this side of the border.[36]

And indeed, other raiders waited to cross the troubled border.

—◆—

England will live to regret her inimical attitude toward us

Among the hundreds of thousands of men who fought for the Union were tens of thousands of Irishmen, some immigrants, others exiles from their native land. Thomas Meagher, for example, had been a leading member of Young Ireland, which had launched yet another doomed revolt against English rule in 1848. His death sentence commuted to exile to Tasmania, he subsequently fled to the United States, where during the Civil War he raised and led the famed Irish brigade of the Union army, rising to the rank of brigadier general. He was not alone in his loathing of the English, nor in fleeing to an America that, if not always kind to Irish immigrants, gave them rights and opportunities unthinkable in their homeland.

Many of these veterans, officers and enlisted men alike, at loose ends after the war, joined the Fenian movement, an offshoot of the Irish Republican Brotherhood, which aimed at achieving Irish independence through the use of violence. One strand of the Fenian movement operated in the United States, plotting the overthrow of British rule in Canada as a precursor to the liberation of Ireland itself. Its members would be the last seriously to contemplate the Great Warpath as an avenue for invasion.

The Fenians were, as was so often the case in the history of Irish independence movements, internally divided and often penetrated by British (and, increasingly, Canadian) secret agents. In 1865 the British broke up the Irish Republican Brotherhood in Ireland, but that left the American Fenians untouched. In April 1866, scarcely a year after the end of the Civil War, they mounted their first invasion of Canada following a grandiose plan conceived by "Fighting Tom" Sweeny, a major general in the United States Army who had lost his right arm in the Mexican War, and who had fought throughout the Civil War, commanding a division under Sherman during the Georgia campaign.

Sweeny's grandiose plan envisaged no fewer than three invasion routes into Canada—one from Chicago across Lakes Michigan and Huron, composed of four infantry regiments; one from Cleveland and Buffalo, across Lake Erie to Toronto, with five infantry regiments; and, up the Great Warpath, a thrust of no fewer than seventeen infantry and five cavalry regiments.[37] In a welter of confusion, disorganization, and disagreement, the Fenian scheme shriveled into one crossing of the frontier near Buffalo, by about six hundred men, although several hundred more had started out. In a sharp engagement at Ridgeway, Canada, on June 2, 1866, the Fenians defeated the local militia, but then retired at word of advancing Canadian and British reinforcements. A second major crossing of the border in 1870 met even less success, and the Fenian raids petered out, although not without considerable friction along the New York and Vermont borders.

The Fenians failed for a number of reasons, quite apart from their own limitations as insurrectionists. The sheer implausibility of their project was probably the most important element: Canadians had no particular reason to establish New Hibernia (the name of the independent Irish state some of the Fenians dreamed of) on their side of the Atlantic, or to welcome armed Americans swarming over their borders. Efficient intelligence work by Canadian agents operating in the United States denied these Irish romantics any hope of surprise, and Canadian militia and British regulars could cope handily with such military challenges as they posed. And the fact was that the United States government, although not entirely free from *schadenfreude* at British protests about the presence of malevolent bands of armed men in a neighboring state, did not wish to destabilize Canada or cause a war. Ulysses S. Grant deprecated British violation, as he saw it, of the duty of neutrality during the Civil War, particularly with regard to border crossers from Canada. "But their wrong doing is no justification for our following their example," and he directed his subordinates to "prevent all armed and equipped military organizations from going from the United States into Canada."[38] He repeated this instruction forcibly during the Fenian crisis.

"Between two peoples and two states there can be such tensions, such a mass of inflammable material, that the slightest quarrel can produce a wholly disproportionate effect—a real explosion."[39] Thus Carl von Clausewitz, philosopher of war. Countries do not always, indeed, do not often go to war on the basis of cool calculation. More often than not, someone tosses a match into a pile of tinder that has accumulated over years, if not decades, and it ignites. Lieutenant Young, General Dix, Fenian commanders, and Justice Coursol all played with fire. Fortunately, level-headed leaders on all three sides—American, British, and Canadian—were quick with the water buckets when that happened.

The sources of antipathy between the United States and the British empire, including Canada, were profound, rooted in history, ideology, and interest. Particularly during the Civil War, it was in the British interest, abstractly considered, to see the Great Republic broken up, as Bagehot had sadly believed. Americans could be excused the belief after the Civil War that Britain had acted, however halfheartedly, in accordance with such a policy, and that they now had in their hands the ability to drive the old country from North America for good. Lincoln himself had bitterly resented British behavior. "England will live to regret her inimical attitude toward us," he told Grant when he visited the general on the front lines at Petersburg at the end of March 1865. He had swallowed the humiliation over the *Trent,* "believing that England's triumph in the matter would be short-lived," he told his commander, "and that after ending our war successfully we would be so powerful that we could call her to account for all the embarrassments she had inflicted upon us." [40]

Both sides had reasons through the middle of the nineteenth century and beyond to feel aggrieved, suspicious, and hostile. War might have happened, and had it done so, it would almost certainly have erupted along the Great Warpath, the most direct path from the United States to the heart of Canada. And if the Confederates wished to provoke such a war—as some clearly did—there was no better way to do it than to conduct operations like the St. Albans raid.

Those days, however, were coming to an end, even as the tension between the United States and Great Britain worsened. While Lieutenant Colonel Jervois made the case for even more extensive fortification of the core of Canada, Montreal and Quebec, as the British government shipped rifles for the Canadian militia and thousands of soldiers to Canadian garrisons, forces were at work that ultimately removed the possibility of yet more bloody battles along the Great Warpath.

In March 1862, the Canadian parliament had considered a bill to raise an active force of fifty thousand from the militia, with a reserve equally large. The expense would be considerable, but still only a tenth of the provincial revenue. The proposal was whittled down to a fourteen-day-call-up of only thirty thousand men, but even so, on May 20, 1862, the Canadian assembly rejected it. [41] There were many reasons for this outcome, including the collapse of John A. MacDonald into one of his periodic fits of inebriation, and the vote had as much to do with Canadian politics as with high policy, but in truth, it revealed a fundamental divide that had opened up between Canada and Great Britain.

For the British, the Canadian vote bespoke a fecklessness on the part of Canadian politicians, who clamored for British protection but would neither share the burden nor take even minimally effective measures to defend themselves. From the Canadian point of view, the danger of American invasion during or immediately after the Civil War resulted not from American antipathy to Canada per se but from the fraught relations between the United States and Great Britain. Britain's policy toward America had caused the problem; it was Britain's responsibility to cope with its consequences. And in any case, the Canadians doubted rather more than the British the intention of their American neighbors to come storming over the border to annex the provinces by force.

The Civil War and, even more so, the Fenian raids lent impetus to the emergence of a unified Canadian state. Particularly since the revolts of the late 1830s, the British had gradually extended the implementation of "responsible government"—home rule—in Canada. Canadian politicians, led by John A. MacDonald, now pressed for something more: the unification of all the provinces of Canada, including New Brunswick, Nova Scotia, and the Canadian West, into a single, self-governing confederation. In 1867 the British North America Act established the Dominion of Canada, with its own parliament and MacDonald as its first prime minister; in ensuing years other provinces joined the Dominion, starting with Manitoba in 1870 and British Columbia in 1871. Canadian leaders were welding a strong new country together.

Canadian unification appealed to these politicians for a number of reasons, including, possibly, the opportunity for them to play on a much larger stage than was allowed by provincial politics. But they also saw a unified Canada as a bulwark against individual provinces' drifting into American arms, along the lines of the peaceable annexation aspirations that Seward, among others, retained. The appeal of America, not outright invasion from it, was their main fear.

British politicians saw the force of this argument. They also now saw the opportunity to rid themselves of an encumbrance and potentially an embarrassment. If Jervois were right, and the only question in the event of war was whether a British garrison could clear out of Montreal and Quebec in time to avoid having to surrender to tens of thousands of hard-bitten blue-uniformed veterans led by the grim likes of Sherman, Sheridan, and Grant, why spend money on stationing troops where the only operational choice would lie between mere futility and downright humiliation?

Sir Edward Cardwell, British secretary of state for the colonies from 1864 to 1866, who became Prime Minister William Ewart Gladstone's secretary of state for war in 1868, cut to the heart of the matter. The time had come, he declared, to withdraw British forces from Canada altogether. The Canadian government objected. It wanted a small garrison, partly for economic reasons, partly as hostages against the admittedly unlikely eventuality of an American attack on Canada, which would, therefore, mean war with Great Britain. Cardwell, however, was adamant. He wanted thrift, and garrisons were expensive. Moreover, he aimed to create an altogether new system for the British army, which had become precariously dependent on soldiers enlisted for decades at a time, who served most of their tours overseas. Instead, he proposed an army based on shorter active duty enlistments followed by entry into a reserve that could be recalled to the colors. He also aimed to secure a reasonable alternation between service at home and service abroad that would make voluntary enlistment more palatable to young men who may have wished employment and adventure, but not semipermanent exile from the British Isles. And he wanted most of all to give Britain what it had long lacked, a powerful military force in the home islands with which to cope with new threats to her security.

Herein lay the most important changes that would occur in Anglo-American relations during the nineteenth century. The British government had watched with dismay the rise of Germany on the Continent, smashing, as it had, Denmark in 1864, Austria in 1866, and finally France in 1870. England, most of its troops scattered in colonial garrisons or holding down Ireland, had few cards to play on the Continent. At the same time the Crimean War, and the Indian Mutiny in the 1850s, had raised the prospect of other emergencies that would require the deployment of a British expeditionary force, while the naval revolution brought about by steam propulsion and ironclad vessels meant that the easy naval dominance of the post-Napoleonic period had ended. Gone were the strategically unproblematic early days of Victoria's reign; a harder and more difficult geopolitical era had dawned.

In this atmosphere, the British government moved to resolve the lingering animosity between itself and the United States, which was particularly acute over the depredations of Confederate raiders built in Britain, particularly the CSS *Alabama*. In the Treaty of Washington, signed in May 1871, the two parties agreed to arbitration of the dispute and also the expansion of trade. It marked the resolution of most of the outstanding issues between the two countries. In such a world it made even less sense to spend British money on far-flung garrisons in countries that could and should provide for their own defense. And thus it was that on November 11, 1871, the first battalion of the Sixtieth Rifles, the last of Canada's British garrison, marched out of the modernized citadel of

Quebec. More than a century before, the British army had created the Sixtieth—then the Royal American Regiment—to master the challenges of the Great Warpath. It was fitting that it should be the last to leave.

And fitting too that they should leave peacefully, in a nostalgic parade, as the bands played "Auld Lang Syne," for the meaning of this last stage in the Great Warpath's military history lay not in violence, but in a tradition of American statecraft. Contrary to those who believe that after 1815 the United States lived in comfortable isolation from confrontation with anyone but potential victims—the Indians and the Mexicans, most notably—the threat of a third Anglo-American war had been real. Avoiding it required the skill of two generations of American leaders. Soldier-diplomats like Winfield Scott and John Wool, politician-diplomats like William Seward (bellicose enough to appease domestic opinion and get his way, not bellicose enough to cause an unnecessary war), Daniel Webster, and presidents Abraham Lincoln and Ulysses S. Grant were all willing, under certain circumstances, to use force. But all of them understood as well how to restrain it, and how to come to accommodations that would preserve real interests as well as the peace.

May the gates of the temple of Janus . . .
not be opened again for a century!

Military organizations, like very large reptiles, often lumber forward long after their brains have told them to stop, or even turn around. So, construction on one of the three ultramodern forts at Lévis, opposite Quebec, continued until 1872; it was actually fitted with heavy artillery in 1878 during a British war scare with Russia against the exceedingly remote possibility that the Russian navy would somehow slip by the Royal Navy and, with an adventurous heart, sail its way up the St. Lawrence in order to pummel Canada into submission.[42]

American engineers, for their part, continued to mount artillery pieces at Fort Montgomery, which had been reinforced at the time of the Fenian raids. By 1867 it mounted a formidable armament of seventy-five pieces, roughly half and half seacoast artillery and shorter-range howitzers. In 1879, General of the Army William Tecumseh Sherman visited it and approved its massive fortification, "the true key-point of all that frontier," he declared.[43] And several years later, the secretary of war still clamored for its importance as a base from which to invade Canada, should the need arise. But the unforgiving freeze and thaw of upstate New York and the equally unforgiving thrift of congressional appropriators contributed alike to the gradual decay of the fort, which is today a picturesque but moldering ruin barely noticed by tourists en route to a Canadian vacation.

Military planners continued, as planners do, to draw up plans, and clerks continued to file them where professors could later leaf through them. American military intelligence collected information about Canada throughout the 1880s and 1890s, while British military intelligence officers brooded about Fort Montgomery and gloomily predicted that it would likely serve as "a base of operations against Montreal."[44] Briefly, during a diplomatic crisis over the Venezuelan border in 1895, it seemed just possible that Britain and the United States might come to blows. The Canadians—who had blithely ignored an eight-year-old British request for a self-defense plan—used the crisis as an opportunity to order some new rifles from the British government, but otherwise pooh-poohed London's fears.[45] Many Canadian politicians disliked the United States, many did not; few harbored a mortal fear of it.

Still, in some Canadian hearts, anxiety about invasion along the Great Warpath never quite vanished. As the years wore on, Canadian scholars, conquering whatever apprehensions they may have felt about monitoring by American counterintelligence agents, sifted through the American national archives. There they discovered—with a frisson of delight and alarm—draft plans and war college exercises that seemed to them proof that throughout the twentieth century Americans still harbored a desire to lunge up the Great Warpath one more time. During the 1980s, the reactivation of the Tenth Mountain Division and the expansion of Fort Drum, in Watertown, New York, only a few miles from the Canadian border, was all the proof that Professor Floyd Rudmin of Queen's University needed. *Bordering on Aggression: Evidence of US Military Preparations Against Canada* is, for connoisseurs of such literature, an intriguing contribution to the paranoid tradition in Canadian politics, suggesting as it does that with one stroke the elite light infantry of Tenth Mountain

Division could paralyze the Canadian government, cut its military communications, split Canada along Anglo- and Francophone lines, and divide its major population centers.[46] And, the author noted, "that's just for starters." But it says more about the real U.S.-Canadian relationship that Professor Rudmin was an American, a graduate of Bowdoin and veteran of the Peace Corps who had moved to Canada in 1978.

In truth, the Treaty of Washington and the evacuation of the British garrisons from Canada ended a phase of American military history that had lasted two centuries, during which one of the chief strategic preoccupations of what was first a colony, and then a republic, was the northern border. From the last quarter of the seventeenth century until the last quarter of the nineteenth century, Americans' conflict with Canada shaped much of their military culture, their way of war, their understanding of strategy. Thereafter, friction between the countries, as between any neighbors, persisted; serious potential for war did not.

Military history, however, did not quite end along the Great Warpath with what some historians have called the Great Rapprochement between the United States and Great Britain, a closening of relations that embraced Canada as well. In May 1913, Leonard Wood, a doctor turned military leader, a soldier who also harbored political ambitions, wrote to American university and college presidents telling them of the interest of the secretary of war to set up "experimental military camps of instruction" for students during the upcoming summer vacation.[47] The purpose was preparedness, a purpose reinforced when war broke out in Europe a year later. In 1914 four camps were convened, including one with 350 students in Burlington.

After the sinking in May 1915 of the *Lusitania* with a heavy loss of American life raised the possibility of Americans' entering the war, prominent citizens in New York began agitating for preparedness, directed chiefly against Germany. A committee, meeting at the Harvard Club of New York, appointed former president Theodore Roosevelt and several distinguished citizens to prepare a plan for establishing similar summer camps for businessmen. Wood supported it, and in 1915 the new training camps opened. The largest of these camps was held at Plattsburgh, where over six hundred students and then twelve hundred businessmen underwent a month of military training.[48] Other, smaller camps spread around the country, to San Francisco, Chicago, the Northwest, but the Plattsburgh Movement took its name from the encampment there. In 1916 ten thousand volunteers attended ten camps around the country.[49]

Participants in the Plattsburgh Movement came from the Republican elite of New York society and formed a lobby for preparedness and, indeed, for intervention in the world war. Although the Military Training Camp Association that resulted from the movement soon ran afoul of the National Guard—descended from the state militias, and jealous of its own status as the custodian of the citizen-soldier tradition—it helped give birth to the National Defense Act of 1916, which provided for the creation of a Reserve Officers Training Corps (ROTC) in American universities. And it paved the way for the mass mobilization of two world wars. Some of the threads of the Great Warpath military experience—in particular the cult of the citizen-soldier—came together here.

After those world wars, the Great Warpath experienced one last pulse of military activity, a military effort directed, once again, to the north—not toward Canada, this time, but as it were, over its head. In 1955 the United States Air Force's Strategic Air Command activated Plattsburgh Air Force Base as a home for long-range bombers to fly over the North Pole to attack the Soviet Union.[50] And after two years of construction in 1961–62, the 556th Strategic Missile Squadron, based at Plattsburgh, disposed of no fewer than twelve launch sites for Atlas F nuclear-tipped missiles pointed at the Soviet Union—the only such installation east of the Mississippi. Two of those sites—at Champlain, New York, and Swanton, Vermont, lay just along the Canadian border, near villages that had been the site of repeated skirmishing during the Revolution and War of 1812.[51] By the end of the twentieth century, though, those missiles and bombers were long gone. And although after the terrorist attacks of September 11, 2001, the successors of William Seward had reimposed passport restrictions on the open U.S.-Canadian frontier, anyone discussing hostilities of any kind along the Great Warpath could elicit only puzzlement, derision, or antiquarian interest.

When the last serious war along this corridor ended in 1815, few believed that it was indeed such. Fewer still could imagine a world in which the very sources of hostility would so melt away as to make the idea of a resumption of conflict there ludicrous. Yet at least one canny statesman had harbored such an aspiration.

On January 5, 1815, John Quincy Adams had attended his final dinner with the American and British peace commissioners. He and his British counterpart, Sir Henry Goulburn, had finally come to a meeting of minds: Both loathed the local Belgian band that kept interrupting the already tedious state dinner by alternately playing "Hail Columbia" and "God Save the King." Ready at last to bring the dinner to an end, Adams stood to propose the final toast. As he did, he mused on the Roman practice of opening the gates of the god of boundaries when that great republic went to war, and closing them in times of peace. And so, despite his feelings about the band, he proposed a toast to "Ghent, the city of peace; may the gates of the temple of Janus, here closed, not be opened again for a century!" [52]

He turned out to be uncannily correct in his forecast. A century after the Treaty of Ghent the doors of Janus did indeed swing open again, but not where they had just closed in Adams's time, along the Great Warpath, but rather in the country, and not far from the town, where the grumpy commissioners had signed a peace treaty in which they had only slender confidence. And in the conflagration that followed, in a second world war after that, in a Cold War and smoldering struggles against murderous fanatics and megalomaniacal dictators, those nations that had fought one another along the Great Warpath—Frenchmen, Englishmen, and Scots, the native inhabitants of the New World, and above all Americans and Canadians, new peoples who had founded two vast liberal democracies— found themselves not enemies but the closest of allies. It was an outcome that, one suspects, would have elicited at least a grim smile from that most sober of peacemakers.

Legacies

By the early nineteenth century the battles and skirmishes of the Great
Warpath were already becoming the stuff of myth and legend. James Fen-
imore Cooper famously depicted the siege of Fort William Henry in 1757
in *The Last of the Mohicans*, a book that has remained continuously in
print since its publication in 1826. At the end of the nineteenth century,
Francis Parkman captured the imagination of his own and succeeding
generations with a series of works on the struggle between France and
England for control of North America. If today's historians find fault
with some of his scholarship, none can quarrel with his powers of description of people and landscape. And as the storm clouds gathered over Asia
and Europe in the 1930s, Kenneth Roberts, one of the most popular historical novelists of his time, produced massive tales of Rogers' rangers, in
Northwest Passage, and of the 1776 and 1777 campaigns, including the battle of Valcour Island, the fall of Fort Ticonderoga to John Burgoyne, and
the battle of Saratoga. *Rabble in Arms* featured not only Benedict Arnold
as hero, but extraordinarily vivid—and utterly unromantic—accounts of
campaigning along the Warpath. "We stood there silently beneath the
heavy gray skies of Canada," one of his characters recalls of the American
army just after the disaster of the Cedars and shortly before the retreat
from Montreal:

> behind us, squatted over their miserable fires, the dejected soldiers who
> waited for the scant supplies so parsimoniously provided for a hungry
> and frightened army. If this was war, I thought to myself—this muck of
> hunger, distrust, disease, raggedness, cowardice—it was different from
> all my imaginings: so different that a little was already more than enough
> for me.[1]

Roberts, a dyspeptic Down East conservative, had a view of American
politics that he attributed to many of the characters in the books that won
him the Pulitzer Prize. He believed politics were dominated by dema-

gogues, fools, incompetents, and schemers. Roberts was no isolationist, but neither did he desire to see his country embroiled in foreign wars; he was an American patriot, but no optimist about its place in the world.

He was wrong in that. Just as his books found their widest audience, the United States entered the greatest conflict in human history. World War II, with its fleets of aircraft carriers and submarines, its massive amphibious landings, its million-man mechanized armies, and its pulverizing of cities from the air may seems very distant from the struggles of the Great Warpath, with armies reckoned, at most, in the thousands or even merely the hundreds, its battles fought with tomahawks and flintlock muskets, its supplies laboriously hauled by bateau or ox cart. But in fact, the way of war that emerged along the Warpath shaped the manner in which America fought the conflict that brought her to global preeminence.

Anglo-American statesmen of the eighteenth century would have soberly approved of President Roosevelt's insistence on the unconditional surrender of America's enemies, for they, too, had hardened on the destruction of an enemy polity. When Germany's Field Marshal Erwin Rommel wrote admiringly of the American speed of adaptation to armored warfare, he explained it by "their extraordinary sense for the practical and material and by their complete lack of regard for tradition and worthless theories," qualities already apparent in the eighteenth century.[2] The unofficial motto of the United States Army—"whatever it takes"—reflects the spirit of those who fought along the Great Warpath.

Rommel discerned, too, the qualities of technical enterprise and ingenuity that were evident in the construction of the fleets that fought Valcour Island in 1776 and Plattsburgh in 1814. The island campaigns of the Pacific and the landings at Normandy depended, first and foremost, on a mastery of intricate systems of supply, and this reflected a tradition originating in the problem of sustaining thousands of soldiers in the woods. As George Washington and many contemporaries understood, Philip Schuyler might not have been a great battlefield commander, but his ability to sustain an elaborate chain of supply made possible the eventual victory at Saratoga in 1777.[3] If in World War II the United States Army managed to produce effective infantry and armored divisions composed of draftees in an astonishingly brief period, they could thank, in part, the precedent of Robert Rogers reducing the complicated art of patrolling to a manual that an intelligent and willing citizen-soldier could master. And surely, if any countries have ever been "conquered into liberty," as the Continental Congress had written to the doubtful *habitants* of Canada in 1775, they were Germany, Italy, and Japan, occupied and transformed by armies that combined, in paradoxical degree, thoroughness in defeating an enemy and an unlimited, even naïve, commitment to liberating him.

Indeed, the very fact of America's entry into World War II should have surprised no student of the Great Warpath, for that conflict was, despite its name, very far from being the second global conflict. Every preceding global war—the Nine Years' War, the Wars of the Spanish and then of the Austrian Succession, the Seven Years' War, the war of American independence, and the wars of the French Revolution and Empire—had reverberated along the Great Warpath. What is now the United States has never really been isolated from global geopolitics, and never can be.

Since 1945, however, the United States has become a different kind of international player. Despite economic setbacks, despite the rise of other powers, and despite the doubts of many of its elite—some of whom echo Kenneth Roberts more than might make either altogether comfortable—it has become accustomed not merely to global engagement, but to global power. Its armed forces span the globe and overmatch potential rivals in a way that even the Royal Navy in its heyday could not, and that the British army never did. America's unparalleled wealth and dynamism, though diminished, remains. Its culture (including the use of its language) has spread around the world, appealing to some, infuriating others. And although Americans shrink, properly, from the use of the word "empire," and may recoil even more from its implications, the United States looks very much like one to others.

Even as a military power the United States has changed since World War II, and in ways that seem to carry it further from the experience of the Great Warpath. Yes, there are units that carry on the lineage of Rogers' rangers, there are helicopters named after the Iroquois, and ships named after Fort Ticonderoga. But today's American armed forces are huge standing organizations. There are National Guard units (including the "Green Mountain Boys," the Vermont Air National Guard) that originated in the colonial militias, but today's armed forces are dominated by regulars, led overwhelmingly by professionals, and characterized by an

ethos that is very different from that of the part-timers of the Great Warpath. Our wars are now remote, waged in the deserts and cities of Iraq,
the mountains and valleys of Afghanistan; our strategic challenges
unthinkable in eighteenth-century terms—maintaining a balance of
power in Asia, sustaining coalitions of weaker allies, hunting down ter-
rorists in ungoverned lands, preventing or preempting the use of weapons
that can annihilate a city at a single stroke.

Yet much of the Great Warpath legacy endures. After the attacks of
September 11, 2001, some European observers were surprised by the
American reaction abroad, and sought to explain it, in the words of Javier
Solana, then the European Union's high representative for foreign policy,
as follows:

> Europe has been the territory of war, and we have worked to prevent
> war through building relations with other countries. The US has never
> been the territory of war—that's why September 11 was so important: it
> was the first time their territory had been attacked.[4]

Breathtaking ignorance, this—and thus all the more likely to contribute
to a profound misunderstanding of how the United States uses armed
force. From before independence, and along the Great Warpath above all,
the United States has been the territory of war.

Commentators wishing to dismiss the behavior of American policy-
makers as juvenile or excessively bellicose often use the term "cowboys and
Indians." In so doing they make light of the roots of the American way of
war in the frontier conflicts that dominated the first two centuries of
European settlement on these shores.[5] This is a mistake. The American
way of war remains a hybrid of European modes and something far more
improvisational, far less rule-bound. When Navy SEALs killed Osama
bin Laden in Pakistan in 2011, they took part in a tradition of "cross-
border operations" stretching back centuries. Their fellow citizens who,
remembering the horrors of the 9/11 attacks, paid tribute to their courage
and skill were far from being the first generation of Americans whose
lives had been touched by terror.

The characters of the Great Warpath were a remarkably colorful lot.
There remain today a few wily military bureaucrats like Horatio Gates,
but orator-statesmen like Daniel Webster and autodidact philosopher-

adventurers like Ethan Allen are few. Today's villains seem to lack the tragic fascination of Benedict Arnold or the sinister appeal of La Corne St. Luc. And some groups have, alas, faded altogether from view. Americans know less than we ought about the history of Canada, the way in which a small but extraordinarily vigorous French population once contended for primacy in North America, how close we came to a third Anglo-American war in which Canada would have been the battleground, or how incursions from south of the border in the late 1860s shaped our northern neighbor's unification. The tragedy of Native Americans long obscured our understanding of their part in American history. Depicted as either the menacing Other or the helpless victim of European expansion, they have too often been reduced to two-dimensional characters. The Indian story is far more complex than either rendering, has its own tale of independent action, and exhibits more than enough statecraft, courage, and cruelty to merit a tale that is neither lachrymose nor squeamish. Luckily, contemporary ethnohistorians have begun to reconstruct Indian history in a more balanced way, describing with considerable skill cultures and polities that produced few written records of their own. American loyalists, too—losers in a different way in the struggles that created the United States—are gradually making their way back into the American tale.[6]

One can write history from the top down, looking at generals and statesmen, and from the bottom up, looking at soldiers, farmers, and families. At least one historian has suggested the wisdom of writing history from the middle—from the point of view of neither the famous nor the common man and woman, but the leaders and managers who get things done.[7] It is a notion applicable to the Great Warpath as well. The events of the Great Warpath were shaped, to be sure, by the likes of Count Frontenac and Major General John Burgoyne, as well as by the men who experienced in the most direct way the hardships of expeditions across frozen lakes, the fierce shock of inland naval battles at close quarters, the horrors of woodland ambush. But the qualities of character that are the deepest and most enduring legacy of the Great Warpath may be more to be found in characters like stoical and unassuming Seth Warner, leader of the Vermont militia who fought the rear guard battle at Hubbardton, or Jeduthan Baldwin, the self-taught engineer who learned his trade at Fort William Henry in the 1750s, endured smallpox and retreat in the war that followed, but carried on to the final victory at Saratoga in 1777, and even Justus Sherwood, the loyalist who attempted to conduct the dark business of espionage and covert action as decently as one could.

The power and influence of the United States has many sources, most notably the size and vigor of its economy and the appeal of its organizing ideas. But in all of its wars, including those to the present, it has been most effective because of those leaders in the middle, who rose to challenges that they did not expect; who learned trades, including the trade of war, that they had not chosen; and who exhibited perseverance and resilience that they may not have known they had in them. They, and the qualities they represent, are the most valuable and enduring legacy of two centuries of skirmish, battles, and massacres along the Great Warpath.

Abbreviations Used in Notes

AA	Peter Force, *American Archives*, Fourth Series
ANBO	*American National Biography Online*
ASP	*American State Papers*
BFTM	*Bulletin of the Fort Ticonderoga Museum*
CO	Colonial Office records, National Archives, UK
DAR	*Documents on the American Revolution*
DCB	*Dictionary of Canadian Biography*
DHNY	*Documentary History of the State of New York*
DRCHSNY	*Documents Relative to the Colonial History of the State of New York*
Franklin Papers	*Papers of Benjamin Franklin*
GW Papers	*George Washington Papers*
JCC	*Journals of the Continental Congress*
JQA Diary	*Memoirs of John Quincy Adams . . . Diary from 1795 to 1848*
JQA Writings	*Writings of John Quincy Adams*
NDAR	*Naval Documents of the American Revolution*
NW 1812	*The Naval War of 1812: A Documentary History*
OR	*Official Records of the War of the Rebellion*
SBD	*Select British Documents on the War of 1812*
VHS Collections	*Collections of the Vermont Historical Society*
WMQ	*William and Mary Quarterly*, 3rd series
WO	War Office records, Natural Archives, UK

Notes

AUTHOR'S NOTE

1. Francis Parkman, *Montcalm and Wolfe*, in *France and England in North America*, Vol. II (New York: Library of America, 1983), pp. 1138–39.

PROLOGUE—THE GREAT WARPATH

1. Nathaniel Hawthorne, "Old Ticonderoga: A Picture of the Past," in *Tales and Sketches* (New York: Library of America, 1982), p. 387.

2. Nathaniel Hawthorne originally published "Old Ticonderoga" in *American Monthly Magazine*, Vol. I (February 1836): 138–42. It has often been anthologized, and was reprinted in *BFTM* IV, 1 (January 1936): 12–17. Nicholas Westbrook, former director of Fort Ticonderoga, notes that the date of Hawthorne's visit— probably 1832—coincided with a visit by Lee, hence the inference about the author's guide.

3. Drawn from George J. Lankevich, *American Metropolis: A History of New York City* (New York and London: New York University Press, 1998), pp. 1–38.

4. http://www.nysm.nysed.gov/albany/population.html.

5. This, and much of what follows, draws from Elisabeth Tooker, "The League of the Iroquois: Its History, Politics, and Ritual," in Bruce G. Trigger, ed., *Handbook of North American Indians*, Vol. XV, *Northeast* (Washington, D.C.: Smithsonian Institution Press, 1978), pp. 418–41.

6. William Haviland to Jeffery Amherst, January 5, 1760. WO 34/51.

7. Drawn from the account in Samuel de Champlain entry in the *DCB*, and Ian K. Steele, *Warpaths: Invasions of North America* (New York: Oxford University Press, 1994), pp. 59–79. The most recent account is David Hackett Fischer, *Champlain's Dream* (New York: Simon & Schuster, 2008).

8. As noted by Steele, *Warpaths*, p. 64.

9. Fischer, *Champlain's Dream*, p. 271.

10. Fischer's argument, drawing on the extensive work of recent ethnohistorians, in *Champlain's Dream*, pp. 254–80 and passim.

11. For a short account and description of existing sites see Eric B. Schultz and Michael J. Tougias, *King Philip's War* (Woodstock, Vt.: The Countryman Press, 1999). On the war itself, see Douglas Edward Leach, *Flintlock and Tomahawk: New England in King Philip's War* (New York: W. W. Norton, 1958).

12. Data from Nuala Zahedieh, "London and the Colonial Consumer in the Late Seventeenth Century," *The Economic History Review* 47:2 (May 1994): 239–61.

CHAPTER ONE—THE SCHENECTADY RAID, 1690

1. Letter of February 15, 1690, quoted in W. N. P. Dailey, ed., *The Burning of Schenectady: Documentary Records and Historical Notes on the Burning and Massacre, February 8–9, 1690* (Schenectady: 1940).

2. Susan J. Staffa, *Schenectady Genesis: How a Dutch Colonial Village Became an American City, ca. 1661–1880.* Vol. I, *The Colonial Crucible, ca. 1661–1774* (Fleischmanns, N. Y.: Purple Mountain Press, 2004), p. 86.

3. From Cotton Mather, *Decennum Luctuosum,* 1699, in Charles H. Lincoln, ed. *Narratives of the Indian Wars, 1675–1699* (New York: Charles Scribner's Sons, 1913), p. 206.

4. Richard White, *The Middle Ground: Indians, Empires, and Republics in the Great Lakes Region, 1650–1815* (Cambridge: Cambridge University Press, 1991), pp. 4–5.

5. The debate about what motivated the Iroquois, and how strategic they were in their calculations, is a lively one. See, inter alia, Daniel K. Richter, *The Ordeal of the Longhouse: The Peoples of the Iroquois in the Era of European Colonization* (Chapel Hill: University of North Carolina Press, 1992); also Elisabeth Tooker, "The League of the Iroquois: Its History, Politics, and Ritual," in Bruce G. Trigger, ed., *Handbook of North American Indians,* Vol. XV, *Northeast* (Washington, D.C.: Smithsonian Institution, 1978), pp. 418–41; José António Brandão, *"Your Fyre Shall Burn No More": Iroquois Policy Toward New France and Its Native Allies to 1701* (Lincoln: University of Nebraska Press, 1997). See also W. J. Eccles's numerous essays, including "The Fur Trade Frontier, 1663–1700," in *The Canadian Frontier, 1534–1760,* rev. ed. (Albuquerque: University of New Mexico Press, 1983), pp. 103–31, and Chapter 4, "War and Trade, 1683–1713," of *France in America* (Markham, Ontario: Fitzhenry & Whiteside, 1990), pp. 95–124.

6. See the entry, "Brisay de Denonville, Jacques-René de," *DCB,* Vol. II, pp. 98–104.

7. M. de Denonville to M. de Seignelay, "Memoir on the present state of affairs in Canada in reference to the Iroquois War," October 27, 1687, in E. B. O'Callaghan, ed., *Documents Relative to the Colonial History of the State of New York,* 15 vols. (Albany: Weed, Parsons, and Company, 1853–87), Vol. IX, p. 348. Henceforth *DRCHSNY.*

8. See "Project of the Chevalier de Callières," January 1689, *DRCHSNY,* Vol. IX, pp. 404–8.

9. Ibid., p. 286.

10. See the discussion in Gustave Lanctot, *A History of Canada,* Vol. II, *From the Royal Régime to the Treaty of Utrecht, 1663–1713,* Margaret M. Cameron, trans. (Cambridge: Harvard University Press, 1964), pp. 113–14. This account differs somewhat from that in "Brisay de Denonville," *DCB,* Vol. II, p. 102. "Project of the Chevalier de Callières," January 1689, *DRCHSNY,* Vol. IX, pp. 404–8.

11. See the entry, "Buade de Frontenac et de Palluau," *DCB,* Vol. I, pp. 133–42.

12. "Le Moyne d'Iberville," *DCB,* Vol. II, p. 393.

13. Charles de Monseignat, "Narrative of Canada," November 1690, *DRCHSNY,* Vol. IX, p. 469.

14. Thomas E. Burke, Jr., *Mohawk Frontier: The Dutch Community of Schenectady, New York, 1661–1710*, 2nd ed. (Albany: State University of New York Press, 1991), p. 107.

15. Here I follow W. J. Eccles, *Frontenac: The Courtier Governor* (Toronto: McClelland and Stewart, 1959), pp. 229–30.

16. Ibid.

17. Dailey, *Burning of Schenectady*, p. 29.

18. Governor Benjamin Fletcher and the Council of New York to Lieutenant Colonel Lodwick, *DRCHSNY*, Vol. IV, June 13, 1693, p. 33.

19. For an insightful commentary, see Lawrence H. Keeley, *War Before Civilization: The Myth of the Peaceful Savage* (New York: Oxford University Press, 1996), pp. 152–56.

20. Chabert de Joncaire, Louis-Thomas, *DRCHSNY*, Vol. IV, p. 126.

21. Lord Bellomont to the Board of Trade, February 28, 1699, *DRCHSNY*, Vol. IV, p. 608.

22. Lord Bellomont to the Lords of Trade, April 20, 1700, ibid., p. 639.

23. Lord Bellomont to the Lords of Trade, October 28, 1700, ibid., p. 770.

24. Callières, Louis-Hector de, *DCB*, Vol. II, pp. 112–13. The entry (pp. 112–17) is the source for much of what follows.

25. See Gilles Havard, *The Great Peace of Montreal of 1701*, Phyllis Aronoff and Howard Scott, trans. (Montreal: McGill–Queen's University Press, 2001).

26. Robert Livingston to Lords Commissioners for Trade and Foreign Plantations, summer 1703, in *DRCHSNY*, Vol. IV, pp. 1067–69.

27. A wonderful account is Evan Haefeli and Kevin Sweeney, *Captors and Captives: The 1704 French and Indian Raid on Deerfield* (Amherst: University of Massachusetts Press, 2003).

28. Colonel Robert Quary to the Lords of Trade, January 10, 1708, in *DRCHSNY*, Vol. V, p. 30.

29. Ibid., p. 32.

30. Samuel Vetch, "Canada Surveyed," July 27, 1708, in Cecil Headlam et al., eds., *Calendar of State Papers Colonial, America and West Indies*, Vol. XXIV, 1708–1709 (London: HMSO, 1922). Accessed December 22, 2010, http://www.british-history.ac.uk/report.aspx?compid=73784.

31. See Bruce T. McCully, "Catastrophe in the Wilderness: New Light on the Canada Expedition of 1709," *WMQ* 11,3 (July 1954): 441–56.

32. For a full and interesting account, including documents, see Gerald S. Graham, *The Walker Expedition to Quebec, 1711* (London: Navy Records Society, 1953). Vetch's career is described in G. M. Waller, *Samuel Vetch: Colonial Enterpriser* (Chapel Hill: University of North Carolina Press, 1960).

33. Dean R. Snow, "Eastern Abenaki," in Bruce G. Trigger, ed., *North American Indians*, Vol. XV, *Northeast* (Washington: Smithsonian, 1978), pp. 137–47; Gordon M. Day, "Western Abenaki," ibid., pp. 148–59.

34. Francis Parkman, *France and England in North America* (New York: Modern Library, 1983), Vol. II, p. 614. The citation is to *A Half-Century of Conflict*, originally published in 1892, Chapter XVII.

35. The description and account taken from David R. Starbuck, *The Great Warpath: British Military Sites from Albany to Crown Point* (Hanover, N.H.: University Press of New England, 1999), pp. 164–65.

36. *Peter Kalm's Travels in North America: The English Version of 1770*, Adolph Benson, rev. and ed., 2 vols. (New York: Wilson-Erickson, 1937), Vol. II, pp. 392–93; the following story is described in Vol. I, pp. 377–78.

CHAPTER TWO—FORT WILLIAM HENRY, 1757

1. The most recent history of the war is Fred Anderson, *Crucible of War: The Seven Years' War and the Fate of Empire in British North America, 1754–1766* (New York: Alfred A. Knopf, 2000). An older, rather more heroically minded account appears in Vols. VI–VIII of Lawrence Henry Gipson's *The British Empire Before the American Revolution*, collectively titled *The Great War for the Empire* (New York: Alfred A. Knopf, 1946, 1949, 1954).

2. See Jonathan R. Dull, *The French Navy and the Seven Years' War* (Lincoln: University of Nebraska Press, 2005), pp. 1–49.

3. On French policy see Gustave Lanctot, *A History of Canada*, Vol. III, *From the Treaty of Utrecht to the Treaty of Paris, 1713–1763* (Cambridge: Harvard University Press, 1965), pp. 70–152.

4. Ibid., pp. 110–21, covers the economy of prewar Canada.

5. For a good comparison of the colonies see Guy Frégault, *Canada: The War of the Conquest*, Margaret M. Cameron, trans. (Toronto: Oxford University Press, 1969), pp. 1–66. French and British forces are described in W. J. Eccles, "The French forces in North America during the Seven Years' War," and C. P. Stacey, "The British forces in North America during the Seven Years' War," *DCB*, Vol. III, pp. xv–xxx.

6. Douglas Leach, *Roots of Conflict: British Armed Forces and Colonial Americans, 1677–1763* (Chapel Hill: University of North Carolina Press, 1986), pp. 130–31.

7. Ibid., pp. 118–21.

8. For a marvelous description of one particular colonial force, see Fred Anderson's superb *A People's Army: Massachusetts Soldiers and Society in the Seven Years' War* (Chapel Hill: University of North Carolina Press, 1984), passim.

9. See the entry in *DCB*, Vol. IV, pp. 394–98. For a recent biography see Fintan O'Toole, *White Savage: William Johnson and the Invention of America* (Albany: State University of New York, 2005).

10. "Rigaud de Vaudreuil de Cavagnial, Pierre de, Marquis de Vaudreuil," *DCB*, Vol. IV, pp. 662–74.

11. "Dieskau, Jean-Armand," *DCB*, Vol. III, pp. 185–87.

12. "Minutes of General Johnson's Council of War," August 22–23, 1755, *DRCHSNY*, Vol. VI, p. 1001.

13. Major-General Johnson to the Lords of Trade, September 3, 1755, *DRCHSNY*, Vol. VI, p. 995.

14. See Vaudreuil's instruction to Dieskau, August 15, 1755, *DRCHSNY*, Vol. X, pp. 327–30.

15. Baron de Dieskau to Commissary Doreil, August 16, 1775, *DRCHSNY*, Vol. X, p. 312.

16. See Eric Hinderaker, *The Two Hendricks: Unraveling a Mohawk Mystery* (Cambridge: Harvard University Press, 2010).

17. Ian Steele, *Betrayals: Fort William Henry and the "Massacre"* (New York: Oxford University Press, 1990), pp. 57ff.

18. William Johnson, *The Papers of Sir William Johnson*, ed. James Sullivan (Albany: University of the State of New York, 1922), Vol. II, p. 149.

19. On the construction of the fort, see Edward Hamilton, *Fort Ticonderoga: Key to a Continent* (Boston: Little, Brown, 1964), pp. 33–53.

20. For what follows, see "Montcalm, Louis-Joseph de, Marquis de Montcalm," *DCB*, Vol. III, pp. 458–69.

21. Eccles's judgment, ibid., p. 459. Eccles reacts sharply here against Francis Parkman's view of Montcalm as doomed hero.

22. M. de Montcalm to Count d'Argenson, April 24, 1757, *DRCHSNY*, Vol. X, p. 550.

23. "Campaign of 1756 in Canada," *DRCHSNY*, Vol. X, p. 470; see also "Abstract of Despatches from America," pp. 479–80.

24. "Attack on Fort William Henry, 1757," *DRCHSNY*, Vol. X, pp. 544–46.

25. M. de Montcalm to Count d'Argenson, April 24, 1757, ibid., p. 551.

26. M. de Vaudreuil to M. de Moras, July 12, 1757, *DRCHSNY*, Vol. X, pp. 584–86.

27. M. de Bougainville to M. de Paulmy, Montreal, August 19, 1757, *DRCHSNY*, Vol. X, p. 607.

28. Louis Antoine de Bougainville, *Adventure in the Wilderness: The American Journals of Louis Antoine de Bougainville, 1756–1760*, Edward P. Hamilton, ed. and trans. (Norman, Okla.: University of Oklahoma Press, 1964), p. 42.

29. *DRCHSNY*, Vol. X, p. 609.

30. See the summary, "An Account of the Campaign of 1757 in North America," *DRCHSNY*, Vol. X, p. 643.

31. Steele, *Betrayals*, p. 103.

32. Montcalm commentary on campaign, in H. R. Casgrain, ed., *Journal du Marquis de Montcalm Durant ses Campagnes en Canada de 1756 à 1759* (Quebec: Imprimerie de L.-J. Demers & Freere, 1895), pp. 292 passim.

33. Steele, *Betrayals*, pp. 112–13. This is the best study of the massacre by one of the leading scholars of early warfare in North America.

34. Thus Montcalm's report, "Detail of the Campaign of 1757, from the 30th of July to the 4th September," *DRCHSNY*, Vol. X, p. 629.

35. Montcalm commentary, in Casgrain, ed., *Journal du Marquis de Montcalm*, p. 293.

36. M. de Montcalm to Lord Loudoun, August 14, 1757, *DRCHSNY*, Vol. X, p. 619.

37. M. de Montcalm to M. de Paulmy, *DRCHSNY*, Vol. X, p. 630.

38. Bougainville, *Adventure*, p. 152.

39. M. de Montcalm to M. de Paulmy, *DRCHSNY*, Vol. X, p. 597.

40. *DRCHSNY*, Vol. X, p. 660.

41. See Bougainville's dispatch, M. de Bougainville to M. de Paulmy, August 19, 1757, *DRCHSNY*, Vol. X, p. 616.

42. *DRCHSNY*, Vol. X, p. 631.

43. M. de Montcalm to Brigadier-General Webb, *DRCHSNY*, Vol. X, pp. 618–20.

44. Bougainville, *Adventure*, p. 172. Entry for 12–31 August.

45. *London Chronicle* (London, England), October 13–15, 1757, issue 124, p. 2.

46. *Boston Gazette* (Boston, Mass.), August 29, 1757, issue 126, pp. 2–3.

47. For a fascinating discussion of this, see David Hackett Fischer, *Washington's Crossing* (Oxford: Oxford University Press, 2004), pp. 370–77.

48. Cotton Mather, *Decennum Luctuosum*, 1699, reprinted in Charles H. Lincoln, ed., *Narratives of the Indian Wars, 1675–1699* (New York: Charles Scribner's Sons, 1913), p. 206.

CHAPTER THREE—THE BATTLE ON SNOWSHOES, 1758

1. William Johnson to Sir Charles Hardy, October 13, 1755, in James Sullivan, ed., *The Papers of Sir William Johnson*, 14 vols. (Albany: The University of the State of New York, 1922), Vol. II, p. 190.

2. Todish, Timothy, ed., *The Annotated and Illustrated Journals of Major Robert Rogers* (Fleischmanns, N.Y.: Purple Mountain Press, 2002), p. 89.

3. Quoted in John Cuneo, *Robert Rogers of the Rangers* (New York: Oxford University Press, 1959), p. 65.

4. I have relied heavily on Bob Bearor, *The Battle on Snowshoes* (Bowie, Md.: Heritage Books, 1997), for much of what follows.

5. Todish, ed., *Journals*, p. 90.

6. Ibid.

7. Ibid., p. 91.

8. M. Doreil to Marshal de Belle Isle, Quebec, April 30, 1758, *DRCHSNY*, Vol. X.

9. M. de Montcalm to M. de Paulmy, April 10, 1758, *DRCHSNY*, Vol. X, p. 693. Emphasis in the original.

10. M. Doreil to Marshal de Belle Isle, April 30, 1758, *DRCHSNY*, Vol. X, p. 703.

11. Winston S. Churchill, *Marlborough: His Life and Times*, Vol. V, *1705–1708* (New York: Charles Scribner's Sons, 1936), p. 433.

12. The latest, and very good, account of Rogers is John F. Ross, *War on the Run: The Epic Story of Robert Rogers and the Conquest of America's First Frontier* (New York: Bantam Books, 2009).

13. M. Doreil to Marshal de Belle Isle, April 30, 1758, *DRCHSNY*, Vol. X, p. 703.

14. See "Rogers' Rangers and Their Uniforms," in Todish, ed., *Journals*, pp. 293–322.

15. See Burt Garfield Loescher, *The History of Rogers' Rangers*, Vol. I, *The Beginnings, January 1755–April 6, 1758* (San Francisco: Heritage Books, 1946), pp. 116–38. Todish, *Journals*, pp. 58–59, includes Bougainville's account, which admits to eleven killed and twenty-seven wounded.

16. Following drawn from his biography in *DCB*, Vol. IV, pp. 512–14.

17. *DCB*, Vol. III, pp. 399–400.

18. Gertrude Selwyn Kimball, ed., *Correspondence of William Pitt when Secretary of State with Colonial Governors and Military and Naval Commissioners in America*, 2 vols. (London: Macmillan, 1906), Vol. I, p. 76.

19. Fred Anderson, *Crucible of War*, p. 99. I have relied heavily on his account, pp. 94–107.

20. J. W. Fortescue, *A History of the British Army*, Vol. II (London: Macmillan, 1910), pp. 185–86.

21. Pownall to Pitt, August 16, 1757, in Kimball, ed., *Correspondence*, Vol. I, pp. 94–98.

22. Cuneo, *Robert Rogers of the Rangers*, p. 91.

23. On this see David Gates, *The British Light Infantry Arm c. 1790–1815: Its Creation, Training, and Operational Role* (London: B. T. Batsford, 1987), and an older, but still valuable work, J. F. C. Fuller, *British Light Infantry in the Eighteenth Century* (London: Hutchinson & Co., 1925). The best and most recent treatment from the point of view of the British experience in North America is Stephen Brumwell, *Redcoats: The British Soldier and the War in the Americas, 1755–1763* (Cambridge: Cambridge University Press, 2002).

24. Lancelot Théodore Turpin de Crissé, *An Essay on the Art of War*, Joseph Otway, trans. (London: A. Hamilton, 1761), Vol. II, p. 110.

25. Fortescue, *History of the British Army*, Vol. II, p. 329.

26. Fuller, *British Light Infantry*, p. 124.

27. On the remarkable story of the raising of the Royal Americans see Alexander V. Campbell, *The Royal American Regiment: An Atlantic Microcosm, 1755–1772* (Norman, Okla.: Oklahoma University Press, 2010).

28. The regimental history is Lewis Butler, *The Annals of the King's Royal Rifle Corps*, Vol. I, *The Royal Americans* (London: Smith, Elder & Co., 1913).

29. See Richard Walden Hale, Jr., *The Royal Americans* (Ann Arbor: William L. Clements Library, 1944), p. 11.

30. The best edition is Todish, ed., *Journals*.

31. Field Manual 7-8, *The Infantry Rifle Platoon and Squad*. https://atiam.train.army .mil/soldierPortal/atia/adlsc/view/public/4718-1/fm/7-8/toc.htm, accessed 20 December 2005.

32. See Todish, ed., *Journals*, pp. 54–65.

33. Kenneth Roberts, *Northwest Passage* (New York: Doubleday, 1936), pp. 104–6. The wordings are virtually identical.

34. For a thoughtful exploration of the theme of the impact of the colonial military experience on American military culture, see John Grenier, *The First Way of War: American War Making on the Frontier* (Cambridge: Cambridge University Press, 2005).

CHAPTER FOUR—FORT CARILLON, 1758

1. "Diary of Rev. John Cleaveland, Chaplain of Colonel Jonathan Bagley's 3rd Regiment Provincials," *BFTM* X, 3 (1958): 198.

2. The following account is drawn largely from Nicholas Westbrook, ed., "'Like Roaring Lions Breaking from Their Chains': The Highland Regiment at Ticonderoga," *BFTM* XVI, 1 (1998): 16–91; Frederick B. Richards, *The Black Watch at Ticonderoga: Campaigns in the French & Indian War* (Leonaur, 2007); and Ian Macpherson McCulloch, *Sons of the Mountains: The Highland Regiments in the French & Indian War, 1756–1767*, Vol. I, Ch. 5, "The day of agony," pp. 85–111.

3. Letter dated July 19, 1758, in Westbrook, ed., "Roaring Lions," pp. 46–50.

4. Westbrook, ed., "Roaring Lions," pp. 44–45.

5. René Chartrand, *Ticonderoga 1758: Montcalm's Victory Against All Odds* (Westport, Conn.: Praeger, 2004), p. 80.

6. Pownall to Pitt, January 6, 1758, ibid., p. 162.

7. Stanley Pargellis, *Lord Loudoun in North America* (New Haven: Yale University Press, 1933), pp. 108–10; Stephen Brumwell, *Redcoats: The British Soldier and War in the Americas, 1755–1763* (Cambridge: Cambridge University Press, 2002), p. 19.

8. Pitt to General Abercromby, December 30, 1757, in Kimball, ed., *Correspondence of William Pitt*, Vol. I, p. 143.

9. Ibid., pp. 136–40.

10. Gustave Lanctot, *A History of Canada*, Vol. III, *From the Treaty of Utrecht to the Treaty of Paris, 1713–1763*, Margaret M. Cameron, trans. (Cambridge: Harvard University Press, 1965), p. 164.

11. Numbers taken from N. A. M. Rodger, *The Command of the Ocean: A Naval History of Britain 1649–1815* (London: Allen Lane, 2004), p. 608.

12. Ibid., p. 638. For a summary of British naval operations during the Seven Years' War see pp. 257–90.

13. Lanctot, *A History of Canada*, Vol. III, p. 150.

14. Paul David Nelson, "Abercromby, James (1706–1781), army officer and politician," *ODNB*, accessed 2 Feb 2009.

15. "Abercromby, James (1706–23 Apr. 1781)," *ANBO*.

16. *Adventure in the Wilderness: The American Journals of Louis Antoine de Bougainville, 1756–1760*, Edward P. Hamilton, trans. and ed. (Norman, Okla.: University of Oklahoma Press, 1964), p. 227. Journal entry of July 6, 1758.

17. The numbers taken from Chartrand, *Ticonderoga*, p. 29. The numbers, like most pertaining to eighteenth-century armies, are a matter of dispute, however.

18. Chartrand, *Ticonderoga*, p. 30 passim.

19. See the discussion in William R. Nester, *The Epic Battles for Ticonderoga, 1758* (Albany: State University of New York Press, 2008), pp. 117–18.

20. Personal communication from Nicholas Westbrook, who has made the closest study of this battle, and to whom this account is particularly indebted.

21. See, inter alia, Ian Macpherson McCulloch, "'A blanket of inconsistencies . . .' The Battle of Ticonderoga, 2008," *Journal of Military History* 72 (July 2008): 889–900.

22. The identification is Westbrook's, "Roaring Lions," p. 56.

23. Ibid., p. 40.

24. Letter of August 17, 1758, as reproduced in Westbrook, "The Highland Regiment at Ticonderoga," *BFTM* XVI, 1 (1998): 57.

25. Chartrand, *Ticonderoga 1758*, p. 88, possibly drawing on Westbrook, "Roaring Lions."

26. Excerpt from "A Short Account of the Life, Travels, and Adventures of Garrett Albertson, Sr.," *BFTM* IV, 2 (July 1936): 43.

27. Westbrook, "The Highland Regiment at Ticonderoga," p. 69.

28. Ibid., pp. 73–77.

29. Letters reproduced in Ian McCulloch, "'Believe Us, Sir, This Will Impress Few People!' Spin-Doctoring—18th Century Style," *BFTM* XVI,1 (1998): 92–107.

30. "La Corne, Luc de," *DCB*, Vol. IV, p. 426.

31. Nicholas Westbrook, personal communication. Diary of Jesse Parsons, a Connecticut soldier.

32. "Journal of Occurrences in Canada, 1757, 1758," *DRCHSNY*, Vol. X, p. 850.

33. *Adventure in the Wilderness*, p. 237.

34. Montcalm to Belle Isle, July 12, 1758, *DRCHSNY*, Vol. X, pp. 732–33.

35. Doreil to Belle Isle, July 31, 1758, *DRCHSNY*, Vol. X, p. 769. On Doreil, see *DCB*, Vol. III, pp. 187–88.

36. Montcalm to Massiac, July 28, 1758, *DRCHSNY*, Vol. X, p. 756. The Marquis de Massiac was the French minister of marine, responsible for the colonies.

37. "Narrative of the Victory gained over the English on the 8th of July, 1758, by the King's army, under the command of the Marquis de Montcalm," *DRCHSNY*, Vol. X, pp. 788–98.

38. *Adventure in the Wilderness*, pp. 242–43.

39. Ibid., p. 244.

40. "Speeches of the Iroquois, Nepissings, Algonkins, Abenakis and Mississagués, 30th July, 1758," *DRCHSNY*, Vol. X, pp. 805–6.

41. Bigot to Massiac, August 13, 1758, *DRCHSNY*, Vol. X, pp. 812–13.

42. Montcalm to Belle Isle, April 12, 1759, *DRCHSNY*, Vol. X, p. 960.

43. John Shy, *Toward Lexington: The Role of the British Army in the Coming of the American Revolution* (Princeton: Princeton University Press, 1965), pp. 92–93.

44. The account that follows is drawn from CO 5/56, "Military and Naval despatches, July-October 1759," ff. 133–56.

45. "The Amherst Expedition Against Ticonderoga, 1759: Excerpts from the General Orders of the Army," *BFTM* VI, 3 (January 1942): 97.

46. Ibid., p. 93.

47. CO 5/56, "Military and Naval despatches, July–October 1759," f. 155.

48. As quoted in *DCB*, Vol. IV, p. 23.

49. See Montcalm to Assistant Minister of War Cremille, April 12, 1759, *DRCHSNY*, Vol. X, p. 959.

50. The text can be found in *DRCHSNY*, Vol. X, pp. 1107–20.

51. For a good description of the last chapter in the fall of New France, see Guy Frégault, *Canada: The War of the Conquest*, Margaret M. Cameron, trans. (Toronto: Oxford University Press, 1969), pp. 268–95.

52. Benjamin Franklin, "Humourous Reasons for Restoring Canada," *The London Chronicle*, December 27, 1759, as reproduced in *Benjamin Franklin: Writings* (New York: Library of America, 1987), p. 533. Emphasis in the original.

53. For a Canadian perspective on this, see Frégault, *Canada: The War of the Conquest*, pp. 296–318.

54. Ira Gruber, "George III Chooses a Commander in Chief," in Ronald Hoffman and Peter J. Albert, eds., *Arms and Independence: The Military Character of the Revolution* (Charlottesville: University Press of Virginia, 1984), p. 189.

55. William Eyre to Robert Napier, July 10, 1758, in Stanley Pargellis, ed., *Military Affairs in North America, 1748–1765: Selected Documents from the Cumberland Papers in Windsor Castle* (New York: D. Appleton-Century, 1936), p. 419.

56. Douglas Leach, *Roots of Conflict: British Armed Forces and Colonial Americans, 1677–1763* (Chapel Hill: University of North Carolina Press, 1986), pp. 130–31.

57. Peter MacLeod, *Northern Armageddon: The Battle of the Plains of Abraham* (Toronto: Douglas & McIntyre, 2008), p. 26.

58. "Journal of Robert Webster," *BFTM* II, 4 (July 1931): 141. The rest of his journal is reprinted in *BFTM* IX, 5 (Summer 1954): 311–34.

CHAPTER FIVE—ST. JOHNS, 1775

1. Benjamin Franklin to Josiah Quincy, Sr., April 15, 1776, in William B. Wilcox, ed., *The Papers of Benjamin Franklin*, Vol. XXII, *March 23, 1775 through October 27, 1776* (New Haven: Yale University Press, 1982), p. 401.

2. John Carroll to Eleanor Darnall Carroll, May 1, 1776, in Thomas O'Brien Hanley, ed., *The John Carroll Papers*, Vol. I, *1775–1791* (Notre Dame: University of Notre Dame Press, 1976), p. 47.

3. Commissioners to John Hancock, April 5, 1776, in *Franklin Papers*, Vol. XXII, p. 397.

4. Brantz Mayer, ed., *Journal of Charles Carroll of Carrollton, during his Visit to Canada in 1776, as One of the Commissioners from Congress; with a Memoir and Notes* (Baltimore: Maryland Historical Society, 1876), p. 75. Entry of April 22, 1776.

5. *John Carroll Papers*, Vol. I, p. 47.

6. See John Shy, *Toward Lexington: The Role of the British Army in the Coming of the American Revolution* (Princeton: Princeton University Press, 1965).

7. Much of what follows is drawn from Pierre Tousignant, "The integration of the province of Quebec into the British empire, 1763–91, Part I: from the Royal Proclamation to the Quebec Act," in Francess G. Halpenny and Jean Hamelin, eds., *Dictionary of Canadian Biography*, Vol. IV, *1771–1800* (Toronto: University of Toronto Press, 1979), pp. xxxii–xlix.

8. Worthington Chauncey Ford, ed., *Journals of the Continental Congress, 1774–1789*, 34 vols. (Washington, D.C.: U.S. Government Printing Office, 1904–37), Vol. I, pp. 34–35. Henceforth *JCC*.

9. Ibid., p. 106.

10. Ibid., p. 111.

11. Lieut.-Governor Cadwallader Colden to Earl of Dartmouth (No. 6), October 4, 1774, in K.G. Davies, ed., *Documents of the American Revolution 1770–1783*, 21 vols. (Shannon: Irish University Press, 1972–1981), Vol. VIII, p. 204. Henceforth *DAR*.

12. Report by Captain John Montrésor to Maj.-General Frédéric Haldimand on Crown Point and Ticonderoga, May 13, 1774, in *DAR*, Vol. VIII, p. 111.

13. Maj.-General Frédéric Haldimand to Earl of Dartmouth (No. 18), May 15, 1774, in *DAR*, Vol. VIII, p. 112.

14. See *DAR*, Vol. VII, pp. 35ff.

15. Governor Guy Carleton to Lieut.-General Thomas Gage (Secret), *DAR*, Vol. IX, pp. 45–46.

16. Letter to Governor Guy Carleton, April 7, 1775, *DAR*, Vol. IX, p. 93.

17. Hugh Finlay to ??? Ingram, May 29, 1775, in *DAR*, Vol. IX, p. 146.

18. Benedict Arnold to Massachusetts Committee of Public Safety, April 30, 1775, in Peter Force, ed., *American Archives*, Fourth Series (Washington, D.C.: 1837–1855), Vol. II, p. 450. Henceforth *AA*.

19. James Kirby Martin, *Benedict Arnold, Revolutionary Hero: An American Warrior Reconsidered* (New York: New York University Press, 1997), p. 71. Variants include "skunk" or the more likely "bastard" rather than "rat."

20. Ethan Allen to the Congress of the Province of Massachusetts, May 11, 1775, in *AA*, Vol. II, p. 556.

21. Benedict Arnold to the Committee of Safety of Massachusetts, May 11, 1775, in *AA*, Fourth Series, Vol. II, p. 557.

22. Justin H. Smith, *Our Struggle for the Fourteenth Colony* (New York: G. P. Putnam's Sons, 1907), p. 152.

23. Arnold's exploits described in Martin, *Benedict Arnold*, pp. 73–75.

24. See the account in Robert McConnell Hatch, *Thrust for Canada: The American Attempt on Quebec in 1775–1776* (Boston: Houghton Mifflin, 1979), pp. 27–29.

25. "John Brown has arrived in Philadelphia from Ticonderoga," May 20, 1775, in *AA*, Fourth Series, Vol. II, p. 624. Emphasis in the original.

26. *JCC*, Vol. II, p. 69.

27. John Hancock to George Washington, June 28, 1775, in W. W. Abbot, ed., *The Papers of George Washington: Revolutionary War Series*, Vol. I, *June–September 1775* (Charlottesville: University Press of Virginia, 1985), p. 42. Henceforth *GW Papers*.

28. George Washington to Philip Schuyler, September 8, 1775, *GW Papers*, p. 437.

29. George Washington to Benedict Arnold, September 14, 1775, *GW Papers*, p. 456.

30. Earl of Dartmouth to Governor Guy Carleton, no. 18, July 1, 1775, *DAR*, Vol. XI, p. 27.

31. Governor Guy Carleton to Earl of Dartmouth, June 7, 1775, *DAR*, Vol. IX, pp. 158–59.

32. Lieut.-General Thomas Gage to Earl of Dartmouth, June 12 and 25, 1775, *DAR*, Vol. IX, pp. 170, 199.

33. Earl of Dartmouth to Guy Johnson, July 25, 1775, *DAR*, Vol. XI, p. 56.

34. On Montgomery see Hal T. Shelton, *General Richard Montgomery and the American Revolution: From Redcoat to Rebel* (New York: New York University Press, 1994).

35. On St. Johns see Jacques Castonguay, *The Unknown Fort: Saint-Jean Foils Americans*, William J. Cozens, trans. (Montreal: Les Éditions du Lévrier, 1965), and his lengthier, more amply footnoted work, *Les Défis du Fort Saint-Jean: L'Invasion ratée des Américains en 1775* (Saint-Jean: Les Editions du Richilieu, 1975).

36. Colonel Ethan Allen to General Montgomery, September 20, 1775, *AA*, Fourth Series, Vol. III, p. 754. Emphasis in the original.

37. Shelton, *General Richard Montgomery*, pp. 101–3. See also Smith, *Struggle*, Vol. I, pp. 379–94.

38. Gustave Lanctot, *Canada and the American Revolution, 1774–1783*, Margaret M. Cameron, trans. (Cambridge: Harvard University Press, 1967), p. 77.

39. An extraordinary tale, which he told in *Journal du Voyage de M. Saint-Luc de la Corne, Écr. dans le Navire l'Auguste, en l'An 1761* (Quebec: A Coté, 1863).

40. Major Sir Charles Preston, "Narrative of the Siege of St. Johns Canada," in *Report of the Work of the Public Archives for the Years 1914 and 1915* (Ottawa: J. de L. Taché, 1916), Seasonal Paper No. 29a, p. 19.

41. Ibid.

42. Ibid., p. 21.

43. Lieut.-Governor H. T. Cramahé to Earl of Dartmouth, September 21, 1775, *DAR*, Vol. XI, p. 124.

44. Hugh Finlay to Anthony Todd, September 19, 1775, *DAR*, Vol. XI, p. 120.

45. Hugh Finlay to Anthony Todd, November 1, 1775, *DAR*, Vol. XI, p. 170.

46. See Gustave Lanctot, *Canada and the American Revolution, 1774–1783*, Margaret M. Cameron, trans. (Cambridge: Harvard University Press, 1967).

47. "Journal of the Siege and Blockade of Quebec by the American Rebels, in Autumn 1775 and Winter 1776," in Literary and Historical Society of Quebec, *Manuscripts Relating to the Early History of Canada*, fourth series (Quebec: Dawson & Co., 1875), p. 4 and passim.

48. For a biography of Knox see North Callahan, *Henry Knox: General Washington's General* (New York: Rhinehart, 1958).

49. Callahan, *Henry Knox*, pp. 39–40.

50. John Becker, *The Sexagenary: or, Reminiscences of the American Revolution* (Albany, N.Y.: J. Munsell, 1866), p. 27.

51. Ibid., p. 35.

52. Quoted in Callahan, *Henry Knox*, p. 58.

53. "Instructions to the Commissioners appointed to go to Canada," *AA*, Fourth Series, Vol. V, p. 1643.

54. Ibid., p. 1644.

55. Maj. General John Thomas to the Commissioners, May 7, 1776, ibid., pp. 421–23.

56. "Journal of the Siege of Quebec," p. 25.

57. Commissioners to Canada to John Hancock, May 1, 1776, *Franklin Papers*, Vol. XXII, p. 415.

58. Commissioners to Canada to John Hancock, May 6, 1776, *Franklin Papers*, Vol. XXII, p. 418.

59. JCC, Vol. IV, May 22, 1776, pp. 376–78.

60. Benjamin Franklin to Charles Carroll and Samuel Chase, May 27, 1776, *Franklin Papers*, Vol. XXII, p. 440.

61. L. H. Butterfield, ed., *The Adams Papers*, Series I, *Diaries*, Vol. III, *Diary 1782–1804, Autobiography Part One To October 1776* (Cambridge: Harvard University Press, 1961), p. 372.

CHAPTER SIX—VALCOUR ISLAND, 1776

1. Thomas Williams Baldwin, ed., *The Revolutionary Journal of Col. Jeduthan Baldwin, 1775–1778* (Bangor, Me.: The De Burians, 1906), p. 81.

2. Persifer Frazer, "Letters from Ticonderoga, 1776," October 13, 1776, BFTM X, 5 (February 1961): 454.

3. Ibid., August 6, 1776, p. 393.

4. Maj.-General Sir Guy Carleton to Maj.-General Sir William Howe, Crown Point, October 20, 1777, in William Bell Clark, ed., *Naval Documents of the American Revolution*, 11 vols. (Washington, D.C.: Naval Historical Center, 1964–2005), Vol. VI, p. 1336. Henceforth *NDAR*.

5. Maj-General Sir Guy Carleton to Lieutenant General John Burgoyne, October 15, 1776, *NDAR*, Vol. VI, p. 1274.

6. Précis of military documents, CO 5/253, f. 37.

7. Board of Trade and Secretaries of State: America and West Indies, Original Correspondence, 1606–1822, "Précis of documents relating to military operations against the revolted colonists,, 1774–1777," CO 5/253, f. 28.

8. See Piers Mackesy, *The War for America, 1775–1783* (Cambridge: Harvard University Press, 1965), p. 57 and passim.

9. *GW Papers*, Vol. III, p. 81.

10. Washington to Arnold, January 27, 1776, ibid., p. 197.

11. Quoted in ibid., Vol. IV, p. 454.

12. George Washington to John Hancock, June 17, 1776, ibid., Vol. V, p. 20.

13. Gen. Sullivan to Gen. Washington, June 6, 1776, and Gen. Sullivan to Gen. Schuyler, June 12, 1776, in Otis G. Hammond, ed., *Letters and Papers of Major-General John Sullivan, Continental Army* (Concord, N.H.: New Hampshire Historical Society, 1930), Vol. I, pp. 220, 234.

14. Entry of May 24, 1776, *JCC*, Vol. IV, p. 388.

15. Benedict Arnold to John Sullivan, June 10, 1776, *NDAR*, Vol. V, p. 444.

16. James Kirby Martin, *Benedict Arnold, Revolutionary Hero* (New York: New York University Press, 1997), p. 221. This is the best account of Arnold's military exploits in the Revolution.

17. John Adams to Abigail Adams, June 26, 1776, *NDAR*, Vol. V, p. 753.

18. What follows is drawn from Elizabeth A. Fenn, *Pox Americana: The Great Smallpox Epidemic of 1775–82* (New York: Hill and Wang, 2001), pp. 13–43, 62–79.

19. Ibid., p. 63.

20. Philip Schuyler to John Sullivan, June 20, 1776, *NDAR*, Vol. V, pp. 641–42.

21. Benedict Arnold to George Washington, June 25, 1776, *NDAR*, Vol. V, p. 731.

22. Horatio Gates to George Washington, July 17, 1776, *GW Papers*, Vol. V, p. 289.

23. Ambrose Serle to the Earl of Dartmouth, September 5, 1776, *NDAR*, Vol. VI, p. 712.

24. Baldwin, *Journal*, entry of July 17, 1776, p. 60.

25. Here, and for much of the other shipbuilding information, I have relied on Robert Malcomson, *Warships of the Great Lakes, 1754–1834* (Rochester, Kent: Chatham Publishing, 2001). See p. 27.

26. Captain Sir Charles Douglas to Philip Stephens, October 21, 1776, *DAR*, Vol. XII, pp. 237–38. CO 5/125 fo. 353.

27. John Trumbull to Jonathan Trumbull, July 12, 1776, *NDAR*, Vol. V, p. 1035.

28. Philip Schuyler to George Washington, August 18, 1776, *GW Papers*, Vol. VI, p. 67.

29. Horatio Gates Papers, Microfilm Roll 3. First quotation from Samuel Chase to Horatio Gates, August 9, 1776, second from Horatio Gates to John Adams, August 23, 1776. New-York Historical Society. Henceforth *Gates Papers*.

30. Jacobus Wynkoop to Horatio Gates, August 17, 1776, *NDAR*, Vol. VI, p. 216.

31. George Washington to Horatio Gates, July 19, 1776, *GW Papers*, Vol. V, p. 380.

32. Horatio Gates to George Washington, July 29, 1776, *GW Papers*, Vol. V, p. 500.

33. Horatio Gates to Benedict Arnold, August 7, 1776, *NDAR*, Vol. VI, pp 95–96.

34. Benedict Arnold to Horatio Gates, September 2, 1776, *NDAR*, Vol. VI, p. 654.

35. Benedict Arnold to Horatio Gates, September 7, 1776, *NDAR*, Vol. VI, p. 735.

36. Benedict Arnold to Horatio Gates, September 21, 1776, *NDAR*, Vol. VI, p. 925.

37. Benedict Arnold to Horatio Gates, September 18, 1776, *NDAR*, Vol. VI, p. 884.

38. Benedict Arnold to Horatio Gates, September 7, 1776, *NDAR*, Vol. VI, p. 735.

39. Benedict Arnold to Horatio Gates, September 9, 1776, *Gates Papers*, Microfilm roll 3.

40. Benedict Arnold to Horatio Gates, October 1, 1776, *NDAR*, Vol VI, p. 1084.

41. See Douglas R. Cubbison, *The British Artillery in the 1776 Valcour Island and 1777 Saratoga Campaigns* (Fleischmanns, N.Y.: Purple Mountain Press, 2007), pp. 54–65 and passim.

42. Alfred Thayer Mahan, *The Major Operations of the Navies in the American War of Independence* (Boston: Little, Brown, 1913), p. 18.

43. Journal of Captain George Pausch, October 11, 1776, *NDAR*, Vol. VI, p. 1259.

44. Autobiography of Colonel John Trumbull, in *NDAR*, Vol. VI, p. 1261.

45. Richard Stockton to Horatio Gates, October 20, 1776, *Gates Papers*, Reel 4.

46. See John R. Bratten, *The Gondola Philadelphia & the Battle of Lake Champlain* (College Station: Texas A&M University Press, 2002), p. 70.

47. Martin, *Benedict Arnold*, p. 283.

48. Richard Henry Lee to Thomas Jefferson, November 3, 1776, *NDAR*, Vol. VII, p. 29.

49. Horatio Gates to Jonathan Trumbull, October 22, 1776, *Gates Papers*, Reel 4.

50. Mahan, *Major Operations*, p. 13.

51. Quoted in Willard Sterne Randall, *Benedict Arnold: Patriot and Traitor* (New York: William Morrow, 1990), p. 558.

52. This and all else on the commemoration of the Saratoga centennial from William L. Stone, ed., *Memoir of the Centennial Celebration of Burgoyne's Surrender* (Albany: Joel Munsell, 1878).

53. Ibid., p. 132.

54. Ibid., p. 62.

55. On this point see Brian F. Carso, Jr., *"Whom Can We Trust Now?" The Meaning of Treason in the United States, from the Revolution through the Civil War* (Lanham, Md.: Lexington Books, 2006).

CHAPTER SEVEN—HUBBARDTON, 1777

1. Lord George Germain to General Sir William Howe, January 14, 1777, *DAR*, Vol. XIV, p 31.

2. Lord George Germain to Governor Sir Guy Carleton (Separate), March 26, 1777, *DAR*, Vol. XIV, p. 53.

3. Governor Sir Guy Carleton to Lord George Germain, May 20, 1777, *DAR*, Vol. XIV, pp. 87, 123.

4. Reproduced in *DAR*, Vol. XIV, pp. 43–46.

5. Lord George Germain to Governor Sir Guy Carleton (Separate), March 26, 1777, *DAR*, Vol. XIV, p. 54.

6. John Burgoyne, *A State of the Expedition from Canada Laid Before the House of Commons* (London: J. Almon, 1780), p. 8.

7. Lieutenant General John Burgoyne to Lord George Germain, May 15, 1777, *DAR*, Vol. XIV, p. 78.

8. Governor Sir Guy Carleton to Lieutenant General John Burgoyne, May 29, 1777, *DAR*, Vol. XIV, p. 100.

9. See R. Arthur Bowler, *Logistics and the Failure of the British Army in America, 1775–1783* (Princeton: Princeton University Press, 1975), p. 226 and passim.

10. Governor William Tryon to William Knox, April 21, 1777, *DAR*, Vol. XIV, p. 71.

11. Lieutenant General John Burgoyne to Lord George Germain, July 11, 1777, in Burgoyne, *State of the Expedition*, p. xx.

12. Lieutenant General John Burgoyne to General Sir William Howe, August 6, 1777, *DAR*, Vol. XIV, p. 156.

13. Anthony Wayne orderly book, January 3, 1777, *BFTM* III, 6 (July 1933): 256.

14. John Trumbull orderly book, October 15, 1776, *BFTM* III, 2 (July 1933): 112.

15. Anthony Wayne orderly book, November 29, 1776, *BFTM* III, 4 (July 1934): 167 and passim.

16. John W. Krueger, "Troop Life, continued," *BFTM* XIV, 5 (Summer 1984): 277–310. This is the third in a series of articles by Krueger whose full title is "Troop Life at the Champlain Valley Forts During the American Revolution."

17. General Wayne to General Schuyler, February 4, 1777, *BFTM* IV, 1 (January 1936): 22.

18. George Washington to Philip Schuyler, February 9, 1777, *GW Papers*, Vol. VIII, p. 292. For a critique of Washington's decisions, see Edward P. Hamilton, "Was Washington to Blame for the Loss of Ticonderoga in 1777?" *BFTM* XI, 1 (1962): 65–74, and Don R. Gerlach, "The Fall of Ticonderoga in 1777: Who Was Responsible?" *BFTM* XIV, 3 (Summer 1982): 131–57.

19. George Washington to Philip Schuyler, June 16, 1777, *GW Papers*, Vol. X, p. 53.

20. George Washington to Philip Schuyler, March 12, 1777, *GW Papers*, Vol. VIII, pp. 561–62.

21. Ibid.

22. George Washington to Philip Schuyler, June 20, 1777, *GW Papers*, Vol. X, p. 90.

23. Letter from Arthur St. Clair to Philip Schuyler, June 25, 1777, enclosed in Philip Schuyler to George Washington, June 28, 1777, *GW Papers*, Vol. X, p. 142.

24. Alex Storozynski, *The Peasant Prince: Thaddeus Koscuszko and the Age of Revolution* (New York: St. Martin's Press, 2009), pp. 23–31.

25. "A Journal of Carleton's and Burgoyne's Campaigns," *BFTM* XI, 5 (December 1964): 245.

26. Michael R. Barbieri, "'They Will Not Trouble Us Here this Summer,' An Account of some incidents that took place on 17 June 1777 near Fort Ticonderoga," *BFTM* XVI, 3 (2000): 253–71.

27. *Proceedings of a General Court Martial, Held at White Plains in the State of New York, By Order of His Excellency General Washington, Commander in Chief of the Army of the United States of America for the Trial of Major General Arthur St. Clair, August 25, 1778* (Philadelphia: Hall and Sellers, 1778), p. 16. Henceforth *Court Martial of Arthur St. Clair.*

28. Ibid., p. 25.

29. Ibid., p. 22.

30. Ibid., p. 24.

31. Ibid., p. 101.

32. "Journal of Carleton's and Burgoyne's Campaigns," p. 263.

33. "Inquisition of a Spy," *BFTM* X,1 (1957): 245. The full account is on pp. 240–45. See also "Gen. Fraser's Account of Burgoyne's Campaign and the Battle of Hubbardton," *Proceedings of the Vermont Historical Society*, Vol. II (1898), p. 140.

34. See Richard Ketchum, *Saratoga: Turning Point of America's Revolutionary War* (New York: Henry Holt, 1997), p. 143.

35. Ibid. This account is drawn from Fraser.

36. "Gen. Fraser's Account of Burgoyne's Campaign," p. 144.

37. *Court Martial of Arthur St. Clair*, p. 34.

38. Philip Schuyler to George Washington, July 23, 1777, *GW Papers*, Vol. X, p. 381.

39. What follows relies heavily on John Williams, *The Battle of Hubbardton: The American Rebels Stem the Tide* (Montpelier, Vt.: The Vermont Division for Historic Preservation, 1988). It is the definitive account of the battle.

40. See the description in Ketchum, *Saratoga*, pp. 224–25.

41. Burgoyne, *State of the Expedition*, pp. 27–28.

42. Testimony of Lieutenant Colonel Kingston, in Burgoyne, *State of the Expedition*, p. 74.

43. "Gen. Fraser's Account of Burgoyne's Campaign," p. 145.

44. On casualty rates, see Williams, *Hubbardton*, Appendix I, p. 65.

45. As quoted in "Stark, John," *ANBO*, accessed May 16, 2011.

46. Ketchum, *Saratoga*, pp. 274–77, gives a full account.

47. See "Letter XXXV, Camp at Fort Edward, August 6, 1777," in Thomas Anburey, *Travels through the Interior Parts of America* (Boston: Houghton Mifflin, 1923), Vol. I, p. 221.

48. James Kirby Martin, *Benedict Arnold, Revolutionary Hero: An American Warrior Reconsidered* (New York: New York University Press, 1977), p. 400.

49. T.W. Baldwin, ed., *Revolutionary Journal of Jeduthan Baldwin*, p. 125.

50. See Piers Mackesy, *The War for America 1775–1783* (Cambridge: Harvard University Press, 1965), p. 147, for a discussion.

51. Ketchum, *Saratoga*, gives a figure of 5,895 British and Germans.

52. Burgoyne, *State of the Expedition*, p. 102.

53. Ibid., p. 99.

54. Ketchum, *Saratoga*, p. 206.

55. John Adams to Abigail Adams, August 19, 1777, Massachusetts Historical Society, *The Adams Family Papers: An Historical Archive*, http://www.masshist .org/digitaladams/aea/cfm/doc.cfm?id=L17770819jasecond. Accessed May 12, 2010.

56. Oration by the Reverend Thomas Allen, *BFTM* IV, 2 (July 1936): 31–32.

57. *The Court Martial of Arthur St. Clair*, pp. 6–9.

58. Ibid., p. 152.

59. Ibid., p. 157.

60. Ibid., p. 145.

61. Ibid., p. 120. Testimony of Lieutenant Colonel Livingston.

62. Testimony of Colonel Udney Hay, deputy quartermaster general, ibid., p. 54.

63. Testimony of Major Dunn, St. Clair's aide de camp, ibid., p. 111.

64. See John Shy, "The Military Conflict Considered as a Revolutionary War," in *A People Numerous & Armed: Reflections on the Military Struggle for American Independence* (London: Oxford University Press, 1976), pp. 193–224.

65. Memorandum of Benedict Arnold to King George III, 1782, in Isaac N. Arnold, *The Life of Benedict Arnold; His Patriotism and His Treason* (1905; Cranbury, N.J.: The Scholar's Bookshelf, 2005), p. 421. Emphasis in the original.

66. Numbers from Burgoyne, *State of the Expedition*, pp. 9–10. After Ticonderoga, Burgoyne took only twenty six pieces of light artillery and ten heavy pieces, distributing the rest at St. Johns, Ticonderoga, and Fort George.

67. For a short summary, see Francis Paul Prucha, *The Sword of the Republic: The United States Army on the Frontier, 1783–1846* (Bloomington: Indiana University Press, 1969).

CHAPTER EIGHT—PHANTOM CAMPAIGNS, 1782–83

1. See "Joseph-Louis Gill," *DCB*; see also J. C. Huden, "The White Chief of the St. Francis Abenakis—Some Aspects of Border Warfare: 1690–1790," Parts I and II, *Vermont History* 25: 3 and 4 (July and October 1956), pp. 199–210, 337–54.

2. Frédéric Haldimand, "Sketch of the Military State of the Province of Quebec," July 25, 1778, *DAR*, Vol. XV, *Transcripts, 1778*, p. 169.

3. George Washington to Landon Carter, May 30, 1778, *GW Papers*, Vol. XV, pp. 267–68.

4. Haldimand, "Sketch," *DAR*, Vol. XV, p. 170.

5. Alexander Hamilton to George Washington, November 6, 1777, *GW Papers*, Vol. XII, p. 141.

6. Ibid.

7. George Washington to Thomas Conway, November 5, 1777, *GW Papers*, Vol. XI, p. 129. Conway's response the same day is found on pp. 130–31.

8. *JCC*, Vol. X, p. 924.

9. Stanley J. Idzerda, ed., *Lafayette in the Age of the American Revolution: Selected Letters and Papers, 1776–1790*, 5 vols. (Ithaca: Cornell University Press, 1977–83), Vol. I, p. 171. Henceforth *Lafayette Papers*.

10. Ibid., p. 192.

11. Lafayette to Henry Laurens, January 31, 1778, *Lafayette Papers*, Vol. I, p. 268.

12. George Washington to Thomas Nelson, Jr., February 8, 1778, *GW Papers*, Vol. XIII, p. 481.

13. George Washington to Horatio Gates, January 27, 1778, *GW Papers*, Vol. XIII, p. 361.

14. Lafayette to Henry Laurens, February 19, 1778, *Lafayette Papers*, Vol. I, p. 296.

15. Lafayette to Henry Laurens, January 31, 1778, *Lafayette Papers*, Vol. I, p. 296.

16. Lafayette to Baron von Steuben, March 12, 1778, *Lafayette Papers*, Vol. I, p. 352.

17. George Washington to John Armstrong, March 27, 1778, *GW Papers*, Vol. XIV, p. 327.

18. George Washington to the Board of War, August 3, 1778, *GW Papers*, Vol. XVI, p. 228.

19. Entry for October 22, 1778, *JCC*, Vol. XIII, pp. 1039–48.

20. Washington's letters may be found in *GW Papers*, Vol. XVIII, pp. 94–112, 149–51, 404–6. Congress's responses in *JCC*, Vol. XII, pp. 1190–92, 1230.

21. "The Marquis de Lafayette with the troops of the United States of America, to my Children the Savages of Canada," December 18, 1778, *Lafayette Papers*, Vol. II, p. 213.

22. Lafayette to the Comte de Vergennes, July 18, 1779, *Lafayette Papers*, Vol. II, p. 257.

23. See Jonathan R. Dull, *A Diplomatic History of the American Revolution* (New Haven: Yale University Press, 1985), p. 147. See also Alexander Deconde, "The French Alliance in Historical Speculation," in Ronald Hoffman and Peter J. Albert, eds., *Diplomacy and Revolution: The Franco-American Alliance of 1778* (Charlottesville: University Press of Virginia, 1981), pp. 1–38.

24. George Washington to Lafayette, May 19, 1780, *Lafayette Papers*, Vol. III, p. 24.

25. Lafayette to the president of Congress, February 5, 1783, *Lafayette Papers*, Vol. V, p. 84.

26. Memorandum of Governor Frédéric Haldimand, April 14, 1778, *DAR*, Vol. XV, p. 97. See his later statements once he had arrived, e.g., his letter to Germain on October 15, 1778, *DAR*, Vol. XV, p. 220.

27. Commissioners for Quieting Disorders (Carlisle Commission) to Lord George Germain, November 16, 1778, *DAR*, Vol. XV, p. 257.

28. Frédéric Haldimand to George Germain, June 18, 1779, *DAR*, Vol. XVII, p. 147.

29. For Haldimand's fears and assessments, see his letters to Sir Henry Clinton, May 26, 1777, and to George Germain, June 7 and 18, September 13 and 14, *DAR*, Vol. XVII, pp. 135–39, 147, 205–14. The quotations following are drawn from these sources.

30. George Germain to Henry Clinton, March 10, 1778, *DAR*, Vol. XV, p. 58.

31. Ida H. Washington and Paul A. Washington, *Carleton's Raid* (Weybridge, Vt.: Cherry Tree Books, 1977), p. 13. Much of what follows is drawn from this account.

32. Orders to Major Christopher Carleton, Haldimand Papers, British Library, ADD 21,792, f. 3. For a copy of Carleton's report, see Washington and Washington, *Carleton's Raid*, pp. 85–95.

33. Frédéric Haldimand to George Germain, November 21, 1778, *DAR*, Vol. XV, p. 266.

34. For a good short account see Brian Burns, "Carleton in the Valley or the Year of the Burning: Major Christopher Carleton and the Northern Invasion of 1780," *BFTM* XII, 6 (Fall 1980): 398–411.

35. On the war in Indian country, and in particular the Iroquois lands, see Barbara Graymont, *The Iroquois in the American Revolution* (Syracuse: Syracuse University Press, 1972); Colin G. Calloway, *The American Revolution in Indian Country: Crisis and Diversity in Native American Communities* (Cambridge: Cambridge University Press, 1995), especially Chapters 1–3; Joseph T. Glatthaar and James Kirby Martin, *Forgotten Allies: The Oneida Indians and the American Revolution* (New York: Hill & Wang, 2006); and the first chapters of Alan Taylor, *The Divided Ground: Indians,*

Settlers, and the Northern Borderland of the American Revolution (New York: Alfred A. Knopf, 2006).

36. Much of the account of Sherwood's personal history is drawn from Ian Cleghorn Blanshard Pemberton, "Justus Sherwood: Vermont Loyalist, 1747–1798," doctoral dissertation, University of Western Ontario, London, Ontario, 1972. Sherwood's account of his initial meetings with Allen may be found in *Vermont History* 24:1 and 2 (April and July 1956): 101–9, 211–19.

37. George Germain to Frédéric Haldimand, March 17, 1780, *DAR*, Vol. XVIII, p. 63.

38. Benedict Arnold to George Germain, October 28, 1780, *DAR*, Vol. XVIII, p. 213.

39. On this period see Charles A. Jellison, *Ethan Allen: Frontier Rebel* (Syracuse: Syracuse University Press, 1969), pp. 208ff., and Michael Bellesiles, *Revolutionary Outlaws: Ethan Allen and the Struggle for Independence on the Early American Frontier* (Charlottesville: University Press of Virginia, 1993), pp. 166ff.

40. *Collections of the Vermont Historical Society*, Vol. II (Montpelier, Vt.: 1871), pp. 32–33. Henceforth *VHS Collections*. Emphasis in the original.

41. Philip Schuyler to George Washington, October 31, 1780, *VHS Collections*, p. 76.

42. Bellesiles, *Revolutionary Outlaws*, p. 196.

43. Quoted in Jellison, *Ethan Allen*, p. 242.

44. Pemberton, "Justus Sherwood," p. 196.

45. Ibid., p. 199.

46. Text in *VHS Collections*, pp. 181–82.

47. George Washington to Thomas Chittenden, January 1, 1782, *VHS Collections*, p. 229.

48. C (probably Ethan Allen) to Frédéric Haldimand, June 16, 1782, *VHS Collections*, p. 275.

49. *VHS Collections*, pp. 297–323.

50. George Washington to Joseph Jones, February 11, 1783, *VHS Collections*, pp. 324–26.

51. Justus Sherwood or Robert Mathews to Ira Allen, March 25, 1783, *VHS Collections*, p. 335.

52. Ira Allen and Jonas Fay to Governor Frédéric Haldimand, May 29, 1783, *Haldimand Papers*, ADD 21835, f. 158.

CHAPTER NINE—PLATTSBURGH, 1814

1. Diary entry, July 11, 1814, John Quincy Adams, *Memoirs of John Quincy Adams, Comprising Portions of His Diary from 1795 to 1848*, Charles Francis Adams, ed. (Philadelphia: J. B. Lippincott & Co., 1874), Vol. II, p. 657. Henceforth *JQA Diary*.

2. John Quincy Adams to Abigail Adams, January 1, 1812, in *Writings of John Quincy Adams*, Worthington Chauncey Ford, ed. (New York: Macmillan, 1914), Vol. IV, 1811–1813, p. 284. Henceforth *JQA Writings*.

3. JQA to AA, May 1, 1812, *JQA Writings*, Vol. IV, p. 320.

4. Numbers from N. A. M. Rodger, *The Command of the Ocean: A Naval History of Britain, 1649–1815* (London: Allen Lane, 2004), p. 608.

5. See "Protocol of Conference, August 8, 1814," in *American State Papers*, Class I, *Foreign Relations*, Vol. III (Washington, D.C.: Gales and Seaton, 1832), p. 703. Henceforth *ASP*.

6. Sir Alexander Cochrane to Commanding Officers of the North American Station, July 18, 1814, in Michael J. Crawford, ed., *The Naval War of 1812: A Documentary History*, Vol. III, *1814–1815* (Washington, D.C.: Naval Historical Center, 2002), p. 140. Henceforth *NW 1812*, Vol. III.

7. See Donald R. Hickey, *Don't Give Up the Ship! Myths of the War of 1812* (Urbana: University of Illinois Press, 2006), pp. 44–45.

8. James Monroe to Albert Gallatin, John Quincy Adams, and James A. Bayard, June 23, 1813, in William R. Manning, ed., *Diplomatic Correspondence of the United States: Canadian Relations, 1784–1860*, Vol. I, *1784–1820* (Washington, D.C.: Carnegie Endowment for International Peace, 1940), p. 214. Henceforth *Canadian Relations*.

9. Quoted in Donald R. Hickey, *The War of 1812: A Forgotten Conflict* (Urbana: University of Illinois Press, 1989), p. 73. See passim for the role of American ambition to take Canada as a source of war. The standard work remains J. C. A. Stagg, *Mr. Madison's War: Politics, Diplomacy and Warfare in the Early American Republic 1783–1830* (Princeton: Princeton University Press, 1983).

10. On the origins of the war see Hickey, *War of 1812*, pp. 5–51; for a British perspective, Jon Latimer, *1812: War with America* (Cambridge: Harvard University Press, 2007), pp. 13–34. J. Mackay Hitsman, *The Incredible War of 1812: A Military History*, updated by Donald E. Graves (Toronto: Robin Brass Studio, 1999), gives a Canadian perspective, and may be considered, with these other two books, the standard account of the war. Alan Taylor, *The Civil War of 1812: American Citizens, British Subjects, Irish Rebels, & Indian Allies* (New York: Alfred A. Knopf, 2010), is particularly insightful on the mixed populations of the border areas, and their ambivalent relationships.

11. Statistics Canada, http://www.statcan.gc.ca/pub/98-187-x/4064809-eng.htm. Accessed September 17, 2010.

12. C. Edward Skeen, *John Armstrong, Jr., 1758–1843: A Biography* (Syracuse: Syracuse University Press, 1981), p. 160.

13. Quoted in H. N. Muller III, "A Traitorous and Diabolical Traffic," *Vermont History* 44:2 (Spring 1976), p. 91.

14. Thomas McDonough to William Jones, June 29, 1814, *NW 1812*, Vol. III, p. 537. See also p. 538.

15. See Allan S. Everest, *The War of 1812 in the Champlain Valley* (Syracuse: Syracuse University Press, 1981), passim, also U.S. government census data, and Abby Maria Hemenway, ed., *The Vermont Historical Gazetteer* (Burlington, Vt.: A. M. Hemenway, 1868), pp. 106, 502–3.

16. See *Supplementary Despatches, Correspondence, and Memoranda of Field Marshal Arthur Duke of Wellington*, Vol. IX (London: John Murray, 1962), pp. 85, 109, and 137. Henceforth *Supplementary Despatches*.

17. Earl of Bathurst to General Prevost, June 3, 1814, in Hitsman, *The Incredible War of 1812*, p. 290.

18. Entry of August 19, 1814, Adams, *JQA Diary*, Vol III, p. 18.

19. Lieutenant Sidney Smith to Secretary of the Navy, June 16, 1812, in *NW 1812*, Vol I, p. 275.

20. Thomas Macdonough to William Jones, April 11, 1814, in *NW 1812*, Vol. III, p. 428.

21. See C. Winton-Clare, "A Shipbuilder's War," in Morris Zaslow, ed., *The Defended Border: Upper Canada and the War of 1812* (Toronto: Macmillan, 1964), pp. 165–73.

22. William Jones to Thomas Macdonough, July 5, 1814, in *NW 1812*, Vol. III, p. 538.

23. U.S. Department of Commerce, Bureau of the Census, *Historical Statistics of the United States: Colonial Times to 1970* (Washington, D.C.: Government Printing Office, 1975), Part II, p. 750.

24. Daniel D. Tompkins to William Jones, March 10, 1814, *NW 1812*, Vol. III, p. 398.

25. George Prevost to Earl of Bathurst, August 5, 1814, in William Wood, ed., *Select British Documents of the Canadian War of 1812*, Vol. III, Part I (Toronto: The Champlain Society, 1920), p. 345. Henceforth *SBD*.

26. Ibid.

27. Order of August 23, 1814, as quoted in Hitsman, *Incredible War of 1812*, pp. 254–55.

28. See David Fitz-Enz, *The Final Invasion: Plattsburgh, the War of 1812's Most Decisive Battle* (New York: Cooper Square Press, 2001), p. 119.

29. Report of Alexander Macomb to the secretary of war, September 15, 1814, in *SBD*, Vol. III, Part I, p. 357. See Fitz-Enz, *The Final Invasion*, pp. 111–19, on this controversial episode.

30. Exchange of letters between George Prevost and George Downie, September 9, 1814, *NW 1812*, Vol. III, p. 598.

31. David Curtis Skaggs, *Thomas Macdonough: Master of Command in the Early U.S. Navy* (Annapolis: Naval Institute Press, 2003), p. 125.

32. For a brief summary of British naval tactics in this period, see Brian Lavery, *Nelson's Navy: The Ships, Men and Organisation, 1793–1815* (London: Conway Maritime Press, 1989), pp. 295–324.

33. Testimony of Robert Anderson Brydon, master of *Confiance*, at the Plattsburgh Court Martial, August 18–21, 1815. *SBD*, Vol. III, Part I, pp. 412–15 and passim.

34. Kevin J. Crisman, *The Eagle: An American Brig on Lake Champlain during the War of 1812* (Shelburne, Vt.: The New England Press, 1867), p. 62.

35. For good accounts of the battle see Skaggs, *Macdonough*, pp. 109–39; Russell P. Bellico, *Sails and Steam in the Mountains: A Maritime and Military History of Lake George and Lake Champlain* (Fleischmanns, N.Y.: Purple Mountain Press, 1992), pp. 205–36.

36. Daniel Pring to Sir James L. Yeo, September 12, 1814, in *NW 1812*, Vol. III, p. 610.

37. Thomas Macdonough to William Jones, September 13, 1814, in *NW 1812*, Vol. III, p. 615.

38. Thomas Macdonough to William Jones, September 11, 1814, in *NW 1812*, Vol. III, p. 607.

39. George Prevost to Earl of Bathurst, September 11, 1814, in *SBD*, Vol. III, Part I, p. 352.

40. George Prevost to Earl of Bathurst, September 22, 1814, in *SBD*, Vol. III, Part I, p. 365.

41. Alicia Cockburn to Charles Sandys, October 20, 1814, in *SBD*, Vol. III, Part I, p. 389. Emphasis in the original.

42. James Yeo to John Croker, September 24, 1814, in *SBD*, Vol. III, Part I, p. 367.

43. Conclusion of the court-martial, August 21, 1815, in *SBD*, Vol. III, Part I, p. 458.

44. Most notably, see Wesley B. Turner, *British Generals in the War of 1812: High Command in the Canadas* (Montreal: McGill-Queens University Press, 1999), pp. 24–57. See also J. Mackay Hitsman, "Sir George Prevost's Conduct of the Canadian War of 1812," *Report of the Annual Meeting of the Canadian Historical Association*, 41:1 (1962): 34–43.

45. F. Lech Coore to James Yeo, February 26, 1815, *SBD*, Vol. III, Part I, p. 395.

46. Entry of September 1, 1814, *JQA Diary*, Vol. III, p. 28.

47. Liverpool to Castlereagh, September 2, 1814, *Supplementary Despatches*, p. 214.

48. Liverpool to Duke of Wellington, October 28, 1814, *Supplementary Despatches*, p. 284.

49. Henry Goulburn to the Earl of Bathurst, October 21, 1814, *Supplementary Despatches*, p. 366.

50. *Times*, October 22, 1814.

51. John Quincy Adams to Louisa Catherine Adams, November 11, 1814, in *JQA Writings*, Vol. V, p. 182. "The *Times* blubbers," were his words.

52. Duke of Wellington to Lord Liverpool, November 9, 1814, *Supplementary Despatches*, p. 426.

53. Lord Liverpool to Lord Castlereagh, December 23, 1814, *Supplementary Despatches*, p. 495.

54. Henry Goulburn to Earl of Bathurst, November 25, 1814, *Supplementary Despatches*, p. 454.

55. November 27, 1814, *JQA Diary*, Vol. III, p. 78.

56. The judgment of Latimer, *1812*, pp. 404–6, and, in a more nuanced way, of Hickey. See *Don't Give Up the Ship*, pp. 209–355.

57. See, most recently, Gordon Wood, *Empire of Liberty: A History of the Early Republic* (New York: Oxford University Press, 2009), pp. 696–700.

58. John Quincy Adams to Peter Paul Francis de Grand, April 28, 1815, *JQA Writings*, Vol. V, p. 314.

59. See Jon Latimer, *1812: War with America* (Cambridge: Harvard University Press, 2007), p. 402.

60. "The Perpetuation of Our Political Institutions: An Address to the Young Men's Lyceum of Springfield, Illinois," January 27, 1838, in *Abraham Lincoln: Speeches and Writings, 1832–1858* (New York: Library of America, 1989), pp. 28–29.

61. John Quincy Adams to Abigail Adams, December 24, 1814, *JQA Writings*, Vol. V, p. 248.

CHAPTER TEN—RUMORS OF WAR, 1815–71

1. "Memorandum on the Defence of Canada," February 15, 1862, WO 33/11, Paper 165.

2. Ibid.

3. C. P. Stacey, "The Myth of the Unguarded Frontier 1815–1871," *American Historical Review* 56:1 (October 1950): 2.

4. C. P. Stacey, "An American Plan for a Canadian Campaign," *American Historical Review* 46:2 (January 1941): 348–58.

5. The chief source on the Rouse's Point forts is James P. Millard, *Bastions on the Border: The Great Stone Forts at Rouse's Point on Lake Champlain* (South Hero, Vt.: America's Historic Lakes, 2009), passim.

6. Ibid., p. 18.

7. Desmond Morton, *A Military History of Canada from Champlain to the Gulf War*, 3rd ed. (Toronto: McClelland and Stuart, 1992), p. 72.

8. On Wellington's and Smyth's memoranda and reports, see Kenneth Bourne, *Britain and the Balance of Power in North America 1815–1908* (Berkeley: University of California Press, 1967), pp. 34–43; André Charbonneau, *Les Fortifications de l'Isle aux Noix* (Ottawa: Parks Canada, 1994), pp. 159–258.

9. Harwood Perry Hinton, "The Military Career of John Ellis Wool 1812–1863," dissertation, University of Wisconsin, 1960, pp. 143–62 and passim.

10. For a brief account see Francis Paul Prucha, *The Sword of the Republic: The United States Army on the Frontier, 1783–1846* (Bloomington: Indiana University Press, 1969), pp. 311–18.

11. Kenneth R. Stevens, *Border Diplomacy: The Caroline and McLeod Affairs in Anglo-American-Canadian Relations, 1837–1842* (Tuscaloosa: University of Alabama Press, 1989), p. 51.

12. Sir Charles Metcalfe to Lord Stanley, July 4, 1845. WO 1/552, item 265.

13. Duke of Wellington to Lord Stanley, August 25, 1845. WO 1/553, item 241.

14. "Sea Power," in Frederick Merk, *The Oregon Question: Essays in Anglo-American Diplomacy & Politics* (Cambridge: Harvard University Press, 1967), pp. 337–63.

15. See Bourne, *Britain and the Balance of Power in North America*, pp. 238–41.

16. "English Feeling Towards America," *Economist* No. 944 (September 28, 1861), p. 1066.

17. William Seward to Charles Francis Adams, July 30, 1863, in *Diplomatic Correspondence of the United States* (Washington, D.C.: Government Printing Office, 1864), Vol. I, p. 373.

18. Ibid.

19. George Wrottesley, ed., *Life and Correspondence of Field Marshal Sir John Burgoyne*, 2 vols. (London: Richard Bentley, 1873), Vol. II, p. 411.

20. On this subject more broadly, see Robin W. Winks, *Canada and the United States: The Civil War Years* (Baltimore: Johns Hopkins Press, 1960), passim.

21. Lieutenant Colonel Jervois, "Letter to the Secretary of State for War with reference to The Defence of Canada" (London: Her Majesty's Stationery Office, 1865), p. 7.

22. On the Confederate Secret Service see, in particular, William A. Tidwell, *April '65: Confederate Covert Action in the American Civil War* (Kent, Ohio: Kent State University Press, 1995), as well as his remarkable *Come Retribution: The Confederate Secret Service and the Assassination of Lincoln*, with James O. Hall and David Winfred Gaddy (Jackson: University Press of Mississippi, 1988).

23. See the account in John W. Headley, *Confederate Operations in Canada and New York* (New York: Neale, 1906).

24. C. C. Clay to Judah P. Benjamin, August 11, 1864, in *The War of the Rebellion: A Compilation of the Official Records of the Union and Confederate Armies* (Washington, D.C.: Government Printing Office, 1900), Series IV, Vol. 3, p. 586. Henceforth *OR*.

25. Winks, *Canada and the United States*, p. 141.

26. C. C. Clay to Judah P. Benjamin, September 12, 1864, *OR*, Series IV, Vol. 3, p. 639.

27. Jacob Thompson to Judah P. Benjamin, December 3, 1864, *OR*, Series I, Vol. 43, Part II, p. 936.

28. See William S. McFeely, *Grant* (New York: W. W. Norton, 1982), p. 180.

29. Oscar A. Kinchen, *General Bennett H. Young: Confederate Raider and a Man of Many Adventures* (West Hanover, Mass.: The Christopher Publishing House, 1981), p. 38.

30. For accounts of the raid see Cathryn J. Prince, *Burn the Town and Sack the Banks: Confederates Attack Vermont!* (New York: Carroll & Graf, 2006); Oscar A. Kinchen, *Daredevils of the Confederate Army: The Story of the St. Albans Raiders* (Boston: Christopher Publishing House, 1959); Dennis K. Wilson, *Justice Under Pressure: The Saint Albans Raid and Its Aftermath* (Lanham: University Press of America, 1992).

31. John A. Dix to Provost Marshal, Burlington, Vermont, October 19, 1864, *OR*, Series I, Vol. 43, Part II, p. 422.

32. John A. Dix, General Orders, No. 97, December 14, 1864, *OR*, Series I, Vol. 43, Part II, p. 789.

33. Winks, *Canada and the United States*, p. 295.

34. Edwin Stanton to John Dix, December 15, 1864, *OR*, Series I, Vol. 43, Part II, p. 794.

35. Oscar A. Kinchen, *Confederate Operations in Canada and the North: A Little-Known Phase of the American Civil War* (North Quincy, Mass.: Christopher Publishing House, 1970), p. 185.

36. William Seward to Charles Adams, October 24, 1864, *Diplomatic Correspondence 1864–1865*, pp. 341–42.

37. See Brian A. Reid, "'Prepare for Cavalry!' The Battle of Ridgeway, 2 June 1866," in Donald E. Graves, ed., *Fighting for Canada: Seven Battles, 1758–1945* (Toronto: Robin Brass, 2000), pp. 138–41.

38. Ulysses S. Grant to Maj. Gen. Edward O. C. Ord, November 26, 1865, *The Papers of Ulysses S. Grant,* John Y. Simon, ed. (Carbondale: Southern Illinois University Press, 1988), Vol. XV, *May 1–December 31 1865,* p. 421.

39. Carl von Clausewitz, *On War,* Michael Howard and Peter Paret, trans. and eds. (Princeton: Princeton University Press, 1976), p. 81.

40. As recalled by Grant's aide, Horace Porter. *Campaigning with Grant* (New York: The Century Co., 1906), pp. 407–8.

41. See the account in C. P. Stacey, *Canada and the British Army, 1846–1871: A Study in the Practice of Responsible Government* (Toronto: University of Toronto Press, 1963), pp. 126–46.

42. "Lévis Forts National Historic Site of Canada: Silent Cannon," http://www.pc.gc .ca/eng/lhn-nhs/qc/levis/natcul/natcul6.aspx. Accessed October 21, 2010.

43. Millard, *Bastions,* p. 62.

44. Richard A. Preston, *The Defence of the Undefended Border* (Montreal: McGill-Queen's University Press, April 1978), pp. 110ff.; Major C. Barter, "The Military Aspect of the Northern Frontier of the United States, together with Notes on Matters Connected with the Naval and Military Forces of that Country," War Office, n.d., 1893, WO 33/55, p. 206 and passim.

45. Preston, *Defence of the Undefended Border,* pp. 125–40.

46. Floyd Rudmin, *Bordering on Aggression: Evidence of US Military Preparations Against Canada* (Quebec: Voyageur Publishing, 1993), p. 53.

47. Ralph Barton Perry, *The Plattsburg Movement: A Chapter of America's Participation in the World War* (New York: E. P. Dutton & Co., 1921), p. 2.

48. Ibid., pp. 29–30.

49. Allan R. Millett and Peter Maslowski, *For the Common Defense: A Military History of the United States of America* (New York: Free Press, 1993), pp. 349–51.

50. See http://www.strategic-air-command.com/bases/Plattsburgh_AFB.htm. Accessed October 21, 2010.

51. See http://www.atlasmissilesilo.com/556thSMS_Site2.htm. Accessed October 21, 2010.

52. John Quincy Adams, *Memoirs of John Quincy Adams, Comprising Portions of His Diary from 1795 to 1848,* Charles Francis Adams, ed. (Philadelphia: J. B. Lippincott & Co., 1874), Vol. III, p. 139.

LEGACIES

1. Kenneth Roberts, *Rabble in Arms* (1933; New York: Doubleday, 1947), p. 81.

2. B. H. Liddell Hart, ed., *The Rommel Papers,* Paul Findlay, trans. (New York: Harcourt, Brace, 1953), p. 521.

3. See James A. Huston, *The Sinews of War: Army Logistics 1775–1953* (Washington, D.C.: Office of the Chief of Military History, 1966), Chapter 4, "Logistics of the Saratoga Campaign," pp. 44–57.

4. Rachel Sylvester, "War is not justified, EU chief tells US and Britain," *Daily Telegraph,* January 27, 2003, http://www.telegraph.co.uk/news/worldnews/middle east/iraq/1420224/War-is-not-justified-EU-chief-tells-US-and-Britain.html.

5. See John Grenier, *The First Way of War: American War Making on the Frontier, 1607–1814* (New York: Cambridge University Press, 2005).

6. See Maya Jasanoff, *Liberty's Exiles: American Loyalists in the Revolutionary World* (New York: Alfred A. Knopf, 2011).

7. Paul Kennedy, "History from the Middle: The Case of the Second World War," *The Journal of Military History* 74, 1 (January 2010): 35–51.

For Further Exploration

The notes to this book serve the usual function of showing where my facts and, in some cases, interpretations come from. I have decided, however, to dispense with a conventional bibliography, preferring to offer readers a list of some of the books, websites, and physical locations that have informed my own researches and travels. My purpose is to assist those interested in exploring the Great Warpath on their own, be it from the comfort of an armchair or on foot.

Places

With the services of an automobile and some comfortable shoes, one can visit just about all of the sites discussed in this book. I have done so, including a visit to the site of the Battle on Snowshoes at the same time of year as the fight, wearing, of course, snowshoes. Quite apart from the natural beauty of the Champlain valley, one quickly discovers that the ground never quite looks the way it is described in books: Some things that are puzzling on the printed page become clearer when seen from the ground (or even, the water); conversely, new questions arise once one sees for oneself spatial relationships that words may not adequately convey. The traveler must always remember, however, that the ground changes, not only in the obvious ways through construction and excavation, but through shifting amounts and kinds of vegetation. Still, it is striking how much remains even of hastily constructed earth and wood entrenchments and redoubts, even after a quarter millennium.

Historic Schenectady bears little resemblance to the town attacked in 1690, but its old section, the Stockade District, has a charming collection of colonial houses; not many miles away, Johnson Hall was the mansion of Sir William Johnson, who built Fort William Henry. Alas, the reconstructed fort at the south of Lake George is itself more commercial (and in a built-up tourist area) than a purist might like, but the battlefield site of 1755 is now a state park, and worth a look. Whitehall, at the very southern end of Lake Champlain, has a small but interesting maritime museum:

This is, after all, where Arnold built his fleet in the desperate summer of 1776.

The most famous of all sites along the Great Warpath is Fort Ticonderoga, a historical site privately preserved and maintained that antedates the national park system and is not part of it. It is a standard setter in terms of reconstruction and presentation; if you go nowhere else on the Great Warpath, go there. Too few tourists, however, see the nearby sites of Mount Defiance (ascended more easily than Lieutenant Twiss did in 1777) or, across the lake, Vermont's Mount Independence, which has an excellent museum and hiking trails that are well marked. The site of the Battle on Snowshoes is now a golf course. A dozen miles north of Ticonderoga is Crown Point—not a reconstruction, like Fort Ticonderoga, but a spectacular and well-preserved ruin.

Along the Vermont shore of Lake Champlain one can visit the cove where Arnold burned his ships after Valcour Island (Arnold Bay, just south of Buttonmould Bay), and visit the town of Vergennes, where the Brown brothers built the *Saratoga*, the ship that won the battle of Plattsburgh Bay in 1814. Also in Vergennes is the Lake Champlain Maritime Museum, which includes a replica of the gunboat *Philadelphia* from Arnold's fleet and extensive coverage of the battle. A real gem on the Vermont side is the Hubbardton battlefield—not much visited, but well-preserved and evocative. You can walk along the military road beyond Sucker Brook and imagine the first scattering of shots as American sentries detected General Fraser's advance in 1777.

On the New York side one can sail around Valcour Island: doing so helps one appreciate Arnold's genius in stationing his fleet where he did, almost completely masked from detection by the British flotilla sailing south. Plattsburgh Bay and the town itself deserve more attention from visitors and are worth exploring, too. Fort Montgomery at Rouse's Point is on private land, but is easily visible from the highway. Other traces of the military history of the region dot the landscape, including old intercontinental ballistic missile silos.

Finally, the Canadian park system has done a fine job of preserving the string of outposts that guarded Montreal—Isle aux Noix (Fort Lennox), which includes the graves of American soldiers stricken by smallpox; St. Johns, until recently the site of a military academy, where the fortifications besieged by Richard Montgomery in 1775 are clearly to be seen; and Chambly, reconstructed and looking rather as La Corne St. Luc and his colleagues might have seen it before departing southward on a raid in the middle of the eighteenth century. Montreal itself has a number of sites, including the Chateau Ramzay, the American headquarters to which weary Benjamin Franklin and his colleagues came in the spring of 1776, hoping to save the American project of conquering Canada.

The website www.historiclakes.org can help you plan your visits, as can the various official websites of New York, Vermont, and Canada.

Historians

One of the daunting features of writing a book like this is the number of superb historians who have covered this field so very thoroughly. Herewith, a few of my favorites, beginning with two who are out of favor with contemporary historians. Herbert L. Osgood's three volumes on *The American Colonies in the Seventeenth Century*, and four on *The American Colonies in the Eighteenth Century*, appeared in the early decades of the twentieth century. These massive works of administrative, political, and military history emphasize the links between the English colonies and government in London; although today's historians conceive of "Atlantic history" in much broader terms, Osgood blazed a path. Lawrence Henry Gipson's fourteen volumes on *The British Empire before the American Revolution* are a staggering work of scholarship, of a kind much out of fashion, and too imperial for current tastes.

Modern historians like Fred Anderson (*Crucible of War*, a recent history of the Seven Years' War in North America) are far wider ranging in their interpretations, and more likely to see events from multiple points of view. And there are many good scholars out there—for example, Stephen Brumwell on the British army in North America and on Robert Rogers; Richard Ketchum on the Saratoga campaign; Douglas Edward Leach on colonial military history; John Shy on the American Revolution and the buildup to it; Ian K. Steele, whose Canadian sensibilities offer a very different take on, among other things, the Fort William Henry massacre; and Alan Taylor, who has written stunning books spanning the American Revolution and the War of 1812.

The history of French Canada has attracted prolific historians, such as Guy Frégault and W. J. Eccles, the biographer of Frontenac, and more recently D. Peter MacLeod: their take on the Seven Years' War, in particular, could not be more different from that of England- or United States–oriented historians. Jonathan R. Dull, among others, has helped us see strategic events in North America from the point of view of Paris as well. And in recent decades such ethnohistorians as Daniel K. Richter, James Axtell, and Colin G. Calloway have given a far fuller picture of the world as seen from "Indian country," as one prominent book puts it.

And then there are the local historians, often independent scholars, whose careful researches have illuminated many of the fine details of events along the Great Warpath. Russell P. Bellico, in particular, has written several books on the maritime history of Lake Champlain. Journals like *The Bulletin of the Fort Ticonderoga Museum* and *Vermont History* sometimes have real gems of local history, which may be placed in a larger context.

Biographies and Memoirs

Few casual readers of history would think it worth their while to pick up massive, multivolume biographical dictionaries. Thanks to the Internet, however, one no longer has to. The *Oxford Dictionary of National Biography* and *American National Biography Online* are standard works for the United Kingdom and the United States, and are usually accessible through library accounts. The comparable *Dictionary of Canadian Biography* is, however, available to all online. All three dictionaries cover the entire period under discussion here well, with articles of varying length by recognized scholars. Although history is more than biography, it is incomprehensible without it, and those curious about the full life story of, say, La Corne St. Luc will find a great deal to enjoy in these invaluable resources.

Biographies, memoirs, and journals of most of the principal characters of this book abound, so I will content myself with just a few that particularly seized my imagination or might be unusually helpful. *Adventures in the Wilderness: The American Journals of Louis Antoine de Bougainville, 1756–1760* is the journal of Montcalm's chief aide; deeply attached to his chief, he nonetheless did not share all of his prejudices. *The Annotated and Illustrated Journals of Major Robert Rogers* (Timothy J. Todish, ed.) gives not only Rogers' complete rules of ranging, but his account of war in the no-man's-land between Fort Edward and Montreal. Stanley McCrory Pargellis, *Lord Loudoun in North America*, despite its age (it was published in 1933), still stands as an account of how a British commander wrestled with command in the colonies during the Seven Years' War. James Kirby Martin's *Benedict Arnold: Revolutionary Hero* covers Arnold's career until his treason, and follows the more recent trend to a sympathetic account of the most brilliant soldier of the war of American independence. George Athan Billias, ed., *George Washington's Generals and Opponents* provides fine capsule biographies of many key leaders along the Great Warpath. The personal papers of many key leaders, including William Johnson, Benjamin Franklin, the Marquis de Lafayette, and George Washington have been published in scholarly editions whose commentary is as valuable as any secondary work of history.

Documents

Scholars, of course, make a beeline for the documents. But readers of history, if they have access to the right kind of library (or merely a good interlibrary loan service), can get them, too. Increasingly, readers can also find these on the Internet. For general readers the approach should be browsing for the feel of things; only by looking at the texts of letters, reports, and the like can one appreciate the constraints under which statesmen and generals operate, the limits of the information they have, and the foresight they can exercise. If empathy (not sympathy) is the core value of a wise reader of history, the best way to get it is through the documents. Really in-depth research may require trips to archives and repositories, but to a remarkable degree, the documents of the military history of the Great Warpath are available in published editions, online, or in other electronic formats (compact disks, in particular).

The gathering of documents began early with *Documents Relative to the Colonial History of the State of New York*, printed in fourteen volumes from 1853 to 1887. It includes documents from Holland, France, and England, as well as what became the United States. The *Documentary History of the State of New York* (four volumes, 1849–51) covers similar ground. French readers should look at the many volumes of letters (including those of Montcalm and his deputy, the Chevalier Lévis) collected by Henri Raymond Casgrain at the end of the nineteenth century: These are available for free at various websites.

Peter Force's *American Archives*, assembled in the mid–nineteenth century, remains an indispensable source for those interested in the activities of Americans rebelling against the British government in the period 1774–76: Letters, newspaper accounts, and official acts of various kinds are available here. The *Journals of the Continental Congress, 1774–1789* provide an insight into the thinking of the American government, such as it was, while K. G. Davies, ed., *Documents on the American Revolution, 1770–1783* is a wonderful work in twenty-one volumes that provides transcripts of selected documents from the British archives, together with a listing of other relevant sources not provided in full. Back on the American side, *Naval Documents of the American Revolution* gives an account of all the maritime engagements on Lake Champlain through the end of the war. *The Naval War of 1812: A Documentary History* does the same for that conflict, largely though not exclusively from the American point of view, while *Select British Documents of the Canadian War of 1812* does the same on the other side.

One cannot keep up with the resources of the Internet, but this is as good a place as any to suggest that the official sites of the national archives of the United States, United Kingdom, and Canada provide ever-expanding resources, as do the British Library and the Library of Congress, while Google Books and other services digitize and make freely available other sources (*Wellington's Dispatches*, for example) for download and perusal.

Entertainment

Then there are the books to be read for the sheer fun of it. The works suggested here are of a kind that a professional historian would probably not cite, but might surreptitiously enjoy.

Benson J. Lossing, a prolific journalist and illustrator in the middle of the nineteenth century, published his *Pictorial Field-Book of the Revolution* in 1850 and its counterpart, *Pictorial Field-Book of the War of 1812*, in 1859, on the eve of the Civil War. These are splendid mishmashes of anecdote, travelogue, history, biography, and—perhaps most important—copious illustration. There is a wistfulness in his description of some of the Great Warpath sites, many of which were succumbing to development by the time he visited them in the 1840s, as in this depiction of Fort Edward: "There are still very prominent traces of the banks and fosse of the fort, but the growing village will soon spread over and obliterate them forever."* Indeed so: The town of Fort Edward today conceals virtually all of the base from which Americans, Englishmen, and Scots repeatedly advanced north along the Great Warpath.

In the middle of the nineteenth century, Francis Parkman of Boston wrote a series of books on the struggle between France and England for North America: The best known of these works is his two-volume *Montcalm and Wolfe*. His own life a desperate struggle with blindness and loss, he chronicled the climactic struggle for North America between the two European great powers with rare literary skill. Parkman was intoxicated with the landscape of the Great Warpath, which he visited repeatedly and described with care. Thus, he tells his readers:

> The earthen mounds of Fort William Henry still stand by the brink of Lake George; and seated at the sunset of an August day under the pines that cover them, one gazes on a scene of soft and soothing beauty, where dreamy waters reflect the glories of the mountains and the sky.

From the present he slides imperceptibly into 1757:

> As it is to-day, so it was then; all breathed repose and peace. The splash of some leaping trout, or the dipping wing of a passing swallow, alone disturbed the summer calm of that unruffled mirror.†

Immediately, for such was his narrative style, he introduces into this idyllic scene a band of Indian scouts led by La Corne St. Luc who seize, slay, and scalp an unwary party of soldiers near Fort William Henry in advance of Montcalm's siege and the ensuing massacre.

Parkman is much despised today by some historians who find him bigoted, reactionary, and too literary. He was, to some extent, all these things, although a more charitable reading suggests that he had a dark view of most human beings, including the elite of the Boston of his day. And no matter what one thinks of his interpretations, his literary skill

*Benson J. Lossing, *Pictorial Field-Book of the Revolution* (New York: Harper and Brothers, 1850), Vol. I, p. 96 (reprinted 1972).

†Parkman, *France and England in America*, Vol. II (New York: Library of America, 1983) p. 1180.

remains a marvel—which is why he, unlike many of his late-twentieth-century critics, remains in print.

Kenneth Roberts's 1930s novels about the Great Warpath—in particular, *Northwest Passage*, which deals with Rogers' rangers, and *Rabble in Arms*, a tale of the 1776 and 1777 campaigns—first hooked me on this subject. He raged against the inadequacy of historians and despised most ethnic groups, all politicians, most certainly his publishers, but above all book reviewers. His female characters were sometimes flat, and he subordinated his plots to his desire to tell history as he understood it—and to vindicate his heroes, most notoriously, Benedict Arnold.

His great gift lay in accurate and compelling depiction of military life, not limited to campaigns and battles. There are battles and skirmishes in Roberts's books, which he renders exceptionally well. But most of all he provides in *Rabble in Arms* the account of a debacle, redeemed by enormous efforts—the pellmell retreat from Canada in the spring of 1776, the ravages of smallpox, the building of the fleet and its destruction, the fall of Fort Ticonderoga in 1777, the delay of Burgoyne's army, the climactic battle of Saratoga. It is not Homer or Xenophon's *Anabasis*, but that is the scale to which Roberts aspired in his attempt to capture the full range of experience in the camps and on the battlefields of the Revolution.

Where Lossing had a romantic view of the personages who inhabited the Great Warpath, and Parkman an equally romantic view of its landscapes, Roberts had little of either, or rather, he had little use for conventionally patriotic accounts. In talking about the subject of this book with all kinds of people—including historians, generals, and the former senior civil servant in the British Ministry of Defense—I have been struck by how many youthful imaginations Roberts kindled with his fictional rendering of the two great American wars of the eighteenth century.

Benson Lossing spoke with many surviving veterans of the Revolution and the War of 1812; Francis Parkman reports encountering one as a young man; Kenneth Roberts lived to see the Cold War. Astonishingly, these three lives overlapped, reminding us that some of the events chronicled in this book may not be quite so distant from us as one might think. Nor, one may suppose, are their various interpretations of those events the last word, it being quite certain that other storytellers will spin other tales—truth, fiction, or a mix—of the Great Warpath and the nations that fought there.

Acknowledgments

This book could not have been written without the support of the administration and staff of the Paul H. Nitze School of Advanced International Studies (SAIS). Deans Jessica Einhorn and John Harrington contrived to provide teaching relief at just the moments needed to complete the manuscript; the library staff (in particular, the indefatigable Linda Carlson) processed hundreds of interlibrary loan requests promptly and were gentle in reminding me of the inevitable returns; my colleagues Thomas Keaney, John McLaughlin, Mary Habeck, and Thomas Mahnken were staunch in their support, as was Christine Kunkel of the Philip Merrill Center for Strategic Studies, and nothing, but nothing good comes out of the Strategic Studies program, including this book, without the labors of Thayer McKell, who provided indispensable administrative support. Financial support in various forms came from SAIS, the Olin and Smith Richardson Foundations, and Mr. Roger Hertog, to all of whom I am deeply grateful.

I used a number of libraries and depositories, including the National Archives of the United Kingdom (formerly the Public Record Office) and of the United States, the British Library, the Dartmouth College Library, the Lake Champlain Maritime Museum, the Massachusetts Historical Society, the New-York Historical Society, and the Thompson Pell Research Center of Fort Ticonderoga. Their staffs were helpful to a fault. A special word of thanks, however, must go to the superb library of the Society of the Cincinnati in Washington, D.C., and to Ellen Clark and Elizabeth Frengel. That magnificent collection not only answered almost all of my scholarly needs: The place itself provided an unmatched venue for serious research. The society has also been exceptionally generous with maps and illustrations.

There are troops of deer and prides of lions; over the years that went into this book I have been assisted by what one might justly term a persistence of research assistants. Edward Burnett, Simon Chin, Beau Cleland, Christopher Griffin, Katherine Harvey, Michelle High, Liesl Himmelberger, Andrew Kamons, Rod Latham, Eric Lob, Rebecca

Michael, Steven Riccardi, and Rebecca Zimmerman may have doubted whether the Old Man would actually finish the work—but if so, they had the good grace to conceal those concerns, as they diligently dug away. To them, and to all of my students who kept after me to finish the book, many thanks.

In a similar vein, I confess that I have worn out two editors (Bruce Nichols and Hilary Redmon) and one agent (Scott Moyers), all of whom helped shape this book. Alessandra Bastagli of Free Press edited the manuscript with high competence and good humor while Sydney Tanigawa kept the myriad details of production on track. Throughout, Andrew Wylie has been not only agent, but coach and counselor. To these professionals and their coworkers and assistants I owe a great deal.

Friends and colleagues helped me on my way: Three Thomases (Donnelly, Keaney, and Ricks) read and commented perceptively on the entire manuscript, as did Brian Linn and Robert Killebrew. Don Higginbotham's observations on this project, at an early stage, had a greater impact than he may have realized. Kurt Campbell was characteristically forceful in pointing out the merits of *Conquered into Liberty* as a title. I would not have had the pluck necessary to tackle this subject without the encouragement of my dear friend Richard Kohn. He, Stephen Webb, and Nicholas Westbrook, all three eminent historians deeply knowledgeable about the events and issues covered herein, commented minutely, exactingly, and wisely on the draft manuscript. I writhed at the errors of fact, interpretation, and style that they exposed, but paid heed, and the book is infinitely better for their help. Such errors, questionable conclusions, and infelicities as remain are my fault, and no one else's.

To Nicholas Westbrook, the former director of Fort Ticonderoga, goes a special thanks. In addition to his extraordinary scrutiny of the document, I must offer thanks—as do many other historians—for his unstinting friendship, his staggering knowledge of sources, his willingness to walk the grounds of that magical place, and his infectious enthusiasm for its vast and varied history.

As I point out in the section on further reading, I have walked almost every piece of ground discussed in this book. Along the way I have enjoyed the company of many friends and colleagues, present and former students, staff riders and curious tourists. Douglas Merrill deserves special thanks for spending an entire day with me expertly navigating the waters of Lake Champlain in the vicinity of Valcour Island and in Plattsburgh Bay. One learns so much seeing battle sites, and figuring out the action, in the company of intelligent friends, and to all a collective expression of appreciation for their companionship.

A special word of thanks, however, goes to my wife, Judy, our four children, Rafi, Miki, Becky, and Nathan, and our son-in-law Ari. With them I have climbed Mount Defiance and Mount Independence, walked the walls of Crown Point, examined the ruins of the fort at St. Johns and the town square of St. Albans, visited William Johnson's mansion in the woods and Benedict Arnold's headquarters in Montreal, camped near Fort William Henry, and snowshoed where Robert Rogers' men met catastrophe 250 years before. During the time that I have worked on this book, Judy and I have seen our wonderful teenagers grow to adulthood, graduate fine institutions of higher learning, travel the world, engage in public service, go to war and return from it, marry, and even begin having children of their own. Their spirit of adventure, insight and good sense, love and good humor have inspired me, and the joy of their company was not the least of this author's pleasures. With their kind, patient, and wise mother's permission, I affectionately dedicate this book to them.

Map Sources

FACING THE PROLOGUE

William Brassier, *A Survey of Lake Champlain, including Lake George, Crown Point, and St. John: surveyed by order of His Excellency Major-General Sr. Jeffery Amherst, Knight of the most Honble. Order of the Bath, Commander in Chief of His Majesty's forces in North America (now Lord Amherst) by William Brassier, Draughtsman, 1762* [map]. 1:400,000. In: *The American military pocket atlas.* (London: Robt. Sayer and Jno. Bennett, 1776.)

CHAPTER ONE—SCHENECTADY

The Fort of Scanecthade, 1695. Scale not given. In: John Miller. *New Yorke Considered and Improved, 1695, by John Miller; published from the original ms. In the British museum; with introduction and notes by Victor Hugo Paltsits.* (Cleveland: The Burrows Brothers Company, 1903.)

CHAPTER TWO—FORT WILLIAM HENRY

L. Therbu, *Attaques du Fort William-Henri en Amériqué: par les troupes françaises aux ordres du Marquis de Montcalm, prise de ce fort le 7 Août 1757.* (Frankfurt: Georg Joseph Coentgen, 1789.) From the Robert Charles Lawrence Ferguson Collection, the Society of the Cincinnati, Washington, D.C.

CHAPTER THREE—THE BATTLE ON SNOWSHOES

Elias Meyer, *Sketch of the Country Round Tyconderoga.* Scale 1:31,680. From the William L. Clements Library, University of Michigan.

CHAPTER FOUR—FORT CARILLON

L. Therbu, *Attaques des retranchements devant le Fort Carillon en Amériqué: par les anglais commandes par le general Abercrombie contre les françaises aux ordres du Marquis de Montcalm le 8 Juillet 1758.* (Frankfurt: Georg Joseph Coentgen, 1789.) From the Robert Charles Lawrence Ferguson Collection, the Society of the Cincinnati, Washington, D.C.

CHAPTER FIVE—ST. JOHNS

St. Johns as blockaded and besieged, anno 1775 (1775). In: *Report of the Work of the Public Archives for the Years 1914 and 1915*, Arthur G. Doughty, Public Archivist. (Ottawa: J. de L. Taché, Printer to the King's Most Excellent Majesty, 1916), Appendix B, p. 3.

CHAPTER SIX—VALCOUR ISLAND

Attack and defeat of the American fleet under Benedict Arnold, by the King's fleet commanded by Captn. Thos. Pringle, upon Lake Champlain, the 11th of October 1776. (London: William Faden, 1776.) From the Robert Charles Lawrence Fergusson Collection, the Society of the Cincinnati, Washington, D.C.

CHAPTER SEVEN—HUBBARDTON

Plan of the action at Huberton under Brigadier Gen'l Frazer, supported by Major Gen'l Reidesel, on the 7th July 1777. Drawn by P. Gerlach, Deputy Quarter Master General. (London: William Faden, 1780.) From the Robert Charles Lawrence Fergusson Collection, the Society of the Cincinnati, Washington, D.C.

CHAPTER EIGHT—PHANTOM CAMPAIGNS

Bernard Romans, *A Chorographical Map of the Northern Department of North America.* (Amsterdam: Covens and Mortimer and Covens Jr., 1780.)

CHAPTER NINE—PLATTSBURGH

Alexander Macomb, *Sketch of the Enemy's Positions & Batteries at the Siege of Plattsburg from 6th September 1814 to the 11th inclusive.* NARA, RG 107, Map enclosures separated from "Reg. Letters Rec'd (Main Series) 1801–1889," M-136 (8).

CHAPTER TEN—RUMORS OF WAR

J. B. Beers & Co., *Plan of Grand Isle and Franklin Cos. Vermont.* Scale 1:190,080. In: *Illustrated topographical and historical atlas of the State of Vermont.* (New York: H. W. Burgett, 1876), p. 143.

Index

Page numbers in *italics* refer to illustrations.

Rommel, Erwin, 338
Roosevelt, Franklin Delano, 338
Roosevelt, Theodore, 333
Rouse's Point, 3, 281, 308–9, 312, 314
row galleys, 180, 187
Royal Navy, British, 35, 37, 42, 43, 57,
        98, 102, 121, 125, 130, 162, 167,
        174, 179, 185, 239–40, 243, 302,
        331, 339
    in American waters, 311
    in Battle of Plattsburgh, 287–94, 296
    blockade of American ports by, 277,
        295
    buildup of Canadian forces of, 312,
        315
    defeat of Napoleon and, 280, 288–89
    impressment by, 272, 300
    Isle aux Noix base of, 275, 276, 309
    Lake Champlain fleet of, 112, 113,
        120, 137, 143–44, 153, 179,
        184–93, 199, 203, 207, 211, 213,
        235, 239–40, 244, 250, 283–84,
        287–97, 290
    on the St. Lawrence, 275
    supremacy of, 100, 207, 244, 306,
        313, 317
    in War of 1812, 269, 271, 274, 282,
        285–97
Royal Savage, USS, 150, 153, 179–80, 187
Royal Scots, 101
Royal Society, 60
Royalton, Vt., 256
Rudmin, Floyd, 332–33
Rush-Bagot Agreement, 308, 312, 324
Russell, John, 270
Russia, 42, 269–70, 277, 331
Rutland, Vt., 215

Sabbath Day Point, 60, 74, 97, 104
Sacket's Harbor, N.Y., 276, 278, 284, 298
St. Albans, Vt., Confederate raid on, *304*,
        321–25, 328, 330
St. Clair, Arthur, xv, 205–15, 217, 222–
        26, 228–32, 236
Sainte Foy, Battle of, 121, 122, 152
St. Francis (Abenaki village), 71, 93,
        235–36

St. Lawrence River, 3, 7, 8, 24, 26, 32,
        35, 36, 50, 57, 85, 86, 100, 102,
        118, 120, 121, 151, 152, 156, 160,
        172–73, 179, 244, 247, 249, 265,
        275, 276, 309, 331
St. Leger, Barry, xv, 200, 218, 228, 260
Salmon Falls, N.H., 19, 22, 23–24
San Francisco, Calif., 333
Saranac River, 286–87, 294
Saratoga, Battle of, 193–95, 219–20, 221,
        226, 228, 229, 237, 238, 242, 243,
        266, 305, 337, 338, 342
Saratoga, N.Y., 158, 161, 190
Saratoga (Schuylerville), N.Y., 80, 89,
        129, 131, 184
Saratoga, USS, 280, 283, 289, *290*,
        291–94
Saxe, Maréchal de, 42, 49
scalping, 118
    by Indians, 38, 51, 218
    by rangers, 119
Schenectady, N.Y., 7, *16*, 37, 39, 101, 103,
        110, 114
    raid on, 9, 17–19, 22–24, 33, 70, 84
Schermerhoorn, Symon, 17
Schuyler, Peter, xv, 17, 19, 23
Schuyler, Philip, 191, 194–95, 200–201,
        204–5, 217, 226, 236, 238, 245,
        258–59
    background of, 126, 146
    at Fort Ticonderoga, 149, 151, 158,
        207–9, 210, 218
    Franklin and, 129, 131
    and invasion of Canada, 146–47, 149,
        161
    and Lake Champlain campaign,
        176–78
    logistical brilliance of, 151, 158, 175,
        338
    as unpopular with New Englanders,
        181, 218
Schuyler Island, 190
Scotland, 273
    Highlanders from, 95–98, 111, 210
Scott, Winfield, 311, 331
Second New Hampshire, 214
Seddon, James A., xv, 320–21, 323

About the Author

Eliot A. Cohen is the Robert E. Osgood Professor of Strategic Studies at the Paul H. Nitze School of Advanced International Studies (SAIS) of the Johns Hopkins University and founding director of the Philip Merrill Center for Strategic Studies there. A graduate of Harvard College, he received his Ph.D. in political science at Harvard in 1982. After teaching at Harvard and at the Naval War College (Department of Strategy), he served on the policy planning staff of the Office of the Secretary of Defense, coming to SAIS in 1990. His most recent book is *Supreme Command: Soldiers, Statesmen, and Leadership in Wartime* (Free Press, 2002); other books include (with John Gooch) *Military Misfortunes: The Anatomy of Failure in War* (Free Press, 1990). In 1991–93 he directed the U.S. Air Force's official multivolume study of the 1991 Gulf War, the *Gulf War Air Power Survey*. He has served as an officer in the United States Army Reserve, and as a member of the Defense Policy Advisory Board of the Office of the Secretary of Defense as well as other government advisory bodies. From 2007 to 2009 he was Counselor of the Department of State, serving as Secretary Condoleezza Rice's senior adviser on strategic issues.

3/12